# Just tu

# at the mountain

## Multi entry trials & tribulations meandering across Chinese borders

# ANDY SMART

First Edition published by Andrew Smart

Just Turn Left at the Mountain

ISBN 978-0-9926912-8-8

First Edition published by Andy Smart

Cover Image: Playing Pool at Hirvesteg, Lake Khovsgol.

*Dedicated to Heath and Brett. You went way too early guys!*

*Also to Dad who taught me never to give up.*

# About the Author

Andy Smart started working life as a welder fabricator before his career move into teaching in 1990. He then worked in a variety of different positions including secondary education, SEN and teenagers with EBD. In 2005 he opted for a life change, setting down roots in China. He taught EFL in the South of China's Guanxi Autonomous Region and South Korea before moving to Beijing in 2007. Andy still lives and teaches there today and is working on his next book. So far he has been to half of China's 22 provinces.

# Acknowledgements

A huge thanks goes to all of my English friends who helped and encouraged me no-end from thousands of miles away, especially Andrew McConnach, Carol Costello and Graham Smith. Cheers to Cork Graham in the States for steering me through unknown territory from afar. A special thanks goes to Simon Hayes for his invaluable advice which completely changed my way of writing.

Closer to home in China, I am indebted to the countless people that have offered help and guidance in every country that's on the map, especially with directions, travel tips and language. There has never ever been any shortage of people who have wanted to lend a hand and show incredible hospitality over the years. Often chatting to people has been more like a steep mind blowing education that has left me shaking my head in astonishment. To Su Jiang Yong, Han Dou Dou, Jiang Wei and Feng Xiao Lei thank you so much for sharing your experiences with me.

To Professor Wang Chun Guang from the Science and Mining University for taking me to see Beijing's subway under construction.

To Fan and Jason Zhang for your unforgettable kindness when the journey started all those years back in 2005 and your massive discount. To Jason for doing so much running around for me between the Double Moon Hotel and various other places. Also for sorting me out with the 'most wanted' bed in the area.

To Simon and Lindy and all the staff at the Red Lantern Guesthouse in Beijing who really looked after me for months. The RLG became a home from home for a long time and my stay there was an unforgettable experience.

To Gary Peckham and Flora over in Shenzhen for getting me over to South Korea at the last second. Gary is also a total geezer who is a fountain of knowledge about the locale and also knows 'how to get things.'

To Stuart Jones in Beijing for his suggestions and positive vibes.

I will never forget the continual assistance from Nagi Natsagbadam Ulzihutag on both trips to Mongolia. Nagi did so many things to keep the show on the road including the mind blowing time consuming tedious stuff to do with visas. Also to her family and what they did for Nathe and I. They are the warmest and most welcoming people you will meet and I hope that Hirvesteg will continue for many years to come.

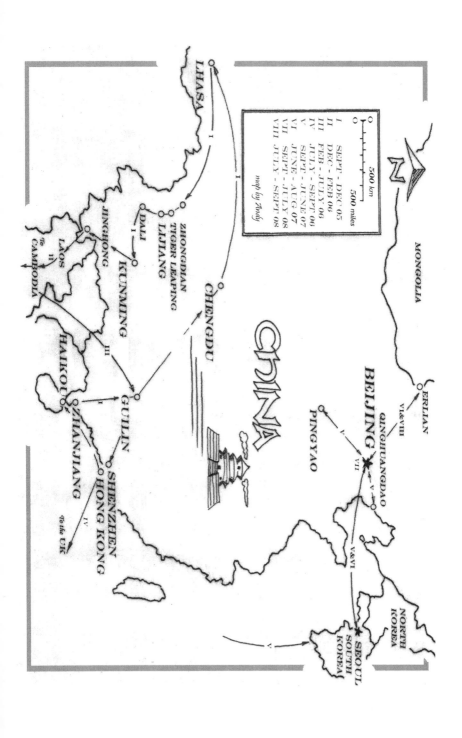

map by Andy

500 km
500 miles

I   SEPT - DEC 05
II   DEC - FEB 06
III   FEB - JULY 06
IV   JULY - SEPT 06
V   SEPT - JUNE 07
VI   JUNE - AUG 07
VII   SEPT - JULY 08
VIII   JULY - SEPT 08

N

MONGOLIA

CHINA

LHASA

ZHONGDIAN
TIGER LEAPING
LIJIANG
DALI

JINGHONG

KUNMING

LAOS
CAMBODIA

HAIKOU

ZHANJIANG

GUILIN

CHENGDU

SHENZHEN
HONG KONG

To the UK

PINGYAO

BEIJING

ERLIAN

QINGHUANGDAO

NORTH
KOREA

SEOUL
SOUTH
KOREA

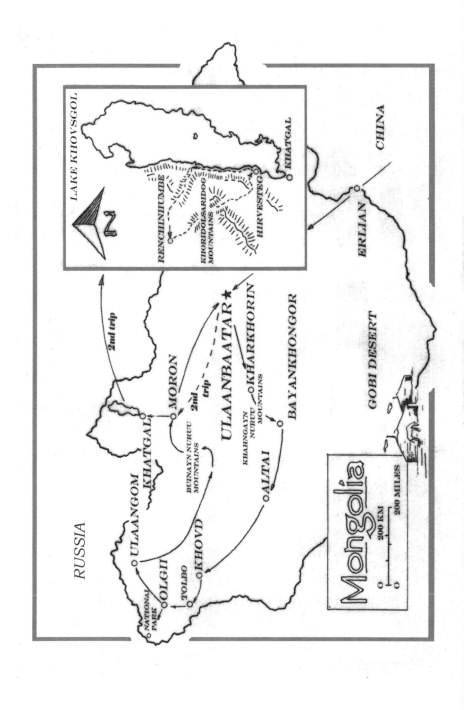

# List of Chapters

1: Meeting the Parents

2: Goodbye Mr Smart
          Part 1 Alternative CV
          Part 2 Reasons to be Cheerful

3: Escape from Zhanjiang
          Part 1 A Shocking Reality
          Part 2 Get out of Dodge

4: Yangers - Doin' It Tomorrow!
          Part 1 A Helpless Tourist
          Part 2 Longsheng Dragon Terraces
          Part 3 Chang-Ge and the Jade Rabbit
          Part 4 First Chinese Haircut

5: Tibet and Chengdu: Touching the Sky
          Part 1 Sichuan Hot Pot
          Part 2 Lhasa
          Part 3 Qomolangma
          Part 4 A Lively Bus Journey into Yunnan

6: Yunnan: Eternal Springtime
          Part 1 Tiger Leaping Gorge, Lijiang and
          Dali
          Part 2 Kunming and Jinghong

7: Laos: Friends in Stereo
          Part 1 Luang Namtha
          Part 2 Luang Prabang, Van Vieng,
          Vientiane and the 4000 Islands

8: Cambodia: Legacy of War
  Part 1 Siem Reap
  Part 2 Phnom Penh, Kampot and Ghost Hunting
  Part 3 Siem Reap

9: Return to Yangers: Square Peg in a Round Hole
  Part 1 Settling Down
  Part 2 A Healthy and Balanced Lifestyle

10: The UK – No Fixed Abode
  Part 1 NFA
  Part 2 Reverse Culture Shock
  Part 3 A Few Other Handy Little Observations
  Part 4 Decisions

11: South Korea: Staring at the Calendar
  Part 1 Continual Study Land
  Part 2 Pei
  Part 3 DMZ and North Korea
  Part 4 Pingyao

12: Mongolia: Where the Eagle Hunters Live
  Part 1 Ulaanbaatar
  Part 2 Way out West

13: China: The Olympics are Coming!
  Part 1 2008
  Part 2 Subway Pandemonium

14: Mongolia II - Just Turn Left at the Mountain!

# 1

# Meeting the Parents

Blam Blam Blam! The heavy handed beating on the door is the usual greeting from the 'fei pin de' or recycling woman. We've been saving our rubbish for weeks and it's a relief to be finally getting rid of it, not only making some space in the kitchen and bedroom but some of it was starting to hum big time. Because you get paid for your rubbish, it's only worth someone's while to come if you collect a large amount and even then you get peanuts for it. Still, it's something to put in the pot for a rainy day and you have to do your bit after all right?

Out on the landing, she sets up a large set of antique cast iron scales with hooks on each end and starts weighing everything; cardboard boxes are always in demand and also any plastic bottle you can lay your hands on. Generally anything goes, including your old clothes and broken electrical items that have given up the ghost. You can tell she's been doing this for a while. Her thick fingers and blackened nails suggest a lifetime of recycling, plus her quilted maroon jacket seems to have been lived in for sometime. She also wears some black leather strapped around her forearms as protection from the heavy lifting that's involved in this kind of work. After the money's handed over, she thrusts the whole lot into a hefty woven bag before leaving.

If you venture into the recycling district around here you're in for an amazing sight. It's an industry that's big in this area, attracting people from all over with their cart loads of everything. Great piles of material get tied down onto small tricycle carts that balance precariously making for a remarkable sight. Their cargo is often so big that it holds up the traffic as the fen pi de slowly pedals down the street. From furniture to great heaving amounts of polystyrene, from varying types of metal to paper, you name it, it's recycled down Shuangqing Lu (road). A continual hub of dusty and noisy activity, business goes on well into the night as lorries line the roadside maxed to capacity with huge sacks of sorted rubbish ready to be taken out of town to their next destination.

This life certainly wasn't what was anticipated when I nervously boarded the plane for China all those years back but it sure is the authentic deal around here in Qinghe! Take the city centre out of the equation and this is how it is right across Beijing. With the first chore of the day out of the way, the next job is to go and fix the puncture the bike got last night. At the bottom of the stair-well I untangle my trusty machine from the assortment of other bikes that are sandwiched together and throw the lock in the basket. As the wifey Suzie and I venture outside, the winter sun is a mere echo behind day two of a new smog bank. Laughably, the powers that be recently issued a statement saying that Beijing had reached its "Blue Sky Days Target" enjoying 274 days of "blue sky" in 2011, fulfilling its annual objective ahead of schedule.

The loud cracking of fireworks explodes nearby marking a wedding going on somewhere in the neighbourhood. From the corner of the apartment complex, the owner of the flower shop Feng Ling attends to her chestnuts roasting away outside on the pavement in half an oil drum. Briefly looking up she nods a good morning in our direction with a smile. Across the road, the usual din from the small supermarket fills the air with its usual boast of cheap zero quality bargains
"Hao xiao xi! Hao xiao xi! (good news) Mei jian shang pin jiu kui jiu (everything is nine kuai nine mao). Baizi (cups) jiu kui jiu, shao shui hu (small tea pots) jiu kui jiu, tuo xie (slippers) jiu kui jiu, dian chi (batteries) jiu kui jiu" are the cheerful words of a girl repeated on a tape loop throughout the day[1].

Once out on the street you are instantly immersed in a hive of activity. Mrs Zhang, a big woman who works in the pharmacy is just going up the steps to the door in her white doctors' coat. Old outdoor pool tables occupy a dirty side street next on the left. A woman on her bicycle wearing tiger patterned pyjamas and slippers navigates past other oncoming cyclists. Endless street venders sell breakfasty omelettes like 'jian-bing' or pork balls and vegetables called 'bao-zi'. Kebabs and burgers local stylee are on the go with smoke and steam billowing out into the cold Beijing morning air. Both men and woman labourers with their yellow safety hats and old clothes chuffin' away on ciggies are on their way to the building site. The obligatory van that tries to squeeze

---

[1] Hello and welcome to the footnotes. I hope you find them entertaining as they are informative. RMB or Yuan is the common currency in China. Normally though people say 'kuai', the English equivalent for saying 'quid' or the American for 'bucks'. Smaller than a kuai is the jiao though most people call it 'mao'. There are ten mao to one kuai. At the time of writing, 1 pound was worth around 15 RMB and 7.5 to the dollar. These days it's dropped down to about 10 RMB to the pound and 6 to the dollar.

itself down another side street brings everything down there to a standstill. People throw their rubbish out from shops directly onto the street while we step through the left over red and white paper remnants from the wedding.

A convoy of over twenty street cleaners cycle past on their tricycle-carts complete with bright blue metal trash boxes loaded with large straw brooms. They're always a sight to see, especially in their day-glow orange jackets and white face masks. Amazingly, there are absolutely no dustbin lorries anywhere in the city, though with Beijing being as massive as it there are no shortage of people ready to do this unenviable job. Turning right we go to the first 'xiu xi xing che de' (bicycle repair man) we see; an old boy who goes about fixing the bike with the utmost efficiency. An equally old looking tailless grey German shepherd guards his master's blackened tool box and growls at anyone that gets too close.

It's been only until recently I moved in with Suzie to her place in Qinghe. Up till then it's been rented accommodation all the way. As per usual, it's the norm to move on a regular basis if you rent a place in Beijing and my case has been no exception. Strangely each move has taken me slowly northwards towards upper suburbia and the district known as Shang-Di which translates to 'Heaven'. Along with this, the lingering desire to settle down there and become an alcoholic with no job has always been pencilled in as one of life's options. With the arrival of married life though, it's all been thrown on the back-burner for the foreseeable future. A few weeks on and the inevitable trip that is the bane of any man's life has arrived as Suzie and I reach the two year wall. I've managed to delay it for as long as possible and with no further cards left up my sleeve things are now fully in motion. It's time to visit the parents!

Their hometown Tangshan represents a vast percentage of what most smaller Chinese cities are like. With its center just a few high rises above five stories, most of it is a vast sprawl of tenement blocks and like Qinghe a far cry from the polish of the business areas and shopping centers of its neighbouring capital just an hour down the road. Here there are few new cars and signs of flashiness anywhere, rather a feeling of simplicity that must be a part of anyone's daily existence.

Suzie's parents show all the courtesies that you get used to when being welcomed into a Chinese home and they are more than friendly. Suzie briefed me in full before we arrived. I should address them formally and not by their names, so it's 'Shu Shu', (Uncle) for the Father and 'A yi', (Auntie) for Mum. Both are retired. Suzie's Dad is an enormous but

3

quiet guy who spent his life doing seven days a week in a factory as an engineer making machine parts. One can only imagine how tough that was. Their apartment is large but with little furniture. The walls are bare and as usual there are no carpets anywhere. No doubt it gets damned cold here in the winter. It's noticeably quiet in this area and the still atmosphere around here is most refreshing compared to the non-stop existence of Beijing. Sitting back on the hard wooden sofa, it's easy to soak it all up.

Before the visit I've been nervously practicing key sentences to say to the folks in my best Mandarin[2] though it turns out that they are totally unable to understand anything I say. A look of puzzlement and bewilderment instantly crosses their faces anytime we try and communicate as they speak 'Fang Yan' a dialect from the East Coast city of Qinhuangdao. Suzie's Mum actually can't speak any Mandarin at all! When the family is in full swing there's no choice but to pretend to look interested in what they are saying and accept the formality of the whole thing; a bit wearing after a few hours for sure.

Dinner time! Yes, the time that is central to anyone when visiting the parents right? It's the moment of truth and the time that's been lurking in the back of my mind for as long as coming here was suggested. Actually, looking at things honestly, this is the big reason why I've schemed my way out of this visit for so long. Suzie's Mum has been busy in the kitchen nearly all afternoon, refusing any help and knocking out the food at an astonishing rate. This includes a great pile of 'jiaozi', the traditional Chinese dumpling eaten in the north; a pastry about as long as your thumb stuffed with pork and vegetables with the edges pinched together. Jiaozi are always good and I breathe a sigh of relief when I see them. Suzie's even taught me how to make them.

Unfortunately I spoke too quickly, having not seen the main dish; a giant plate of boiled pig's feet in soya sauce, something considered a delicacy around here. Mercy! Come back Mum's mashed and highly salted cabbage, all is forgiven! We also have sweet potatoes baked in foil, Chinese cabbage in garlic and green beans with chilli to save the day, though the table is still totally dominated by the pig's trotters. With Mum gesturing to eat with enthusiasm, its time to get stuck in so I tentatively take one in my hands, feeling its weight and fighting back the rising anxiety. The anticipation makes it difficult not to screw my face up with the first tentative bite; it's impossible to eat a pig's trotter

---

[2] Mandarin or Putonghua is the standard language that is supposed to be used across most of China. No matter how good your Mandarin is though, its not difficult find yourself in a place where the dialect is completely different and unrecognisable.

4

and smile at the same time that's for sure. It's pretty chewy and there is no way I can get past a small few slithers, let alone eating a whole one so I leave it on the plate and get on with the veg' hoping it goes unnoticed.

It's been a long journey getting to this time and space; to be truly settled with the missus, our own apartment, a decent job nailed down and accepted by the family (kinda); a tale of trial and error that steers itself blindly across East Asia, stopping occasionally to catch its breath, taking stock then moving on in another random direction. From the outset, it meant binning a thoroughly established life, complete with its daily intricacies of routine and familiarities we take for granted in our structured existences. With virtually no traces of my former self remaining, the only thing left behind was the genuine personality cowering away beneath; utterly useless, spoilt and brought up on an easy life; raised on beer, an expensive weekly shop from the supermarket, takeaway food, weekends off and all done in a relatively uncontaminated environment. The shock of change was far more than I bargained for. The reality of Asia was a sledgehammer to all the preconceptions and romantic dreams, thoroughly pulverising them then chucking them onto the nearest pile of rubbish at the side of the road.

# 2

# Goodbye Mr Smart

## Alternative CV

Life has never been normal. When I die at least I can say that it's been an amazing time filled with ludicrous situations. I am proud of my working CV, but just as proud of my alternative CV which I wouldn't change for five million Tugrik[1]!

I was born in Slough slap-bang next to the M4. Although this was clearly an enlivening place to reside, when I was six my family moved to a small village called Upton St Leonards in Gloucestershire, right beside the M5. Though we had chosen to live alongside a second motorway, this was my first really lucky break in life as it was easy to get away from it all and play in the countryside. Wearing wellington boots most of the time, my friends and I would often return home soaking wet, covered in mud from playing in the stream and the fields.

Of course we made lots of dens in those days. One of the best ones was an eight foot wide hole covered with boards and blankets in the back of Robert Bernie's back garden. Although this was also a heroic effort to dig to Australia, that didn't seem to cut any ice with his parents when they got home, who, upon seeing the huge amount of turf that had been removed from the lawn were not best pleased. My best friend Graham and I collected eels and frogs in buckets and my first pet was an egg I found in the bushes. When Dad broke the news that it was never going to hatch I was devastated. My next pet was a pink sugar mouse which I ate without thinking, filling me with remorse for days after.

My Grandmother was an eccentric woman from Dundee. She was utterly terrifying, especially with her wide-eyed stories of ghosts playing the organ at night in the nearby church. She even wore a wig

---

1 Tugrik is the standard currency of Mongolia. One pound is around 2000 Tugrik. You can get 1 Tugrik notes. What for I have absolutely no idea. When I tried to change my Tugrik into Chinese money the people in the exchange office laughed.

that was passed on to her from her dead neighbour which seemed particularly unnerving. I was more scared of her cooking though. Whenever Dad said we were going to see the Grandparents for the weekend, I'd be filled with foreboding for days. If she made a cup of tea, she would melt digestives into it until it became a paste, then eat it with a tea spoon, something that was particularly hard to watch.

We always thought there was something hmmmm funky about the flavour and consistency of her tea. During one of our visits Mum leant over to me when Gran and Granddad were out of the room.

"God, this tea is really awful!" she whispered to me, screwing her face up tightly. "Go and have a look in the kitchen to see what tea this is."

Not being able to face anymore of Gran's strange lukewarm syrupy tea, we both decided to take the window of opportunity and do a quick reccy' together. In the larder, to our horror we discovered that she had been saving all the left over tea dregs in a plastic bowl. Whenever there were guests, she would simply re-heat it and used over again in an effort to be frugal. There must have been tea in there from way-back and the realisation left us recoiling for the rest of the day.

My sister Jane is 10 years older than me. I thought Jane and her friends were more than cool. While I was running around in my little bedroom making airplane noises with my Airfix kits, she was discovering Marc Bolan and Jimi Hendrix. One day I saw there was a trilby in her bedroom.

"Where did you get the hat from Jane?" I asked curiously.

"We went to see a band called Queen last night at the Cheltenham Town Hall" she replied smugly. "They aren't that famous but you never know hey. That's the singer's hat. At the end he threw it into the crowd and I caught it."

The next day, there was suddenly a terrible shriek from downstairs; "No Muuuuum No!" Jane was more than upset.

"You can't keep that filthy hat in the house" Mum said firmly, thrusting it into the bin. "It's probably got fleas."

My Father's hobby was flying big model airplanes and he had joined several clubs. Being fanatical about this, if he ever gave himself any spare time he would always be found in the shed making some new creation. One Saturday, he said that I had to go with him and his friends for some competition or event. What he'd neglected to tell anyone was that they were down to do the entertainments before the 1979 FA Cup Final between Arsenal and Manchester United.

Having never been to a football match before, upon approaching Wembley Stadium and the penny finally dropped, I became filled with utter panic. I had to wear the Arsenal colours,

7

running on to the pitch before the game as the team mascot. After being faced with the roaring din of the crowd, I was sick in the tunnel. Looking up with watering eyes and half my dinner left down the wall, there was Gordon McQueen one of United's defenders, a red faced giant of a man warming up without his boots on right in front of me. Later Dickie Davies accidentally broke my autograph book in two and of course there was Arsenal's winner hitting the back of the net; the first bit of footie I'll ever remember.

I also have to write a few things about Mum. We all love our Mums right? Mum is totally the greatest; always cheerful, positive and the funniest person ever. She worked as a cashier in the Co-op for a few years and would often talk loudly in her sleep shouting
    "That's two pound fifty-eight please. Do you want it in a bag?"

One afternoon, when driving home in her little silver Honda Civic automatic, we came to these temporary signs saying "No Entry" and "No Through Road". Of course Mum kept going and at once we became part of the Gloucester Carnival, sandwiched between two slow moving floats, as people in highly decorated costumes waved to the crowd. One of the more embarrassing moments I can tell you. A difficult car to make yourself look small in for sure!

When I was fourteen, Mum decided that it was important for me to have a can of beer every night as she said it was healthy. She would say, "Andrew! Its time for your beer!" and I would reply "Yes Mum", at that moment loving her more than ever. One day she said it was time to count the change we'd been saving in these great big Teacher's whisky bottles. She said I could have all the money in one and she was going to treat herself with the money from the other. I can't recall how much it was, but certainly remember that Friday when she came home from doing the shopping, sneaking a whole box of thirty two cans of Carlsberg Special Brew upstairs to my bedroom so Dad didn't see. Oh how I loved my Mum so that day (and so did all my friends).

Leaving Upton St Leonards, I moved to Birmingham to do my first college qualification, a foundation course certificate in Art and Design. You needed this before doing a BA in any kind of art and I soon proved that I was good for doing sweet FA apart from getting stoned every night. Although I passed the course, the tutor said my work was and I quote "shite" and he was hmmm, correct in that statement in every way. Needless to say absolutely no college would accept me so having no other choice was forced into taking a year out and build up my portfolio - yeah right!

In order to fuel my motivation to study I moved to Moseley, just south of the city centre; a strange place filled with all kinds of bizarre people taking all kinds of strange substances. It is and always will be one of the oddest places you could come across. People would consume seemingly any chemical they could lay their hands on and there were many truly crazed head-cases hanging around then. There was one guy who would walk up and down the same bit of pavement all day, shouting that he was an eagle. Also the local home for people with learning difficulties would allow a lot of the residents to go out during the day. Curiously, they seemed to blend in with the environment quite naturally and often the boundaries surrounding 'sanity' in Moseley seemed to be hazy at best. All in all, Moseley was a fairly desperate place. People took whichever drug was on offer because they generally had nothing. The queues for signing-on down at the DHSS[2] were always too long and I guess that if you were wheelin' and dealin' at least you some sort of focus and purpose in life. Mainly though, being in a continual drug related stupor just covered up those giant sad cracks of nothingness in life that lay ahead along a barren pathway with no promise.

Back to the serious business of college and I continued to be refused by every course on the list. I can understand that. I was a total mess. Moseley was a full-on intense place and the need to get out was becoming urgent. Failure would have meant at least another year in the land of lunacy. The last interview was at Leicester Polytechnic. It was the final throw of the dice and things were not going at all well. One of the interviewers was a chap called Ken Ford who had learnt his trade under the sculptor Aristide Maillol. Clearly exasperated by my lack of knowledge on anything sculptural, he gave me one last question.
     "What is the division between mass and space?" he asked in an increasingly pained voice.
     "Surface" I somehow managed to splutter out.
     "Gooooood" he beamed with relief.
There is no doubt that the most important seconds of my life had just whizzed by.

In many ways though, Leicester was just as bad as Moseley. There was an enormous scene going on and with a delicate mixture of extreme forms of anti-social behaviour things were again simply too hectic. One day I came home to hear my friend Mick, who made it his life's mission to be in a permanent state of annihilation, call out from upstairs,

---

[2] The Department of Health and Social Security was responsible for the welfare system in the UK until 1988. It was then replaced by the Department of Social Security until 2001. This was replaced by the Department for Work and Pensions.

"Andy. Can you help me" came a wailing drunken voice from above. As I reached the top of the landing he stumbled backwards all the way down through the bathroom door, flipped over the sink and disappeared head first out of window. Crashing through the roof of the shed, the door burst open and he fell out covered in dust, wood and masonry. He then collapsed against the wheelie bin which in turn deposited its full load of rotting matter all over him before he passed out in the middle of the yard. Certainly a sight that sticks in the mind forever!

Finishing college, unable to make a go of things in the art world, I started work as a welder fabricator, also doing evening classes to improve my skill level and learnt how to really graft[3] for the first time. I would get up at 5.30 in the morning and get home at 9.30pm hoping the missus had cooked (yeah right!) With all the heavy machinery around it was also a fairly dangerous life. One of my work mates had had his arm cut halfway through by a circular saw, then sewn back on again and there were no guards on any of the machinery. If Health and Safety ever came, the foreman had a button under his desk to sound the alarm. To top it all, I had identical recurring nightmares that my arms were cut off in the metal guillotine, waking up in sheets of sweat. In the end, having a metal shard drilled out of my eye was the total clincher. The memory of that drill bit as it slowly made its way to my eye will never leave, that and the nurses direct and assertive voice

"Don't move!"

Eventually things just got too much, so I split from the whole Leicester scene down to Brighton where I did my PGCE teaching certificate, coming second in the whole year. At last, I found something I was good at. The first teaching practice was at a school in Crawley. On the first day the Head of Faculty said that the previous student teacher had broken down and started crying in the middle of class. The kids new they had a new student teacher and they were "waiting for me!" That morning was both unforgettable and riotous, but at least I did better than my predecessor. The next day I made the whole class wait outside in a line until there was some sort of order, then controlled the whole thing with meticulous precision. After ninety minutes, even the worst behaved offenders looked slightly stunned and confused that they had actually produced some work.

Brighton could be quite a full-on place at times, coming into contact with homeless people and heroin users for the first time. There were squats everywhere and these two guys who went begging everyday

---

[3] British English for 'hard work'.

became my best mates. When we first met, they were sleeping outside a bakery every night in cardboard boxes, using polystyrene for warmth. If they hadn't begged enough money, they would go to the nearest supermarket and when no one else was looking, stuff themselves with pasties or sausage rolls as quickly as possible before walking out. Later they managed to get housing benefit, in a place down the same road as me. You got so little money as a student teacher then, that they would cook me dinner with what cash they had blagged that day.

One weekend while my mate Heath was visiting, we were walking up the steeply inclined Trafalgar Street, when it felt like it was starting to rain. Looking upwards, some guy on the bridge above was just putting his tackle away and we realized simultaneously that some guy had just pissed on us. Racing to the station, we found the offender, demanding an apology but none was given.

The guy told me to where to go in his most colourful language and that he knew where he could get a knife.

"Go ahead! Get your knife and see what happens" I replied in so many words, following him filled with curiosity to The Traveller's Fare coffee shop. Grabbing one of those white plastic knives in one hand and a Kenko coffee sign in the other, he lunged at me yelling out loud, "graaaaaaaaa!" Unfortunately he'd forgotten about Heath who had cleverly manoeuvred himself behind him, taking great delight in kicking him in the arse as hard as he could. I had never seen anyone's legs go up in the air and do the splits like that before and as he hit the deck the old bill[4] chased us out and we hid in the church yard. Amazingly I saw this guy's face in The Big Issue[5] magazine later that month as the "Star Vendor". How did he manage that I wonder?

Never got on with the South, that and the demands placed on a teacher in their probationary year were totally overwhelming. They dumped three subjects in my lap to teach from the outset. Aside from Art, one of them 'Design Technology' was brand spanking new and straight off the drawing board from the Department of Education. The third one, 'Graphic Communication' I hadn't had any experience in teaching at all. This therefore meant planning three times over for five year groups and developing detailed lesson plans for each project.

Along with this came a massive and unnecessary amount of paperwork which had to be squared away in immaculate order. Someone in some government think tank with obviously zero teaching experience brought in the great idea of continual assessment in order to raise standards. This meant the kids had to do a mid-term self-

---

[4] Informal British English for 'the police'.
[5] A magazine to support the homeless sold across the UK.

assessment during class that needed to be done in triplicate. The teacher was then to collect them in, split up each one into its various component parts and file them, the kids keeping one copy for themselves. At the end of each project a final assessment would be done in the same manner, plus a formal teacher evaluation. Of course with three subjects came three sets of meetings to add to those all staff had to attend. Mondays were the worst. They would start with a full staff meeting and then school assembly in the morning. At lunchtime we would have a department meeting squeezed in between other duties. In the evening there would be another full staff meeting followed by a faculty meeting. With all the new 'innovations' from above, these meetings would drag on for a painfully long time. As a commuter, as it got close to 7 o'clock your focus would be heavily on your watch rather than the meeting. By 7.30 as the Head of Faculty would be rounding things off with the obligatory "Any more questions before we go?" There would always be someone to jump in at the last second with "Just one more quick thing!" leaving you contorting in absolute torment for another fifteen minutes.

Another remarkable thing about life as a professional was the unexpectedly high level of gossip that went down between other members of staff. Like some negative vortex you would find yourself being drawn into various backstabbing or piss taking conversations on numerous occasions during the day. All in all this strange culture of negative self-empowerment went way over the boundaries of adult behaviour and it became a key ingredient in the downward spiral of disillusionment.

Breaking from the whole thing, the missus and I moved to Bath and I got a job washing dishes for a few years. Dropping out, sure, but washing dishes is a full on and demanding job, especially if you pulled a split shift and to be honest I loved it; there was no stress, I felt alive and started laughing again. You needed some serious staying power and when that bistro kicked into action you worked hard. After work, at about 2am we would be super wired up, legging it sharpish round the corner to The Huntsman to get absolutely comatose. It was the only pub open during those hours, so everyone from all over town would go there and have a thoroughly great time. The carpet was actually sticky so much beer had been spilt on it over the years. Indeed the Huntsman is still a legend to this day.

I then broke my wrist one night after a forty eight hour non-stop binge with my mate Heath when putting my arm out and missing the bed. That was the last straw! Life was at an extreme once again and something had to be done. Even the head chef down the bistro was

12

getting puzzled at my lingering in the kitchen. The feeling that it was time to hang up my apron and hand over the scourer to another dish pig became incessant nagging; professional life and responsibility was once more beckoning.

## Reasons to be Cheerful

I can't remember January 1$^{st}$ 2005. In that respect it means that New Year's Eve was a good one. Yes mate! DJ Dad's at the Ashley Court Hotel in Bristol was one of the best mixes of hip hop you could party to. At midnight my mates Big Andy, Mhari and I looked out from above on Ashley Down to see every firework going off simultaneously. Everyone went for it big stylee until our brain cells had completely left the premises with frontal lobes reduced to the state of a black mush.

There are so many amazing things about the UK. That we can express ourselves in such a diverse number of ways is a blessing. I am so lucky to come from a country which has such a wealth of interesting and extrovert people who are unique in so many ways. The party scene and festivals in Somerset are truly special in the world and have been a part of my life since I was fourteen. I always loved the outdoors, hiking, caving, camping and living in the back of my battered old blue Peugeot 405 estate diesel, (minus the turbo) visiting mates.

One of the many notable times worth a mention here was a trip to Scotland, hiking up Ben Nevis with Heath. On the summit, we came across three Chinese students cowering in the steel shelter, taking refuge from the bad weather. Wearing only jeans, sports shoes, and jackets and carrying no water, the wind and cold had got the better of them. It was here, as we descended together, the first seed of interest in China started to germinate. After exchanging e-mail addresses we managed to keep in touch from then on, even meeting up later on in Beijing.

        Once back down from the mountain, the trip quickly fell apart as Heath and I got ratted[6] down the local[7], waking up the whole camp site. At 3ish, Heath set off the car alarm, then fell on top of a tent occupied by six female students next door to us. To say they weren't best pleased is the understatement of the decade. In the morning, we were woken from our alcoholic stupor by two Scottish guys talking in strong and deep accents right outside the tent;

---

[6] Informal British English for 'extremely drunk'
[7] British English for a nearby pub. A 'pub' is British English for a 'bar'

"If I ever see those f*cking English c*nts who woke us up last night, I'll rip their f*cking heads off!"

Needless to say, it was only until lunchtime that we cautiously emerged, discovering that there was not one remaining tent left in the field.

All in all, life in the UK was never a bad existence really. Indeed there were countless moments that made life really worth living. But there's a flipside to everything! I had long previously learnt from the old man that the only possible course of action in life was to work hard, I mean ridiculously hard, to get promoted and be as middle class as possible. Dad was a self-employed interior designer and his routine was the same every day; coming home from the office, having his dinner and then falling asleep on the sofa, head back, mouth wide open, snoring at maximum volume for one hour. Incredibly he would then haul himself up, get back in the car and go back to work until the early hours.

We only ever went on one holiday together as a family and that was when I was fifteen, to Barry Island in South Wales on a caravan site for a weekend. Mum got absolutely ratted and thought she was falling down a cliff, waking up the whole camp site in the night.

"Oh my God. Oh my God. I'm going down. I'm going down" she wailed at the top of her voice. As Dad and I raced over we found she was actually just lying down on a bit of an incline with a fence behind her, but in the dark as she clutched onto a few handfuls of grass she thought the end was near. The only real holiday we got was one time with just Mum and I down in Weymouth while Dad just stayed at home and worked.

I do remember that Mum and Dad went down the pub very occasionally. Bizarrely, Dad would drive the ten minutes down the road to the King's Head and park the car in the car park facing the hedge. After ordering one Heineken each for themselves and a lemonade for me they would sit in the car to drink them. Dad would bark "Drink it slowly" to me and after fifteen minutes they would go home again. Even after all these years I still can't get my head around that one at all and have never met anyone else who sits in their car to have a pint[8].

Despite all the warning signs and lessons provided by my Father, I pursued his work ethic with all seriousness at the expense of all else. In the last few years in England, I entered into a self-imposed vacuum of sameness. I was merely one of the thousands of utterly stressed and overworked teachers trying to pace themselves between each term. People would always comment on how teacher's holidays were too

---

[8] Standard measurement of beer in the UK served in a pint glass. You can also order 'a half' which means half a pint.

long, but really they were over in no time. Even the summer holidays seemed to finish quickly. You would spend about two weeks getting over the exhaustion, and then have a two week island of feeling normal again. This would be the only time you would feel truly alive all year. After that, two weeks of preparation would lie ahead for the next term and those long winter months. This would give you a continual 'Sunday downer feeling' throughout the remainder of the holiday. For a couple of stretches I had the misfortune of doing supply teaching. Of course like most teaching agencies, they boasted that it paid extremely well on an hourly rate and that you would experience many different schools over a broad area. In reality though, no amount of money would ever remedy the complete uninterrupted shock to your senses that you would suffer while you were out on a job. Actually most of the schools should have had a sign outside saying "Welcome to Hell" warning you as to what would be waiting for you.

The first place had two burnt out cars on the playing field that must have been left there from the weekend. That day there were over fifteen teachers off sick and I wondered how many were off due to stress. I've never seen so many supply teachers gathered together in one place as the co-coordinator handed out maps of the school to get us to our classrooms. There was even a teacher retching in the toilet before first class, no doubt down to anxiety.

There were three full-on fights on the way to the classroom. Along the central downstairs corridor two year 10 or 11s laid into each other on the floor. One lad was in a full headlock as teachers walked past doing absolutely nothing. One teacher even stepped over them. Carefully making my own way past the two I turned, looked down delivering a hearty "Morning" in my best teacher's voice. For a split second both halted their horizontal battle, looked up and replied simultaneously "Morning Sir" before returning to their more important matters.

The school was enormous and it took a while to find the right classroom. The sad little map was a dead give-away to any student that another supply teacher was on the way. Eventually I got to the door of the classroom; a portal to some other dimension of despair that would have to be endured for a whole day. The kids had all let themselves in and already a minor riot had started. There were no pictures on the walls as they had been all torn down. Only the pinned or taped up corners remained to suggest something creative happened in there at one time. In fact there was nothing of value in there whatsoever.

Another fight had started; one big lad had another in the second headlock of the day and was punching him at point-blank in the face. Blam, blam blam blam; these were hard punches.

"Excuse me, can you stop that" I barked pathetically a couple of times with no avail; this confrontation was far more hard-core than the one in the corridor.

"WHY ARE YOU PUNCHING HIM?" I aimed directly at the red faced and incensed lad who was in control.

"He's got my pen Sir"

"OK" I turned to the other, "Give him his pen back. Come on. Give it back."

The two stopped their melee and upon return of the aforesaid chewed up Bic Biro they were friends again as if nothing had happened.

"Are you a Supply Teacher Sir?" enquired one of the girls.

"Yes. My name's Mr Smart. I'm here to teach DT for the day" I smiled.

"May as well go home then" one lad said in a distinct 'can't be arsed' tone, pulling out a packet of Marlboroughs from his pocket and shoving one into his mouth. Putting on his jacket, he headed for the door, "Sorry Sir. But you know how it is."

Sure I knew. Their usual teacher was once again absent. Yet another agency worker who they didn't know had shown up to do absolutely nothing with them apart from try and exercise some sort of classroom management and make up the numbers. Without any resources, the concept of learning had become redundant. El lame O! Two other students followed him, giving me the choice to either stop them leaving or stop the rest from throwing each other's bags out of the window and hurling expletives to another class across the block. Oh the joy. And that was only the first fifteen minutes of the day!

At home that evening, lying on my bed and looking at the ceiling, I wondered how on earth I was going to do supply teaching on a regular basis. I was annihilated after only one day and some little shite had keyed my car. You have to develop a relationship with the kids in order to get any respect from them and therefore work. As someone who is there for only one day you have absolutely no chance.

Determined not to give up, things didn't get any better as the agency started bull-shitting me about what subject it was that day and then feigning they'd made a mistake. "Well now you're there you may as well do the class right?" was the usual line; a standard tactic in order to cover the less desirable classes. I even ended up teaching Year 10 Girls Badminton at a particularly 'serious' inner-city school. Amazingly, the Head of PE insisted that it was my job to go into the changing rooms and introduce myself, not caring one iota of how unprepared I was.

Waiting inside were thirty girls sat in two lines on the benches in tiny pleated skirts, white socks, sports shoes, long permed-dyed hair and excessive make-up. Each one chewed heavily on gum like a machine, some blowing pink bubbles as they looked me up and down with faint contempt and a "What the f*ck?" look for another nothing-teacher. Seeing as the agency hadn't told me about any of this, I hadn't even brought a pair of trainers with me. Instead I was wearing the cheapest white shirt ever, tucked into a pair of second-hand blue trousers over a pair of black DM's. I was given a whistle on a piece of string to wear around my neck, merely adding to the impression that Mr Anorak was in the house.

"Hello. I'm Mr Smart, your teacher for today" I croaked nervously. With no timetable provided and an attempt to small-talk I asked "Can someone tell me when your next period starts please?" While they all immediately broke out into fits of uncontrolled laughter, I on the other hand only wished I could jump into the nearest wheelie-bin, wait for the bin-men to come along and dump me on the tip.

Trying to find something more long term I attended an interview for a temporary contract to cover someone's "sickness". From the quiet safety of the empty CDT department, across the way you could see in one classroom, a teacher having numerous objects being thrown at him. Next door, a boy was jumping up and down on a desk and a football was being hurled at the wall. In another, the books were being ripped up and just being chucked into the air like confetti. The whole morning not a single stroke of control seemed to be occurring and the last line of defence was when the Head Teacher arrived. There was absolutely no sense of order there whatsoever and I was more than happy to just walk straight back out again.

In one of my first-full time posts, the Head of Faculty told me flatly that I should have
"no other life now that this was my career"
and never a truer word has been spoken. The absolutely exhausting treadmill of planning, teaching, paperwork and meeting after arseing meeting served to do nothing but suck you dry until you were just in a daily fight to do anything to keep your morale up and from burning out. On Saturdays, there was absolutely no chance of getting out of bed at all. If I did manage to get up and make it outside, then it would have only been to walk blankly around Tesco in Nailsea pushing a trolley around to get food in for another samey week. Night after night of feeling utterly smashed, mullered and cream-crackered[9], just keeping your shit together so the kids wouldn't walk all over you at school the next day.

---

[9] 'Knackered': Informal British English for 'exhausted'. Can also say 'cream crackered'.

The Peugeot was always in need of attention. I had to sell my lovely Yamaha YZF 750 bike after being forced out of one job that I was doing really well at and loved. Stitched up or what! Funny how it happened one week before my probationary year was due to run out. Exactly the same thing happened to the guy before me and it outraged the other staff there. Wonderfully, the staff got a huge petition together to help state my case and their disdain for such bad practice but it never changed anything. I left officially "redundant" a week into December (ho ho ho!) And of course there was the pin board which seemed to be continually covered in bills like a Christmas tree, nice! No matter how much I earned it seemed impossible to save up for anything, refusing to use the credit card to cover up the cracks and make everything look ok.

About six months later, a great job came my way with a private company that offered accommodation and education to kids with extreme behaviour and drug problems. For the next two years, I had the pleasure of working with some of the most talented and utterly streetwise professionals you can imagine. Their focus was placed solely on pointing these young offenders in the right direction instead of leading a life in and out of the cells. The value of such schools cannot be understated and there should be far more of them about. Though it was a tough job and one that required maximum patience, when you helped those kids do something that they were genuinely proud of, it made everything seem worthwhile.

The School itself was located down the notorious Stapleton Road and to say this part of Bristol is hmmmm, 'wild' is another one of those giant understatements. Ah, how I reminisce upon those zestful afternoons; sitting outside with the kids, watching the Armed Response Unit blast up and down the road at top speed in their black unmarked vehicles. They even came and said hello one day and showed us all the hardware they kept in the boot. Quite a nice little selection of shotguns and machine guns really! I guess a pain when it came to fitting all the shopping in as well right?
    The tip of the day round the neighbourhood was to try not to go out around there at night. Sounds bland, but it's really is crack central around there, that and all the prostitutes hanging around to get some money to fuel their habit. Next to the school was a small cul-de-sac. There would be two stolen cars, each with a side window put in and parked up there at all times; one to use for a quick one round the corner, full of used condoms and tissues and the other full of dirty old needles and crack pipes, yeeeeech. When the council finally did come and take the vehicles away, another two would quickly replace them.

There is a particular road junction that always sticks in my mind along the route to work. It would be from East in Gordano on the M5 to the M4 and then the M32 every morning; same same but occasionally just really similar. People mouthing off in their protective little metal shells; I mean you don't often see people shouting at each other as they walk down the street do you? But with that comforting barrier of being in your car everyone becomes an f*cking wanker!

So you come off the M32 down to the Stapleton Rd and wait at the lights under the flyover. It was sitting there in my car staring at the concrete supports of the flyover before work that really started to do it. Every day I would ask myself "Is this REALLY it?"

And then the unthinkable happened. Sometime in January, we were called into the office to meet the receivers. A week into January 2005 the job had come to an unexpected and abrupt end. The boss had gone on holiday and hadn't returned. He had left the company in a total mess financially and all of us completely stuffed. Vanishing into thin air, we never saw him again. There was even a photo of him on the front page of the Bristol Evening Post saying "Have You Seen This Man?" Yeah mate, happy arseing New Year to you too! We always knew that it was getting harder and harder for us to get payment from various councils, but hadn't realised how broke the company was. One emergency meeting after another only served to bring us down just that little bit more. Some people working there had big families to support and there were the kids. The final day when they had to leave was truly one of the most terrible days you will experience. Two of the lads barricaded themselves into their room. I mean they didn't want to go, none of them did.

Having already thought that at some point I would have to leave the country, as time went on, the notion that it may have to be a permanent move abroad became the only option. I had done just about everything possible job wise and the stress was becoming intolerable. When the company folded though, it was like some vague and stupid dream had imploded up its arse. Luckily, I hadn't told many people about this absurd idea, just as well hey! Out and signing-on down at Western-super-Mare Job Centre; so enlivening! I would get home so depressed, that all I could do was lie on my bed with a t-shirt over my head and pretend it wasn't happening, and this went on and on and on. I got a job hauling rocks in a wheel barrow into a skip for a while. That was nice!

One day the Job Centre said that it was possible to claim some extra money to help with the shopping and petrol, so I waited for an hour. Finally, the woman told me that she would arrange a time and come to the supermarket and petrol station, paying for it with me at the checkout. This would be so I wouldn't "misspend the money." She said she would be wearing her bloody job centre uniform too, aaaagh! With a double helping of humiliation and feeling utterly deflated, they'd made me wait so long that there was even a parking ticket slapped on the windscreen when I got to the car park! Oh well, another one for the pin board!

I don't know when, but at some point a grand arrived from the receivers and I slapped it into my account. The moment that cheque cleared I was in that travel agents like a rocket; money is like water through my fingers and thought of the grand dwindling away on bills sent a shudder through me as it all became quite clear. "Look mate, you've got no choice. This shit's gotta end and end today" were my feelings and that was it! I remember Amy down the travel agents saying "There you go! You've done it" and handing me the receipt. Sheeeeeeeet! It was then I started telling people I was going to China. Everyone thought I was off my trolley!

PREPARATIONS
Wow! Is leaving the country painstaking! I got a great temporary job, again teaching teenagers with varying behaviour problems. It was a really nice place with great staff and great kids, oh and I continued to come home utterly shafted again. I crossed as many bills off the list as possible (though did do a runner on some of them). Chucking all of my stuff away over a period of weeks down the skip, I moved into the living room.

Buying the biggest map of China that could be found, I stuck it up on the wall in front of the bed, starting to think about where to go and what to do there. Having never considered the vastness of this enormous country before, upon seeing the map for the first time with its huge number of towns and cities and immense empty expanses, all excitement quickly turned into bewilderment. In the end, my poor brain gave up the ghost. To say my plans were vague to the point of having no idea, or about as clear as the waters of Burnham-on-Sea would have been a fair assessment at this time. Starting in the southernmost part of China on the cosy looking island of Hainan, (this choice being made entirely on the fact that it looked small and therefore quantifiable, ignoring the fact that it's almost as big as the next neighbouring island of Taiwan), I would then "go north" for one year with the following objectives: firstly, find a place to settle down and build a new life, secondly, to experience a world "untouched by modernisation and progress". You are joking aren't you?

20

I also started seeing a Chinese family once a week before hitting the road; just a few hours each week in a small effort to get a taste of the Chinese way of doing things. They rented a room in a shared suburban house nearby with a number of other Chinese families. During those valuable few hours I learnt the following things: everyone in the household was incredibly hospitable, it was impossible to understand a word of anything they said and they lived in one room though seemingly oblivious to be living in such cramped conditions. Mum and Dad worked all hours including night shifts, rotating hours between them so they could look after their boy. A teacher came every day to give him private English lessons. They sent at least half of their money to their family back home. Their shared kitchen frightened me to death and the food was so awful it was clearly from another dimension filling me with dread of what awaited me on the other side.

There was another, more cunning part to this superbly crafted plan that got tacked on a couple of months before D-Day. Not only would I be hitting the road, but it wouldn't be alone. I would find a Chinese girlfriend on the internet who I would meet over there. We would hang out then go travelling together, before finally getting an apartment and living forever in perfect bliss and harmony, all wrapped up in one convenient package. Holy Shit! In this case theory went way beyond the bounds of all realism.

Of course it's common these days to search for a partner on the internet and it became somewhat of an addiction checking out the various profiles of different women in China who were looking for a Western partner. Easy life! First, find some half decent photos where you look at least vaguely respectable and then write something about what a great person you are. Definitely don't mention that you have no job, savings, house or car but focus instead on romance and your dreams of a new life together. Also don't mention that the entirety of your belongings now fits into one stylish trolley-bag and a rucksack, the items of the highest value being a personal CD player and a cheapo camera with no memory card you bought from Argos.

"What are you looking for?" was the ultimate ego inflating question; "Friends, travel partner, casual dating, long term relationship or marriage?" Oh decisions decisions! After twenty four impatient hours waiting for my profile to be accepted it was tally-ho and off into the twilight zone of cyber dating and my mail box suddenly became filled with mail from women that you would normally cross the road to avoid. Of course this is why people come to these websites in the first place, that or asking you to send you some money to help with their poor grandmother's hip operation. Existing in a world of pure naivety I told myself that I knew exactly what I was doing and at my age I could spot any form of deception a mile off.

After a few letters with one would-be soul mate from Nanning in the south of China, my hopes were quite high that I'd at last met my true match. One morning I went online with excitement to see she had sent me some more photos. Leaning against a wonderful Chinese pavilion set against rich green tropical vegetation, there she was again to greet me while I enjoyed my first brew of the day. As they were high resolution, it meant that I could zoom in and get a really close look at who I'd been chatting to for the past seven days. To my horror though, it turned out that not only did she have a set of teeth like Janet Street-Porter, they were also hideously rotten with a delicate combination of colours varying from brown to grey thus dispelling any further fantasy of a romantic and passionate embrace upon our meeting.

A few patient weeks later though, I'd finally found a girl called Chu Yan, a secretary who lived in Zhanjiang; the same city that would be visiting at the beginning of the trip. With dialogue in full swing, there was even enough time to send some letters by post instead of e-mails. It seemed amazing to be getting real mail from someone in China. To be learning about someone's life and their family intensified my obsession with the whole project and I proceeded onwards at full speed, now completely blinkered to any notion that things may not quite work out how I imagined.

PREVIOUS TRAVEL EXPERIENCE
Around this time two of my best pals Big Andy and Mhairi moved in and really kept my head together. Planning the trip, buying equipment, getting all those lovely jabs such as rabies and Japanese encephalitis, just making sure that everything had been done, to be honest I could feel my growing anxiety about the whole thing. Everyone's reaction was "China? Why the hell do you wanna go to China?" Travel wise my experience was, hmmmm, limited to say the least. I hadn't used my passport and had never been to an airport. I had never applied for a visa and the whole travel thing remained something terrifying I chosen to avoid thinking about.

I did go to Italy for a week once, on a coach with college as a student. It was amazing seeing Venice and Florence; the art and architecture the most beautiful and stunning you could ever imagine in terms of aesthetics. Just a week though; a blur of travel tiredness and a week on a bus as part of a tour is hardly travelling right?

The only other venture to another country was back in the Brighton days. One Friday, Heath came to stay for the weekend. I had this new map of Europe and we noticed that Holland was really close to England. If we just went across the English Channel to France, you could get the train along the coast and be there in no time. Withdrawing a few hundred quid from my account we were off having opened the map only hours earlier.

By late afternoon we were on the ferry going to France. Strange really! I mean why we didn't catch the ferry to Holland, seeing as we were going to Holland is still beyond me. We just thought it would be quicker going to France. I remember on the ferry asking Heath if he had done much travelling before and it quickly transpired that we had absolutely no idea what we were doing at all. At that moment, I recall seeing a look of fear in Heaths eyes, something you rarely saw.

At Calais everyone was herded onto a train to Paris where we instantly got lost. No one would give us directions to the next train station in Paris. When we got there four gendarmes swooped down and marched us to an out of the way office, visibly satisfied at having a couple of Brits to pass their time with. Towering above us and looking completely intimidating in their black uniforms our welcoming committee proceeded to interrogate us, treating is with utter contempt. I had ripped up combat trousers on and had really long hair, while Heath looked like the skinhead from hell.

"Where is your lugeeege?" one of the officers asked in a no doubt Parisian accent. We had no bags or anything, so when I pulled out a pair of socks from my pocket and placed them into his open hands it didn't go down too well at all. Along with that I had a melted Marathon Bar[10], three packets of Fisherman's Friends along with half a pocket of loose ones covered in fluff, some loose change, wallet, condoms, a length of toilet paper, tooth brush also covered in fluff, rolling tobacco and three packets of torn up blue Rizlas which did us no favours at all. Having unwittingly dented his Gallic pride an animated conversation in French proceeded amongst them for a minute before the officer barked his next orders

"Turn around and face the wall. Now take off your clothes…and now bend oveur"

"F*ck! What are they gonna do to us?" I fretted in anticipation of what was about to happen. One of them, a woman who was the splitting image of Fatima Whitbread, said something and they all burst out laughing. Though all they were doing was humiliating us, I was more relieved that nothing serious had just gone down.

We spent over half our money on the train ticket from France to Holland and on the train we were searched again. In terms of a simple trip to a neighbouring country we handled it disastrously, even managing to sleep on some open wasteland one night and behind a rubbish skip the next. On the way back, the old bill searched us again

---

[10] Marathon was the original British English name for Snickers Bar

and they even ripped up the seats on the train. We had, for yet another unfathomable reason bought return tickets to Paris.

In Paris someone from England gave us the rest of the money for the tickets from Paris to Calais. When we finally got back, looking completely annihilated, my girlfriend was more than pissed off as I forgot to tell her we were going. It was my birthday as well (sorry mate!)

Back to reality and before leaving for China, as the days before take-off disappeared, the number of sleepless nights increased. Rather than excitement about going on such an incredible journey, I began to shepherd a feeling of impending doom about the whole thing. At night a vast web of miniature nightmares would plague me until the early hours about the journey or what may happen at the other end. I could miss the bus therefore miss the plane. Unable to afford another ticket it would mean returning back home and piecing the original life back together again; a disaster! I could get lost at the airport! My bags could go missing ending up in Somalia, their contents being distributed amongst an exited crowd of locals. I could go missing in China and end up living in a small village for years without being found. Maybe I would just die; a wasted sad body lying limply at the side of the road pressed against the kerb while uncaring people pass by with no thought of this person's sad tale. My only solace was the thought that Chu Yan would be there at the end of the long and dangerous flight to open armed to take care of me.

Every morning I would wake up surrounded by the chaos of moving out. An overwhelming feeling that I was being stripped bare with no material objects to reflect my identity extended the apprehension into new depths. My pictures were all gone, revealing bare white walls, the bookshelf was mostly empty as was the mantel piece and window ledge. Heath came to visit just a week or so before and man was I up tight then, having lost the ability to make conversation. Wound up like a spring, unable to hardly think, I was in a right old mess. The night before, I gave finally my Peugeot away then walked down to The Little Tipple for my last few cans of McEwans. On the way there I collapsed in a heap of uncontrollable dry retching such was the terror of the imminent ordeal that led ahead. It was like my world was ending, and it was, big time!

The next day I would be on my way to China. Holy shit!

# 3

# Escape from Zhanjiang

China is divided up into a series of twenty-two provinces similar to counties like the West Midlands and Shropshire only far bigger. There is also Taiwan which is counted as the twenty-third (for sure that one is argued over until the cows come home). Each province is individual and unique, so language, customs and even climate can be very different. There are other parts which are not seen as provinces; municipalities like Beijing and Tianjin are also counted separately. There are also vast areas that are claimed as 'autonomous' regions such as Xinjiang and Xizang/Tibet (yeah right!) In fact, there are many other huge regions with their own complete and separate identities all over the place.

The journey starts on the huge island of Hainan, which is the most southern of all provinces in China. Its main city is called Haikou and is twice as big as Bristol with a population of a million give or take a few hundred thousand. Often people ask how long I spent there and are understandably stunned upon hearing it was only one day! After all, it is one of the top holiday resorts in China. People save up for a long time to be able to get their once-in-a-lifetime chance to go to this dream location. People choose to get married in Hainan or go on their honeymoon there. Generally if you go to Hainan its something you're going to tell people about and cherish for the rest of your life. So far I've been to twenty two provinces in China, having always said how important it is to stick around and get used to the way of life wherever you go. So why on earth did I go for one day? I have absolutely no idea about this other than a total lack of forethought. I took a staggering three photos of this amazing area and went for one casual stroll. Phew, talk about soaking it up.

Culture Shock: I really don't quite know what I was thinking, but in my mind both Haikou and Zhanjiang were both sleepy little seaside ports with quaint teahouses overlooking fishermen in their antiquated little wooden boats. Needless to say it didn't quite turn out that way and within one hour of touch down things were all in a bit of a panic. Firstly, I was then thirty nine and really stuck in my ways. I have always found acceptance of change difficult anyway and each year is merely more cement in my inflexible brick wall.

Secondly, this was no holiday where you would be back at work in a few weeks with all your favourite creature comforts waiting at home upon your return right? Having chucked away all worldly possessions, this was a break for a "new life", so it was not surprising that my mood plummeted upon reaching the apartment in Zhanjiang. Though it was merely intended as a brief two week stop over, standing in front of the encrusted toilet and being greeted through the broken window by a pile of rotting tampons on the window ledge, was hardly the majestic image of the East I had hoped to have found. Before you turn inside out at that image, you have to remember that most of Asia doesn't have the sanitised packaged health warning sell-by-date way of life that we are used to. Often you will see things that go way beyond a health risk, especially piles of rubbish dumped everywhere when you get into the suburbs.

Leading nicely on to number three, I'd always tried to project a fairly streetwise image of myself, having lived out of bins, the skip round the back of my local supermarket and the veg thrown on the floor when the open-air market closed in Leicester, but this was in another realm. The food still freaks me here at times and even now if I'm presented with a boiled chicken, all white with the head and feet still attached, it's really difficult to chew and swallow. Our supermarkets are just too cushty[1] and that's all there is to it. How on earth can we live without chicken nuggets in a crispy crumb hey?

If you order something that you know you can eat then guard it with your life. People will lean over and help themselves to it. There is no concept of 'this is my food' in China; people will normally share each dish, deciding what to order together. If you are unlucky enough to be sat at a big circular table that rotates, (common in China so that everyone can have a go at everything), then the only way you can preserve your food is by physically lifting the plate up off of the table, which at times can be seen as bad manners. If not then it quickly disappears into oblivion in front of your very eyes.

Next, leading to full on panic stations, of course was my virtual total lack of Chinese speaking ability. I had really tried to learn some basic Chinese (kinda), going to lessons after work every Monday. I do remember coming out of those lessons with my brain absolutely fried, leaning against the car, sparking a ciggie and thinking
"Shit, that's difficult!"

---

[1] Informal British English for comfortable or a good situation.

Things didn't go well at all really, and in the end the teacher stormed that she

"could teach a child easier!"

Not only was it difficult but she was teaching grammar to me. Of course grammar is integral to any language, but being able to say to a taxi driver "the red pen is on the table" or "the big blue plane is bigger than the white car" isn't particularly helpful in any situation. As D-Day got ever closer my concern in this vital area understandably turned into panic; "Excuse me Sir! Did you know that pencil is very long?" That was what I was armed with when I went to China.

Lastly though, and this is the real clincher, was the disastrous relationship with the internet girl Chu Yan and the ensuing nightmare that lasted throughout the whole time in Zhanjiang. It's amazing what ridiculous things we do in life; the kind of tale that only ever comes out after the fifth pint with your best mates. One friend of mine said he went with this girl that was so unattractive that he pulled a pillow over her head while they were shagging. Another mate got caught in the kitchen by his missus naked, shitting in the cat litter tray he was so pissed; not a pretty sight I'm sure.

We all have these stories and this is definitely one of those that will always be found in that deep archive of shame, (I do seem to have a lot of them). To think I could find Mrs Right online still utterly amazes me. I do know people who have successfully met their other-half via various dating sites; one of my friends even married someone they met online and they live quite happily together. The difference is they all had the luxury of hit and miss whereas in this case there was absolutely no room for backing out.

In all aspects of the trip, I lived in a rose-tinted blinkered fantasy world that came crashing down the moment of walking through customs in Zhanjiang airport.

# A Shocking Reality: 9<sup>th</sup> September 2005

Alright there! Well, at last after nine months of planning and talking about it, I've finally put my money where my mouth is, writing this from Zhanjiang in the south of China. Yes, I am here, I've done it and find this absolutely unbelievable! This place is totally nuts, like being on another planet. Sure, you know that everything is going to be completely different, but nothing you can ever read or hear can prepare you for the reality of it!

Anyway, I arrived at Hong Kong airport (what a place) to see my first East Asian rolling hills. The luggage went walkies for two hours leaving me decidedly uptight but with great relief eventually it materialised. Took the flight to Hainan Island and the 'town' of Haikou, which I thought was going to be a small seaside port like Weymouth. Turns out to be the biggest sprawling place you could possibly imagine. The roads are immense with four lanes each side and there were three crashes on the way to the hotel. Some of the most falling apart, rusting, weirdest homemade motor devices on the planet are driven around here; some with no hood; just a totally exposed engine. One had ploughed into this brand new Beemer. From the twenty third floor of the lovely air-conditioned five star hotel room, you could not see the limits of Hainan, just thousands of grey decaying tenement blocks looking really hard core. I distinctly remember at that moment thinking, "Ha! My flat in Zhanjiang won't be like that" with an assured smugness!

With half the restaurant looking at me, I ordered my first Chinese dinner after four hours total crash out.

"Ni Hao, xiang shenme?" (Hello, what would you like?) asked the waiter, handing me the menu. Though it was all written in Chinese at least it had pictures of some of the various dishes, so I could at least point to what I wanted.

"I'll have that one" was all I could muster in response, feeling already overcome by such a simple task as getting something to eat.

"Hao le, hao le. Zhi you yi ge. Ni  bu xiang biede ma?" (Fine, but it's only one dish. don't you want anything else?) the waiter curiously inquired or something to similar that effect.

"That one" was the flat toned minimal response, pointing for a second time. By now even my English seemed to have fallen by the way-side.

As the food arrived was I in for a shock or what! Instead of the chicken and rice I thought I'd ordered, a bowl of this stuff was served up which had a really unpleasant smell to it. It had some weird white rubbery corkscrew thing in it and looked absolutely nothing like the photo in the menu. I think it was some kind of sea food which I've always found seriously stomach churning, but managed to get about a third of it down then went for a walk.

Caused quite a commotion on the way out! The waiter became suddenly agitated as I tried to pay but leaving the money on the table I headed for the door as fast as possible unable to get to grips with what was going on. It was only until I was well down the road when the penny dropped that the soup may well have been just a starter.

Everyone stared at you as there were no other Western people on the island. Walking through the park to the waterfront and taking the first look at the South China Sea was everything that you could hope for. The parks were immaculate; like being in Kew Gardens, the sunset totally beautiful with a typical wooden junk sailing slowly across it. Hundreds of people did their exercises including martial arts with no overweight people at all. Families cycled past on tandems and tricycles.

Booking a flight at the airport to Zhanjiang was an event in itself, deciding not to go for the ferry then the train as planned and freely admit that I totally bottled it. At the ticket office I managed to create yet another scene. No one had a clue what I was going on about (months of learning Chinese certainly paying off there alright) but somehow I got a result, seeing this as the first achievement of the journey!

Anyway, with the initial hurdle of actually starting the trip out of the way, now it was time to finally meet Chu Yan. On the plane journey a sense of anxiety began to build. I guess the jet lag had a lot to do with keeping it at bay, but as we got closer to touch-down, the feeling that this could all go horribly wrong suddenly let loose.

The arrangement was that along with Chu Yan, a translator Mrs Feng (pronounced Fung) a fluent English speaker, would also be there. After picking the bags up at Arrivals I looked up to see two female figures silhouetted against the sun-glare outside; one tall and the other less than half her size who started excitedly waving to me. Clearly this was my welcoming committee. Oh dear!

They say that looks don't count for everything but you have to admit that there are always times where we all blow this theory well out of the water right? Although Chu Yan had sent me some photos, they looked nothing like her whatsoever. They must have been taken a lot earlier as now her face was absolutely plastered in acne. With huge Dennis Taylor-like-glasses and tiny eyes, her attempts at compensating for her miniature size with the highest of high heels seemed OTT to say the least. So there's me with a painted smile across my face the size of a canoe. "At last we meet" was all I could think of to say.

"Nice to meet you too" Chu Yan replied, leaning over and shaking hands with a thoroughly excited demeanor about her.

At that moment two things descended; a sinking feeling of intense disappointment but worse was the realisation that I'd be spending my time for the foreseeable future with who I can only describe as a 'human mole', SHEEEET! As time visibly slowed down, here was definitely one of those moments where you would rather fall off a cliff than be in this present incarnation.

Feng in contrast, a stunning, elegant woman with straight black hair down to her arse and looks to die for then made her introduction in perfect British English.

"Very glad to meet you. I hope you had a pleasant journey" also shaking my hand with a polite smile. "Let's get a taxi and go straight to your apartment. You must be tired" At that she turned and led the way. It seemed that she had done all of this before and her 'matter-of-fact' manner spoke volumes.

Leaving the airport, Chu Yan immediately held my hand and also throughout the whole ride to the apartment. While we occupied the back seat, Feng sat up front. When the taxi pulled away she donned her sunglasses giving her a model-like quality. As the hot Zhanjiang air blew through the open window fanning her hair back, I tried desperately not to make any comparisons with the person sitting next to me.

Suddenly, Feng turned around, lifted her shades and made strong and deliberate eye contact with me,

"Chu Yan has made a lot of effort to get the apartment ready. I hope you don't let her down."

As the hairs stood up on the back of my neck, clearly she knew her shit. "Don't worry about that" I stammered. "So how long have you been a translator for?" blatantly trying to change the subject.

"Oh, a few years now. I've been helping Westerners getting married here in Zhanjiang for some time. Chu Yan's been really practicing her English for you. You will find she's a really nice person."

"Married?" This single word set instant multiple sirens off resonating inside my heaving skull and I battled to show any effects of my alarm to Feng, managing to maintain a smile as best I could. Even so it rendered me unable to reply and speechless for the rest of the journey.

Big BIG major SHITE! The taxi pulled up at what can only be described as the armpit of the universe. A series of endless identical ageing concrete housing blocks tightly bunched together was to be the new neighbourhood for the foreseeable future. With morale plummeting as fast as a burning B-17, I wondered what I had been imagining this moment would be like; a nice wooden cabin with an Aga cooker overlooking a lake? Maybe something more traditional with sliding screens for doors and curved tiled roofing in quiet suburbia.

With puke on the stair-well, bare electrical wire hanging everywhere and graffitied walls, it was easy to feel worried about leaving all my gear there but at least the door had a hefty lock on it. The flat turned out to be a small single room with a very short wooden bed as hard as concrete and no mattress; tough for one person to live in, let alone two. The kitchen looked like it had never been used and was shared communally with everyone on that floor, as was the toilet that looked like it had never been cleaned. By the time we sat down, I was already in a state of complete shock about the whole thing.

Before the trip a friend had advised me to take photos of friends and family along which I proceeded to show Chu Yan and Feng. As we knelt on the floor together in front of my open bags, Chu Yan pressed herself as close as physically possible to me, while Feng sat beside us on a small chair and leant over to look. Hard work focusing on the photos with Feng's perfect legs right next to me; wearing black leggings which ended just below the knee, though her matching black heels were far more modest than Chu Yan's they seemed to totally belong on this woman.

They viewed all the snaps from England with interest and also a lot of my travel gear. Fair-play to Chu Yan; she really had been doing her homework, showing that her English wasn't half bad. Communication didn't seem as hard as anticipated, especially with a dictionary and pen and paper.

"What is this?" asked Chu Yan, pulling out the diary; an unnecessarily large book with blank pages and a colourful Buddha picture on the cover.

"Oh, just my diary" I shrugged casually.

"Diary?"

"Ri ji" said Feng towards Chu Yan.

"Ohhhhh, diary!" And at that they both started reading with great interest. Amazing hey? What ever happened to "Is it alright if I have a quick look?" Luckily I'd only started it the day before in the hotel so there wasn't much in there. Even so, feeling decidedly uncomfortable with them absorbing my heart-felt thoughts and feelings, I quickly changed the subject, directing their attention to the karabine attached to the bags. I'd brought them to link any luggage to my belt in crowded stations for safety so no one could run off with them.

"For travel" I explained, giving a quick demo.

"I hope soon we can travel" said Chu Yan. "It is my dream."

"Yes me too" my smile now becoming painful while my brain had been reduced to the state of runny scrambled eggs. Today had now become just a series of heart palpitations and there was the distinct feeling that it wasn't going to get any better. The wheels had now been set in motion and there didn't seem to be any brakes. Mercy!

After half an hour and pleasant formalities out of the way though, that time I was dreading had arrived and Feng said she would be leaving.

"I'll leave you two alone then. I hope you will be very happy together."

As soon as she was out the door Chu Yan threw her arms around me and announced "I loooove you!" Oh my God!

Blessed relief! Feng returned early evening and took us out that night. The night air is relentlessly hot and humid. People don't just stare at you, they gawp and turn their heads as you pass by. Some even stop and laugh. We were watching a group of dancers in the park in colourful red and yellow silk costumes when I turned my head to see this guy right next to me staring point blank. With eyes wide-open, he looked me up and down in utter disbelief like the aliens had just landed. I guess they had to him.

We went to the grubbiest dirtiest restaurant in the world. Dinner was served on the most stained table cloth you will ever see. Everyone was wiping their chopsticks or 'kuaizi' and washing them in the hot water for their tea. They offered dove as a starter I but gave that one a miss; the blackened meat looking wholly inedible. The whole place is totally overwhelming. City centres are okay as in the past after a couple of hours it's always been easy to escape to the tranquillity of Cedar Close and have a bit of a nap. You're having a laugh mate! Imagine doubling the number of people out in Bristol city centre on a Friday night and then doubling it again and you may get close. Your head feels like it's going to implode. Tenement blocks everywhere, bright lights, strangely Brightonesque near the water front and just total and utter pandemonium, aaaaaagh!

Back at the flat, the decision that evening to clear out of Zhanjiang ASAP was made pretty fast. After less than twelve hours it was time to make an immediate assessment of this dire situation. I chain smoked heavily outside on the landing that night while running through the various options. Through the bars across the window a big tropical storm came in to view over the rooftops with low rumbles murmuring in the distance.

Half an hour of self-absorbed pacing up and down later, it seemed the near future could be broken down into two separate possibilities; give her the news directly or do a runner. Concentrating with as much energy as possible on the latter, I worked out that the choice of an immediate evac' could have three variations: Runner 1: Leave in the middle of the night. Hardly likely under the circumstances. Runner 2: Say I'm going on a day trip by myself and make an instant b-line for the station? What would I do with my bags though? How would I get them out of the apartment without being discovered? If I did do it, it would have to be while she was at work though some covert research into the whereabouts of the train or bus station would have to be made. Also what time they leave, where you buy your tickets from and how much they would be was information that should be gathered in advance of the blitz-out. Runner 3: Maybe I could just jump into the nearest taxi, say "to the next town" in Chinese and just drive the hell out of there.

In the end after a whole packet of high tar deliberation, having as much energy as a dying shrew at that moment was the clincher in shelving the disappearing act as a worst case scenario. Instead, I decided to pick my moment and tell her straight despite the risks. Allowing my mind to wander once more, the possible dangers of what may happen ran riot around my poor aching cranium. Maybe an enraged crowd would gather outside the apartment block awaiting the family. Upon their arrival they would take me away to somewhere out of the way where the torture would commence. I wondered how many other Westerners had also gone down this one way cul-de-sac and where they were being kept.

I was hoping she would be asleep when I went back in. Fat chance of that! Not only did she wait up, but it turned out that in the evenings Ms Mole transformed into a human limpet resulting in the worst most fitful night's sleep in ages. I mean it's hot enough there anyway at anytime, but she seemed to cling to me the whole night, irritably resisting any attempts made to pry her off. To top it all, the neighbours were all extremely loud. For some reason they had their TV on max every night and the walls were so wafer thin, they offered no protection for your ears.

In the morning, once outside in the light of day, although seriously hot, the streets had cleared; still busy, but do-able. Chu Yan had taken the day off of work and we had breakfast in a restaurant that even served toast. Strange watching Madame eat. She would lean downwards towards the plate and then hold the toast up close to her mouth in both hands. Making quick tiny bites with closed eyes I was now positive of her rodent lineage and imagined the whole family gathered around the table eating in the same fashion in some burrow somewhere.

While we were eating breakfast, a Western guy unexpectedly walked in with a Chinese woman following closely behind. Sitting at a table across the other side of the restaurant he had the looks of a young Val Kilmer while sporting a blond crew cut.

"Hey buddy, how's it hangin'?" he bellowed across the way from his table.

"Great thanks, just knackered from the jet lag, I'm Andy what's your name dude?"

"Call me Keys" he replied with a broad smile, "Just got here huu?"

"Yep, still getting used to it. What are you doing here?"

"Oh, I just come here once a year for a few weeks" he explained nonchalantly. "I mainly come here to pick up girls and party" he beamed turning his head and making eye contact at close range to the girl sitting next to him. Certainly an amazing sight for any man, her tight silk red dress hugged her perfect curves like it was painted on and her red lipstick was made to match. Her abundant hair had been perfectly tied up in a bunch on top of her head revealing a long and elegant neck line. Smokin' was the only way to describe her and for a brief second they were almost nose to nose as she smiled back.

Returning his attention back to our table "Are you here to get married then?" he delivered like some hammer blow, "Most Western guys I see here are".

"Oh we're just good friends" I stuttered, unwilling to commit myself in any shape or form despite the consequences of such a statement.

"Well good luck for whatever bud" he ended, now focusing on their breakfast as it was brought to the table.

When Chu Yan's face bunched up into a big frown it was never a pretty sight at the best of times and it was my first experience of this painful sight. After leaving the restaurant Madame walked ten paces ahead in a strop, my "Its still early days" explanation merely aggravating the situation so the next fifteen minutes continued in painful silence.

Onwards with the day we continued our walk down by the water front which seemed to melt the frosty atmosphere from earlier. Amazing to think that this was China and the first time my cluttered mind could start taking it all in. Enjoying breathing in the warm sea air, the sound of sea gulls was a welcome replacement to the previous night's barrage. Water gently lapped against the side of the sea-walls, an invitation to fall into a wave of uncaring tiredness. People slowly cycled past on rickety bikes and the sense of space away from concrete central was a tonic to the nerves. Old-dilapidated boats tied up to the shore, gently moving up and down together with passing waves. Rusting brown hulks that looked like they would never go to sea again remained permanently moored.

It was this time that I planned to drop the bad news to Chu Yan and just get it over with, but in some amazing quirk of bad timing she suddenly delivered a major blow to the scheme.

"We must go home now!"

"Oh, how come? I'm having a great time today. Can't we stay out here for a bit longer?" Anything to returning to the confines of that tiny apartment after all.

"No! My family will visit. We must go" said Chu Yan firmly as she started to turn back. Not only was I suddenly suffering yet another coronary, this pissed me off no end. We had agreed before I left England that the family would be kept at bay and I could only think that this was some sort of strategic move on her part to speed up the process of getting us together.

Like an air-raid warning siren going off in my head for a few minutes, once more I'd soared into a high state of panic. I mean meeting the parents at anytime is a big one, but with someone who you were preparing to dump a few seconds earlier? All I wanted to do was bail-out at 40,000 feet and forget the parachute. With my poor jet-lagged and stressed out brain doing what it could under the circumstances, I managed to come up with the first of many golden excuses I would employ during the next week or so:

"My Chinese is still not good enough and I would be too embarrassed when meeting the family. If you could teach me some more Chinese for a few weeks then that would be fine".

Luckily, though clearly annoyed once again, she got on her phone and told her Mum. Phew! Her bombshell had me so shaken though that there was little choice to abort Plan-A until another opportune moment.

We resumed the walk, getting close to the water though with a second helping of the silent treatment and knitted forehead. For another half an hour, Her Majesty refused to talk once again. Obviously this was a behavioral pattern that no doubt I would become very accustomed to in the days to come. In total relief from the previous events and another wave of exhaustion, I succumbed to a total crash out in a park under the shade of some palm trees. Annoyingly though Ms Limpet, having by this time mellowed out, still managed to attach herself to me, even in the blistering afternoon heat. One super-irritating habit she had was to hold hands where ever we went. I found myself continually looking for reasons to let go, but even when my hand was free, there would be an inevitable tug at my shirt reminding me. If I suggested I didn't want to, the frown from hell would immediately re-appear.

Anyway, later, with a big sigh of relief, Feng showed up looking as stunning as ever taking us to this huge sea food restaurant to meet some of her friends and also a supersized American guy called Dan that she was helping out. Dan was taking this woman called Li back to the States to marry and this was the first time they had met. She couldn't speak a word of English and the pair looked decidedly awkward, especially as Dan did not know a word of Chinese! He had just bought an electronic dictionary and they sat next to each other figuring out their primary mode of communication for the foreseeable future. They looked happy enough though and all in all it was a pretty good evening.

One wall of the restaurant consisted of nothing but fish tanks filled with live sea creatures. There were so many, there could have been every species of sea life on display, including small turtles and sea urchins. Actually, experiences aside I've never been able to eat sea-food in any shape or form and it makes me turn green the moment it gets close.

I remember even as a child, those painful Saturday evenings when Mum would bang a plate of her carbonized fish down on the table. My Dad would shout "EAT IT" and I would cry loudly. Unfortunately, though I was able to order chicken and some greens it was brought to the table quite early on. Though this would normally be a good thing if you were as ravenous as I was, within seconds everyone had helped themselves to it and it quickly vanished before my eyes. It's the custom to share your food here and take what you want from any plate on the table. The next dish was this enormous platter of sea worms, hmmmmm not my thing really!

Oh the woe! Chu Yan cried loudly last night for hours blubbering out "You Don't Loooove Meeeee" in a wailing voice.

Even after shoving in my ear plugs as far as they would go, she made impossible for me to go to sleep. "You're damned right" was all I could think of, that and the worst nightmare scenario of having a family of 'mole children'. On that thought, for sure, tomorrow was going to be the day to bring this whole painful episode to a close.

Having hardly slept, Chu Yan was up early already wearing her favourite mega-frown. With barely a chance to open my eyes, she said she had to go to work. "Wait here!" was the sharp good morning greeting. At that, she slammed the door and I could hear the key turning in the lock. It's amazing what can snap you out of slumber and like a rocket I was out of bed, checking to see if I really had been locked in. With great relief the door opened so at least I wasn't a prisoner in that tiny room for the day. Peering nervously outside, the coast was clear so I went straight to a heavyweight session of diary writing before breakfast. Therapy or what!

After leaving a note on the door saying when I'd be back, it was onwards with enjoying the first day in this huge city by myself. Relief! The streets are maxed out to capacity here, with the worst road lunacy you will ever see in your life. I started by running across these roads, but if you don't manage to get all the way across, you soon find yourself stranded and faced both ways by a huge volume of oncoming traffic. As a result the best thing to do is closely follow people as they cross, who are obviously experts at navigating the gaps between vehicles.

Finding the same restaurant as before, I got the toast in and then went to an internet café. There was an e-mail waiting from Mum. Actually it was the first one she had ever written and with it the endearing image of her slowly typing it with two fingers, her nose inches away from the key-board. It took a long time to persuade her to start using the internet; "Just send me a post card" was her argument. Even when we finally got to the internet café, it took ten minutes to get her to learn to double-click. I had to write the whole procedure for sending mail down in black and white for her on a sheet of A4. Mum's e-mail said that everything was ok and not to worry about anything as "Kevin was helping her". "Who the hell's Kevin?" I wondered.

After spending a few more hours soaking up the bliss of the water front again, it was time to take a closer look at a Chinese building site which are fascinating places. No attention spared to the old health and safety regulations here mate. Scaffolding is made out of bamboo poles tied together with string. Ladders are made out of nailed together wood. No step ladders so far. They work all night and the sites are lit up with steam and smoke giving quite a top atmospheric effect. There are some road works at the end of the street. This guy has been sitting in this small crane for days doing absolutely nothing. Mind you he seems to sleep a lot and yesterday was reading the paper, phew! Some of the construction workers live on site under tarps. Dedication to work alright. No sickies in China.

Reluctantly arriving back at the 'fun-palace', there was Ms Mole sitting there reading the diary....aaaaagh! She must have spent quite some time rifling around to find it. Neglecting to say she'd be back at lunchtime, she had been waiting all afternoon. How long she'd been trying to decipher my inane rantings I can only guess. Whether she understood it or she was just pissed-off at waiting all day, either way she was wearing the frown of all frowns. Maybe it was just the taste of freedom that disagreed.

With virtually no time to even sit down after a day's wandering around in the heat, she announced that she had invited some of her friends to join us and were already on their way. No sooner had they arrived, Chu Yan was holding hands with a fierce grip and lapping up the attention. Of course her friends all wanted to know about her new man, something I had no choice but to go along with. From then on, the friends have shown up every day on the dot to keep us company and I can only think that this had been some calculated tactic to keep me in place.

In the evening we went to the cinema because they wanted to see Air Force One with Harrison Ford (as you do). When the film started it was only Willy Wonka and the frigging Chocolate Factory wasn't it! The film they wanted had finished a month ago but the poster was still up!

Other stuff, oddments and other unusual observations in no particular order:

You have to use chopsticks for every meal. It doesn't make much difference if you make a mess as everyone does. Still getting served food I can't eat, like one time there was a little bird in the soup! One of the waitresses in a familiar restaurant kept smirking at my crap attempts to use chopsticks. Having developed quite a rapport with her and making her laugh in my pigeon Chinese, I beckoned her over and said "Wo jiao shemne?" She looked a bit weirded-out and after repeating it a few times, walked off looking highly confused. I then realised that I had been saying "Who am I?" to the poor girl.

The Chinese TV is also mad. They have the football on but they intersplice the Premiership with the Championship and then half way through the highlights there are some comedy sketches with guys poncing around in fluffy animal suits with loads of canned laughter.

Every shop is open from 8am to 11 pm. The department stores are the most immense multi-storey places you can imagine that sell absolutely everything, well all except envelopes which after three days are proving to be illusive. These places are all absolutely heaving and you'll often find yourself with little space to move. With people shouting at the top of their voices it's almost impossible to hear yourself think. Believe me you don't need to be pushing a shopping trolley around here I can tell you.

Funnily enough, after all the worry and utter terror when arriving on Saturday, things are starting to level out a bit. I've made friends with a bloke called Mr Wang, the owner of this shop on the corner that sells cheap beer (well we're all entitled to the odd one now and again). Tsingtao is the most popular brew in China and isn't half bad as it goes. It comes in these whopping great 600ml bottles and costs two kuai. That's less than twenty pence so you can't complain about that. He even puts a special table outside of his shop with an umbrella. Its great sitting there watching the world go by. Every night loads of OAP's do aerobics to traditional Chinese music in the precinct over the road, that's really something a bit special to watch.

Woke up feeling really chilled having seemingly put all the worries aside for the time being. The people here make you feel really at home. Along with the best nights sleep in weeks my dreams are enormous. It's great not to be drinking every night and with growing confidence about things, I now strut around like a Western peacock saying hello and good morning as often as possible, Crocodile Dundee stylee. People greff[1] really loudly all the time and everywhere even right next to you when you are eating in the restaurant which is definitely hard to handle.

Met this Aussie in the street who knew all the details on the best, cheapest ways to get to Yangshuo in Guilin. The big headache is how to get away from here on my own without creating a big scene. I really don't want to have a giant bust-up before I go, especially with the friends hovering about all day and the potential of family members on stand-by. My brain is on overtime trying to work everything out, including how to get to the train station and buy a ticket for one. There is one on Sunday at 12.30am and it's a sleeper train.
Reckon I'll feel like I'm really on my way then. Until then life is about dealing with this all-consuming stress and maintaining the power of rational thought. I cannot wait to get away from here, to be going north and really getting into the trip. It's going to be an awesome one for sure.

BRING IT ON!

---

[1] Greffing is everywhere in China and is similar to spitting except before you do it, you make a huge snorting noise as you bring everything up from your sinuses and throat. Get used to it if you can. The worst is in restaurants or when you're in a taxi. If you're in a taxi and the driver winds down the window, take cover immediately. Cover your ears, look away and make sure your not downwind if you're sitting on the back seat.

# Get out of Dodge: 14<sup>th</sup> September 2005

Zhanjiang turned out to be an incredible, unforgettable experience, but to say I'm glad to have put it in the past is surely the understatement of the decade. After using every bit of energy to get out of dodge, now it's over the feeling of space and freedom feels vast. I am totally free! After a week of Zhanjiang, this was clearly not the start to the trip that was envisaged. There's no doubt that Chu Yan knew that things weren't heading in the right direction but she sure wasn't going to let me go without putting up some major resistance.

One day she and her friends took me to a small zoo to find animals stuffed into tiny dirty foul-smelling, dark black cages covered in shite with no water. There was one decidedly ill-looking deer, very bony and unhappy in the intense heat. I was really upset about this. Call me an ageing wet hippy, but after sitting watching the deer in the tranquillity of Longwood on the Mendips, it maxed me out big time.

Retreating to the park next door, we got some ice creams in and found some benches out of the sun; a perfect remedy for the poor Westerner to calm down. It was also there, surrounded by all her friends that Chu Yan suddenly announced that she would soon be quitting her job and go travelling with me. Of course this was all done in Chinese and I had absolutely no idea what she was going on about, other than her friends seemed all very animated and happy. One even came over and shook my hand, "Gong xi, Gong xi" (congratulations) he cried.

"What did you just say?" I asked Chu Yan, trying to gleefully go along with the whole thing.

"Tomorrow I will tell my boss I will leave. Then we can go together"

As a wave of approval went round, all I could think of was whether I was going to keel over with another heart attack or not. In that split second, with stress levels instantly hitting a new all-time high, it seemed that there would be surely no way to talk my way out of this new hole. Like a window into terror, my visualisations of the family and friends waving us off at the train station were like the happy ending of a film. It really was going to become reality if something wasn't done about it double time.

As the evening approached, like some saving angel Feng showed up and was able to translate my next scheme I'd been concocting throughout the afternoon. The line went as follows:

"I've been here in Zhanjiang for too long already and have itchy feet and really need to get going. I will go ahead of Chu Yan then meet her at a laer date but will miss her very much. I would really appreciate it if her friends can take me to the train station so I can find out when the train goes and where to buy a ticket." Class! The look on Feng's face wore a strong look of disbelief in my story but she translated the whole thing. Although the line was as wafer thin as a sheet of No-Frills toilet paper, the cunning use of the friends was a stroke of genius. Turning the tables around, in true Chinese style they instantly went to work and like lightning we were down the train station where they sorted me out.

Unlike the airport, there were no signs in English and the atmosphere was completely different. The whole place had a worn and dilapidated feeling about it and hadn't seen a coat of paint in a long time. People were unable to queue up, shouting and pushing-in, even though there were metal railings to keep the masses in order. There was one platform for one train so things started to become a bit easier to comprehend. I got all the information that was needed, taking notes on everything down to the letter. This included how to ask the taxi driver to go to the airport for a quick getaway, written in Chinese in case he couldn't understand. Result! Throughout the whole time Ms Mole could not keep that terrible frown at bay, as she realised her friends were unknowingly assisting me in my bid to escape.

On the flip-side to the whole nightmare Chu Yan and I did have some nice times together. Once we were out and about and seeing the sights, the tension at least for the time being seemed to go away. Chu Yan's friends had been fantastic. Everyone did so much and showed so much hospitality, helping me out and showing me round.

On the final day, we went out of Zhanjiang on the bus together to go to a park. Loads of people stared and some on the nearest seats chatted with me, curious as to the extent of my Chinese. In the countryside fly tipping is all the rage. Great piles of rubbish are dumped everywhere and as the aging little bus juddered its way along, it kicked up vast amounts of paper and old carrier bags in its dusty wake.

From the bus stop Chu Yan then flagged down a rickshaw to go the rest of the way. There are rickshaws all over the place and they flood the traffic lanes helping to add to the already congested roads. A lot are still pedal powered but most consist of motorized three wheelers with a green body of thin metal and canvass over a skeleton of stainless steel. Each one has a small door round the back with just enough space for two people to squeeze in. To be honest I'd been hoping to avoid going by rickshaw as they look so unsafe but it's so easy to find one and they're really cheap. As the driver tears off as fast as he can, throwing road safety firmly out of the window, you really feel like your fate is in the hands of the Gods, wholly expecting to be involved in a smash up at any second.

With great relief and legs like jelly, we found the park; a nice quiet space with no people anywhere. At the ticket office, the discovery was that it cost 100 kuai to get in. I find parks pretty boring and for the equivalent of over fifteen quid, it was difficult to restrain my typical moany behaviour, but when we got in, holy shit!

Once inside, long steep slopes led smoothly down to a massive circular volcanic lake called Huguang Yan. The whole area was covered in lush sub-tropical vegetation, the forest buzzed with life and working our way down to the water line, the humidity noticeably increased. Apparently you could drink the water but judging from what the local environment had already offered, I decided to opt out of the taste test.

In every direction, enormous Chinese dragon statues would be there to angrily bear down upon you. Brightly coloured pagodas and a vast labyrinth of stone steps and pathways allowed you to wander all day to your heart's content. Hundreds of small six sided pavilions awaited in the surrounding hills, linking the different routes if it was time to sit down and take a break. Some hid in the woods engulfed in twisted undergrowth.

Some boasted a breathtaking view. After doing some great walking through the trees, I noticed that we'd been walking obliviously through a network of the biggest, most colourful and nastiest looking spiders known to mankind. There were just smaller than a dinner plate. I was more careful after that and backed out very slowly.

An amazing Chinese temple known as Lengyan protruded out from the forest, working its way high up the steep hillside. The priests were all very chatty, though I didn't have a clue what they were going on about apart from the fact that it cost 180 kuai to be blessed, hmmmm! Still, it really was more of what I had in mind when choosing to come to China; a relief to know that it's not all just crazy roads and apartment blocks.

Once again the Chinese demonstrated their complete lack of Health and Safety standards, something that felt really refreshing. The boat cruise round the lake turned out to be a complete white knuckle ride as the owner threw it into full throttle and tore off at full whack. He took great delight into throwing it into the tightest turns possible while everyone screamed at the top of their voices. The other attractions were also completely dangerous like neglected narrow wooden walkways over ditches, slippery with the humidity. No doubt plenty of visitors had already gone skew-whiff damaging important parts of their body, especially in the kids play area.

With our time at the lake drawing to a close we decided to go down to the shore one last time. It's quite amazing how quick the weather can change in the south of China and while we made our way along the bank a massive electrical storm descended. As the sky blackened, the wind suddenly died and all became strangely silent. A faint low rumble of thunder in the background suggested that a big one was on its way. Triggering a feeling of impending doom, we quickened our pace. As per usual Madame had worn her super high heels so was unable to run when the rain hit. Being totally caught out in the open Chu Yan pulled out her umbrella; a tiny pink and blue one which we attempted to use as a shelter. I seem to recall somewhere, someone saying that hiding under an umbrella is not quite top of the pops in these circumstances, but what can you do hey? Within seconds it seemed that bolt after bolt of lightning was coming down ear splittingly close like an air-strike.

The storm was so immediately fierce with the rain hammering down vertically that a carpet of warm water washed down over our feet. With the expectancy of becoming a human barbeque we continued heading for the nearest cover as fast as possible; some spectacle I can tell you as Chu Yan made her way pathetically tip toeing through the deluge in her shoes.

All in all it was a fantastic day. Trouble was when arriving back in Zhanjiang, the need to get out of Dodge was really building. The thought of getting on that train and what would happen was by now my one and only thought. After the restaurant, I hit Mr Wang's big stylee, saying I would be back in half an hour; anything to avoid going back to the apartment. By 2.30 in the morning, the locals were pretty amazed at how much of the local brew I'd got through and how totally and utterly arseholed someone could get. Getting back to the flat, Madame had been waiting-up the whole time and was not a happy bunny. Once again she'd been reading my diary having left it open next to the bed. Since the last episode though, I'd been writing about what a great time we were having and how well we were getting on in the clearest of handwriting. The thought that she had just absorbed some quality disinformation brought some minor satisfaction.

That night was a tough one though and all the Tsingtao in the world couldn't get me to sleep. The nightmare scenarios had become worse. I now visualised an angry shouting mob carrying flaming torches, chasing me down the street towards the station with the trolley bag rattling behind. Another worry about missing the train and being marooned for another day. Would I be going to the station alone or not? Maybe Feng would come along to deliver one last icy look of doubt into my eyes? Maybe Her Majesty would somehow sabotage my operation or even decide to come along at the last second, throwing a few clothes into a bag and declaring that "nothing else mattered!"

Anyway, Sunday midnight cometh. Chu Yan insisted on seeing me off though with relief, noticeably only brought her handbag. She held hands in the taxi until the last. This time the station was absolutely packed to the rafters fuelling my already frayed nerves and what made things worse was remembering that everyone there was also going on the same train. Shite! Talk about a stampede when the gates opened. Madness! At least the sudden torrent of people gave me the opportunity to make one last excuse in avoiding any goodbye speeches. As people shoved and pushed their way forward all that could be done was twist around and spare a wave before climbing on board.

Finding the right compartment was an event in itself. The aisle was completely jammed with passengers and their luggage, all shouting and going crazy in some form of strange panic to find their places. As it was an over-night train, at least half of its carriages were made-up of sleeper cabins with two three-storey bunk beds either side. As the train pulled away there was just enough time to catch a last glimpse of Chu Yan on the platform; her eyes welling-up. I have to admit that for the previous twenty-four hours I'd been harbouring a sense of mounting guilt but there was nothing that could be done about it and within minutes of departure, a feeling of utter relief replaced the familiar mixture of negativity and stress that had been possessing me for weeks. Though the whole saga had left me totally exhausted, I was out of there, able to start again. Thank f*ck for that!

It was a crazy night on that train with everyone jammed in like sardines, but far cheaper than catching the plane. Mind you, there was this old woman on the bed next door who was ill and kept making these horrendous noises from her lungs all night. At one point she got too close, sharing her halitosis with me. I spent the whole night worrying about going to go down with some rare Asian sickness.

By morning things had become far more chilled out, and the journey was a really enjoyable one. Looking out and watching the Chinese countryside go by, you could really feel that we were moving inland filling me with excitement The people in the compartment started to warm to me when saying good morning to them. At last Guilin. Made it! Sense of achievement. Next was the bus to Yangshuo. This is the first major place on the list to visit; somewhere I have read about so much about and seen so many pictures of in the past nine months. To think I'd be seeing it for real instead!

# 4

# Yangers - Doin' it Tomorrow!

Yangers, the name given to the town of Yangshuo by the local Westerner ex-pats, is a place straight out of paradise. As the sun sets on a warm autumn evening, any roof-top view will take hold of your senses immersing you into a state of bliss. All your worldly stress and worry will be completely lifted while you're in this nirvana. Breathe in and close your eyes, reflect on your past for a moment, then forget everything.

The scenery is some of the most stunning you will see in your life. The small town itself sits comfortably below the classic limestone hills of the Guangxi Antonymous Region. There are around 20,000 of these hills in Yangshuo County. At dusk, they seem to march purposefully towards the horizon, as if each one is a giant towering single life form. Set against the dimming sky, their sharp angled silhouettes seem to magnify your already heightened appreciation of space, perspective and depth to this magical place. It's easy to encounter a perfect moment in Yangers for sure.

The town itself consists of small buildings, offering the passer-by a glimpse of what it may have been like before China discovered the high-rise block. An intricate network of narrow alleyways, Yangers only really only has two main roads that run off from the main highway, Die Cui Road and Xi Jie or West Street, so it's easy to go off the beaten track and see how the other-half live. In terms of aesthetics, you are confronted by a combination of traditional architecture and industrious existence as the locals go about their daily business. The Li River threads its way lazily by and there are countless places to visit by bicycle out of town such as old villages, farmlands, caves and of course Yangers is famous for its rock climbing.

Whilst visiting such an amazing place, Westerners also get to do what Westerners seem to love doing best; that is lying in bed late, eating big breakfasts, a little shopping followed by lunch, perhaps a nap or sightseeing, eating and then going to bed late after getting arseholed with the possibility of a shag. You can moan that your wireless connection isn't that great or that the apple pie down West Street wasn't as good as they said. The bars are great on a hot evening. In such a thoroughly good mood it's easy to find yourself inevitably being drawn towards your already favourite designated drinking hole where the friends you met last night are already on their next mission of defilement.

It's easy to get stuck in Yangers. Indeed it's a strange place for that. If you've been on the road soaking up the adventure you are suddenly faced with the total opposite. Yangers is cushty with a capital C. I mean why not put off doing anything you had planned until the day after tomorrow. Time does not exist in Yangers. When the day after tomorrow quickly arrives, you've normally already forgotten what you were gonna do anyway so why not go down the bar instead. Ahhhh, Yangers!

At certain key times in the year, many people from surrounding areas will descend on Yangshuo. My stay luckily coincided with the Mid-Autumn Festival which is one of two holidays Chinese people will get in the year and has been around for about 3,000 years (the other being the Spring Festival aka Chinese New Year). It normally lasts around two weeks and celebrates the end of the summer and the harvest. There are two calendars in China, the solar one like ours and the lunar one. The celebration is based on the latter so that the moon will be at its fullest during the holiday. Chinese people get so little time off and work all hours, so the general level of excitement is massive. Noise levels go through the roof and there are tour parties everywhere. If it's your first time you will easily enjoy the wonderful atmosphere of a Chinese festival. Down the main drag of West Street it is hard to move, it's just a blessing that most people will be tucked away in bed by 12pm. Having said that they are also up at the crack of dawn. Oh the joy!

## A Helpless Tourist: 20th September 2005

The Australian guy in Zhanjiang said to avoid the touts at Guilin bus station at all costs and go to the ticket office. Like a mug though I've been immediately sucked in by the first person shouting the word Yangshuo and end-up sitting on the most dilapidated crate you will ever see. For over an hour we wait in the station while the sun heats the bus like a microwave oven. At last, after all the seats have been taken we slowly move off only to find the driver pulls over every five minutes at every stop along the way. Still, who am I to complain? The view around here is unbelievable and by the time we reach Yangers I am excited beyond belief.

Waiting for the stampede to finish as the passengers all try to disembark at the same time, it's nice to get off the bus slowly with no shoving or pushing. My bags were first in the small trunk anyway and it takes a while to retrieve them. To my horror they've been squashed in with sacks of rice and luggage which had been forced inside to allow the door to close. Still, nothing too breakable in there I guess.

With the wheels of the trolley bag now rattling behind me once again, it's time to bravely venture forth into another unknown. From early morning until late its pandemonium in Yangers bus terminal; dusty vehicles of all shapes and sizes beep their horns. People shout at the tops of their voices and generally, the din of the whole place can be overpowering.

Almost recoiling from the volume and overload of information, I beeline it to the nearest exit and proceed to stand at the side of the road looking utterly clueless about what I am doing. At this point at least ten taxi drivers surround me all shouting and gesturing, obviously amused at the dazed look that has appeared across my face. This is surely the case of spot the totally useless tourist time.

"Qu nar?" (Where do you want to go?) As per usual, unable to understand anything they are saying, like a complete idiot, I decide to get out my guide book out. As I rifle around in my rucksack at the side of the street in broad day light, they close in like hungry vultures rubbing their hands together at the prospect of an easy killing. Reaching the correct page number, I hold up the book and point to the guesthouse on the little map I'd previously bookmarked. El lame-O!

"I want to go HERE. HERE? You know here?"

Taking the guidebook, three of them deliberate as if some major undertaking is lying ahead. "Er shi kuai" (twenty kuai) says one holding two fingers up.

"San shi kuai" (thirty kuai) says another with a big grin on his face.

"Wu shi kuai" (fifty kuai) and they burst into laughter. Having been completely mullered by the touts[1] I take the cheapest one just wanting to get out of there as fast as possible. My brain has been left pickled and they have done their work well. He grabs the trolley bag, carelessly throwing it into the back of his open rickshaw before jumping on and starting the engine.

---

[1] Touts will be found everywhere in China especially in the main tourist areas. If you are a Westerner they will always try it on with you. Prices may start at an unreasonably high level in case they get lucky. The best advice is to ignore touts completely and move on to a clear area where you can think. Touts will normally be flogging rip off taxi rides, tickets for tourist areas and trying to get you into crap guesthouses that no one else wants to stay in.

Talk about learning the hard way. I guess that's the only way to do it at times right? We pelt down the road at breakneck speed for no more than two minutes, turn right, then he stops outside the hotel and that was it; no more than a five kuai ride! Holding out his hand, he demands the money, "ER SHI" smiling profusely; evidently satisfied at fleecing another green Westerner.

Still shaking from my humiliation, the relief to be in the cool of the foyer lasts for all but ten seconds. The guesthouse has been recommended in my guidebook as "having welcoming staff with a relaxed reception area" and I've been envisaging my comfortable room on the journey over. For sure it's relaxed; the girl behind the counter can't give a rat's arse about me and is far more interested in chatting to her friend on QQ[2]. It seems this is more of an inconvenience to her.

"Ni Hao (hello) Do you have a room please?" I ask in a crap helpless tone.

"No Room!" she snaps, without taking her eyes off of the computer screen.

"Don't you have anything?"

"Later maybe!" Clearly she's highly irritated by this terrible disturbance.

"Oh, ok" my voice by now reduced to more of a pathetic mumble. Now met with silence and sadly hovering at the counter for a moment, my mind is a blank.

"Later!" she barks suddenly, now engaging eye contact in a minimal effort to remove the tourist from their lingering. I almost jump back with surprise at this undeserved and unexpected salvo and leave like some sad little puppy with his tail between its legs. Holy f*ck!

Back out on the busy street in the blistering sunshine, I have to admit that there's something wholly uncool about lugging a trolley bag down the street, especially in front of crowded restaurants with everyone looking at you. From seeing no Westerners anywhere for weeks, they are everywhere in Yangshuo and I can feel a lot of eyes locked on me as I forlornly make my way by. Strangely in Yangers, the locals are so used to seeing foreigners that most don't bat an eyelid at all. It's actually the Westerners that stare at other Westerners with a blank look on their faces. How strange is that hey?

The main drag consists of West Street and the smaller Xian Qian Street nearer the Li River. Unexpectedly there is a McDonalds[3] at the top of the road; a sure sign that 'progress' is in full march. Mixed in with the

---

[2] QQ: The Chinese equivalent of Yahoo or MSN messenger.
[3] In China McDonalds is called 'Mai Dang Lao', KFC is called 'Kan De Ji' and Pizza Hut is called 'Pizza Dian'.

traditional architecture that you were hoping to see, the big rounded day-glow yellow 'M' is completely out of place.

Further on the pedestrian area quickly becomes choked with tour parties and visitors perusing the souvenir shops, eateries and hostels. With its haphazard jumble of small buildings huddling together closely hemmed in by such terrific countryside, all grumbles instantly go straight out of the window though. It's easy to fall in love with this place, especially after the big city experience of Zhanjiang.

Breaking out into some quietness, I wander into a fairly empty cobbled area. Most residents wisely take refuge from the heat around lunch time and often you will see people sleeping spark out in any shady areas. Peering into another hotel, the guy behind the desk is face down and snoring at full volume so I make my way on.

Eventually a friendly looking woman calls out from across the way, "Hey there. Do you need a room?" A nice feeling to be wanted by someone and she introduces herself as Fanny, one of the owners of the Double Moon Hotel.

"Only two nights. I'm sorry after we are fully booked for the holiday"

"What holiday's that?" I stupidly reply, knowing absolutely nothing about this.

"The Autumn Festival will start soon. Many people will come and everywhere will be busy" she laughs. "Don't you know?"

Oh dear. More lameness on my part. Turns out that the second biggest holiday in China is well on its way and I'll be smack bang in the middle of it. Hours of research in advance certainly paid off there didn't it. To top it all off Fan' said that room prices will go through the roof, rendering some places unaffordable on this limited budget. Most will be triple rate. Still, mustn't grumble. It's more like a great fluke of timing to be here as the celebrations are about to kick-off and I get excited every time I think about it.

Until then it's just mustard being able to crash-out on a decent bed under air-con in front of the telly; heaven! Fan's husband Mr Zhang or Jason as he likes to be called came and said hello. He's a policeman at the station round the corner and seems like a decent bloke. Sitting outside the hotel, it's great just watching the world go by with them, taking in this amazing new environment. Having now recharged the batteries I can thoroughly pretend that the last few weeks never happened including the Yangers welcoming committee.

How on earth can things get any better? After drawing a blank at every hotel to look for a room, this American guy put me on to the most terrific place called Monkey Jane's Guest House. It's not hard to miss

49

the way-in to MJ's. A yellow sign above a small entrance on the main drag is the only indication of what awaits. Find your way through the narrow tangle of old stone alleyways and if there's no one downstairs to meet you, go round the back and keep going up the stairs all the way to the top.

At the doorway, the coolest Western dudes under the sun said hi. More like a family, they'd been living at MJ's for months making it their home from home, seemingly abandoning any of their future plans for travelling. Understandable; the whole place is pure nirvana! They sorted out the most amazing room with a view out over Yangshuo that blows your head off. Upstairs opens up to a roof top bar with great sounds and a pool table. People come from all over to party most nights. In the morning you'll see bodies lying everywhere, spun out on the local brew all looking dreadful.

The bar is one or two floors above most of the other buildings, and you get a 360 degree panoramic view of just about everywhere across the thousands of small old rooftops to the hills at the edge of town. Down in the western part, the pagoda in the park rises up through the treetops and on the opposite side you can watch the life on the river all day. Man, can I not wait to move in there or what! Just totally and utterly awesome are the only words available describing what you see from the roof-top bar.

One of the first things you do when you get to Yangers is hire a bike out, get out of town and into the countryside. Just the tonic if you are hanging from the last night's abuse of the liver. Get to the top of the road and turn left for Moon Hill. Most people go that way but beware; the hawks await your arrival. Turn right and you quickly hit open expressway; scary!

The first time is the worst. When the heavy lorries and buses blast by at top speed, it all feels a bit precarious, almost as if you are going to be sucked in behind them in their wake and taken all the way to Guilin. What with their huge air horns blasting away or ageing suspension banging away into potholes, you can normally hear them coming a mile off. This means that mentally you will at least have a few seconds to prepare yourself for another dose of adrenalin. Once they go crashing past, the natural reaction is to instinctively make yourself as small as possible, grip those handlebars like your life depends on it, in a hope that you don't become suddenly airborne.

As soon as you're off the road though, it instantly turns into dirt tracks and you can start to breathe a great sigh of relief. At last your out there proper. It's also blissfully quiet. As the way ahead split up amongst the hills and farmland, I cycled on, uncaring about getting totally lost. Past the irrigated patchwork of rice fields connected by raised pathways and into hamlets of small buildings.

Stopping by a river an old man carried his grandson on his back across to the other side. A guy in a blue shirt shepherded his water buffalo lazily along the bank with nowhere to go in a hurry. Nearby houses remained silent with only a mixture of tools, wood piles, buckets and baskets left outside to show any sign of life. Roof tops were often corrugated sections of metal. Many were weighted down with bricks or stones so not to get blown away in the wind. Around the each doorway red paper signs in Chinese characters were pinned up for good luck. All in all as much as a Brit can say they love being in the countryside, you have to take your hat off and start to see how completely poor it is out here.

With the late afternoon sun setting as a reminder that it was time to make tracks I followed the sound of distant traffic guided my way. Back on tarmac, all sense of direction left the premises and I cycled aimlessly before unexpectedly getting directions from a hugely attractive woman called Mei standing at the side of the road. In tiny pink hot pants and white high heels it was kind of surreal seeing her standing there in the middle of nowhere. Politely turning down her kind offer to go into the nearby hut and share tea with her, I made my way back. All in all that has to be one of the best bike rides ever!

Had some intense moments with the local grub lately. A lot of the food is very hot, making you feel quite high and the locals find it all highly amusing. Yesterday, I was invited for a meal round the corner at someone's place and anticipation of it built up all day; this was not going be the safe restaurant food I've grown accustomed to.

Getting there early, they asked me to help in the kitchen, mercy! Most of the food was brought in clear polythene bags that had been sitting in the market place all day in the heat. One of the main dishes was an enormous helping of dark brown slime and bones that got poured out from a hole in the corner of this big bag. There was a great plate of black river snails, a platter of pig's knuckles and one of pig's ears. There were also unidentifiable meat parts of some sorts, but luckily at least there were some spinach-like greens in garlic to come to the rescue.

The kitchen itself was pretty much the standard in Yangers; stone walls, stone floor and a stove powered by a gas cylinder underneath. When it runs out someone on a tricycle cart or motorbike will deliver a replacement, slung precariously over one side. The food was cooked at lightning speed in a giant wok and the smoke from the chillies quickly found its way down the back of my sinuses. When one dish was finished, the wok was quickly wiped with an old minging[4] cloth and the next one quickly done; stir frying proper! For sure you don't want to be allergic to nuts over here. Nearly everything was fried in peanut oil.

How I made it through the meal I don't know. Sticking to the stuff that could be recognized, I managed to keep it down with a pleasant smile on my face. Kept belching the weirdest unpleasantness for the rest of the evening though and another guest spent the night heaving up the snails. Nice!

Had another big learning curve today; waking up with the ultimate hangover from absolute hell and in mad searing heat. It was a belter today. The three weeks of hitting the local beer must have created some sort of toxic build up in my system. Yes, most of us defile ourselves on a regular basis, but this is all a bit out of control in Yangers, especially at MJ's. Someone said that the locals clean their beer bottles using formaldehyde and whatever it is, has hit my head with a major paranoia trip about everything. Are those really ants crawling all over the place in my hotel room or what? Been driving me to lunacy all night and day.

In a bid to keep my head together I've started to look for chilled spaces to hang out to get away from it all. Actually it's harder than you think. It's virtually impossible to get any headspace in Yangers other than hiding in your room and feeling like a lame-arse.

Finally I found a quiet spot next to a small river that meets with the Li that's really nice. It's Yanger's only French bar but is also famous for having no customers in it, so is ideal for my needs. Out the back there is a side door with a wooden veranda jutting out over the water's edge; perfect. On my first night-off from the madness, I got chatting to one of the bar maids called A Qiao (I dare you to pronounce that) and we instantly hit it off. A Qiao is tall, has long dark curly hair and her English is pretty good.

"Hey, your English is great. Where did you learn it?" I pried.

"Oh, from my American boyfriend. He was a good teacher."

"Really? Well I look forward to meeting him sometime" was my sincerest sounding reply. "Where is he these days?" I snooped, delving even further and feeling that by this time I had entered into full on chat-up mode.

"We split up recently. I don't think he'll be back"

"That's too bad. I Hope you don't mind me asking what happened?"

---

[4] Informal British English for 'very dirty'. Also used as 'minger' for someone who is deeply unattractive.

"That's ok. He was drunk every night. Westerners all seem to get drunk, I don't know why. Chinese people will only have one or two bottles, but foreigners always drink a lot more. One night he was drunk so I hit him in the back of the head with my shoe while he was on the sofa"

"Really?" I grinned. "Was he alright?"

"No. I knocked him out and he had to go to hospital. You don't get drunk do you?" she asked, fixing a sudden and intense eye to eye glare at me.

"No no no. Only ever a few" I replied nervously holding my fourth bottle and already trying not to sway around. "Must have been a hell of a swing" was all I could think. Since that moment needless to say I've kept a distance with A Qiao though we've become good friends.

"How long have you been in Yangshuo for? Do you like it here?" were but a few of my bland openers that evening.

"Just a few months. It's ok. Maybe I'll move on to Yunnan, but it's better than before. I used to work in a factory in Shenzhen for for for...making........cigarette machines."

"Ah, you mean lighters?" taking mine out from my pocket.

"Dui Dui Dui (correct).That was difficult work. Maybe ten hours every day."

"What, no weekends off?" I asked in a crap moment of lameness

"Most people work every day in China" she laughed. "You have to make money here you know."

"Of course" I added, as if I knew what I was talking about. "If it's ok, can I ask how much money you made?"

"No problem. In the cigarette factory I could make twenty kuai but then I got another job making parts for computers. That was better; I could make thirty in that place."

"An hour?" the stupidity now becoming really quite fluent.

"A day!" she roared.

Amazing hey. That's thirty pence an hour top rate. I don't think you'll find a minimum wage around here mate. Just to think where all of my Chinese made products come from; people like A Qiao working seven days a week for ten hours a day. I mean in the UK it would be unthinkable not getting my weekly lie-in with a decent Tetley tea at the side of the bed. That followed by a second brew in front of Football Focus with just your boxers on.

"You know some workers will live in the factory and sleep for only a few hours then start work again. Many will work much more than ten hours. That is their life. They will work and save money then send it to their families"

"Don't people get any time off at all?"

"The holiday is coming. You know that. And then there is the Spring Festival. Some people get two weeks at that time." she replied, now sounding vaguely irritated.

Actually I meant Sundays, bank holidays, the odd day off; anything to break up the seven day week but the need to put your feet up in front of the telly is seen as more like a waste of time in China. Why waste time when you could be out there on an earner right?

"People work hard in China because we remember before when we had nothing.

My family live in the countryside. When I was very young     my Grandmother would go into the forest to find food. She would find fungus and some, some some.......How to say? Like from under a tree.

"Roots?"

"Dui Dui Dui. We had no meat and often no rice. If we got rice we would save it for a special time. This was the same everywhere for a long time. Many families would have nothing to eat."

And so endeth the lesson. No wonder everyone smiles around here. Seriously, Chinese people are the happiest bunch you will meet no matter how skint[5] they are. Everyone seems to smile. If you think I'm talking out of my arse then get yours over here and take a look for yourself. For some strange reason I didn't get wankered that evening. Whether it was not wanting to end up in A&E from one of A Qiao's special right hooks or just being totally humbled. Either way I went home as a deflated Western tourist who doesn't know the real meaning of hardship.

Right! With itchy feet to get moving already, the solution seems to be to head off for as long as it takes but seeing as I've already paid to stay here for three weeks (Lord help me), I'll be returning to Yangshuo. Travelling light and heading out into the agricultural heart of this region, the trip will start from Guilin, to Longsheng and then the famous rice terraces in the mountains of Pingan to find the Dong people. Apparently they all get up in the morning and put on their traditional blue clothes including full head dress complete with horns. Am I calm about this? You're having a laugh mate!

---

[5] Informal British English for having no money/ broke

54

## Longsheng Dragon Terraces - 26<sup>th</sup> September 2005

Well, I just got back from Pingan, a village in the Longji rice terraces, near Longsheng, kinda north of here. Some things didn't happen though, so return a bit disappointed. The only people wearing anything like traditional clothing were at the gates to the rice terraces selling tickets to get in and there was not one horn in sight. Oh dear! I also ended up travelling as part of a group, with Johanna from London, James from Canada and Yuval from Israel who also go to the roof top bar. Although, the idea was to go alone, it was awesome hanging with them and later in the day their company was really appreciated.

The journey to Longsheng was eventful; it soon ceased to be the normal Chinese bus journey you get down the main road. First, a woman with a moving bag got on the bus. It contained a chicken and a duck, presumably for dinner. This was a long bus journey alright and the duck stuck its head out of the bag the whole time, shaking with fear and rasping in the intense heat the whole time. We climbed higher and higher into the mountains which was breath taking stuff. All the while, the driver kept making ludicrous overtaking maneuvers on blind bends with a sheer drop on one side, often firmly glued to his mobile phone at the same time!

Longsheng
What a shit hole! I can only guess it's because it has the only main road around and there seems to be more traffic than people. Got the vibe to get out of there double time, but seeing as it's already lunch time, the guys start to look for somewhere to eat.

"How about this place?" asks Johanna already going towards one of the small open street diners like it's a done deal.

"What in that rancid smeg pit from hell?" I think. Seeing as the others are following though, another lesson in local food is clearly on its way.

The group decision is to order noodles, but when the food arrives, the gelatinous mass that is quivering away on each place looks wholly inedible. Maybe it's something to do with the lukewarm brown sauce or that it just looks like someone else's leftovers reheated. Either way, each mouthful is met with an accompanying grimace from each of us followed by a look of concentration while the swallowing commences.

Like many places, the kitchen is just a small area up front, big enough to get a couple of woks fired up, with the ingredients strewn everywhere on the floor and on a few shelves. Without warning the chef suddenly goes crazy right next to us, snapping us out of our gastronomic heaven. He's a tall powerhouse of a guy with wild eyes, bare-chested and pumped right up. Who knows what's pissed him off, but he jumps up waving a huge meat cleaver around, shouting at the top of his voice. Briefly turning his attention to us, he bellows something out in quick-fire Chinese at point blank range right into our faces.

"Faaaaaack!" James is the only one to say anything as we all instinctively recoil as far as possible while remaining seated. Talk about feeling small and helpless. Luckily for us, he then turns and focuses on one of the waitresses, chasing her outside still wielding the cleaver. You can hear his insane rantings right up the street causing a huge commotion. I go out to see what was happening, when he runs back down the street at me. Holy shit! Retreating back into the restaurant double time, we look for something to defend ourselves with.

"Quick. Grab anything you can" shouts Yuval, picking up a chair and we all follow suit. Blocking the doorway, the chef is still going absolutely nuts really keeping us penned in; we are going nowhere. There is a way out round the back but we burst into the next room, disturbing a bunch of guys playing cards who glare back strongly. One of them has a white eye with a huge scar running across it. Even when we have the chance to leave, we still haven't paid and are not just gonna do a runner on it. Eventually the old bill[1] show up and quickly do their stuff on him, as three of them cuff him over the back of their car. We emerge pretty shaken and dive into the first taxi that drives past, relieved to make a quick get-away. The taxi driver's girlfriend Cherry says that her uncle lives where we were going and insists that we stay there. Although it's that old familiar line that gets pulled on all tourists, this time we're not complaining. As we drive away still in shock, the Carpenters "Every shing-aling-aling look they're starting to sing" is playing on CD. Surreal!

Up and up we drove, along more winding narrow roads with an incredible drop down to the bottom. There was also an accompanying feeling of being a very long way from home now for the first time. When the taxi stopped, a long climb lay ahead that continued up to the first house. Locals offered to carry you in these brightly coloured sedan chairs, but unfortunately for them, we declined. Instead they had to take an enormous whale of a woman to the top and we could see them all struggling away as we hiked past.

---

[1] Informal British English meaning 'the police'.

Cherry's uncle's house was an amazing wooden structure with a breathtaking sight of the mountains from our room. As soon as it was possible to dump our gear, we were out as fast as possible, making our way to a high point to get the best view of the rice terraces as the sun set. Rice terraces are a traditional method of farming in the mountains that can be found across China and South East Asia. Where flat land is unavailable, irrigated steps have been carved into the hills to grow the rice and other crops. As the steps follow the contour of the land, this five hundred year old way of engineering is more like some great optical illusion; vibrant with energy and playing tricks with your senses. The locals call them 'the Dragon Terraces' for they snake away into the distance like the backbone of an ancient dragon. From early evening to sundown, sit back and watch a truly mesmerising display of changing colour and light across the valleys.

Words don't thoroughly describe the terraces; the incredible symmetry; colour; sense of space and tranquillity; stunning is a 195% understatement mate! We ended up in a locals place for tea, eating my first chicken's feet and rice cooked in bamboo! I may be getting a bit braver. At least it was all fresh this time.

I was squatting down in the toilet, when coming face to face with this enormous brown huntsman spider on the wall inches away from my nose. It had this weird menacing grin on its face. Not knowing whether or not it was a jumping spider, I moved very slowly away. The Uncle tried swatting it with his broom, but he somehow missed and the spider legged it. Shite, now it was really pissed off. So glad to have put the mozzy net up, but a real ordeal every time we wanted to use the loo[2]. Like there it was in the morning grinning away. I guess it must have been its manor or something! Outside in the heat a million insects made the biggest racket for miles. The countryside had never sounded so alive. There were giant multi-coloured millipedes and praying mantises everywhere which really are that bad tempered!

Along the way we also encountered the most fearsome waitress in Asia. A tall woman with a long white dress and high heels, she had a frown which made her look like a Klingon and a stare that said "What the f*ck are you looking at?"

"Fu yuan, (waitress). Excuse me, could I have a fork please?" I asked politely; the others had been given forks.

"NO FORK, NO FORK!" she replied in a loud and snappy voice before storming off. Later, James made the big BIG mistake of asking for ham and cheese with his omelette.

"NO HAM AND CHEESE! CHEESE ONLY! HAM ONLY!"

---

[2] Common spoken British English for W.C.

"I'll pay extra for it" he said almost apologetically.
"HAM ONLY!" she bellowed, leaning towards him.

Every time she came near the table glaring at us we cowered in trepidation. One time she brought the wrong tea. Oh dear, another shouting scene, but by this time, it had become kind of enjoyable. We did a lot of hiking while we were there, taking in the scenery; one morning getting up at 6.00am to see the sunrise. Outside, I noticed that the house nearby that had had no roof the previous night suddenly did, tiles and all. All the locals were out in the fields grafting. Many make their living as porters as much of their gear has to be carried up and a very unhappy pig was being carried tied up by its four legs and slung over a pole, squealing away.

Visited a very old village called Longji Zhuang Zai; an afternoons trek from the guesthouse. The locals looked a bit blown away when we got there, but a few words in Chinese seemed to connect. The whole place was the most aesthetically balanced place you could imagine, with vegetable plants growing between and on top of the buildings; tomatoes, watermelons, pumpkins, marrows, chilli plants, beans and fruit trees were in abundance everywhere. The irrigation system around there was the most intricate and perfect series of waterways you will ever come across, feeding each layer of terrace as they coiled their way up the hillside. Certainly a place that will stick in your mind forever.

# Chang Ge and the Jade Rabbit: 3rd October 2005

Alf, the owner of the Buffalo Bar took me on a guided tour of the backstreets of Yangshuo today. Whoa! Was I in for a shocker or what; seeing how the other half lives away from the touristy areas, encountering my first bit of in the street 'dentistry'. This woman sat there with her mouth open while an old bloke hacked away at her open mouth with what only looked like a filed down six inch nail. These are also the kind of streets that can really stink and have tons of rubbish lying around, so it was even more of a shocker to find a guy having surgery done on his back; the skin peeled well apart like curtains; the 'doctor' with a horrific set of tools on the floor around him.

Alf also took me past the indoor market so later that day I returned out of curiosity. Picking up as much courage as possible, taking one last deep breath of fresh air I then quickly ventured into another dimension. Massive and dimly lit, the surroundings seemed to be absorbed by deep shadows as far as the eye could see. It was like you were looking through a dark sepia camera lens or something. The ceiling seemed horribly low leading to a constricting sensation penetrating the top of your head and down into your throat. The air had a thickness to it, hot and layered with a million unbreathable aromas. People loomed out of dark places.

Thousands of sacks of raw ingredients filled every space containing seeds, pulses, pods and powders of many colours, dried animals, fish, squid and octopus. Live fish were kept in boxes of less than one foot high and ten feet square strewn across the floor haphazardly. They squirmed and rasped to get out as there was no room for them. Clear tubes were fed into the boxes to oxygenate the stale warm water and keep them alive. Dead and dying animals were all over in their hundreds; some nailed to benches before being torn apart; entrails hung from the ceiling and off the bench edges draped across the floor. Dogs had been hung up looking totally contorted in their final agonising death mask, marble white with their guts hanging out[1]. One was being cooked with a blow torch, a common way to do a quick barbeque. Carnage everywhere; red, brown, blue, a blow fly paradise.

---

[1] If you go out into the countryside, you will see animals running around together; chickens, ducks, small pigs and dogs are all raised together in the same place. Dogs are treated the same as any other farm animals in the south of China and also the extreme north by the Korean population, especially in Jilin. Some people say that dog meat is especially delicious.

At that point I shifted double time as my guts themselves were about to give up on me so I stumbled out gasping for air and to look at the sky.

Anyway less of that, I'm feeling sick all over again. Yesterday A Qiao and I got to the top of Green Lotus Peak, a high point in Yangshuo. Dragonflies buzzed about everywhere and the view from the top is phenomenal. Today, another hike took me to highest peak in the area, known loosely as TV Tower Hill. Wow was it worth it or what and I'm still in a ridiculously good mood from the whole thing. It was another one of those great moments, where you just couldn't take in that this is all happening, feeling seriously chuffed[2] about everything. To think of all those hours spent on the M32 motorway stuck in traffic. From the top, you get to see for miles in every direction including the river snaking off into the distance. There was also a great graffiti wall up there, with hundreds of names carved in it. Finding some old keys, I left my own inscription.

Watched the cormorant fishing last night. The fishing boats are normally long and slender with a small cabin along the middle though some can be simple bamboo rafts. Lit by dim lantern-light, the fisherman will quietly make his way out to the centre of the river. With the cormorants attached to a line they dive in and go hunting under the water. If they're successful, the guy pulls them in, takes the fish from their mouth and sends them back. Not sure whether to enjoy watching this really as the birds are tied around the neck so they can't eat what they catch. It is an amazing site though and is a traditional way of life on the river that's been going on for centuries; certainly something you don't see very often.

Well the Mid-Autumn Festival started officially yesterday and the streets are absolutely heaving every night. Everywhere you go there are brightly coloured red paper lanterns which really add to the atmosphere, a reminder that this really is China. Amazing! There are even flying lanterns lit with candles that people let off into the sky, drifting off high into the darkness.

It's also called the Moon Festival and celebrations will peak when the moon is at its fullest. The holiday is best known for its 'moon cakes' which are on sale everywhere you look. You can buy them individually or in special boxes to give as presents and they come in a variety of sweet or savoury flavours. Sometimes there will be a salty egg in the middle so watch out. I can't get on with the meat one's at all and they are often be made with lard which may explain why you're

---

unable to move afterwards. One's always enough. Eat two at your own risk.

There are plenty of stories surrounding the festival that have been around for centuries. The main one goes that a beautiful woman called Chan Ge found her husband's pill of immortality and "accidentally" took it. She overdosed and floated to the moon where she still lives today with her friend the jade rabbit. I reckon they'd definitely sell well in clubs at the weekend in the UK. Anyway, the legend of Chan-Ge is remembered by everyone on China and her face can often be found on moon cakes. People also burn incense in her name either in temples or special places set aside at home.

Actually, though there are few real holidays where people get time off in China, it seems that the calendar is packed full of festivals which all have their own special significance. So far there has been 'Teacher's Day' on September 10th, though nothing much happened. I guess it's just a time to respect your teacher and be nice to them. If only they had that one in England hey! There is also 'Double Nine Day' which is held on the September 9th, when, I am informed, "all the old people go out and climb the mountain". Phew! I now have images in my head of thousands of pensioners massing in the center of each city and passing out with coronaries on the way up; some spectacle I'm sure. There is also a 'Double Seven Day' which is Chinese Valentine's Day and 'Double Eleven Day' which is also called 'Singles Day' where unmarried people look for their partner.

People are descending on Yangers like you wouldn't believe. Coach load upon coach load of people fill the bus station. It's like there is no space left anymore. There are huge groups of Chinese tourists in big tour parties from all over the place. They all wear the same coloured baseball hats and follow someone with the same coloured flag; it looks insane. I think I'm gonna get my own flag and lead them off the jetty into the Li River. Often they'll go completely OTT. I mean there we are standing outside the Buffalo Bar signing autographs. I mean can you believe that! I must have signed about forty autographs last night. They make you feel famous. Surreal is a major understatement there. Also this guy came up and offered me a teaching post as he's the head of Guilin University. He wouldn't let it go. There he is at 11o'clock banging on the hotel room door and there's me looking like shit and smelling like a brewery. Think of how long it takes to get a teaching job in the UK!

In another bid to find some head space I walked along the river to the five hundred year old village called Shi Ban Qiao, set in rolling lush green countryside, next to the river. Wow. What a place! More of a community, the locals share all the rice fields and fruit trees. Orchards for giant grapefruit bigger than your hand surround the place and you can feel like you can breathe again after the hoards back in town. There are a hundred and forty-six people in this village and there are only four surnames between them; Wang, Xu, Li and Zhang.

My feet by this time were minging so badly it was starting to get quite upsetting. I mean an odour so powerful and strong it would have stopped an elephant in its tracks. Those bloody sandals! Wash 'em, wash your feet, then ten minutes later minging again! If you have plastic sandals you end up scrubbing them everyday, but even so on this walk my feet started to go brown in their own slime, hmmmm, nice! I mean the aroma follows you everywhere you go with an accompanying pain barrier created by those straps rubbing all day[3].

Went into the travel agents late afternoon. There were three really nice women in there having to inhale my minging feet. Talk about really embarrassing. Anyway the problem has been remedied now after inserting a pair of odour eaters in each sandal with some red insulation tape to hold them in place. Footwear aside though, I proudly left the office with one ticket in my hand to Chengdu. With controllable excitement and fingers crossed, it will be Tibet for the 16th of October. Some people are saying that some parts of Tibet are already closed off due to the early onset of cold weather including Everest Base Camp. Doubts aside, all say that the journey from Tibet to Nepal and into India is the most amazing trip through the Himalayas that you will ever have in your life. Hmmmm, not a bad idea that!

---

[3] If you do go to Asia, whatever you do, definitely do not buy a pair of plastic sandals as they will kill your feet. Why these things are on sale in out-door shops I have no idea. Definitely buy a pair of flip flops for around town and wash 'em when you shower every evening with an old tooth brush or your mate's one when they aren't looking. If you're out in the countryside get some decent walking shoes and not boots.

# First Chinese Haircut: 14th October 2005

Nervously wandering around looking for a place to get a haircut, the worry that I may be entering the twilight zone of hairdressing is a weight on my mind.

Because of this I've been putting it off for way too long and the cake like mat of styleless hair on my head has been getting beyond control lately. I run into this Scottish guy at the top of West Street who says that he knows of an excellent place.

"Just follow me. It's not far so it's nee bother" he insists in a broad Glaswegian accent. "She does a great job, professional like."

"Can she speak English?" I fret, now focused on my new acquaintances rough looking number-one cut. "I need to tell her how I want it mate you know?"

"Dooooon't worry about it mate. You'll be fine. She speaks great English and it's cheap. That's the main thing right?" he assures positively.

Hmmm! Having now been pulled into something I'm feeling decidedly unsure about, I go along with it, hoping that this guy's enthusiasm matches the ability of the hairdresser. "It's just down here." Leading me towards one of the side streets, he beckons to an old crone, making the gesture for haircut with his fingers.

"Here she is. Just let her do the job and you'll be out of here in nee time. Take it easy pal" and he's off!

Now left alone, the old woman leads me by the sleeve up this small dim alleyway, round some more corners to a long mirror leaning against the wall and accompanying small pink plastic chair.

"Zuo, zuo, zuo, ni zuo" (you sit) she excitedly rattles, trying to pull me by the arm into the seat. Suddenly loads of locals seem to descend, also motioning for me to sit down, hmmmm! I am hemmed in by people all loudly talking to me at once in Chinese. The crowd then part, giving way to this mad looking woman who comes running down some steps wielding a large pair of scissors stroke shears. F*ck that! I do my first Chinese runner and leg it back to daylight. Not the best start in the world, but at least my long hair is still intact. No basin or skin-head cut today!

A bit later I bump into this woman I know with an unpronounceable name, but speaks ok English. She takes me to a more normal looking hairdressing salon along the main road, where she asks for a wash and cut. Easy peasy, yeah and lemon squeezy! Yeah right! After sitting down, the strangest looking bug eyed woman from the planet Zanusi appears from a small room, then proceeds to lather up my scalp and give the most totally painful head massage you could ever possibly imagine. It is absolutely agonizing and I begin to wonder how much pressure my cranium can actually take before reaching its maximum crush capacity. I try to get her to stop and so does my friend, but my cries of pain don't slow her down one tiny bit. In the end I start swearing very loudly, until finally she finishes. My friend does say it was only supposed to be a haircut, but then weird bug eyed woman starts to massage my shoulders, digging her thumbs in as hard as she can.

Jumping out of the chair, there I am standing up looking like a right f*cking idiot with my hair all soaped up and this small black shiny towel thing round my shoulders, shouting "I just wanna frigging haircut!" At last this other woman washes the soap out, again very painfully. I am wondering how it's possible for hair follicles to withstand such an onslaught and if I'm going to have any hair left at the end of the day. At last this guy comes out and starts cutting my hair. He does seem to know what he was doing, but this is China not Central Studios! My hair is looking more Chinese by the second, but I manage to communicate to him how I want it. I now sit here with my new short and slightly Chinese haircut, sporting what I can only describe as a pair of Mao wings that just won't go away! I don't know how they do it, but every time I try and brush them flat, they spring back up again. Phew. Do I really have to go through that every month?

Noise Pollution and Personal Space: I struggled out of my room today after a twenty four hour food poisoning session. I suppose everyone gets it a few times when they are travelling and I am tripping my box off today. It's mad lying in such a noisy hotel though. Normally it's pretty quiet, but it is the Autumn Festival after all. The place is fully booked and everyone is just so totally full on its ridiculous! Chinese tourists don't ever shut a door, they slam them. They ALL do. It sounds like when they are slamming that door they're putting everything they have into it. Every hotel I've been in has it. Families and friends are all up at bloody 6am and shouting from room to room. Kids learn how to slam doors at an early age and generally a single Chinese family is capable of generating a total cacophony around them.

If you're on a bus for god knows how long, it's hard enough to get any sleep anyway, but when the driver continually honks his super loud air horn throughout the whole journey it's seriously taking the piss. Back in the UK we use our car horns sparingly right? I mean if we do, fellow drivers can quickly get the hump and see red. Over here, it doesn't always mean 'get out of the way'. It can also mean, 'Watch out, we're coming past'. On a busy day all you can hear is a thousand car and bus horns beeping. On the Li River during the festival, there were at least ten tour boats going past at any one time, each one had a horn blowing. Is this really necessary? If they didn't sound their horns would they really collide? Is the bottom of the Li River a strange graveyard of tour boats that had no horn?

I was on the sleeper train when at 2am this guy leans over me and starts having quite a loud conversation with his wife. I mean Hello! Can you see I'm here? Can you see I WAS asleep! In the internet cafe, you'll be online and someone will lean across you and start having a conversation. Like I was in this public loo, standing there just finishing taking a leak, when this guy comes in and starts cleaning the same bowl with this big brush. I was out of there sharpish I can tell you.

Generally people are a lot louder in China and that's all there is too it. It must be because it's always so crowded. Where ever you go there are normally at least three times as many people. That means the queues are three times longer, public places, especially restaurants are three times over the limit, there's three times more cars on the road and three times as many screaming children. Mercy! Add this to the 'do not disturb' mentality of the Westerner and you have one big moany old git. You called sir?


Other stuff: Oddments and other unusual observations in no particular order:

I've been trying to teach one of my fave waitresses the menu in English. She was doing well until she got to the bit with cheese on it. Bless her; she is totally unable to say the word cheese. Instead she says the word "JEEEEZ". Don't think I'll be having the cheese sandwiches or cheese omelets anymore and especially the quarter pounder cheese burgers. Saw this guy 'playing' with a rat outside a bar today. Watching in amazement, he had two big sticks and was beating it, much to the delight of the locals who were all laughing away, clearly enjoying the whole spectacle. Just outside of the guesthouse, there were loads of ducks tied up and just left on the pavement all day in the blistering heat, their beaks also bound. I don't think they're too clued up on animal-rights down this neck of the woods, that's for sure. People eat dog around here and there used to be three cute ones tied up around the corner down an alley way. The next day there were two and then just one remained, looking lonely and craving affection. The day after, that one was gone too. Often it all looks terrible through the eyes of this green Westerner and I find myself judging everything as if we all are so perfect. Dogs are just treated the same as any animal down here though and that's normally only something for the dinner plate.

Chinese people really make a lot of noise when they're eating. People say that they do it as a way of showing you're really enjoying your food. It's one thing that my Western ears just can't get used to and has the equivalent effect of running your nails down a black board. People will get their heads right down into the plate, slurping and munching with their mouths open like there is no tomorrow. Watch out if someone is eating noodles and don't forget to wear your raincoat. I was having lunch with some Dutch people when this woman on the next table started sucking heavily on this big piece of vertebrae from her soup. Clearly absorbed in her own world, she dropped the bone onto the table from her mouth and belched loudly. Luckily, my friends matching look of disbelief made the whole thing comical, especially when the woman bent over the bone using her lips as a kind of vacuum cleaner to suck it back up again and continue slurping.

People have drips on the street here if they are feeling ill. You can them sitting there with a bottle full of anti-biotics hanging inverted from a bamboo pole and a tube running into their arms as cars drive past. Amazing hey! Anti-biotic drips are seemingly the solution to nearly every ailment in these parts including a bad back or a cold.

Grilled pigs tongue in soya sauce only 10p each. Very reasonable considering how big they are!

Well today is the last day in Yangshuo and I leave with mixed emotions about this place. Firstly it was not what I expected at all. I love it here but it's like a vortex that won't let go. I must admit, that after the trauma of Ms Mole and Zhanjiang, it's been a good place to unwind. It's seriously beautiful and on paper the lifestyle is a fantastic one. Just imagine living in Yangshuo, with a flat and a job. Amazing hey? The trouble is, it's easy to fall into old habits and I wonder if it's really a place that you could come back and seriously live in.

It's been almost three months since working and it's nice finally not worrying if you should be doing something. Have I chilled out though? Well it's been just total pandemonium most of the time and my internal organs are definitely wondering what on earth has just happened to them. Imagine being Bill Murray in Ground Hog Day only every day you wake up and hit that alarm clock it's with the worst hangover you ever had. Mercy! Last time at MJ's, Jane had offered the whole crowd living in her guesthouse free accommodation and beer for as long as they wanted if they stayed and worked for her. When I left them they were getting totally annihilated.

People come and go in Yangers. Of course there are the locals who will be here forever, then there are the travellers who stay in the vortex happily for months, and the ones that stay for a week or just a few days. You make great friends and start to establish yourself, but then after having an unexpected and unbelievable experience with them, it's finally your turn to split too. Saying goodbye to Fan and Jason was tough going. I'll also miss Alf and his wife Ming Fang already. Not used to being hugged from such a big Australian geezer.

You literally have to wrench yourself free from Yangers and it feels great to be breaking away. I had forgotten what a buzz it was to be on the road again. The idea is to travel so let's get this show on the road shall we!

# 5

# Tibet and Chengdu: Touching the Sky

## Chengdu:

Sichuan is without a shadow' one of the most highly regarded provinces in China. It's famous for the Giant Pandas, its super spicy food similar to eating napalm and one of China's holy of mountains called Emeishan. There is also a giant Buddha carved into a cliff face near the city of Leshan and at over two hundred and thirty feet high it is the tallest carved Buddha on the planet. I was amazed to find that Sichuan is 'twinned' with Leicestershire, though quickly discovered that strangely they are nothing like each other in any way and found not one Pukka Pie[1] anywhere.

You could spend a whole lifetime getting to know Sichuan as it is an absolutely huge place. It lies east of Tibet and dips down into a basin surrounded by mountains. From Sichuan the Tibetan Plateau rises steeply and the change in altitude is enormous. In the north-west is a vast and spectacular mountainous region filled with small towns and villages completely out of touch with the modern world. This includes the Minshan mountain range in Huanglong and also the Wolong National Nature Reserve in Wenchuan County, the centre of the 2008 earthquake.

Chengdu is the capital of Sichuan and is one of the main staging points for people who want to get into Tibet. Sadly, this usually means travellers will often miss out on many of the fascinating and amazing things it has to offer due to the limits of time, cash and the desire to keep moving west. To date, one of my biggest regrets is not sticking around for longer.

---

[1] With the company slogans "Socialise with Pukka Pies" and "Pukka Pies Don't Compromise" these famous meat delicacies are sold in chip shops and at football grounds across the UK.

## Sichuan Hot Pot: 17<sup>th</sup> October 2005

Everything went one hundred percent perfect today, arriving at Mix Guesthouse in Chengdu without a scratch. I was pretty chuffed, getting an express ticket to Guilin, a taxi to the airport with the Chinese vocab' being really helpful. I didn't feel like a frightened chicken any more.
      The journey was the best yet, getting rushes of self-achievement and disbelief that this is really happening. The plane flew over two layers of white and pink cloud drenched with sunbeams and below it the Sichuan Province! If only it could have slowed down a bit or gone round in a few circles, maybe even a bit of low level; a view you could gaze into all day. There is also a feeling of complete helplessness when you are at the check-in and your luggage is taken off of you. I'm always wondering if it's going to be there at the other end.

Mix is pretty cool and there are people from all over the world there, just the place to be when your tired, dehydrated or your face feels like a sun dried prune It's very noisy on my floor though, including more door slamming, hmmmm, I wonder why that is?

Chengdu! Totally unbelievable city and not what was expected at all. The travel book said it was a beautiful city that was untouched from Western influences. Like hell it is! Its high-rise central with thousands of cars. The driving is far worse than anything you can ever witness, with cars swerving from lane to lane all over the place. They also drive fast, so sitting in the front of a taxi is yet another nail-biter. It is also the most cosmopolitan city you could imagine, with coffee shops and fast food restaurants on every corner. The women dress in ridiculous high heeled boots with matching short skirts. The school kids all wear shell suits as their uniform, either in blue and white, or red and white. Kinda cool really clart. The buildings are shiny and new with neon signs everywhere. Skyscrapers line the enormous streets and vanish into the smog.

The next day I took a trip over to see the Giant Pandas in a huge nature reserve with an Israeli couple who were also staying at Mix, Michal and Ronen. It was a great experience. Never seen an animal that just eats all day! The Panda is famous as an endangered species due to its inability to breed. So far Pandas have been given Viagra to no effect and also been made to watch blue 'panda porn' movies in an effort to get them to reproduce. To me they just seemed to be mega lazy and couldn't be arsed to mate. One male just led on its back with its fat stomach protruding upward next to a pile of bamboo. After eating one stick of bamboo it would look utterly full and bloated like it just couldn't possibly eat anymore. Obviously it had been eating continually all day. It would then once more notice the bamboo pile and reluctantly reach over and have just 'one more one'. Weirdly, people line up to have their photo taken with a panda. In order to do this they have to wear a germ free one piece plastic suit, including gloves and elasticised hood. Some strange sight that must be to have that on your mantelpiece, especially a family shot.

On the way back we stopped wandered about the city centre for about seven hours soaking up the new environment. There are eleven million people in this place. It turns out to be the most massive endless expanse you will experience. Photos don't do it justice at all, especially due to the intense pollution from all those exhaust fumes. The taste lingers on your palate and up your sinuses for hours after.

The guys wanted to go and get pizza. When we arrived we were greeted by the staff at the door all wearing witches costumes, who for some reason were already celebrating Halloween in a big way. Their main dish was 'Deep sea eel pizza', ingredients: cheese, eel sauce (yummy), eel slices, onion and pepper. Sounds kinda irresistible really!

A twenty four hour gut rot I've been suffering from has now become a five-dayer, so had the pleasure of sampling over twelve public toilets today, some really grim. One had just two rows of holes in the ground and NO partitioning what so ever. Because it was in the centre of town, it was packed out and everyone could see everyone else squatting down, nice! Still feeling terrible and desperately hoping that it goes soon. I've been looking forward to coming to Chengdu for a year now, and can't waste time lying in bed. This place is incredible.

It's really apparent in Chengdu that a lot of taxi drivers get lost really easily, and when they are off it's really difficult to stop them. I got into one taxi and blam there we go in the wrong direction and its hard work to get the driver to turn round. You can't blame my terrible Chinese this time though. Mix even gives his guests maps specifically to give to taxi drivers and everything is written down in Mandarin. It's not that they are trying to rip you off or anything, as in China there are no shortage of passengers waiting for a ride on any corner, it just seems like a lot of drivers just don't know the way.

One day my stomach was still feeling highly volatile, so got a taxi to do the equivalent of a fifteen minute walk instead. Half an hour later we'd gone around the statue of Chairman Mao four times. I stopped the taxi and immediately got into another taxi. The driver looked at the map and said he had forgotten his glasses. I gave him five kuai and got into a third taxi feeling worse. This guy then took me through the Green Lotus Market by accident, one of the biggest open air markets in Chengdu, completely skirting around the destination in an anti-clockwise direction by about half a mile. The taxi became thoroughly pinned, unable to move in the heaving market while the driver beeped his horn trying to do a U-turn. All the while, I was clenching so hard I could have exploded a walnut between my cheeks, by this time gripped in a state of panic. Somehow we drove through the whole of the Green Lotus. I tell you a Chinese khazi never looked as good as it did when I got back to Mix.

Just starting two days much needed R+R today, having just come off of Emei-Shan, one of China's holy mountains. I'm sooooo knackered I can hardly move, or talk, or think, in fact all body functions may cease imminently. Great! Life as per normal then. Just gimme a bed pan, a nurse and a stretcher bearer.

Wednesday: Left Chengdu for Emei in a wall of smog travelling with this sorted guy called Justin from Holland. When the bus got out into the country it was just as bad. Apparently burning fossil fuels is another biggy out here, though it also depends on the weather conditions. After some intense haggling over our room we went for some grub. Oh dear! There just seemed to be a group of eight restaurants in Emei, the staff all outside trying their best to get us to come in and eat at their place. For some reason, upon checking them out, each one had exactly the same printed menus.

Reckon I've got used to the food these days and normally it's not bad, especially the spicy stuff, but that evening's was seriously hardcore. The main meals on each menu were as follows: salted pigs tongue, pig's heart in mashed garlic, pig's head in soy sauce (tempting), tripe in soy sauce, pig's lung Sichuan style, sautéed pig's stomach, stir-fry chitterlings, pig's hoof soup and egg in fermented glutinous rice. With little choice in the matter we succumbed and ordered some food, then watched the cook as he did Justin's grub, who had ordered chicken.

The chef got a whole chicken partially cooked out of the fridge. He then baked it for five minutes, boiled it, immersed it in cold water and then dipped it in a big vat of sugar. This chicken on the plate was utterly inedible and still red in the middle. My chicken clearly was not chicken. People ask what the worst or strangest food I have eaten has been, but honestly sometimes you just don't know what it is that's confronting you on the plate. It may have been stomach that night as it was white and furry. The going was getting tougher and tougher when then this little chubby guy sitting opposite greffed big style and drooled it downwards into a rag on his lap. That was end of meal I can tell you!

Thursday: Up at 6.00am. We got on a bus to the base of the mountain with, oh no a Chinese tour party! I mean they were shouting and arguing with the tour guide about something, very animated for nearly the whole journey .Possibly they didn't get their free breakfast. The bus was packed to capacity and the aisle disappeared with fold down seats so no expense spared there for health and safety. Breakfast consisted of the hottest pot noodles known to mankind, while watching about three hundred Chinese people in tour groups going crazy to get to the front of the queue to get in. Pandemonium! This was definitely NOT what was planned (so what's new mate). You had to buy two tickets for a whopping 180 kuai and get an ID photo taken. There was a "tickets price complaining hot line" as well. The only way to get on to the mountain was by cable car, 'queuing up' with this crazy mass of tourists and all that at 7.00am.

Relief! Once off the car, they all buggered off to the nearest temple and we departed along the path and up the mountain to be left in peace and quiet for the rest of the trek. On the way there were donkeys carrying incredibly heavy loads. They all looked very unhappy and continually being slapped round the legs with shovels and sticks to keep them moving. Guys in packs of thirty to forty carried huge blocks of stone in teams of three, with a single manager coordinating them. All in all, every kind of material was being taken up this mountain; coal, electrical equipment and building materials. After only a few hours, I started feeling absolutely mullered, but these guys were still going strong.

Getting higher, our packs of food inflated like balloons because of the air pressure. A bit further up we walked into a thick cloud bank so I slapped my waterproofs on. Through the trees the path suddenly opened up to some amazing Chinese temples, certainly everything you would hope to find; atmospheric, peaceful and transcendental. Sitting there in the darkened courtyard drinking hot green tea with the rain dripping from the curved rooftops is surely what it's all about.

There are shed loads of aggressive monkeys on the mountain so we were told to carry sticks to get rid of them. At one of the temples out of the muggy whiteness, a dark shape appeared. F*cking monkey coming straight for us at 12 o'clock! I used every expletive in my dictionary at the top of my voice and charged at it. It kind of growled at me bared its teeth before swiftly retreating. These monkeys will steal anything that's not properly squared away, seriously, so we kept our cameras firmly out of sight. This was an ongoing thing, but not so heavy once you got into the gist of things. A bit worrying when they appeared in packs though. One monkey had cleverly concealed itself up on the roof of a hut. With great dexterity and skill it managed to lean down and open the rucksack of someone just ahead, half-inching[2] his biscuits. Years of practice no doubt! Anyway, with legs like complete jelly and completely mullered, we found a small hotel near the top. We went through a lot of pain barriers on the way up, but we did it. How anyone can get to the top of a real 'mountain mountain' is totally beyond me. Friday: Woke up and went for the summit! What a total mind numbing anti-climax that was! I mean it was six in the morning and this guy was shouting at a large number of excited tourists with a frigging megaphone. They were there in swarms and had come up by bus and then cable car. Also the cloud still hadn't broken so you couldn't see anything! On the bright side, as trips go it was ok; the trek on the way up was totally spectacular after all with fantastic views. I did leave with some disappointment though. Clearly all the places I've planned to see cost an arm and a leg and there are hundreds of tourists everywhere. That crosses-off the trip to see the giant Buddha at Leshan as apparently it's just totally full on there. You just need to be braver, scrap most of the destinations that are on the agenda in order to find somewhere with no crowds.

Sunday: Had the world's greatest lie-in with three pints of Tetley tea in bed. All the Chinese people here think it's crazy, especially when they see the milk being poured into it. They also say that it is definitely NOT tea! With calf muscles aching like mad and feeling utterly exhausted, it was just mustard lying in bed lolling in and out of consciousness. A great contentment and intense satisfaction from the past few days made the pain worthwhile. The room was by this time completely covered in gear strewn everywhere, merely adding to the feeling, cool as!

Dinner at your own risk
My friend Rui visited this afternoon. She's back in Chengdu as it's her home town and one of the reasons why I became interested in China. One night, July-ish last year in the early hours, an invitation to put her on my messenger's contact list popped up on the computer screen and that was it! Next day, I bought a book on China, and although she soon left for a new life in Sweden, I was hooked. Today it's like completing the circle and amazing finally getting to meet her after all this time.

So Rui shows up with her sister Xiao Xiao and after introductions they take me out to a local restaurant to sample the legendary Chengdu hot pot or 'Huo Guo'. In China, Chengdu is famous for this and there are hot pot houses everywhere. If you ask anyone, anywhere, what is the most well-known dish in the country, it will always get the vote. I always thought that hot pot was something that your Mum does in a

---

[2] London rhyming slang for the verb 'to pinch' meaning to steal something

casserole dish, (yeah right!) What anyone has neglected to tell me is that huo guo translates into 'Fire Dish'.

In the taxi I ask them why people drive with such lunacy here. "They seem to swerve without looking. I've never seen driving as bad as this anywhere".

"Actually you are mistaken." bats Rui. "It is because they are so skillful. Chengdu drivers are some of the best in the world." she boasts.

"Does that mean I can relax when the driver turns wildly into a busy main road without looking? They must have special intuitive powers" I think with more than a hint of sarcasm.

"Do you like Sichuan food?" asks Xiao Xiao from the front seat?

"I've only had the food in the guesthouse so far. So I don't really know. Does that count?"

Rui then leans closer to her sister, says a few sentences in Chinese and both of them burst out laughing. Feeling a bit left out of the loop, I enquire what the joke is about.

"You are in China, but haven't had Sichuan food before?" adds Xiao Xiao.

"No, this is my first time." and at that, big grins appear across their faces until they start laughing again. Even the taxi driver gets in on it, having I assume, asked what was so funny. In the end he too is roaring with laughter while Mc Twat here sits there trying to smile through the whole thing.

"Well I am sure you will find this will be an experience you will not forget" says Rui in a slightly patronising tone, holding back the hysterics.

Entering the restaurant, I follow behind the girls, wondering what is about to happen with a rising sense of concern. The first thing I notice is that the table has a large hole in it about the size of a washing-up bowl and a gas burner underneath. A large stainless steel basin divided into two halves is brought in and placed carefully in the hole. One part of the basin has a white broth with vegetables and half a fish in it. The other part contains a dark crimson soup with a million chilies or 'la jiao' floating in it. There is also traditional 'Chinese medicine' in there that looks like seed pods of some kind.      The waiter then brings over a plate of maybe a quarter-kilo of thick bright red chilli paste loaded with seeds on a plate and scrapes the whole thing in too. The flame is then lit under the table and the soup remains boiling away throughout.

"My God! We're not really going to be eating that? I fret in disbelief. "That could actually be quite dangerous".

"Don't worry. I think Westerners aren't used to such spicy food. You can always have the fish soup. It's very mild" reassures Rui, having seen my growing straight-faced look of seriousness.

"I don't like fish, but it's ok. We English love it spicy" I declare defensively, referring to our love of Indian food. "I can handle it".

Raw meat and vegetables on separate plates are ordered, including a selection of tofu from a trolley. Platter after platter of raw foods come to the table such as potato, cauliflower, Chinese cabbage, 'Ou' (lotus root) and a variety of greens all sliced and ready to go. Various cuts of meat including duck's stomach and duck's throat appear.

"I hope you're hungry. We've ordered a lot of food." says Xiao Xiao before giving me my first lesson. "Take something in your 'kuaizi' (chopsticks) and put it into the soup...Like this. It's so hot, everything cooks very quickly. The meat doesn't take long. Try the duck's stomach. It's delicious". Taking out the now grey rubbery meat from the broth, she then dips it into a brown bowl of sesame paste before downing it.

I've never been a great stomach eater but go along with it, trying to hide my reluctance. Blowing on it in a hope of cooling it down before the moment of truth, the girls watch intently as I pop it into my mouth hoping I won't wretch and embarrass myself. At first it doesn't seem so bad. Though it is still red hot temperature-wise and chewy as hell it's not so bad; the sesame really makes a difference. Suddenly the chillies kick in though; a searing acid rips down my throat and up my nose followed by the weirdest combination of tongue numbing tastes presumably from the medicine. I contort uncontrollably while my eyes water.

"Are you ok?" chuckles Rui; a look of satisfaction across her face.

"I'm fine" I splutter, wiping my nose with a tissue.

"You can't stop now. It gets better the more you eat it. Try the duck's throat". Duck's throat is especially nasty looking since it resembles a giant coiled up red and white glistening worm on the plate. It's actually cut into three foot lengths, which Xiao Xiao shows me how to eat. You have to hold it up at arm's length with the chopsticks before dunking into the hotpot. Some task eating that as you lower the quivering steaming tentacle into your wide open mouth. Never again I can tell you.

Rui and Xiao Xiao keep eating for over an hour without showing any signs of discomfort until every bit of food has been cleared. Talk about having a cast-iron stomach. I, on the other hand last about fifteen minutes before the chilli gets the better of me. To top it all, the whole meal is washed down with a big jug of prune juice which they say "is very good for the digestion". While writing this, my head is still spinning with weird tastes and aromas, my nose and sinuses are on fire and my guts have followed suit by shutting down all normal functions. It is by far the hottest thing you will ever experience. You can always tell when a Western person has just eaten hot pot. As they walk through the door of the guesthouse, a red face, streaming nose, mouth open and that 'about to sneeze' look is always a dead giveaway! That and an accompanying air of helplessness.


Other stuff: Oddments and other unusual observations in no particular order.

There was a military parade on TV the other day. There were tanks, missile launchers and the like, all in columns, all the soldiers saluting their leader as they filed past. What got me was that the whole thing was being led by about a hundred soldiers on white mopeds at the front. How intimidating they must look charging in across the battlefield. Terrifying!

There was this item on the Chinese National News: A coach had come off a flyover and into another bus below. Many people were killed and the scene was horrific. In the UK this would be headline stuff for weeks right? Instead this was used as a catchment item at the end of the news, kinda like the dog that can roller-skate or the duck that can control a herd of sheep. Unbelievably, cameras were allowed onto the scene minutes after it happened and on to the bus, also following the survivors as they were stretchered into ambulances contorted in agony and shock. There's so much about this place I still can't get my head round. You spend your whole time in awe of this crazy place. There is an almost opposite way of thinking in this country and it's utterly fascinating. I don't think you could ever get bored with it.

Right! My investigations into Tibet are getting intense. It's getting close. I have put ads up on the walls of varying hostels for anyone who wants to sell any of the gear after returning from Tibet and is heading for warmer climes; outdoor gear is a rip-off here. This morning, this guy who's just come from Mongolia knocked on the door and sold me a load of his gear for 200 kuai, having seen one of the signs on a wall somewhere. I'm well happy. The past two days have been dedicated to scrounging and blagging as much stuff as possible for the trip, wandering around the centre of Chengdu trying to get the last bits and pieces. Got the altitude sickness pills and made contact with someone who is already up there and wants to go trekking. I can't believe how exited I am now. COME ON!

**Tibet:**

Looking back on Tibet the first thing that always springs to mind is the total excitement and happiness from being in such an amazing place. In terms of countryside there were no trees or forests and normally the terrain was stark. Its lakes though were more like bright dazzling mirrors. The clouds seemed so close that you could reach up into the sky and run your hands through them. We sang and laughed a lot wherever my friends and I went. All in all I have never been so in the moment for such a prolonged period of time, felt so complete and so happy in my whole life.

**Lhasa: 26<sup>th</sup> October 2005**

Well I'm in total heaven at the moment. I've hit the jackpot; the mother load; the absolute total dog's bollocks. I've done it........I'M IN LHASA....TIBET! YES YES YES!

Phew, where to start? 5am; a vague memory of someone banging on the door for the wake-up call. Rolling out of bed, hitting the floor fully clothed, grabbing my stuff then suddenly out in the refreshing cool of the darkness and into a minibus along with two others, Raff and Katrine from Belgium. The driver stopped for a few more people and sped through the 'for once' empty streets of Chengdu. The trip on the plane over the Tibetan Plateau was the most spectacular view you could imagine; a thousand snowcapped peaks under the clouds, glittering in the sunrise; the sky electric blue. Further on the first really big mountains started to appear, like giants forcing their way upwards with immense power through the clouds. I remember thinking, "Andy mate. What have you done?"

At Lhasa airport after an hour of haggling over the bus journey to get into town and being messed around big time we'd still gone nowhere. Even the old bill showed up, so we buggered off and eventually got a bus to ourselves on the quiet and off we went. Oh my god, the countryside is truly breath taking; big wide open spaces surrounded by mountains, hugging blue clear lakes. The altitude is doing weird things to everybody. Its 4,500 feet above sea level so you often feel really out of breath and strangely high as a kite. Also the UV is awesome; it's very bright, so don't forget the shades and a hat. Gotta chill for a couple of days to get used to all this before starting to go higher I rekon. After that, it's time to start going on short one-day hikes into the hills for a bit, before being more ambitious.

The plan is to find a four-wheel drive via Everest Base Camp and then maybe go through to Nepal but there's no rush. This is truly a time to savour. The hotel room is the best one so far. There are traditional Tibetan style images such as tigers and deer painted directly onto the walls; it's beautiful! There is the greatest view of the mountains from the balcony. Raff and Katrine are hilarious company. Their favourite pastime back home is building and racing stock cars, then smashing them up. There's also a Dutch couple, Steven and Jon from Yangshuo at the roof top bar. We even met again at Mix in Chengdu, terrific though they are also suffering from the altitude at the moment with pounding headaches.

Sleeping is well trippy due to the altitude. You keep waking up dying for water, feeling well dehydrated and then having crazy dreams. In the morning, I am woken up by this local Tibetan woman called Tomo. She knocks on the door, lets herself in, takes my laundry (poor woman) and fills up this big metal thermos with boiling water from a huge kettle next to the bed. I manage to say good morning in Tibetan to her and she nervously mumbles Tibetan prayer under her breath before hurriedly leaving.

The streets of Lhasa have a strange mix of people. There are Tibetan monks in small groups wandering about everywhere in their burgundy robes, locals in traditional colourful clothes, and people who live outside the city in the countryside looking as rugged as you like. You'll see some Chinese locals in Western looking clothes and the odd Westerner in brightly coloured day glow outdoor gear[1].

At the same time you will see lots of beggars in Lhasa. Some just come up and say "MONEY!" Well at least they are up front about it. There are whole families begging in places and some will follow you down the street, hoping to exploit the tourist's weaknesses. Some seem to do surprisingly well, openly counting their cash as they have their dinner. I went to for a dump yesterday and this beggar follows me into the loo. Standing up to give myself a wipe, there he is grinning away at me holding his hand out, over the four foot high partition. He was lucky I didn't think he wanted my used bog roll. So there I am saying to this guy "Look mate I AM wiping my arse! Go away!" which he kindly did about two minutes later. Maybe he was just dammed kinky or something.

---

[1] From this point Han-Chinese will be referred to as 'Chinese' to distinguish them from Tibetan people. On paper Tibetans are also defined as Chinese citizens, but Han-Chinese people are very different in appearance, behaviour and customs. Han-Chinese are the largest ethnic group in China, constituting for 92% of the population.

Local Tibetans walk casually around holding prayer wheels spinning clockwise on sticks in front of them. These are cylinders with sacred prayers or mantra on them and can be seen all over the place in Tibet as they are a really important part of Buddhist tradition. Most common are the hand held ones you spin in daily life and big metal ones you spin as you pass by. Often at the entrance to a holy place you will find a great row of them. Some places have enormous prayer wheels with buildings especially constructed.

It is said that rotating the prayer wheel is the same as actually saying a prayer and is helps you increase your karma and purify your bad karma. They are also supposed to calm your mind and take you to a peaceful meditative headspace. I wonder if it was statistically proven that they worked they would catch on in the West, especially at job interviews and high pressure positions. Sounds crazy, but even the Dali Lama himself has said that if you put a prayer on your computer then your hard disc will spin it in the same manner as a prayer wheel, therefore cleansing your office or surrounding space.

The first port of call on anyone's list is to visit the Dalai Lama's old place called the Potala Palace; an absolutely enormous building, towering above Lhasa in the blue sky. Must have taken them a long time to build (he says knowledgeably). The history goes that Dalai Lama was forced to flee from Tibet in 1959 because there was a high chance the Chinese Government were going to arrest him. The last time he was at home, more than 30,000 Tibetans surrounded the palace in order to maintain his safety, allowing his escape. Amazing hey? During the next few years 'The Great Leap Forward' saw the destruction of 6000 monasteries and between 400,000 and 1.2 million Tibetan deaths. It was a disaster that also saw the deaths of tens of millions of Chinese people.

No photos can be taken inside the palace as it's seen to be disrespectful and its especially bad luck if you take ones of the big statues. Saw the burial chambers of the 4th, 5th, 6th, 7th and 8th Dalai Lamas; each room totally awe inspiring; all over twenty five feet high; gold everywhere and embellished in vibrant colour. The aesthetic value of this place is overwhelming; the colours staggering, bright and coordinated; flickering candles illuminate dark corners twenty four hours a day; statues in their thousands in gold; it just went on and on and on.

Menu of the day: Yak is in in a big way. I was going to go for yak steak today but with no appetite due to the altitude, it's hard to get anything down. At the moment "sunflower and yak's tongue" is in. Also "snow mountain spicy lungs" and yak tripe. Weird! Funny how everywhere has its own smell. Unfortunately its one of those things that you just can't take with you or record. China was very noticeable for that at times; the same smells in every city, especially down south. The same goes for Tibet. Maybe it's because of all of the yak meat everywhere. Yak is massively important to the Tibetans. Every part of the yak is used after it has been killed including the blood and hair. Yak dung is also dried and used for fires.

You will also see shops that sell nothing but yak butter at every turn. The big two foot yellow blocks are often piled high, adding to the display of colour down the street. Yak butter is central to the way of life. Yak butter lamps are not only used for daily living, but have an important place in ceremonies, also illuminating temples and holy places. If you are offered the typical tea known as 'po cha' it will have yak butter as one of its most important ingredients, keeping out the intense cold on those long, well below zero nights. The staple dish in Tibet is 'tsampa', made of salted tea pounded together with yak butter.

Been spending a lot of time in the old part of Lhasa; what an amazing place. So much going on. The people all smile at you and make you feel at home. Throughout the labyrinth of narrow streets, the shops and open air markets are like no other on the trip so far. Brightly decorated cloth is sold in abundance and the whole place is alive with colour everywhere you look, especially the burgundy and ochre that's worn by the monks. From end to end, along each lane you will see brilliant prayer flags hung between the buildings. There are also large umbrellas put up to protect each stall from the elements, in fact there are so many they almost touch, forming a canopy at head height. All in all, it seems Tibetans have a real natural eye for colour, displayed in a manner you won't ever forget.

Nearby is the Jokhang Temple[2], also known as Tshuglakhang, (cathedral). What a crazy place; although its gates were closed, people still threw themselves on the floor again and again in front of it. Surviving many chapters in history, this is the holiest temple in Tibet and you certainly know it, as the pilgrims go totally ballistic when they get there. It's some sight I can tell you!

Later, my Chinese friend Amy, who I met via the internet in Chengdu, came along on a trip to the Drepung Monastery. My travel book is so inaccurate it doesn't get anything right, which is why we spent an hour in the wrong place waiting for a bus that doesn't exist. Money well spent there for sure! Also it says that the monastery is less than a mile

---

[2] The Potala Palace was built in 637 and the Jokhang in 642 by King Songtsan Gampo. It is said he is the man who brought Buddhism to Tibet.

away from the main road; yeh right! Blessed relief to have blagged a lift off of this teenager driving a tractor. I mean we just kept going on and on up into the mountains.

Built in 1416, the Drepung used to be the largest monastery in the world housing up to then a thousand monks and is absolutely huge! The sense of space at this altitude far out of the city is staggering and met hand in hand with a powerful sense of aesthetics. The monks had made their own solar powered kettle boiling devices out of sheet metal, looking like great silver butterflies with the pot hanging in the middle. It was an incredibly quiet and reflective place but we were scratching our heads as to where all the monks had gone. Later on we from a dark candle lit room with a giant gold Buddha, a noise that can only be described as a cross between football crowd celebrating a goal and a swarm of bees started to filter through to us.

"What on earth is that?" I asked Amy.

"I really don't know" she replied, clearly equally as baffled and instinctively starting to follow the sound. Exploring further, we managed to sneak a sight out of a shutter, through a small gap. Below in a large courtyard filled with trees, there were all the monks going absolutely crazy in their hundreds, leaping around, shouting and gesturing to each other and chanting their heads off.

"My God! What are they doing?" I asked again.

"I have no idea about this" she laughed. "I've never seen anything like it before".

At this point two guys nearest to us started hitting each other over the head with a book. It actually looked quite painful and certainly one of the more bizarre things you will set eyes on; like they were trying to bang the prayers through each other's skull or something. Perhaps we should adopt this method in secondary schools depending on their ranking in the league tables? Hmmm, now there's a thought and a half.

Finally we got to the highest point of the temple; huge flag poles towering above, a massive court yard and the mountains leading off far into the distance. You just don't get a better feeling, I can tell you. On the way back, we got a lift on the back of a flat-bed pickup. The driver insisted that he did not turn the engine on in order to save petrol, so we coasted down the hill at a ridiculous speed with little control. We passed a similar vehicle that had overturned and the police had just arrived. No doubt he was going without power too! Talk about clenching hard. Reality check double time!

From monasteries to supermarkets, later that evening while getting some shopping in, my observation antennas naturally went up and I started taking notes. There are two small ones in Lhasa and they are kinda like Happy Shopper or the Co-op[3]. Firstly, for sure seeing monks in supermarkets is not a common sight anywhere, but there were loads of them in there, all in their burgundy robes and yellow sashes. Some had baskets or pushing trolleys and one was on his mobile phone. One showed up on his Honda 400 and parked up outside. Another came up, shook hands and said hello.

There was a lovely deli-counter pick and mix and for a set price you could fill up a plastic tub with the usual variety of Chinese nightmares. There were even white boiled ducks heads behind the counter that day, yum! There are seafood Pringles and a whole section that sells nothing but glucose.

I decided to treat myself to some shaving foam. In order to buy shaving foam you have to get one of the staff to go to the shaving foam behind this glass counter. He gives you a ticket which you then take to the check out. You pay and the cashier then separates the ticket and you get two carbon copies and two receipts that they staple together. You then have to take them back to the original guy. He then opens the glass counter and then gives you two cans of shaving foam that you didn't realise that you paid for.

It's been impossible to find a bath tub anywhere since hitting the road, so it was more than amazing when Raff and Katrine revealed there was one hidden away in their hotel room. That feeling of submerging your head under the hot water sure is one you just can't beat ........ahhhhh pure heaven. Woke up and just sat there looking at the mountains over the first brew of the day. Everything seems to be the best ever at the moment, and today it was best breakfast. Everything you do feels so great!

I met these totally sound people, Michelle, Alex and Roz from Canada, who teach outdoor activities in Vancouver. We're going to do a seven-day trip out of Lhasa tomorrow by jeep that will take us over a hundred and fifty miles out and to various remote places including Everest Base Camp. Amazingly it rained last night and in the morning the mountains were frozen white. All those books and films and documentaries that have been filling my head for so long and now here it is in this wonderful moment!

Another early and sleepless night in anticipation awaits. OH SHIT!

---

[3] Since the opening of the railway in 2006 the larger Baiyi supermarket was opened as part of Lhasa's 'development'.

## Qomolangma: 30<sup>th</sup> October 2005

In Lhasa, the Canadians and I go to have a look at the jeep that we'd put a deposit on. When we arrive at the office, the guy that's sorting it is strangely unwilling to let us see it.

"It is being used today. When you go, then you will see it."

"No see, no money! Understand?" barks Roz. "You said the jeep would be here and we could see it" and at that she plants herself in a chair with her arms folded. Nice one! Following suit, we all sit there defiantly until reluctantly he picks up the phone, getting the driver to bring it in.

Finally, a pretty tired looking machine with over 400K on the clock arrives. "No wonder he didn't want us to see it" remarks Alex. "That is one old jeep!" I'm sure any machine around here takes a hell of a pounding and this one is no exception.

"Smashed lights, no tread on the tyres..." Roz has already started making a mental list of defects. "Let's see the engine."

The driver, clearly pissed off, says something to the manager who then translates. "He said the engine is ok. No need to have a look. It is good. We use this vehicle every day" sounding increasingly irritated.

"We want to see the engine. If we can't see it that's just ridiculous" launches Roz, now throwing about her assertiveness. "We're going to be driving all the way to Everest base Camp and back and we can't see the engine? Absolutely no way!"

At that moment Alex finishes his inspection of the under-side; "Looks like the suspension's shot too" At that the driver who supposedly can't speak any English bursts into a rage along with the manager who disappears into the office leaving us outside. Roz isn't having any of it though and she follows him in, rolling her sleeves up for another round.

"Right, we want another one" she insists

"Yeh and another driver" Michelle interjects. I think we've all had enough of the driver's behaviour by now.

"If you want another jeep, you have to pay for it. It's hard to get another one right now. They all being used" Evidently this is a favourite line of his.

We spend some heavy moments arguing with the guy, but refuse to hand over any more money until we get another that looks like it's going to go the distance. After stubbornly sitting there for three hours, all is looking grim in mudsville for a while and it is the first down moment I've really experienced on the trip. Feel like we are out for the count, suddenly through the gates growls a half decent looking Toyota and we all simultaneously jump out of our seats in excitement.

The 4x4 is as good as it sounds and the driver called Phuntsok seems friendly enough with a big smile. Wearing a black leather jacket and sporting a dark pair of shades, he looks more like mafia than a driver. As we sign the contract with the manager, Phuntsok leans against the jeep and sparks up a ciggie. "He can't speak any English but don't worry, he's a good man" says the boss, giving him the thumbs up. The trip was on! Hats off to Roz and her complete never-say-die attitude. Throughout the whole time she never lost her temper or threw one expletive. I learnt something that afternoon. People will take tourists to the f*cking cleaners if they can out here and you should never be afraid to roll up your sleeves and give back entirely what they dish out.

The afternoon's shopping was better than any other supermarket shop. The hotel room became filled with supplies in boxes for the trip. Saying goodbye to Raff, Katrine, Steven and Jon was really difficult. They're off to Nepal. Maybe I'll see them then, but getting back into China is difficult; it's best to go to India or Vietnam from there[1]. Seeing someone off is the only disagreeable side to travelling.

Sunday23rd. An early start. Phuntsok showed up and suddenly we were out of Lhasa heading out into the mountains just past first-light.
     "This is awesome. I can't believe how high we are" I remarked.
     "These are just the foothills" Alex pointed out, "Long way to go yet buddy".
     "You mean these enormous mountains?" I thought. WAAAAAAA! Previous experiences have taken me high on various trips, but seriously, we just went up and up and didn't seem to be stopping for anything. I guess that's the Himalayas for you.
     Reaching Mt Kangbala summit by road at 4,990 metres, overlooking a crystal turquoise lake, prayer flags fluttered everywhere against a crisp blue sky. Onwards we drove for the next seven hours through stunning Tibetan landscape. Stopping for lunch at Nakartse, the locals looked at us like we were from another planet surrounding the jeep, but actually this was nothing they hadn't seen before. Unexpectedly, someone herded us into an upstairs restaurant absolutely full of Westerners, all out doing various trips. For some reason none looked happy. Maybe the sight of so many others on similar trips took their sense of adventure away.
     Driving into a really high mountain pass the weather suddenly took a turn for the worse as the wind funnelled through the valley.

---

[1] Of course going from Nepal to Vietnam is the obvious choice of routes of any traveller. They are after all so close as to be neighbours. Just one of the many puzzling and wildly inaccurate pieces of advice I have given out along the way.

Throughout the day though, after passing countless piles of rocks covered with prayer flags known as Mani prayer mounds, Michelle and I decided to get out and take some photos. The idea is that each rock has an inscription in it, and as you pass by, you drop another carving into it for a safe journey.certainly not the best idea in the world to get out at that time. The wind was so biting we were almost instantly running back to the 4x4 for cover, lame hey! Yak herds; hundreds of black dots all over the stark brown landscape on the way to the first port of call, Gyantse!

Though Gyangze is one of the largest towns in Tibet, it feels more like a small place that has somehow lost itself in the middle of nowhere. For a 'city' of sixty thousand it sure is quiet. After climbing up the fortress called the Dzong, you can look out across the open landscape that surrounds the town. The land feels so vast it feels like it's trying to suffocate and compress Gyangze until it's about to vanish.

There was a very strange feeling about being in Gyangze that you just couldn't put your finger on. It started to bite big time and eventually the guys also started to feel it. Maybe it was something to do with Gyangze's history, when back in 1904 Colonel Francis Younghusband led the British Expedition to Tibet through there. He had to fight his way to Lhasa for months and the Dzong was a major obstacle in his way that needed to be taken in order to progress. Finally, after laying siege to the fortress and the use of cannon and Gatling guns, the walls were breached, the Tibetan troops retreated and the British soldiers advanced to Lhasa. After doing a few empty deals, the Brits went home having achieved very little, though they proclaimed to have "won the war".

Still trying to come to terms with the quietness and wondering where everyone had gone, we went to a nearly restaurant for dinner. There were no customers, well maybe; there were a few guys near the kitchen who looked like they spent all day there doing very little. With no music, no noise and no sign of service, they all stopped chatting and stared at us as if it was a 'locals only' zone and we shouldn't be in there. A strangely awkward feeling verging on the surreal descended. Eventually a waitress did come out and take our order, exhibiting body language like she had better things to be doing.

Feeling more uncomfortable by the second, while we waited for our food, someone greffed fiercely in the kitchen; a really loud and long one, then another and another. The chef was obviously clearing some major phlegm from his throat. He must have greffed about ten times in the space of a few minutes.

"You don't suppose they're doing that into our food do you?" wondered Alex." I just hope it's not mine that comes out first".

Soon after Alex and Roz's milk tea was brought in. The look on their faces was unforgettable, especially as the tea was unusually frothy. Michelle and I promptly had the greatest laughing fit of all time. As the food arrived my face was firmly planted in my folded arms on the table with everyone crying with laughter. Needless to say, we could hardly eat our food such was the image of the chef drooling away in it.

The odd feeling that night intensified. In the dark, buxom Tibetan women hung out of windows from above shouting things at us, well me and Alex most likely.

"I think your luck's in there mate" I nervously joked to Alex as we walked back to the guesthouse. Packs of growling dogs followed as we proceeded over rubble and garbage strewn across empty roads and waste ground, (glad for those rabies jabs). We were all relieved to be moving on the next day really.

24th October: Set off early again, sun rising, watching the people in the fields, the villages, the mountains, the traffic along the road, farm vehicles overloaded to the max. Phuntsok stopped to visit his friend's farm, so there was plenty of time to walk out and experience the whole picture, even helping a guy change his tractor wheel. This vast amazing, beautiful place! All along the way Phuntsok played this groovy Tibetan pop music, and we all grooved along with it. Another amazing seven hour drive.

SHIGATSE: As the second largest city in Tibet with a population of around 80,000, you can easily walk from the centre to the outskirts in less than half an hour. Like most Tibetan towns, there are few places over two storeys and small white washed buildings form narrow dusty streets that don't seem to have ever seen any change. Walking along the winding prayer path around the monastery in the overlooking hills, views of the rugged inspiring landscape gave way to moments of true introspection.

Later we discovered a great place to sit and chill on top of the hotel roof, looking down upon the whole city. A power cut engulfed Shigatse in the evening; candles and lamplight became the only source of illumination, while dogs howled and barked creating a strange atmosphere. Alex had cabbage curry (the wanker), taking great delight in firing off the biggest farts known to mankind all night. Just round the corner was the Sling Shot Bar; the most highly decorated local joint you will ever drink in, with a huge picture of Everest on the wall. There were locals so pissed they couldn't stay on their seats and the barmaids kept sitting them back up then giving them refills.

On two occasions this bloke fell across the table and smashed all the glasses. Once again the barmaids got him upright and poured fresh drinks.

25th October: This day we set off for Shekar, the last village before the north side of Everest. Without warning, Phuntsok suddenly veered off of the tarmac and the journey became eleven hours of the most unbelievable off-roading you could experience. Officially this was on a road, but it was the Friendship Highway between Tibet and Nepal we are talking about here. At this time, the whole thing was seriously 'under construction' and has to be the most knackered strip of dry mud you will ever come across. Often, its huge craters and potholes would make it look more like it had been hit by an airstrike. Frequently you would be met with a diversion, followed by another diversion and then another. Sometimes, after leaving the road, you would be forced to take a diversion from the diversion you just made, leaving you wondering if you were actually going in the right direction at all.

Through white planes of desert walled in by the mountains, a vast expanse of space, followed by hill climbing, hill climbing and more hill climbing. The lakes are so blue they are almost purple. We had dinner along the way at Lhatse; what a total dive. More like the Tibetan equivalent of Watford Gap, Lhatse seems to be a stopover for any lorry driver that is passing through. Trucks blast through kicking up great clouds of dust in their wake leaving everything with a thoroughly natural coating of grime. This Dutch couple had been stuck there for three days and looked filthy and utterly depressed. They'd got off their bus and it had gone without them. I remember thinking, "Where the hell am I?"

And on today's menu in Lhatse, we have for your delectation the following Tibetan delicacies translated into the most colourful English: "Steamed bum wish meet stuffed, bear's paw bean curd veggie, cold three delicacies (carrot soy noodles), screamed carp, chicken shreds with strange flavour, shredded meat with fish taste, crispy rice crust with three fresh ingredients, Sichuan glutinous rice balls, bran curd vegetable soup, whole snake like pot and soft shelled turtle pot". Well there's nothing like a bit of variety in your diet right?

Back on the road and along the way rocks had been placed for miles to separate lanes. Various jeeps had broken down at the side of the road, though mainly due to drivers being reckless with some surprisingly bad mechanics going on to accompany. Phuntsok got a number of them going and was always there to help. Then, after going through a pass 5,200 meters above sea level, suddenly there was a huge sign on metal columns towering above the road saying "Welcome to Qomolangma National Park". It was bloody freezing and the incoming wind blew a gale from the surrounding mountains and landscape. A thousand prayer flags snapping against the air current covered the structure from top to bottom, their colours faded from the sun. Many had been tied along lines which snaked outward, whirling and thrashing like living tendrils trying to break free.

Both the Tibetans and Nepalese see the mountain as the most sacred and holy place on the planet. Before anyone starts climbing a Puja ceremony is done for a blessing from the mountain for a safe journey. A lama will create an altar and burn juniper for purification while they chant and give prayers. All the most important climbing equipment will be blessed while offerings to the Gods such as yak butter and chocolate may be made. Near the end of the ceremony people may throw Tsampa (barley flour) into the air and rub it onto each other's faces for good luck that they may survive the trip and see each other again.

Qomolangma (Mother Goddess of the Universe) is the original Tibetan name for Everest. It's also known as Sagarmatha (Goddess of the Universe) by the Nepalese and been called Zhumulama by the Chinese for hundreds of years. Everest is the name given by the Royal Geographical Society after Sir George Everest, the vice president in the not so distant past. He actually didn't want the mountain to bear his name at all and his surname is pronounced 'Iverest'. Best stick to an original name like Qomolangma for the rest of the trip then.

Phuntsok: It's impossible to carry on without writing something about our driver. What a top bloke. We couldn't have got anyone better; he is so all about it. We love his mad Tibetan music as we drive along. Everywhere we go people know him, and we've done some big distances. Sometimes he took us through check points with no permits. The officials would flag us down and see who it was driving and then wave us through with smiles on their faces; he saved us a lot of money. Sleeping in every bar and restaurant, he would win every gambling game and seemed to have a women in every town we went to. In Shekar he negotiated our hotel rooms with this right wanker of a hotel manager for us and then pulled a fast one on him in the morning. He gave me the keys to his 4x4 and tried to lend me some money out of his wallet. There's much more about this guy, like a real feeling that he's looking out for us. We love him to bits!

26th October: Got up well early. We hated Shekar and all the blaggers that immediately pounce on you, trying to shred every last kuai out of yet another Westerner. The shit overpriced food gives me the chance to use my hidden supply of spam sausages to go with our pot noodles, passing them round to my reluctant Canadian friends. They love the Tetley tea that Mum has sent though and we drink gallons of it. All in all, we are well glad to get away from Shekar as soon possible at the crack of dawn.

Arriving at another check point as the sun is rising, Phuntsok does a quick deal with a load of cigarettes to get our permits and we're off. Driving up and up for an hour, suddenly we go over the top and there is the most utterly unbelievable sight you will ever see. Against a crisp blue Himalayan early morning, there are suddenly a hundred really big glittering snow coated mountains sitting proudly above the clouds; Lohtse (8501m); Makalu (8463m); Cho Oy O (8501m) and Qomolangma at 8848 metres above sea-level. This is truly the most utterly beautiful and awesome sight in the world. I admit I cried to myself, having been obsessed with this place for years; some of my heroes are still up there on that mountain. There was the plume of snow curling up into the sky from the summit of Qomolangma carried up into the jet stream as it sat so proudly above the others.

At that moment, we all totally understood why people want to climb this huge mountain despite such a great risks. You could just feel it and feel it strongly, as if being hypnotically pulling towards it.

"I want to climb it right now" said Alex. "I want to train for a year and get up there ASAP!"

For many it's an obsession of a lifetime that's led them to come back time and time again to peruse their dream no matter what the cost. Even people with various 'disabilities' have fought to get to the highest place on earth. In 1998 a British American called Tom Whittaker, who had lost his right foot became the first disabled person to successfully reach the summit. Later in 2001 Erik Weihenmayer from the States was the first blind person to do it. In 2006 the New Zealander Mark Inglis did it with two artificial legs. Just as remarkable, Min Bahadur Sherchan from Nepal became the oldest person to get to the summit at the ripe old age of 76 in 2001. Amazing hey?

It's well documented why it's so dangerous and incredibly difficult to complete the circuit to the summit and back. Qomolangma is the highest graveyard in the world after all, with so many frozen bodies up there that we've lost count. Around two hundred is the rough guess. Because the air is so cold and dry they become mummified and well preserved. Some have are so well known that they have been renamed and used as landmarks. Tsewang Paljor an Indian climber is now known as 'Green Boots' because of the fluorescent green boots he is wearing. Another climber Hannelore Schmatz, could be seen for years after she died, sitting against her gear with her eyes open and her hair being blown in the wind.

I've always been fascinated with Qomolangma. Ever since 1856 when a British survey named it as Peak VX, Qomolangma has been a place of mystique and legend. From the outset, the earliest successful summit attempt by Sir Edmund Hillary and Tenzing Norgay in 1953 still remains steeped in controversy over who got there first. It has been suggested that George Mallory and Andrew Irvine who died on the mountain could have made it much earlier in 1924. Though they have found Mallory's body, the hunt still continues for Irvine and his camera that may hold proof of the victory.

From stories of courage and heroism such as Reinhold Messner and Peter Habeler's amazing ascent without oxygen in 1978, these days Qomolangma also has tales of less scrupulous behaviour, such are people's obsession with reaching the top. For a fee anyone can have a go at it. Some companies offer a wide selection of choices for the would-be mountaineer. One boasts an executive 1:1 package with your own Western guide for 100,000 dollars or even an "express package" which guarantees you get to the top much faster than normal, including a helicopter to take you to base camp. Some companies can cancel an expedition if they deem conditions to be unfavourable on the mountain at that time. If that's the case then the customer will lose their entire fee which is normally in the region of 50,000 dollars.

Not so long back only one expedition would be allowed on the mountain at any one time, but with restrictions now slackened to allow for the big money it's possible to see a vast number of people all snaking up the slopes like ants following the same path at the same time. Some may have only minimal climbing experience and hold everyone up behind them at crucial moments. By the time the top of the mountain is in sight, some will stop at nothing to reach it. Known as 'summit fever' having been living on the slopes for months, enduring immense hardships and paying a hefty wedge[2] many refuse to turn back if they are told to abort if it's too late or too dangerous by their leaders. There are stories of people shouting "I've paid 50 grand for this trip, you can't stop me" or even punching their Sherpa[3].

---

[2] Informal British English for an amount of money
[3] Name of mountain-dwelling people of Nepal, India and Tibet. Also called Sharwa

The most famous episode in Qomolangma's climbing history must surely be in 1996 when eight people died in one day. In total fifteen people died during the season and blame has been thrown around everywhere. This resulted in many books written by various climbers trying to clear their names. One famous TV personality, the then Sandy Pitman was apparently ordered to be 'short roped' to a Sherpa as she was too tired to go any further. In reality this really meant that she was dragged to the summit before celebrating her victory. It is said that during the expedition two climbers actually shagged half way up, completely freaking the guides out who saw this as a huge act of disrespect to Qomolangma herself and a sign of imminent doom for anyone on the mountain. Bad luck aside, it is generally thought that inept management and so many people trying to get up at one time were the main reasons for the tragedy.

The list of facts and figures about Qomolangma goes on. The 1996 disaster saw the world's highest rescue by a helicopter at approximately 20,000 feet (6,096 meters) by Nepalese Lt. Col. Madan Khatri Chhetri. The helicopter, an old Russian Mi-17 was able to stay in position for only a few seconds before plummeting like a rock back down to a safe altitude. On May 14, 2005, test pilot Didier Delsalle, of the French company Eurocopter made Everest history by actually landing on the summit.

There is over 50 tons of rubbish on its slopes including a helicopter. Oxygen cylinders and camp waste lie everywhere at each camp. There's so much rubbish that it's sometimes called the world's highest rubbish tip!

Apparently there are even ghosts up there, including a friendly climber that helps people down who are in trouble and even Irvine himself who you may find suddenly sitting in your tent.

Everest Base Camp
Back on the road, the way on hairpins perilously and continuously. Phuntsok's driving is impeccable though, past huge ice fields too bright to look at even with sunglasses. After waiting for hours at another check point, Phuntsok pulls yet another blag, pissing off some other drivers and saving us a wedge. Over the last hill and there it is. OH MY WORD! Qomolangma is massive! It rises above us miles away, still so big to fill your line of vision from top to bottom and so, so beautiful.

Getting a room in the small guesthouse there, we chuck our stuff in and were off! Roll on the greatest hike you can imagine. I have five layers on my body, a balaclava and two pairs of gloves. The path winds up hugging a river but Qomolangma is always up front; you just can't take your eyes off it. It just gets bigger and bigger, it is staggering. Every few steps you are hacking for oxygen, never feeling so out of breath before and the temptation to continually drink is overpowering. The detail of the mountain is so clear; we couldn't have hoped for a better day. I can see the ridge that Pete Boardman lies. Pete was found two years ago; he sits there looking down the south face. I think his best mate Joe Tasker who he was climbing with must fallen, so Pete decided to stay a while. We finally get to Everest Base Camp at 5180 metres. Utterly shagged from just the walk up there, I am in awe at how anyone can get to the summit, especially without oxygen. I mean that is another 3000 metres above us!

Qomolangma is alive. Every part of it is alive. Snow plumes spout from it all over, snaking high into the sky, the light is continually changing, waves of snow fly from the summit into the jet stream from the death zone. From the top of a hill, amongst a mass of prayer flags and the coldest of cold winds, I close up inside my many layers of clothing and sit there for an age just looking, it is an unbelievable sight. Finally, getting back to the guest house and the Rongbuk Monastery (the highest in the world), we are all completely done in and shaking. As the sun sets, the light turns Qomolangma to a brilliant gold pyramid. At night you can see a million stars, so white, so bright, like being in outer space, only broken by its massive silhouette. One of those days you wish would never end.

27th October: After a fitful night's sleep, I awoke with the headache from hell. The altitude really had got to me feeling more like wearing a crash helmet made from pain. It was absolute agony and yet another reminder of what people go through up there on the mountain. Off we went in the dark at 7.00am. Alex suddenly became a surrogate father for a couple of hours as Phuntsok took a two year old boy down the pass for someone to hand over to his mother in a nearby village. Thankfully he never cried once, just sitting there with these big eyes staring at Alex in amazement. Back down the Friendship Highway.......WAAAAAA! Eleven hours back to Shigatse. If you breakdown here it is an unforgiving place. Dust, dust and more dust. People live in tents and work every day on this road. It is a brutal, relentless environment. In the 4x4 we were continually thrown about and battered senseless, often leaving our seats and becoming airborne.

28th October: Amazing! Up early ready to head back to Lhasa, the trip was suddenly cut short because the route had become frozen with three jeeps already coming off the road badly. Phuntsok then appeared with a translator who said that we couldn't leave for Lhasa until 3.00pm. Shite!

"More bad news I am afraid. The Panchen Lama died in his sleep and the identity of the new 15th Panchen Lama has been revealed. He is on his way to Shigatse and he will pass this way going to the monastery. I think it would be better if you waited until tomorrow. Your driver says he is very sorry, but there is nothing he can do about it". Quite mind-blowing I would say. Outside Shigatse was absolutely buzzing. Hundreds of kids were being led out of schools in lines of two. People were quickly filling the streets, flooding in from all over in their thousands. The town went on major shut down; the police on crowd control and street cleaners washed the roads. The Canadians were fantastic, playing with the kids and captivating the locals. It was absolute pandemonium and we were more than happy to be a part of it. As the day went on, the anticipation became almost tactile. When at last the convoy appeared at the end of the street, the crowd went completely ballistic. It was incredible and I got a good view of the main man as his motor went right past, covered in white silk prayer flags along with about forty other vehicles to the Monastery. Phew, what a day to remember.

Contrary to the above, he is actually the 11th Panchen Lama and is definitely not dead. Just goes to say, you can't believe everything you hear. The occasion was merely a very rare visit by the existing 'Panchen Lama'. The Panchen Lama is the No2 Lama around, second to The Dalai Lama in Tibetan Buddhism. There are two Panchen Lamas though; the Tibetan Panchen Lama who vanished in 1995 and has never been seen again; the present one was decided by the Chinese government by drawing a name out of a golden urn in some kind of lottery.

29th October: Seeing as the trip had been cut short, Phuntsok offered to take us out for the day the Ganden Monastery just east of Lhasa (Ganden meaning 'peaceful'). Although it was built in the 1400s and looks as old as any other, it actually had the crap bombed out of it in 1959 and had to be rebuilt from scratch. Ganden is another place set high up in the hills and you must take a long, steep and winding zigzag route to get there. From an overlooking peak, huge juniper fires smoke twenty four hours a day and thousands of prayer flags flutter in the breeze. In the distance, the big mountains on the horizon in their hundreds form huge valleys with blue rivers snaking away; rice terraces and villages dotted about are engulfed by the hills. For me this truly reflective moment brought with it a strong feeling of something ending and not knowing what could be just around the corner.

Saying goodbye to Phuntsok was difficult. We've so far recommended him to two groups of travellers and all done letters to give to his boss saying how good he is; he is by far the soundest and best driver compared to any other we saw along the way.

So ends 1500 miles of the most remarkable Tibetan landscape and culture you can possibly imagine. Crazy things have happened along the way and I've lived my dream to go to Qomolangma. Wondering what to do next. To be honest I am completely stuck. I really want to go to Nepal trekking, but I've heard it's nearly impossible to get back into China. At this moment China is still really the main idea. If I went to Nepal I would have to leave via Vietnam or another neighbouring country and then Laos for Christmas, then China[4].

Who knows hey!

---

[4] If anyone discovers this mythical border crossing between Nepal and Vietnam please dial 911 and ask for assistance and counselling. Maybe there is an interdimensional portal that opens at specific times during rare planetary alignments.

## A Lively Little Bus Journey into Yunnan
## 6<sup>th</sup> November 2005

Well, once again it's where do you start? Phew! Well today I woke up in bed on a heated blanket (toasty) in a really nice place called Zhongdian, one of the most northerly towns in the Yunnan Province of China. In the end, sticking to the original plan and blowing out the Nepal idea, I took the 'twenty four hour' sleeper bus from Lhasa and what a crazy totally insane journey that one turned out to be.

Having just descended from 4,500 metres to 3,000 metres there is also a strong accompanying feeling of euphoria that's come with it. Everyone says that the resulting increase in your red blood count makes you as high as a Boeing 747 and I am now very happy to agree with this. At the moment I'm speeding like I'm late for work the second time this week. I am Eddie the Eagle. My head is racing with ideas and thoughts at mach ten. I am an inter-ballistic road runner on amphetamines. I'm Rudolph the red nosed reindeer. I'm tip of the top and cream of the crop with Slipknot, Plastic Bertrand and Lene Lovich mixed together in my head all at once. I can safely say, I'm having so much fun, my lucky number's definitely just won!

1st November: 'Twenty Four Hour' Sleeper Bus from Lhasa to Zhongdian. So here I am on the sleeper bus going to Zhongdian, along with Carmen and Jorn from Holland, and Manu from France. Firstly, the locals can't believe that there are Western people on the bus; this is not a normal occurrence here and they can't stop talking about us especially as Carmen and Jorn both have short white-blond hair. We are getting major attention and stick out like a sore thumb. Secondly, I've never seen a bus like this. Inside there are three rows of bunk beds with stainless steel frames, one row against each side of the bus and one row in the middle, leaving two very narrow aisles. My gear is under the bed and the thermos is tied to a small rack near the feet-end. I am on a bottom bed against the window, central on the left hand side, nice. The bed is very small, narrow and you have to bend your legs when lying down. There's a guy who is eating sunflower seeds to the right and spits the empty shells on the floor. Let's hope he doesn't start greffing. All the beds have little blue quilts with cute little smiling dalmatians on them. Looking down the bus, there are over forty Tibetans all tucked into these with their heads poking out.

Once we are off the Tibetan landscape rolls by again; the yak herds; the flat planes and farm land; the small villages; the blue sky and the snow-capped peaks. The new Tibetan stylee thermos has become an essential part of the kit. It's great getting tea and hot meals together while you're on the move, though can get well messy at times, especially when the bus goes around a sharp corner or into a pothole. I'm full of nerves about this trip and keep wondering what's going to happen. Had this gut feeling of imminent doom for two days and now the choice has been made, there is nothing to do but let the drivers do their thing.

There's now snow on the ground and it's really cold which easily transfers up into your body, even within the safe confines of the bus, duvets and all. Ice covers the road big time. We are up on a high pass through the mountains and already at the scene of an accident. A minibus has come off the road and there is a great pile up of traffic. Shit! We're only three hours into the trip. The drivers are immediately putting chains on the wheels, on a bus for God's sake. They really look like they know what they are doing though. I on the other hand, slip over on my arse like a right idiot.

We are caught up on this pass for ages. Two purple lorries are stuck and the drivers are shoving dirt under the tyres. Even if we get moving it's gonna be well cold and frozen tonight for sure. When we eventually continue the chains slap against the wheel arches like a grandfather clock. Someone just said that the bus takes THREE DAYS to get to Zhongdian, not twenty four hours, mercy! At least most of the people are Tibetan not Chinese so it's really quiet onboard.

Reaching our first check point at 1.45 in the afternoon, my Western friends and I all keep a very low profile and the bus gets through with no problems[1]. At a nearby restaurant they serve hot water in paper cups with spam and chilli noodles. There are two drivers; one drives and the other advises as the road is so dangerous. It is very narrow and winding with a huge drop down one side. Chatting with the locals on the bus is going really well and this woman Liu Yi is helping out with the translation.

There are rock falls obstructing the way on but the driver is tanking down the road, often just driving straight through and over them, scary! Second town, don't know where. Lorries are double parked and won't move. One of the drivers likes rocks and we frequently stop so he can collect them. When we're on the move he cleans them and if he doesn't like them throws them out of the window. The bed might be too short but it's awesome lying here looking out of the window watching Tibet roll by for hour after hour. Am I cursed?

---

[1] If you are not a Chinese national, travelling without a permit is kind of dodgy. I mean 'kind of', as no one really seems to know what's going to happen if you travel outside Lhasa without one. Some one said that the bus ticket counts as a permit, (yeah right!) The police can basically do what they like with you if they catch you out and that's all there is to it.

There's an old woman behind my head and she's making the worst greffing noises known to mankind. In fact half the people on the bus are at it, continually spitting on the floor and out of the windows.

Moving out of the familiar Tibetan landscape, the road now cuts through huge valleys with hills covered in forest turning from green to orange in the autumn sun. With great snow-capped peaks rising up in the distance, this is bliss. Stopping at some town somewhere, everyone, men, women and children all piss in a line against a wall.

6.00pm and we reach the town of Bayi. The streets are wide and long with hundreds of prayer flags hung across. The chap next door opens a vacuum packed package of tongue and promptly starts munching and slobbering noisily away. He then swaps with his mate and spends hours with his head out of the window puking wildly out the bus.

The first thing that springs to mind around here is the word SPECTACULAR! Having never considered this bus journey to be anything but a way to get from A to B, this is now completely staggering. After only six hours into the journey, Carmen and Jorn's travel book describes this as "an epic once in a life time journey taking you through breathtaking landscape". Not a bad discovery to make after you've already started the trip! Turns out that we're going to be going through a dozen serious mountain passes higher than 5000 metres and past glaciers.

2nd November, 9.00am: Another beaten-up weather-worn town surrounded by beautiful mountains. The sun is rising and it's all good. Last night though, while everyone on the bus was asleep, the road had got suddenly seriously bad. It is another road under construction like the Friendship Highway after all, and if they detonated TNT on this road, in places it wouldn't make any difference. There are now three drivers; one drives, one sleeps and one advises. There are also four of their mates who sit up front and assist in everything. They are a very tight crew. I sit up watching their immense skill at getting this hulking bus up the road for hours; they are awesome. Most of the time the bus is only doing between 5 and 10 mph and hardly ever getting into second gear. They drive into bends really slowly and then reverse out of it. This manoeuver may be done several times before we can make it around.

At 11.00pm I'm off to sleep, somehow, as this trip is another really hellishly bumpy one. 11.20 pm: We are woken by all the driving crew shouting to get off the bus. I swagger down the steps and into the freezing blackness and immediately met by an unbelievable scene. The

97

road has disintegrated into a mire of deep mud. It curves at forty five degrees downwards and to the right is a sheer drop into nowhere. Clearly this is a very VERY long way down.

A lorry is trying to get up this crazy slope and is totally stuck half way. There are at least thirty people trying to push the lorry up. It looks really dangerous; people shouting' gesturing in the dark, snow, smoke, the engine revving and cutting out repeatedly, lurching forwards for a few inches and then rolling backwards. At one point it seems for sure that it's going over the side and taking everyone with it. In the end the driver gives up and it rolls backwards to the bottom at a crazy break neck speed to where there are another ten or so lorries also jammed up.

We are then made to walk in single file from the bus down this hill illuminated by its head lights precariously close to the drop. As we start to go down Liu Yi says that this is one of the most dangerous roads in Tibet, therefore one of the most dangerous in the world I guess.

"You're not f*cking joking" I mumble under my breath.

At the bottom we wait for the bus with trepidation. "Where's Carmen?" I ask Jorn and Manu upon discovering her absence.

"She wanted to stay on the bus. She said it was too cold to get out of bed" shrugged Jorn nervously.

At that, our attentions all immediately turn to the bus as it kicks into gear. Moving cautiously forward, inch by painful inch it starts down the hill. As the bus hits the incline, its top-heavy double decker weight and super soft suspension makes it lean right over. At this point there is no doubt that the bus is going over the edge, but the driver instantly quickens his pace, correcting the steering and goes for it. Maybe he has no choice, but it's the ballsiest thing you will ever see. Blessed relief to see the bus suddenly right itself and come flying down the track. Mercy! It's only the evening of day one. Oh shit!

It's still around midnight and it is dark and snowing. Back on board all the Tibetans are instantly tucked in under their dalmatian duvets and sound asleep. I, on the other hand, am now wide awake filled with nerves, so sit behind the drivers wondering what's going to happen next. At 1.00am the bus stops at a long and high bridge. Again we have to get off the bus and my friends and I hide in the dark from the guards. A lorry is coming over very slowly and carefully.

When it finally gets over, we again walk in single file in the dark across the bridge. This bridge is old, it has big gaping holes in it and some of the wood is clearly rotten. We all walk carefully along the left hand side, holding onto the wooden rails in case our feet go through. It's a slow walk and feels like it's never going to end. On the other side, we turn round and watch as the bus kicks into gear and inches over this death trap of a bridge. Oh man! I wonder how it can support any weight at all and you can hear the timbers creaking and moaning under the stress. The relief when it gets over is almost tactile. The rest of the night I plan my escape from the bus in case it started to go over the edge, visualising rolling out of the open window.

It's now 9.45am and there is at least a 1000 foot drop on the right. We are overtaking lorries on blind bends through their huge dust clouds and the sun makes it even worse. This is pure lunacy! We are passing this lorry and it's so close that the vehicles lock together and all you can hear is the scraping of metal on metal. The windows bow inwards and some look like they are going to explode so I dive off the bed into the aisle (yeech). Bad move! The amount of rubbish on the floor is outrageous. We are like a giant moving bin on wheels and it shifts from side to side with every crazy bend we make.

11.30am, Bangda: Skinny animals and rubbish everywhere! 2.00pm Dzongang: As we are leaving I dig out the DVD that I bought in Lhasa. It's the music that Phuntsok was playing all the time on the Everest Base Camp Trip. One of the drivers gives me a grin and the thumbs up and when it's on the crew up front all sing along to it at the tops of their voices. They know all the words. The guy next door, the one who didn't get sick on the tongue is called Wo Xiangsheng, which translated means 'Mr I'. He's a good bloke and he only greffs on his mate's side of the bed now and not mine. How thoughtful!

8.00pm, Markham: It's dark, it's cold and we are all mentally exhausted. This is the last Tibetan town before entering the province of Yunnan. As we drive in, Manu suddenly jumps up and shouts in his French accent
"MARKHAM! F*CKING MARKHAM!"
Two weeks ago Manu was arrested by the Chinese police for being here, fined and sent back two days to Chengdu. We are all nervous about this place and there is a rising anticipation as the bus draws closer then reaches the outskirts. The one and only thought is to get out ASAP. Not so long back Westerners were absolutely forbidden to set foot in Markham and the rules now are hazy at least. As soon as we get into the bus station there are police around the bus checking everyone out. We just stay on the bus, making ourselves small under the blankets until they leave. The driving crew then announce that they will be staying in Markham overnight. Terrific!

In a nearby restaurant, the old bill come in and just stare at us. We say hello but get no reply. They just continue to stare, deliberate quietly between themselves and then with great relief, head off in the direction of the police station, spooky! Bollocks to that! Returning as quickly as possible, we make a b-line for the safety of the bus and stay there for the rest of the night.

Back on board, it's still cold but actually not too bad. There's a good vibe about and one of the drivers passes around some clear spirit in a green bottle a bit like paint stripper. It goes quiet as everyone nods off, then at about 2.00am suddenly there are six new passengers that board the bus and they are all Chinese, great! With loads of big packages they bring onboard, they keep falling into everyone who's in bed. They talk so loudly with no regard for anyone else who is trying to sleep and like a load of hamsters on speed are unable to settle down for one second. After an hour of loud conversation between them and getting on and off the bus, they attempt to get into bed and sleep, yeah right! They all seem to have these big crackly packages they are messing around with and being really noisy. In the end, three feet away from them I shout "SHUT THE F*CK UP!" and the bus goes immediately quiet, nice! Something's just get through any language barriers I guess.

3rd November: The fumes in the bus station are so bad I use my sexy balaclava to cover my nose and look like a local. Markham is certainly not the best of places and we are very glad to get out. Last day on the bus today! The sun is bright and the countryside is terracotta; all the farm houses, earth and trees are this colour. There are huge rice terraces going down the mountains and beautiful villages along the way. They put their crops in huge piles to dry on flat rooftops. The snow just adds to it all; so different from the Chinese terraces. The bus may as well be a dustbin lorry now and everyone is seriously minging. There's a new guy next to Mr Wo. He was sick in the bus station and he's sick now, very loudly out of the window and in a bag while still in his bed, aaaaagh!

Over another 5000m pass! Snowcapped mountains looking stunning as ever. Midday at Yanjing: Great green terraces and white farm buildings dotted everywhere on the hills. At 1.30pm we stop at the Mingyong Glacier. Wow, what a magnificent sight! The rest of the trip seems to be merely an unbroken flow of time that we need to finish in order to reach our destination. As we finally hit smooth roads, the drivers go for it and hammer perilously fast around hairpin bends through more mountain passes.

# 6

# Yunnan Eternal Springtime

This is truly a special and unique province in China. Its name translates to 'Clouds in the South' and is most famous for its moderate and spring-like climate. Indeed it is also known as 'The Province of Eternal Spring'. If ever there was a place to bring you down into calmness after the excitement of Tibet, this is the place to do it.

Bordering Vietnam, Myanmar and Laos, though Yunnan is such a vast place, it seems to be tucked away in the bottom left hand corner of China as if hiding and quietly going about its business. It remains sleepily unconcerned as the East Coast tries so hard to push forward in its relentless pursuit of development. Only until recently has it become easy to travel into this area and many people fled here when the Japanese occupied large parts of China during the Second World War. Even now, although many still head for its most famous of places (Chinese people loooove to party in Lijiang), comparatively it's quiet.

Kunming is the only city that even tries to compete with the other big places, but even then upon arrival these attempts feel a bit half-hearted. And why would you want to? From every town where ever you stand you are always aware of the vastness and beauty of the surrounding countryside. Yunnan is hugely mountainous and boasts a terrific diversity of animal and plant life. Its climate ranges from frozen summits in the north to the palm trees of the sub tropics in the south. It is known mainly for its green and fertile farmlands and can be seen as one giant and vast garden.

## Tiger Leaping Gorge, Lijiang and Dali
## 16th November 2005

The last month has been crazy so I spent a couple of days getting over the bus trip in Zhongdian also called Shangri-la, having been renamed in an effort to make it more popular for tourists. It's not just any old Chinese city though. It's a staggeringly beautiful old town that still keeps its traditional Tibetan architecture. When you're enjoying the first brew of the day, the mountains that you've just come from form a panoramic display, reminding you of your journey and what it took to get here.

There's also the biggest prayer wheel you will ever see on top of a nearby hill, taking three people to push it. I guess the bigger the wheel, the bigger the prayer must be. Maybe they should make super large prayer wheels for the passengers about to get on the sleeper buses down at the station.

You know when the bin men are coming as the lorry plays those old favourite tunes really loudly, 'There's no Place like Home, My Fair Lady, Oh my Darlin' Clementine, Happy Birthday to You' and you can hear it from blocks away. They must be very cheerful bin men. Machetes four pound fifty; very reasonable; there are knife shops everywhere in Zhongdian and you can also buy a variety of different swords. I knew there was something missing from the trolley bag.

It's also another sad day, having just said goodbye to Carmen, Jorn and Manu. As the downside of travelling; it's not just about missing your friends but it makes you feel a bit needy when you part company and your all on your own, kinda like you've softened up or something. The group mentality always gives you a false sense of strength. You just have to put your head down and get on with it though.

Pushing on south from Zhongdian to Lijiang, a brief detour gets added to the itinerary to see Tiger Leaping Gorge. Located on the Jingsha River it's around 18 km long and one of the deepest canyons in the world. The gorge is surrounded by mountains and snowy peaks and if you like hiking, welcome to paradise. Get off the bus at Qiaotou, a small town nearby on the main Lijiang road. A fifteen minute walk towards the gorge will take you to a line of hostels and cheap guesthouses.

Tiger Leaping Gorge is a fantastic place. To see the best if it, you have to do a two day trek up high with breathtaking landscape. Although it mullers you out big time it's certainly not a bad way to spend a Monday, especially if you stay overnight in a great place called the Tea

Horse Guesthouse. Most inhabitants who live in this region are Nakhi (or Naxi) people, one of the fifty six ethnic minority groups in China. They make their living mainly from farming, but these days are happy for any tourist to drop buy and spend a few kuai. Leading a seemingly self-sufficient lifestyle, the buildings form a court yard giving shelter from the wind and allowing vegetables to dry in the sun. Baskets full of drying produce and potted trailing plants fill every ledge and corner, while pumpkins and squashes cover the steps to the guest's area.

Just unbelievable; when you wake up, the first thing you see is dazzling scenery framed by the window, all from the warmth of your colorful Nakhi bedspread. It's just a total feel-good factor before you even got up around here. The next day, hiking along to the Half Way Guest House, you can crap in the toilet they claim as having the "best view in the world." I must admit it was pretty damned cool squatting there overlooking glittering mountains against a blue sky.

Lastly for ten kuai you can go to the bottom of the Gorge. This is an awesome spot well worth the effort to get down there as the river is so completely powerful. So far at many places along the way there have been crowds of Chinese people who wear top of the range outdoor gear. They will always catch minibuses or cable cars to any view point and ten minutes later they are on their way back after they have taken their photos. No chance of that here! In order to reach the bottom of the gorge you have to go waaaaaaay down a long tough path. Of course this is also the only way back so all you see are Chinese hikers having major heart attacks, rasping for breath flaked out everywhere.

Blagging a lift in a minibus for just a few kuai, I took one last look at this stunning place and wondered how long it would still be there for. Someone at the guesthouse said that there are plans to build a number of dams in the area which would most likely see the end of the gorge. Although one project was scrapped by the local government, it was merely moved just outside the province so plans could continue. Similar to the Three Gorges Dam over in Chongqing it would mean 100,000 Nakhi people would have to move and yet another way of life destroyed forever; a shame to be leaving such a magical place with such a somber note.

A couple of hours down the road is the ancient Nakhi city of Lijiang. Split down the middle, great efforts have been made to keep the old part of town separate from the typical Chinese modern style. It's easy to get lost in the vast maze of fantastic old architecture, cobbled streets, canals and bridges. There are no cars allowed in this area, so if you decide to rest your legs outside any of the coffee shops, you can sit there unhassled and blissed out all day.

If you're ever staying in Lijiang then definitely make a point of hanging out at Mama's Guesthouse. I was tipped off from Raff and Katrine, wrote it down and I've been looking forward to it ever since. The owners Mama and Papa Naxi are well known not only for their amazing hospitality but especially for the amount of food Mama will pile up in front of you at dinner time. All she wants to do is to feed her guests, then feed them again. Half of the food is for free and if not its really cheap. Plate after plate keeps coming until things go past the uncomfortable stage but she insists you eat all of it. After all, it's considered bad manners and extremely wasteful to leave anything in China.

Often I'll go into my room and there will be some food left on the table. Twice now, there has been a knock at the door, it's opened a few inches and then an arm has reached inside, quickly depositing some fruit on the floor. It has all the creature comforts, including a hot shower at last, its own loo and the dinner table right outside the door. Mama sets each table for six and you are sat with new people every meal time. You are pushed into meeting people here, it's fantastic. Annoyingly, all the pillows on the chairs keep sticking to the Velcro on my trousers, so when I stand up there will be one stuck to my arse. They're only little pillows so the first time it happened I didn't notice until I was virtually out the gate. How cool can you get!

They don't call Mama 'Mama' for nothing. Mama Naxi will look after and help her guests out with an energy that you just won't find in any other place. You will even see her hugging unsuspecting guests who she really likes so it's best to keep a low profile as much as possible. One guy called Adam from the States needed to phone home and she spent over two hours helping him. On the other side there is Papa; a mellow and quiet guy who is happy to sit there all day, smoke ciggies and do absolutely nothing while wifey runs around barking orders at the staff with the energy of an express train.

Visited the Black Dragon Pool today; a beautiful lake lined with willow trees that is so crystal clear, the long wooden rowing boats look like they are floating on air instead of water. It boasts one of the most famous views in China, with its curved white marble bridge arching over to the 'Moon Embracing Pavilion'. The Jade Snow Mountain rises up behind to a lofty 5.5 thousand meters and the reflection in the lake forms a picture of perfect symmetry. Stumbling across a traditional Nakhi calligraphy school nearby, they didn't mind people wandering about the empty classrooms at all so you could take your time studying the Nakhi pictogram-writing covering the walls. Being in a Chinese art room was a humbling experience, especially when the teacher showed up. He looked very old, had a long white beard and red silk robes.

The evenings in Lijiang are pandemonium. There are thousands of Chinese people on the streets getting aresholed on two beers and going nuts. They form huge circles in the centre of town and then do something a bit like the hokey-cokey.

Dunno what the day is today. The 11th my watch says, but that doesn't mean much. Went cycling out of Lijiang with my new friends I met round Mama's dinner table; Adam, Ev' from Canada and Yvonne from Holland. What a terrific day! Down a long straight road with the Jade Mountain up front, we cycled to a village called Baisha and saw some old but unimpressive frescos, then met this guy called Doctor Ho who is famous in the medical world. Apparently he has a cure for cancer and saves people all the time.

You certainly knew which place was Dr Ho's since he waits for visitors outside in his white doctor's coat. As we arrived he was already shaking our hands while we tried to get off our bikes, virtually dragging poor Eve up the steps; talk about personality. He is also certainly not a guy that is shy of photos. Normally taking a photo involves a slight edge of unease if it's of a person you don't know. Dr Ho on the other hand, encourages you to take your cameras out and photograph him. He loves the attention and is more than happy to let people snap away as much as possible.

If you ever wind up at Dr Ho's you'll find that his clinic is a lively place. The white shelves of blue and red plastic buckets are filled with different blends of dried herbs that he collects from all over the mountains.. There is a counter that is covered with half a ton of mail from all around the globe and he waved his thank you letters from recovered cancer sufferers under our noses with the upmost enthusiasm.

He's eighty three but amazingly looks like a young sixty five, having seen a lot of history in his lifetime, including the Japanese occupation and surviving the Great Leap Forward. How on earth can someone have so much get up and go at that age? Before leaving, he gave everyone a checkup and prescribed different types of his special 'healthy tea'. Maybe there's still hope for me yet!

Big mistake! We should have eaten before going to Dr Ho's and instead left it until well past 2pm. Of course being totally ravenous, everyone ordered way too much food in the restaurant. Completely bloated out, the cycle ride back was a painfully slow one, then bang on the dot, there's Mama slapping the food down on the table again.

"Oh please, I can't take anymore" moaned Yvonne in discomfort after the first half an hour. As Ev responded, trying not to laugh with a mouth full of food she couldn't swallow, another plate of fried aubergine was banged down on the table.

"Xiang mifan shenme?" (want more rice), the waitress asked with a huge steaming pot full under one arm.

"Oh God no!" Adam quickly replied.

I don't think I've eaten that much food in one day before, well not since Mum got a freebie down the Beefeater when she found some glass in her prawn cocktail. It's just not normal to only have three hours between meals. Apologetically leaving the table with some food remaining, my distended gut felt more like one of those old space-hoppers for hours afterwards.

Leaving was also a memorable occasion. On the way from the guesthouse, Mama came up and gave us a good luck necklace, a bag of fruit and delivered a series of bone crushing hugs. Her staff carried all our stuff to the bus stop and even Papa managed to motivate himself to come along and wave goodbye. Sweet as! Mountains and scenery aside, out of everything that happened in Lijiang, 6pm at Mama's Guesthouse will always be the most memorable time.

The next stop was the famous town of Dali though it turned out to be quite disappointing to be honest. Like I'm sitting there out front of a restaurant eating my dinner, as crowds of Chinese tourists flocked by in their tour groups all gawping away. People came up trying to sell all kinds of unwanted stuff, followed by a lorry that stopped right outside dumping a huge load of bricks in the street and pavement. It kicked up a billowing cloud of dust which enveloped the tables adding to the flavour and texture of the food. Very nice!

Monday! Another great cycling day, out of Dali and into the countryside. Yunnan is lush, green and filled with colour. Ev', Adam and I went down to Erhai Lake, the seventh largest in China, named so because it is said that it's shaped like an ear. If you translate 'er hai' exactly, it becomes 'ear sea'. Cycling through the fields and seeing the locals going about their business was far more that we imagined. Yunnan is more like a living patchwork of colour that stretches off to the horizon. Upon arriving at the water's edge, the rest of the afternoon was spent painting and taking in the lazy autumn-rays, bliss!

Since arriving in Dali, myself and the friends I made at Mama's have been staying at a place called the No5 Guesthouse. This was another recommendation from Raff and Katrine, though this time not the best of ones. It's so big, with so many guests that the staff don't give much of a monkey's about anyone. There are just so many people coming in and out and it's so oversized that the contrast with Mama's is huge. Zero personal attention here mate I can tell you.

It didn't go well from the outset, with issues of communication causing most of the problems. Things started to get to extreme levels where with mad arguments over tiny problems. One morning all I wanted was two fried eggs for breakfast and there were ten of them going spare. We were there at five to ten, but because they made us wait ten minutes they wouldn't serve us with this woman shouting

"No Breakfast, No Breakfast! Breakfast at 10!" and it goes on. Eventually I got two eggs but no toast! I asked for toast and she shouted at the top of her voice "NO TOAST, NO TOAST".

To be honest, I'm getting sick of not being able to speak Chinese now. Being unable to communicate effectively gets you into all kinds of embarrassing and stupid situations, causing commotion after commotion and therefore the attention of half the neighbourhood. I wonder what people say when they hear it?

"Hey, what's going on over there?"

"Just another foreigner being an arsehole, that's all." most likely. Normally there's a big scene whether it's in a restaurant, hotel or guesthouse, especially when it comes to getting a mug of decent English tea in. Chinese green tea is pretty good as it goes, it's just that you start to crave things from back home and that includes a Tetley every morning that's all.

Example 1: One morning in the Kirey restaurant in Lhasa I ask the waitress Kandzhu the usual request.

"Can I have a pot of tea with these two tea bags in it please?" handing her a couple of Tetley's and pointing to the tea pot.

She replies, "Pot? Pot? Pot?"

I say, "Yes, That pot!" pointing and put the tea bags in her hand.

"Pot?" she says again and I say, "Yes! That pot! Can I have a glass of milk please?"

She replies, "Milk?"

"Yes, Milk!" I say, then walk back to the table. I then see that Kandzhu is on the phone ordering the milk, who then puts both tea bags in a glass with some hot water. I'm over there in a flash behind the bar as I virtually live there anyway, get the tea pot and pour the lot into it and top it up. The milk then takes half an hour to arrive in a tiny cup. You can only get one cup of tea out of it and it goes on and on. Quite often I will find myself in a kitchen with the chefs and waitresses going nuts.

Example 2: While in Mix Guesthouse, after an immense hassle of getting a brew together, I make the big mistake of ordering a couple of bacon sarnies. So they serve one bacon sarnie. In it are two tiny pieces of bacon. Each one is roughly two inches by a half an inch inside two normal sized dry bits of bread. It's very easy to become like John Cleese in these instances. There I am in the kitchen again going "No, no, no! Two bacon sandwiches please. One, two!" holding up my fingers and saying it in Chinese.

"Shenme yisi?" (What does this mean?) puzzles one of the waiters.

"Liang ge" (two of), I finally remember.

They all go, "Ohhhhhh, two!"

"Yes" I say. "Two! Hen hao. Xie xie" (very good and thank you). At last two sarnies arrive, but only one has anything in it. The other one is empty. Pointing to the first sarny and the lack of bacon in the second, the chef then takes one of the pieces of bacon with his bare hands and puts it between the two blank pieces of bread, so now there is one bit of bacon in each sandwich ...AAAAAGH!

There's no way you can continue with this argument. Everyone means really well and will do their best running around for you. Chinese people will go nuts to help, often going right out of their way to lend a hand. It's maddening though because it always happens over the smallest of things. The golden rule at any time, clearly, is to stick to the menu. Menus will often have pictures of the food in them anyway so us lame arses who can't speak enough Chinese can point to what we want instead.

Example 3: So I'm in Lhasa when I go to the corner shop to buy some tissues.

"Can I have some tissues please?" I ask, pointing at the tissues.

"Shenme yisi?" the usual response.

Getting out the sad little overworked phrasebook, I point to the correct vocabulary.

"Wo mei you" (I don't have) the shop owner replies.

"Xiang zhe ge" (want this one), I insist. Once more pointing to the tissues. The shop owner's friends join in and between them they get more and more animated, until after five painful minutes they reluctantly sell them to me.

"F*cking xie xie" I angrily snap, opening the packet in front of them to find it is really a packet of tampons. At that they all burst out into uncontrolled laughter. Oh the shame!

God I need to sort my Chinese out double quick. I am trying, but it all seems kinda halfhearted when you're on the move all the time. Often you will find that a traveller's Mandarin is embarrassingly appalling. Anyway it doesn't matter too much after all, as your going back to your home country soon right? Trouble is that's not on the agenda. It's the people who really have started to settle down or have been to college to study it that can speak the Chinese around here!

On the last afternoon in Dali we went up Mt Cangshan which sits just west of town; a great time with an absolutely fantastic view of the lake and surrounding areas. After an amazing day exploring and hiking we made our way back in the early evening humidity. About half way down something big and insect like jolted me out of my hiker's delight, caught in the back of my hoody. Clearly annoyed at its capture I could feel its legs and body squirming to get free with a loud accompanying buzzing sound. With alarm bells instantly ringing, at full speed I attempted to get my sweater off before it was too late but to no avail. An intense needle of searing pain suddenly went stabbing into the back of my neck causing me to shout expletives at the top of my voice. Within seconds, the pain had spread across my head and back with a burning sensation, forcing me to my knees in the middle of the track.

Adam hesitantly fished through the sweater to find the offending creature; an Asian giant hornet. Holy shit! This huge black and orange beast was easily larger than my middle finger and though it had delivered its sting it was still alive and going strong. Folding up the sweater, Adam hesitantly moved it away from the path some feet away before letting it go. Asian giant hornets are not something to be taken lightly. They are super aggressive fierce predators that have a quarter of an inch sting delivering a blast of venom so strong it can dissolve human tissue. A single dose by these things can kill you even if you're not allergic to wasp stings and around forty people die each year from them. Now convulsing and squirming in the dirt, my mouth started to open on its own accord. Crazy; I just couldn't close it causing me to panic blindly. By now the pain was an absolutely searing agony and I started retching myself inside out.

Unable to do anything there, my friends carried me down to the roadside and looked some help. Incredible! Where are all those hundreds of taxi's when you need one?Finally we got a lift and in a blur of overwhelming pain I found myself back at the hotel while everyone went out to look for some medicine on a "Save Andy" mission. Unfortunately the only thing they could come up with was a local snakebite remedy and a few antihistamine tablets. A weird and trippy night's sleep commenced but luckily my body started to detoxify and by morning, though my neck was still sharply acid like, at least some form of sanity had returned. That was definitely a lucky one!

Doing the sleeper train to Kunming tonight. Adam who already did the same journey said he had a Chinese guy trying to cuddle him. Maybe my luck will be in tonight hey. Got that expectant travelling-again feeling and well excited about the next part of the trip. Never thought about leaving China but it feels that South East Asia is definitely beckoning.

The antennas are still up though and at some point as the cash runs out I'll really have to have a serious go at putting down some roots somewhere.

Dali has been a drifty, dossy haze of eating and drinking cheap beer and hanging with some incredibly sound people. So much has happened and everyone has been continually laughing. Chinese 'corn whiskey' is only two kuai a bottle! Why? Because the bottles are recycled ones from the hospital and come in all shapes and sizes.....hmmmm, doesn't sound too tempting really does it.

Yvonne and I have a theory that as we get closer to leaving China it's getting noisier and noisier. This morning a loud group of builders woke everyone up, smashing the room next door in with sledge hammers, nice! They've been standing right outside at the crack of dawn, having loud conversations and shouting over the building work. The guesthouse plays deafening Chinese music over the top of that. There's also building work going on out the back and dogs bark continually. They brought a lorry in and dumped a ton of gravel outside. Dali is undoubtedly the noisiest place you can imagine. Still, we will not move out until the last. We will not be defeated! I just predict that the next guesthouse in Kunming will have pneumatic drills thundering away outside and the locals arguing at the tops of their voices.

## Kunming and Jinghong: 23rd November 2005

Well, here we are in Kunming. The sleeper train was quite something. The station in New Dali was absolutely heaving with people all stampeding for the same train. Staring out of the window at the lights outside somewhere in the darkness; rollin' on again. Crazy, seeing the Chinese people getting up in the morning, all flocking around the wash basins by the dozen; the guys all wearing the same coloured grey-blue one piece thermal underwear with their socks tucked in. A cover of The Bee Gees 'How Deep is your Love' on saxophone was played on the tannoy system before the train pulled in.

At 6.30am and Yvonne and I ended up this backpacker's place having said goodbye to our friends in Dali. God I really hate dorms! There was a guy shagging some tart over in the corner and three pissed-up French people, two of which were also going for it in the bunk directly above. One guy had rotten feet and another had thrown up next to his bed. Needless to say with all the activity going on and an unbearable stink sleeping was kinda difficult!

There's a great display of stuff on the wall in the restaurant that belonged to the Flying Tigers including some of their old flying jackets. The Tigers were an American mercenary squadron based over here during the Second World War. With huge snarling teeth painted on the sides of their machines and complete recklessness, they terrorised the Japanese on a daily basis. On the back of the jackets is their 'blood chit', a red and white square patch with Chinese characters that says "This foreign person has come to help the war effort. Soldiers and civilians, one and all, should rescue, protect, and provide him with medical care."

Happily leaving the stench of the dorm we quickly moved to the Camellia Hotel. Actually it's not as flash as it sounds. In fact the rooms were the grimmest, darkest closets known to mankind with a serious downer quality about them but it was right next to the consulate and well handy if you need to sort your visas for Laos out.

Kunming itself is another heaving city; really hectic with huge supermarkets and office blocks. It still maintains its traditional side though, and if you want to get away from the noise of the city then the Green Lake Park is the place to go. Filled with large groups singing and playing traditional music, people playing Chinese chess under the trees, exercising or just relaxing in pavilions drinking green tea, at last you get a traditional flavour of what the city used to be about. If you want to find some personal space, just go to the bamboo island, or chill-out on a bench next to the pond filled with gold fish and koi carp. Not a bad way to spend the afternoon.

As cities go Kunming's is a fairly pleasant place and at night it's lit up brilliantly with coloured lights like a Christmas tree; that's really something. The Chinese woman's dress sense is more OTT than in any other town. At night some even wear silver, with silver thigh length boots and mini-skirts. Some of the clubs are like being in a space craft. If you do go into one then you an either pay a huge amount of money for the table and drink all you like for the night or you can buy your beer in individual bottles. This can be especially annoying as not only are the bottles tiny and expensive, you order your beer from a waiter. He will then take your order, give you a written ticket, bring the beers back after ten minutes and then you have to go to the counter to pay for them. After five minutes you've finished your beer already and if want another one, you have to find a waiter and go through the whole process all over again. On a busy night you can wait up to half an hour between beers so locals may well hit the baijiu instead.

Aside from beer, baijiu, which translates to 'white wine' is the number two drink in China. Made from rice or sorghum, a type of cereal, this clear spirit in every supermarket and corner shop you will go in. It's normally about sixty percent alcohol and incredibly cheap. The most common type is called 'erguotou' and a lot of guys will buy a small 100ml bottle for during dinner that costs around five kuai, that's about fifty pence. The next most popular is 'maotai' which is the kind of thing drunk by your boss at business lunches and amazingly has won awards. What for remains a mystery, as so far all baijiu tastes more like cellulose thinners, rewarding you with a complete blinder the next day.

Here's a little tip. If someone ever offers you baijiu, try and avoid it at all costs. Even climbing out of the toilet window is preferable to a night on the baijiu. Mercy! Unfortunately we were five stories up, so with no escape possible, when some locals insisted they join us for a baijiu bucket it was game over. Woke up in a completely different hotel and it's been a haaaaard day today alright I can tell you.

Please turn it off; they are now already playing Western Christmas carols in Chinese everywhere now, especially Jingle Bells. I just hope they haven't discovered Slade. Christmas is coming, but as usual it never smiles on the less fortunate. It's weird; there are all these high-tech flashy buildings everywhere and then there are loads of crippled people on the pavement asking for money. I don't use the word 'crippled' lightly here, as the truth is that a lot of the beggars are deliberately mutilated in order to become professional beggars. Often kids will have their legs and arms broken and twisted so they become beggars for life. It's something we noticed in the modern part of Lijiang and after seeing it here, it seems like its common place all over the country.

So while people go in and out of department stores, there will be this guy with no arms and legs having been dumped on the steps all day crying out for money. At the end of the day he will be collected and taken back to a bed for the night. He will have a boss who will take the money. I've seen it all so far I can tell you; from the terribly burnt, to those who can only crawl about on a homemade skateboard and children that have been snatched from their parents. For some reason the old bill do absolutely nothing about this problem. I have heard that China is the land of the back hander and maybe this is one example of it. There are also professional beggars, who go home and take off their rags and put on decent clothes. Either way, even though a lot of genuinely poor people come in from the countryside with nothing to their name, having real reasons to live at the side of the street, generally begging has a reputation as being fake.

23rd November, Twelve Hour Sleeper Bus to Jinghong: The taxi takes us to the bus station where there is supposed to be this guy with the tickets. Predictably, there's no one there except a band of full-on women with an attitude, shouting at us about God knows what. Eventually, with much relief, the guy appears and takes us to the bus. My bed is near the back on the bottom bunk and in the middle row. This is a totally different bus from my lovely Tibetan posse from Lhasa. This after all is a Chinese bus and don't you know it. It's the usual pandemonium only compressed into a very small space.

There are at least forty people on this bus, so we are in pretty close contact with each other. I am on the bottom bunk in the centre, right near the back. Across the back there is a line of people sleeping together from side to side, so it means there are two pairs of feet; one each side of my face. Trouble is everyone has had to take their shoes off on the bus, so you get to smell peoples' socks in all their glory at point blank range. Boy do they stink and frequently brush and stick into the side of my face...aaaagh! The sock on the left foot belonging to the guy on my right has a hole in it exposing his big toe, making it even more appealing. One guy keeps breaking wind big time and the smell of farts, bad breath and feet already makes it difficult to breathe.

It's also very noisy. Why does everyone feel the need to shout all the time? There are a couple of Chinese movies which quiets everyone down, but when the bus stops for a break there's this rush of everyone trying to get off at once and there are people climbing and sitting on me. When I return some wanker has nicked my pillow. Later this family gets on, so there is a crying two-year-old next door with his dad shouting at him at 12 o'clock. People have their mobiles on all night and when they finally answer they talk at the top of their voices like they want the whole world to know what they are saying.

By 1.00am I already feel the need to wash really heavily, feeling utterly contaminated by other people, especially my face. At 2.00am the bus stops and the driver is clearly lost. I just lie there too tired to give a rat's arse. Everything stinks. People greff on the carpet loudly and there's no air to breathe.

7.00am: Waking up in a seriously good mood, there is the last bit of Babylon's Burning by The Ruts racing around in my head over and over. Outside, the view is amazing. We move from views of rice terraces going off into the distance, then over long winding dirt tracks disappearing into thick forest with big logging operations going on. This is Grizzly Adam's country Chinese stylee alright. Outside there is a weird convoy of buses and huge lorries sandwiched together, all inching their way down a long and incredibly steep untarmacked hill; crazy stuff! I don't trust bus journeys one bit now. Ev saw a big crash on her way to Dali. Two buses had had a head to head and there were bodies all over the road. In Kunming we met two Brits who had been on one of them, vowing never to travel by Chinese bus ever again. All in all, the penny has dropped that sleeper busses are a really hazardous way to travel.

Ah good old sleep deprivation; seems to keep coming around in waves every few days now. Still the new tea bags are fantastic and with the new Coffee Mate it tastes so creamy. How can that be? I don't know, but it does! Suddenly we are hit right up the arse by a lorry and the sound and vibration seems to explode down the entire length of the bus. The whole back end is smashed up big time and the driver ends up squaring up with the lorry driver. It looked like we were going over the edge for sure that time.

We move onto another highway under construction. These are everywhere as soon most of the outlying small towns will become cities. In all the places visited on the trip so far there has been massive construction going on so it's easy to see how China is growing. As we go down a hill towards a pass there is smoke pouring out from the wheel arches of each bus like a bonfire. How those brakes don't melt down is another mystery. Just pure madness!

Jinghong: Yvonne and I emerged from the bus with a tired but big sigh of relief. The journey sure was a stressful one and we were both minging big time. Blam! What a transition; it was sweltering in Jinghong. There we were in November with a blue sky, hot sun, surrounded by palm trees; just the perfect place to be in order to get our shit together for Laos. The hotel room was total heaven, I mean absolute perfection. It had a large balcony plus a table and chairs looking out onto more palm trees. With the washing hung out on a line to dry and kit strewn all over the place, a serious sorting out operation commenced; chucking clothes out and adding to the med kit all the time. Unable to keep our eyes open, it was quite easy to doze off at any time. Woke up with tea in bed and a decent shower. Oh my god, such utter bliss. The next evening we went for a slow walk in the late sun along the Mekong River. This was the quietest and most chilled out city so far; so sleepy with no Chinese tour groups anywhere. Having said that, as we were sitting there a jeep had a head-on with an ambulance in front of us. Crazy driving, but somehow everyone was okay.

Of course being in a completely different country English books were hard to find so most tended to be total rubbish. It is often a traveller's hobby trying to come across something to read, often swapping their old books with people they meet along the way. Feeling left out of the loop, the other day I bought the epic 'Battle Tank 2, War Hammer'. What a load of crap that was! It was so awful that absolutely no one wanted to swap their book for it.

Went out of town to a small place called Ganlanba the next day; a white knuckle ride in a knackered little bus up into the hills above the Mekong. Quite a dump really; dusty, smeggy, utterly depressing with empty rickshaws buzzing around like dirty beetles. Locals sat around all over the place doing absolutely nothing. Not too bad though, as a hike away from there leads you to green and rich countryside and the village of Manzha, home to the Dai people.

Walking along the river huge butterflies and dragonflies zipped by, water buffalo lazily wallowed in the water while banana trees bloomed with big purple flowers. There were these two lads who had devised an ingenious way of catching fish. They had two poles with electric cables taped down them attached to a car battery. This was carried by one of them on his back. At the end of the poles there were two prongs which they zapped the fish with in the water before scooping them up in a net.

WAAAAA! The ancient village had hordes of Chinese tourists flocking everywhere led by a tour group leader with a megaphone. Someone had put a giant fence up and charged tickets to get in. Shite! The village was beautiful though; old wooden buildings on stilts sat amongst the palm trees and jungle. There was an open-air theatre and with a great performance by about forty lovely dance girls in yellow and blue silk costumes, fantastic! Ate my first bamboo; nice, though felt a bit like a panda at the time. I did wonder though, what it must be like having a ticket office erected nearby and suddenly thousands of people walk by taking photos of you while you go about your business. Imagine that while you were mowing your lawn or washing your car. No doubt some rich bastard is making a mint out of it somewhere. The goal now is totally to find a people out in the middle of nowhere unspoilt by tourism. Can't be that difficult can it?

In the evening we went to the night market. This is simply another one of those great places to be; heaving with people around tables eating and drinking in dim light, buskers, fly pitchers and loads of kebab stalls. A big group of locals invited us to their table. They had a huge spread of food and shared the lot with us. There was a baked pineapple stuffed with rice; well nice. Round the corner, a huge table of locals celebrated this guy's birthday. Everyone ended up totally annihilated on baijiu and covered in cream cake. On someone's birthday it is traditional in the South of China to grab a handful of cream cake and spread it all over your friends face and head.

Finally we ended up in Mengla after a four-hour bus ride nearer the border. It was so noisy that you could hardly hear yourself think, inside and outside. Everything was so loud it was incredible, with loads of deafening Karaoke bars, people talking at the tops of their voices like they were shouting at each other. The traffic was intense as hundreds of lorries passed directly through the centre of town blasting their horns. Clearly the locals had hearing impediments. And yes, there was a pneumatic drill tearing up the road outside the hotel just to add to it.

On the way, Yvonne turned into the lunatic on the bus after taking too many travel sickness pills, shouting "Ni hao" (hello) at the cows out of the window in a drug induced rant. After that it all went downhill as she started to complain she needed to stop to take a leak for a second time. Eventually, as it got to the painful stage she cried out "Oh my Gaaaad. Oh my Gaaaad. I don't vaaaant. I don't vaaaant" in her broad Dutch accent. This woman puked along the entire length of the bus all down the windows so we had to look at its quivering gelatinous tendrils for nearly the whole trip, very nice!

Mengla was the last port of call in China before the border. Weird! China is without a doubt the craziest place you can imagine, but for some strange reason I miss it already. Some mad mad times have been happening and although your patience is continually pushed to the limit, I feel utterly compelled to return. Roll on Laos!

# 7

# Laos – Friends in Stereo

Am I a moany old git? Of course! That argument is now nailed down in one fell swoop.

Strange and unexpected place was Laos. Though you enter into a world of poverty, from the start, Laos is no shit hole. Its towns and villages are well maintained and people work hard to make sure their families are okay. Laos has a peaceful edge to it and if you take time to say Hi then you will find that it's a sincerely welcoming place.

Lets be honest though, clearly there are two sides to Laos. Firstly, coming in from the north via China, the quietness is kinda overwhelming; there's no one shouting on their mobile, no pneumatic drills and no door slamming. It took me days to get used to it. I mean the occasional car would go by, kicking up dust as it went, but often it was so quiet you could hear things from far away. To add to it, a couple of the guys we were hangin' with rarely spoke, especially around the dinner table. Sleepy is a giant understatement here, rather deeply soporific. If you want to see a Laos where people do their own thing then stay up in the north as much as possible. The scenery is also amazing with huge expanses of jungle and wildlife.

Split it down the middle though and you'll easily see the other side of Laos; the southern side. It's based on tourism and that's all there is to it, taking me completely by surprise. Tourism is big in the south and the country benefits from this continual cash injection. That's tourism! Some places would not exist if it wasn't for the tourist industry and in fact have been built solely for this purpose.

Most dictionaries define a tourist as 'someone who visits a place for pleasure or interest when they are on holiday'. Of course therefore I definitely fall heavily into this vast definitional crevasse, and if that's so, I can only define myself firmly as a reluctant one. So why all this aversion then?

Well, lurking in the darkest depths of this abyss lie the following categories (this also applies to people moving in and out of Cambodia):

1. These come across the border purely on a visa run with little or no interest in getting to know the culture. If Laos was any other country it wouldn't matter. It's nothing more than a novelty to be there. You enter via Thailand and exit back into Thailand after a few days with a new Thai stamp in your passport. With no real aim you will have gone to exactly the same places that everyone else has been to.

2. A very interesting and highly debated phenomena is the use of a certain well known travel guide (WKTG). We all use them; indeed I have six on my shelf right now. I guess they make me feel kinda safe having them around. They are good to have if you are making your first inroads into planning to go to a country you haven't been to before. Sadly though and here lies the argument, people often don't use the WKTG as a guide, instead following everything in each town to the letter so are awarded the title 'NAFI' or 'No Ambition and F*ck all Imagination'.

Example: A restaurant as recommended by that WKTG was so crowded that you couldn't get a table. The NAFIs were literally standing there waiting and having the cheek to look vaguely irritated by the whole thing; it was heaving. Next door was a perfectly good restaurant; the staff were all polite, the surroundings were comfortable and the food was okay but it was virtually empty. There were only two people in there.

Another example: A friend and I walked into a new town armed with our WKTG. It recommended a guesthouse so we went there. It was so crowded with NAFIs though it was unpleasant. It may have been a nice place at one time, but after being mentioned in the WKTG it had become overpopulated, noisy, dirty and unfriendly. Just walking minutes down the road we came upon a row of perfectly good guesthouses; cheap, clean and quiet.

If you are in a tourist town then sit back and watch the NAFIs as they walk in, faces glued to those pages, their destination Based Entirely Around Nothing other Than On A Single Travel book, (which loosely spells 'beans on toast'). In their determination to find that great recommendation a NAFI will go past numerous other places that could certainly do with the money and are perfectly okay. Get a few beers with your mates and check 'em out as they go by. Great fun!

Can't knock SE Asia though. With the swarm of people that descend on this neck of the woods, it's an awesome place to make friends. Funny that most people I met were originally travelling alone but gradually we became some giant amorphic pack of head cases and laughing became our regular diet. This addictive lifestyle is a familiar sight in Laos and it's hard to drop when you're having so much fun. You feel utterly in tune with your mates and will quite often say to yourself that you're simply having the best time of your life.

If you do go to Laos and like me follow the crowd then most likely you will wind up going to the most popular tourist destinations because they got a mention in the WKTG. This includes endlessly wandering around looking for restaurants, hostels, things to see and places to go all as recommended. Don't hope to find much authenticity about these places and don't kid yourself that the money you spend while you're there makes much of a difference. If you go to a restaurant your money is no doubt going into the pocket of a big operator who pays the staff absolutely bugger all. Most will work all hours and go home to appalling poverty. Maybe that's why you never get to see them eating a pizza and French fries.

If you do want to see how most people live, you have to cut loose, bin your WKTG and get speaking to the people who serve you in any shop. For sure they will instantly invite you to their place. Suddenly you will be on a real adventure. Your eyes will be wide open and you'll start remembering everything you did with a clarity that will stick in your mind forever. You'll be communicating with local people out of town instead of just buying a packet of twenty at the corner shop, your fourth beer Lao or booking a room. Your itinerary is no longer dependent on what other people want to do and you're life has immediately become fluid.

Independent Travelling: When you travel by yourself your experiences of cultures are heightened. Feelings become richer. True emotions are no longer repressed and can be felt far down to their source. Being on the road is one time when you can become truly in touch with yourself. Think about it; how often do you really do anything by yourself for longer than a few hours? We are surrounded by other people. We accommodate other people continuously throughout our day. Even if you travel with only one other person, then your attention is often directed towards your travelling partner and not what's going on around you.

If you are alone you are faced only by yourself. You have no one else to blame if anything goes wrong or something pisses you off. If you have bad luck then you have to deal with it sharpish and not dump on the next person next to you. You are completely reflected back on yourself like your standing in front of a giant mirror. It's stunning how the child can be brought out in all of us if we don't get our way. How many of us are deeply terrified of facing who we really are. I'm not saying we are all fake, rather what we see at face value is often only 95% of the real person. This is why so many people stay together in boring relationships. It's not through any other reason than being faced with a giant void that is your own life if you were suddenly on your own.

There are also some feelings that we only ever get to experience when we are alone. There are no names for these feelings or ways to describe them and often they have no point of reference. These truly singular introspective moments can never be found when you are in the company of others. It takes time for them to surface so you can't just go and cut loose for a few hours. You have to be brave enough to stick it out and see what emerges.

Independent travelling is like looking at a painting by Raphael while being in the Uffizi Gallery as opposed to a picture you saw in a book. The colours are stunning and the onlooker will instantly have a great emotional response when confronted with something so vibrant. In this way your experience of the world can become almost tactile, with a richness where you are able to touch other cultures. After all, that's what you hit the road for in the first place I am sure right?

Phew! Lost the plot then for sure! Beat me with a stick right now. Laos was okay. Just full of NAFIs and a bit beans on toast that's all.

## Luang Namtha: 9<sup>th</sup> December 2005

AAAAGH! Another crazy bus journey with special magic roads that disappear in front of your very eyes. A bus with strange interdimensional abilities like the Tardis where you will never see so much stuff and people fit into such a small confined place at one time. Nothing like being squashed up against a sack of meat on a blazing hot day. Nice! Oh, and another full-on argument as the bus ran into a brand new Beamer at 8.00am in the bus station. Hmmmm, nice driving mate!

Laos: I now realise that I know absolutely NOTHING about this place; the customs, the language (I keep wanting to talk in Chinese all the time) the terrain, anything! I mean a single kuai is the equivalent of 1,337.5 kip which is the local currency. A quid is around 12,500 kip and a dollar around 8000, sheeeet! It's weird paying for things with such a huge amount of money. I mean my first meal cost 22,000 kip, the hotel room costs 40,000 a day and the internet costs 20,000 an hour...AAAAGH! Even more confusing is that they also use US dollars here which is supposed to be 'a more convenient way of paying'. Like hell it is! Actually I quickly found out that if you pay with dollars than you may well be losing money while the recipient will be secretly rubbing their hands together. Always best to pay with kip and keep those dollar bills in case of emergencies.

Laos in fact has a world record, though not one any other country would hope to beat, and that is the record for having the most ordnance dropped on it than anywhere else in the world. You know these guys have had it tough in Laos! In the 60s and 70s the might of the good old US of A military delivered massive air strikes here, dropping five million tons of bombs on them. There are still old unexploded bombs everywhere as you move into the south eastern areas. They also dumped 200,000 gallons of Agent Orange on it courtesy of Monsanto, over a period of ten years in order to destroy the forest that the enemy was using for cover. They did drop a variety of different colours though, such as Agent White, Purple, Pink, Green and Blue for destroying the rice fields.

Luang Namtha: The first port of call in a new country. It's extremely quiet here. After the final chaos of China, the stillness of this place is almost hard to handle, actually ........mmmmmmmmmm...no! It's amazing! This is the third largest town in Laos and our third storey guesthouse is the highest building here. It's surrounded by dense forests and hills. Oh, and it's seriously hot. The hottest place yet.

Down by the river some kids were really having fun playing on a bamboo raft, some of them fishing with spears. They came over to say hello and we messed around for the rest of the afternoon together. Farmers grazed their water buffalo and I watched in amazement as the most unlikely of farming vehicles somehow made it across the river. Hmmmm think I'm gonna do very little for a while and just take it all in.

The food is unbelievable. There are so many flavours going on and in each meal it's hard to know what's going on in your mouth; aromatic and mind blowingly hot. Even breakfast feels like your face is being torn off of your head at times.

Good luck or what! It was the Laos National Day yesterday. Spending the evening with some of the locals we had a fantastic time. I swear that these are the friendliest bunch of people you will ever come across. Some of them took me to sample the local Lao Hot Pot; well interesting, though was unable to eat too many of those big three inch square slabs of pig fat. Lao beer is twice as drinkable as any Chinese one and is really easy to get down. Ended up completely lost in this small town, as a thick mist comes out in the early hours. Well that's my excuse anyway.

Weird head trip! These people are the best. They are so welcoming. Most people are farmers and they work hard to make an existence. People come in from villages and farms from all over the place on mopeds and old farm vehicles to Luang Namtha. So there I am after changing all of my Chinese money down the bank, walking down the road with one million one hundred and five thousand, five hundred and thirty kip stuffed in my pockets. You try keeping your cash out of sight and walking naturally with that amount of paper shoved down your strides. It's just not possible. Just can't really get my head around that one at all yet.

The hotel room looks out across the roof tops of the town and over to the surrounding hills. The owner found it hysterical that I got locked out in the middle of the night. It's all just so good natured here. I absolutely am totally in love with this place already. Went to see Luang Namtha in Laos League football match. One of the most enjoyable games you will see. Those guys put everything into it under a glaring red hot sun. Though the stadium was tiny, the atmosphere was still brilliant. I was so into it shouting "Get in there my son" that some of the guys took me to watch it from next to one of the nets, sheltered under two giant umbrellas, top people! Luang Namtha won 2-1 and celebrated their arses off. The whole match had a commentator and it was blasted out all over town over a tannoy system including at the open air market.

After tea we went walking just out of town down by the river as the sun set. Wooden huts and palm trees silhouetted against an orange sky, insects buzzing in warm air. Oh my word, this place is an absolute paradise.

Cracked it! Got a bike and cycled out of town. In ten minutes you are onto narrow rough tracks and in twenty you're out into the countryside. It's so peaceful that I end up just slowly pushing the bike absorbing the place. There are rice fields, stilted buildings and the mountains in the distance. Above, two big hawks circle high up on the thermals. Moving on, three guys in t-shirts and shorts come out of the woods carrying AK-47's, both casting a strong look at me. Luckily I manage to remember good morning in Lao, "Sabaa-dii don sou" and they nod back and walk past.

"Hello, where are you from?" this young guy asks from the opposite side of the track, the standard opener for many Asian people when they engage a foreigner.
    "I'm from England. How about you?" I joke.
With a big smile, he introduces himself as Noi and that he lives in the nearby village.
    "Is it ok to walk with you?" he asks politely.
    "Sure, no problem. Have you always lived here Noi?"
    "Yes, my father used to work in that factory" he replies as we start off, pointing to a long row of open-thatched buildings that stretch along parallel to the track. Most are unused empty shells, but some still have some signs of activity.
    "They make..." at that Noi opens a shoulder bag he's been carrying and takes out an old red dictionary. With its corners rounded and bent outwards, this dictionary must have had a lot of use. "...Bricks!" he grins, clearly satisfied that he's found the right word.
    On closer inspection I can just make out the old mud kilns inside each structure, surrounded by the detritus of the past which spreads out into the fields.
    "What does he do now?"
    "Oh, he has no job so now we live off of farming. It is difficult for us to make money but we have always been farmers. It is the same for everyone. Is that your bicycle?" he asks, suddenly changing the subject.
    "Uhh, no actually I hired it from the hotel" I reply almost apologetically.
    "Hire" Noi has his head in his dictionary again. "Ah, hire! How much was it?"
    Unable to lie about this crap state of affairs, I deliver as close to the honest truth to him as I can go. "Around 50,000 kip" actually

30,000 lower than I paid as I knew there was no way he'd seen that kind of money on a long time.

"For that much you should buy it" He says looking surprised. "I only need it for today. I'll have to take it back later" I answer feeling increasingly awkward with each passing word.

Eventually we arrive at his house; another thatched hut on stilts surrounded by banana trees and green foliage. It has a fence, pathway and a front gate separating it from his neighbours. "This is where I live" he proudly announces "and this is my father Gwaan" Noi's Dad, who's been sitting on the front steps watching the world go by looks visibly taken aback upon seeing a Westerner materialise in his front yard. Jumping up, he shakes my hand while speaking nine to the dozen.

"My Father says he is very pleased to meet you. He hopes you can come back and meet our family. Maybe we can go to the uplands now and come back later. You should lock up your bicycle. People will borrow here and leave it in town" he laughs.

At that we were off to the "uplands". I wonder how 'up' the uplands could be as it does seem quite high from where I'm standing. There also seems to be an awful lot of jungle up there and I have the complete towny thought that "If it's a long way there, we'll have to spend all that time coming back down again the same way too".

We just keep on walking, on and on and up into the immense jungle. For miles the path is lined with great funnel webs home to spiders tarantula stylee. The walk goes on forever and is a fantastic experience; huge trees tightly packed with high canopies, valleys and river crossings, oh my word!

On the way, he takes me on a detour along a virtually nonexistent trail into the scrub to his mate Mak's hut. Inside it is spacious, made more so due to the lack of any furniture apart from a couple of knackered looking bamboo tables and a few old chairs. Holes fill the roof and light penetrates, forming beams in the cool darkness as my eyes adjust.

"He makes a special drink" Noi reveals as we sits down at the table. "We call it the Whiskey of Laos".

At that Mak appears with a bottle of his finest, three glasses and a wry smile on his face. From the moment I lay eyes on the bottle I know this isn't going to be a pleasant experience. It contains a clear vodka like liquid with some plants and berries at the bottom; the top covered with a handful of silver foil held on by an elastic band.

"Actually, I'd rather not" I mumble, but there is no way I am going to stop Mak's obvious enthusiasm for getting a foreign person to sample his home made embalming fluid. The dusty glasses are about two times bigger than a normal shot glass which Noi wipes with the end of his sleeve.

"Ok enough, enough, ENOUGH" are my failed attempts at stopping Mak from filling the glass to the top.

"What's in it?" I ask, already screwing my face up in anticipation.

"It is made from herbs from the forest. It is medicine that is good for your body".

"Medicine?" I contemplate; I think that word gets commonly bantered around over in Asia. I also worry that homemade brews like this can contain kinds of chemicals to give them a stronger edge.

As I hold it up in front of my face, in terms of bouquet, the most prominent thing you can smell is something between soil and cow shit, maybe just from the bottle; hardly the most tempting of aromas. A slight froth and skin has already formed on the top. Maybe it's still fermenting. Even so, time waits for no one and I fire it down the hatch as hard as possible in an effort to avoid touching my taste buds, instantly gagging as a burning sensation spreads downwards, across my face, and into my nose. My skin rapidly feels like I've spent too much time under the sun.

"Holy F*ck!"

This is one of the most unpleasant things you could ever possibly taste. Refusing to down the second one that Mak has already poured out, I quickly say my thanks and leave as soon as possible, stumbling down the track as my guts turn themselves inside out. Strangely Noi didn't drink anything, something that I find a bit irritating. "Whiskey of Laos my arse" I think as we head away. Certainly not something you would give to your Gran as a Christmas gift, maybe just your boss if you wanted a quiet stress-free day at the office.

We finally reach Noi's objective. A remote village called Smaa-Lenton high up in the hills. From the track, the view out across the jungle canopy is incredible, especially in the late afternoon sunshine. The maze of old stilted huts determinedly clings on to the side of the hill and as we work our way through, the place seems strangely quiet. "I wonder how these places can take on a storm?" I ponder, noting their look of fragility. Eventually a few people come out and stand there watching us from behind fences. I must say that I'm pretty dumbstruck and don't have a clue what to say. Noi does do some translation but I really get the vibe that we don't need to be there. Feeling way out of my depth and more uncomfortable by the second, taking out my camera for a couple of shots is clearly a big mistake.

"Is it ok to be here?" I nervously press. They seem reluctant to speak to Noi and for some reason he also looks uneasy, "Maybe we should go soon" and at that we're off.

On the way back, two girls in their early teens join us from another path. "This is my sister Nam and her friend" announces Noi. Nam wears a dirty yellow t-shirt with a pink panda on it. Across the top of her head she has a long braded strap from palm leaves that's tied to a sack of rice hanging against her back. Her friend has the same set-up.

"Man that looks heavy!" I remark.

"They will take the rice into town. Don't worry. They are strong." explains Noi.

After walking back together, Nam and her friend continue onwards without looking tired while I join Gwaan, his mother Mangsee and youngest sister. Their house, a single spacious room made from woven palms creates a pleasant and relaxing environment. Apart from a few baskets though, the only other furniture is six beds, each with a few items of clothing hanging from a line attached to the wall. "Shit, that's all the clothes they've got" I notice. Together we sit on the floor which is covered by a patchwork of coloured mats.

"How many people are in your family?" I ask.

"There are seven. I have two younger sisters and two older brothers".

"And you live here together?" I inquire.

"Yes, but often my brothers will stay in town"

Certainly a humbling experience; sitting there trying to absorb this brief glimpse into life as we absolutely do not know it in the UK. I mean I still know people who drive round the corner to the shops because they can't be arsed to walk. Before leaving I ask if I can take some photos of Noi and his family. Of course they say it's ok, but I can't escape a feeling of total crapness as I snap away.

Saying goodbye, I quietly passed Noi ten dollars. I'm still unsure of my feelings about giving money but let's just say it was something that had to be done. I felt well screwed up inside and for the rest of the day, trying to focus on the incredible hospitality I'd just experienced instead of anything negative. Whatever though, from then on I'd be seeing Laos and the rest of SE Asia through new eyes in a strange mixture of guilt and respect.

## Luang Prabang, Vang Vieng, Vientiane, and the 4000 Islands
## 19th December 2005

Time to leave Luang Namtha. We decided that there was no way that we could handle another bus journey, so Yvonne and I opted to take a four day boat trip instead. This would stop at three places on the way, taking us through the Golden Triangle[1] to the city of Luang Prabang. It's true though, no day is ever what you expect it to be when you wake up in the morning for sure. Within minutes of getting to the pick-up point of the boat trip, the whole thing was off. Two others that were supposed to be coming hadn't showed up and it was "boat trip cancelled!" Nice!

So it was down to, yes that's right, the bus station, AGAIN! At least it we could get off at the half way point, Huay Xai and pick up the boat from there; small consolation! Not only that, but the ride was not even in a bus, just in a crappy little sawngthaew. This is basically a flatbed van with a frame thrown over the back then a tarp thrown over the frame. Inside are two boards to sit on in a space about 5x10 feet. Shite! Another ten hours on bad roads.

The only saving grace was that most of the trip went through one of Laos' national parks. Fantastic views from the back end of an open vehicle gave it an extra dimension, but was it hard or was it hard! I mean ten hours of being severely jolted and bashed around against this metal frame, getting stuck in rivers and stopping at impassable roads. Ten hours of being compressed into this small space with seventeen people along with a huge amount of baggage including four sacks of rice; yes the driver kept stopping and loading more and more stuff on until we couldn't move. Ten hours of suffering from the worst cramp from hell. Ten hours of breathing in dust and fumes. The whole trip felt like we were in an eternal cloud of dirt along another road under construction. Every lorry that came past rendered visibility to zero, in a vehicle that would have failed the emissions test ten times over.

After five hours I was more tired and pummeled than any ride so far. No one could talk or keep their eyes open. Seriously hangin' or what! By the time we got to Huay Xai it was dark and my limbs were killing me. We staggered into the nearest hotel across the street, utterly filthy, hair grey-red from the dust. The thermos and some of my kit went in the bin, in fact a lot of it is on its way out now including my Salomon walking boots, rucksack and trousers. So arsing tired again! We sat

---

[1] Where Myanmar, Laos and Thailand meet. It is notorious for the opium industry. Can also include Vietnam.

there speechless, motionless and seriously mingin' in the lobby in front of a European fashion show on the telly. Kinda surreal really and I had images of me and Yvonne hobbling along the cat-walk towing my trolley bag behind to a wild stand up reception from the dinner dressed audience.

The Trolley Bag: I now love my trolley bag which has now taken on the colour of the earth plus the addition of new big umbrella which is strapped to it. So far this journey has been rough on the old trolley bag. Sometimes it's been pulled across surfaces which have been long and rocky and I've wondered on many occasions when the wheels are going to explode. It seems that ninety nine percent of travellers out here have these enormous rucksacks with waterproof covers on them. I've been laughed at and had the piss taken but I know inside it is some serious kit that it's doubtful they have. Of course it's a pain in the arse when confronted by stairs which do seem to be in the most inconvenient of places especially hotels, underpasses and overpasses.

Checking into a lush thatched wooden bungalow with a veranda surrounded by palm trees, the evening was paradise. A mixture of contentedness and tiredness, sitting there as the red ants used the washing line as their new highway and the salamanders chirped away under the strip light eating the midges.

Got up well early to the usual cockerel cacophony to go to the morning market and get a few things for the boat trip. Not much on offer there, even the vegetables looked past it. There were also dead rats on sale or small clear bags of rat blood. It's amazing what people really live on out here.

Down at the waterfront Yvonne and I waited for the slow boat down the Mekong River to Pakbeng (eight hours) and then on to Luang Prabang (another eight hours); a two day journey with no pot holes and dust. Just sitting there watching it all go by and drifting off while staring at the wake. Aaaah, waiting for the boat in a great restaurant, looking across the Mekong as the sun came up, oh man!

Unfortunately this early morning heaven only lasted for half an hour. Suddenly a massive tour group of Westerners appeared and took over the restaurant. I mean there must have been sixty of them wearing large orange badges and being led around like sheep. They all bought their tickets from a travel agent and paid twice the price. Everything was being done for them.

"There is nowhere to get food on the way. If you don't have anything then you must buy something from this restaurant" the tour guide stated dramatically.

At that two waitresses brought in a great pile of ridiculously over-priced baguettes wrapped up in cling-film and the crowd pounced. It was totally unbearable. I mean it just took the whole edge off the journey. Some of them were sticking their cameras in the faces of every local they saw. These three guys in front of us moaned about the trip continually and of course we did stop several times along the way where we could buy something to eat.

Pakbeng: This is basically a single street that waits for the slow boat to come in every evening and each Westerner is a big dollar sign. Don't get me wrong; tourism injects a massive amount of money into Laos, but it felt so crap being part of a tour group. After tea we wandered up and down looking for something to do. Old habits die hard though so parking our arses on the nearest bench and downing as many beers as possible was just the remedy. As the sun went down some of the guys from the boat were also wandering past looking for something to do. In the end, there were about fifteen people sitting on the road with us getting mullered on Beer Lao. Some night! Made some cracking friends, including Hronne, a cute blond girl who works in a slaughterhouse in Iceland, Andre, an Icelandic fisherman, Mad Eric from Sweden and Matt from Devon in the UK who's a stand-up comedian.

The boat trip the next day was very different. Most of the passengers stayed firmly in their seats looking miserable while we commandeered the back of the boat and had a riot. Another strange phenomenon you can see along this stretch of the Mekong are the 'rocket boats' and they frequently blasted by shattering the quietness. A rocket boat is basically a canoe with a huge outboard motor. If you want to get to Luang Prabang in one day this is the way you do it though they are notorious for tipping over at speeds of over 40mph. Passengers wear crash helmets, earplugs and for the whole six hour journey will be crammed together with knees up to their chins. There are even stories of boatmen playing chicken with each other. I spoke to one guy who had just finished his trip on one of these things and was a total wreck, shaking all over with nervous and physical exhaustion. Give me the slow boat any day!

Luang Prabang sure is a chilled-out place. It feels just like being on holiday at the moment and definitely avoiding going anywhere near a bus or a bad road is at the top of the itinerary. There are magnificent temples all down the street, I mean absolutely beautiful. Tall majestic pillars meet you at the doorways. Gold leaf stenciled murals work with simple bright vibrant colours while careful mosaics dance and create soothing movement. A Lao temple's most striking feature surely must be its proud sweeping-tiered rooflines protruding high up into the blue sky. Tiled in terracotta and lined with green and gold these are images that stay with you long after your trip is over.

The Mekong is round the corner and the night market is like walking into some dream world. All the stalls are lit up with single light bulbs hanging on the end of long wires from angled poles like fishing rods. There is colour everywhere and the people who live here show hospitality that is almost too much to comprehend.

Evening meals consist of going down to the market where you can eat anything you're able fit on your plate for 5000 kip and you eat by candlelight. Paying for anything is always the worst part of the day. If you have to shell out for a meal with a group of people, there is always a vast pile of kip on the table, and seeing as it's so difficult to work out, ninety nine percent of the time it's the wrong amount.

The guesthouse we are staying in is a really nice one. It has a veranda where you can look out across the palm trees and see the coloured rooftops poking out. The people from the roadside beer sesh' in Pakbeng have stayed together plus a few new faces. So far there are four Danes, three Swedes, four Dutch, two Brits, two French and our lone Canadian Ev! Amazingly she checked in to the room next door in a town absolutely full of guesthouses just out of pure coincidence. We're all so happy to be together again. Ev is a legend for her clumsiness. Yesterday outside a restaurant she suddenly went flying off some steps like a missile, knocking two great urns over with plants in. I mean one minute she was there and then gone the next. She was ok but quite some sight to see lying on the floor all covered in soil and foliage.

Yesterday Ev and I spent the afternoon chatting to these two monks Kamseng and Nang outside a temple, helping them with some English vocabulary they were practicing from their note books. They told us that a lot of guys become a monk at an early age for four years before they get a job as its one of the only ways to get an education. It costs fifty dollars a year which is mega expensive for them and their families will spend years saving the money up for it. Monks are a common sight in Luang Prabang. Some frequent the internet café, so maybe online either side of you with their orange robes and yellow sashes, mostly playing computer games.

Weird! So we're sitting there outside the temple when a great big party of around twenty tourists show up and they start taking photos. I guess you just have to get your monk shot in right?

"Do you mind moving out of the way so we can take some of these two guys?" asks an outspoken man, armed with his giant black

Olympus super deluxe power-shot with interchangeable zoom lens hanging around his neck.

"Sure buddy" I reply. Ev and I leave our seats and shift to one side. The pack proceeds to gather into formation, creating a crescent shape around the two unsuspecting monks. Some even get down on one knee to get a better shot.

"You know they never asked the monks" notices Ev. "Do you think they mind?"
For a painful few minutes, the sound of snapping shutters becomes unbearable. Finally as the show grinds to a halt, Ev and I return to helping them with their pronunciation.

"What you got there?" asks one of the tour group, staring down our backs.

"Just some English practice" grinds Ev in an unusually short sounding tone.

"Hey that's really interesting can I help?" he asks in a minimal effort to make contact with his subject matter.

"Yes" says Kamseng. "How to say this?" This draws the guy right in, leaning over us in order to get a better look. As he holds up the little book, Ev and I also get closer to see what the word is.

"Masturbation!"
Lost for words, the gentleman quickly withdraws stony faced. "I don't think I can help you with that one buddy" while Ev and I contort in an uncontrollable laughing fit.

Another Monday, moving further on down south. It's up early to get a really mellow bus ride to Vang Vieng. Oh, the tuk tuk[2] driver just stopped in the middle of nowhere on the way to the bus station and tried to rip us off. Wouldn't take us any further until we paid him another 40,000 kip; the usual shit then. Big arguments and bad vibes until finally getting on the bus. Anyway shit happens I guess.

More like a third world equivalent of Butlins, Vang Vieng is basically a holiday town packed full of Westerners on vacation. The only difference is that at least Butlins has to abide by the minimum wage.

"I'll be there for yooooou, I will-be-there for you. I'll be there for yooooou, I will-be-there for you" is the first thing you hear when you get off the bus.

"Holy shit is that 'Friends' I can hear?" I wondered. Following the noise from the bus station and out into the main street we stood there in amazement. The main drag turned out to be one dusty strip of gravel and dirt, lined with bars that show nothing but Friends all day

---

[2] A tuk tuk is a small motorised tricycle that is the SE Asian equivalent of a taxi. Make sure you nail the price of any journey down with the driver before you go.

and night on a big screen. Normally they don't play music at all until much later so down the road you get Friends from both sides in stereo. El lame o!

The view from the balcony in the hotel was a striking view of limestone karst hills reminiscent of those in Yangshuo and equally as dramatic. The problem was, the whole thing was ruined by the sound of Friends blasting out in the background, especially when the theme tune got to that part that has that twangy guitar jingle. After dreaming of getting far away from the city and visualizing jungle adventures, how many visitors must have asked themselves the same question "Is this really what I came all this way for?"

Most people will tell you strictly do not eat any pizzas or drink any milkshakes in Vang Vieng as they are full of really strong weed. Everyone who has tried one here says they had the worst and most paranoid time of their lives. Oh, also these absolutely disgusting magic mushroom milkshakes. They're actually milk, field mushrooms and weed blended together. You can buy Lao wine in 'buckets' down here, filled with snakes and straws sticking out of the top. The kebabs are foul; mostly stomach and offal as the best part of the animal is for local usage. You can get this stuff called M150 which is twice as strong as Red Bull and you mix it in with your Lao rice wine for a full on evening. Shove that in your bucket and you're away my son!

Aside from annihilation and destruction of as many brain cells as possible, you can also go down Tham Phu Kham Cave or take a dip in the Blue Lagoon to cool off. Also Vang Vieng is mostly known for its 'tubing'. This means floating down the river on an inflated tractor inner tube and getting as arseholed as possible along the way. Actually, most people say its great fun and have a wail of a time. Be careful though, as there are loads of newspaper reports of people have got too pissed and drowned.

Opting out and steering clear I decided to save my staying power for the evenings carnage. A few minutes from the main strip, a really nice river criss-crossed by rickety old wooden bridges invited you to cross. At night the river became illuminated by endless rows of coloured light bulbs. In this sense this place was more like heaven! You could sit on wooden platforms over the water and chill out with a beer immersed in the evening's humidity, or if you were up for it, cross the river to an island, party big time and get thoroughly smashed. Best get over there as soon as possible then right?

Our friends love hearing stories about my relatives. One day, I told them one about my Auntie Carol and Uncle Roger, who became famous for a day when they got into the national newspapers. The story goes that after a neighbour sent them some anonymous hate mail about their Christmas lights hanging outside their new house, Carol was so furious she sent the letter to her local paper. They in turn, sent it to a number of big national newspapers including the Independent. Have a look online under "Yule cannot be serious" in the Sun or "Hate mail at Christmas because of outdoor Christmas lights!" When you see it, there will be Auntie Carol looking well angry like she's about to deck someone. Matt was so absorbed with it that he made it his mission to make Auntie Carol's photo the desktop background for as many computers as he could find during the remainder of our time in Laos. For a lengthy spell Auntie Carol became something of an obsession for him and he seemed like it was all he ever went on about.

So we were round the fire on the island when two people Tash and Stu from the UK appeared out of the darkness, sat down and joined us. "What part of the UK are you from?" I asked.

"Cheltenham."

And at that Matt was in there like a shot "Auntie Carol lives there! Do you know Auntie Carol then?"

"Carol who?"

"Carol Knapp."

"I know Dave Knapp. We used to be classmates. Ring any bells?"

Turned out that Stu was best mates with my cousin Dave and has met Auntie Carol a few times, therefore going full-circle in a second. At that everyone who had been hearing her name for the past few days went absolutely ballistic, especially Matt. Talk about coincidence or what! Sometimes the weirdest things happen when you're on the road.

Tuesday! Oh no! How can anyone feel so annihilated? The absolute hangover from hell! Tequila and Beer Lao, a collapsing bench leaving everyone sprawling on the floor on top of each other for the rest of the night, but the next day? Mercy! Shaking with nausea in the baking hot sun with big time paranoia and when you have a bad day everything seems to go tits up when you are travelling. Like ordering breakfast at 1.00pm and then nothing happens. After three quarters of an hour Matt went into the kitchen to find that the chef was asleep and absolutely nothing was taking place. As we left, the woman who served us came out and followed us down the road shouting at the top of her voice. By 2.30 the only other place that was open for business served virtually inedible food accompanied by 'Friends' at full volume. Certainly not the best of hangover cures.

Blessed relief to escape Vang Vieng; I just couldn't take it anymore. A few hours away down the road to the south is Vientiane, the capital of Laos. After the cities of China this really seems like a quiet and sleepy little town and a perfect to recharge the batteries before the next part of the trip. The street outside the guesthouse was actually very noisy but that's really an exception. For some unfathomable reason, every so often the whole top floor of the guesthouse would vibrate. Never had a vibrating room before! On the whole though, it's just a pretty mellow place next to the Mekong with few people about.

While you're there you have to visit the Pha That Luang. This beautiful gold 45 metre stupa[3] is the most important national monument in Laos and it's exhilarating to see it. It really is something a bit special and against the clear blue Lao sky it is a positively dazzling sight. This is sculpture in its highest form without ever trying to be 'art'.

Ah shopping! It's the little things in life that make you happy. Replacing your kit brings you right up; a new razor after three months; anti histamine tablets for those nasty bites; powdered milk; unbreakable tea cup and four emergency Snickers bars. In Vientiane the best place to go is the Talat Sao market. You won't feel more in touch with the local way of life than wandering around a SE Asian market; the colours, the smells, (though the meat market is always hard work), the sounds, the activity and the people. Talat Sao is a massive and mad place that you can spend hours getting lost in. Haggling is great fun and so is the banter that goes with it. Imagine going to Tesco and the cashier deliberately gives you half your change to try it on.

The 4000 Islands: Five hundred miles later, we, plus our new friend Georgina from the UK arrived in Pakse, Southern Laos at 6.00am suffering from more sleep dep. Lolling around the bus station at an open-air restaurant I managed to do the laundry, get chilli in my eyes, lose Matt and Hronne, thus taking a trip to the police station and then have breakfast. A tuk-tuk ride to the noisiest and dustiest bus station in the world led Matt to buy us all dust masks.

Don't stick around in Pakse as it's such a total dive. Instead take a sawngthaew ride for three hours where you will arrive at the landing at Si Phan Don; about as far south as in gets in Laos. This is called the 4000 Islands, a truly marvelous place and definitely worth the effort.Here, the Mekong suddenly fans out creating a vast network of islands and channels.

---

[3] A stupa is kinda hard to describe as they vary in shape and size. Some can be domed in shape with a significant pinnacle on the top. They are Buddhist monuments which have important relics.

The boat ended up at Don Det Island, an unbelievable location to hang out for Christmas. Living in a communal stilted house with a great chill-out space, it had its own veranda with hammock and a wooden deckchair looking out over farming land and palm trees. The beds had pink mozzie nets and shutters on the windows. There were only four hours of generator created light every night, so paraffin lights flickered away most of the time.

Went walking with Georgina across to the other island to a waterfall and then took a boat trip towards the Cambodian border to see the Irrawaddy Dolphins. They are pretty rare and there are about fifty of them living in the area. On an early evening amongst the islands, seeing the dolphins is a truly brilliant thing to see. Had that 'miles away from home' feeling as the sun set over the jungle. We caught a lift home on the back of some motorbikes as it was getting dark. Clenching hard or what! One of the guys taking us home must have been all of twelve years old but rode the bike with the utmost skill across the loose pebbled track.

Christmas Day was a two edged sword really. Sure it's Christmas; ding dong merrily on high and all that. Christmas dinner itself was fantastic and Ev, Georgina and Hronne all looked stunning. We had turkey by the kilo followed by pineapple and watermelon, then cocktails and beer Lao. This top Aussie couple, Rob and Mel gave everyone presents from a sack and I got a toothbrush. These guys got a sound system together and everyone danced and got messed up on the beach until the early hours. As the sun started coming up people said their goodbyes as the next day we would be mostly splitting up.

The trouble was, the whole time we were surrounded by the locals all looking on wondering what the hell was going on. I bought this guy called Boon a beer which he downed in less than a minute like he had been on the desert for a month with no water. Within minutes he'd become my best buddy just because I'd bought him a beer and he proudly carried the second around like some prize in front of his mates. I reckon a single beer is probably well out of most peoples' price range around here. And turkey by the kilo! What's all that about then hey? People have next to nothing around here and I couldn't help that same old feeling that I'd had throughout the whole time in Laos that we were rubbing their noses in it.

Arriving back at the guesthouse, the family who were already awake invited me in to their place. Talk about a mellow contrast to the sound system of the beach. While the man of the house Munee mindfully fixed one of the fishing nets hanging from the ceiling, his missus Puban rolled a fat ciggie with some killer tobacco which, much to their amusement completely floored me.

A few more beers to those flickering lamplights watching the sunrise; a reflective way to see out the last evening in Laos out on the balcony in the hammock. Nice! I leave Laos feeling to be lucky to have visited such a calm and peaceful country. The people there are the most hospitable and friendly you will meet and I already miss their kindness.

# 8

# Cambodia – Legacy of War

It's amazing what we see and what we don't really get to see in our lives. Many of us are completely sheltered from the reality that the world is generally a tough place for most. We get to watch the poor, starving and diseased on TV and think "Oh that's so terrible" then as soon as it's finished we choose to forget about it instantaneously and wonder whether to go out and get an Indian or order a pizza. This is no judgment on anyone; life must go on all the same.

If you check out 'A Village of a thousand people' on the internet though, most sites say pretty much the same thing. Generally, in the world people have crap living conditions, don't eat well enough and don't get to go to school. 'We' in the Western world of course are aware of how lucky we are, but understandably still get bogged down with paying those frigging bills. We have lives to lead and jobs to go to every day, fair and square. All the same, on the whole we simply just don't get to see how the other side live.

I do remember something happening in Cambodia when I was a teenager, though I actually assumed it was in Africa. It was during children's TV on John Craven's News Round I first learned about it if I remember. Somehow, John Craven managed to talk about some really sensitive world issues showing images of what is really happening on the planet. This was at 5pm sandwiched between Jackanory, Dinky Dog and Rolf Harris's Cartoon Time. Amazingly John Craven helped to raise three million pounds to help the suffering going on there.

Still, no matter how much we watch and stash away in our subconscious, it does not substitute for the reality of what is really happening. The most full-on account of one of the darkest times in world history is the film 'The Killing Fields', but even that is but the merest of whispers of the real truth. Imagine every terrible thing that could happen to a place and combine them, that is Cambodia in the 70s and 80s.

I can't even start to think about the fear that you would feel if you knew some people were coming your way to put people into forced labour; your friends and family taken out and dispatched in front of your eyes in the most brutal manner. This is but one aspect of this nightmare.

When I crossed the border, it was simply a 'delightful' experience. I really couldn't remember much about Cambodia, other than vague memories from the news and the assumption that it probably got the shit kicked out of it like Laos. As time moved on the realisation that something more than terrible had recently happened there quickly grew. It was like a weight ever pressing down that got heavier and heavier. The more I learnt the more I couldn't believe what had happened and what is still happening there to this date.

When you come to Cambodia remember where you are. Take a few minutes alone, away from any company and think long and hard about this place. You have one month on your visa so please don't go through it in one week. Here is a rare opportunity to see the legacy of war at its worst.

## Siem Reap: 3<sup>rd</sup> January 2006

Well I'm in a state of shock! After days of deliberation, the next course of action turned out to be Cambodia, though to go into the various reasons would take a week. Once again, all that can be said is that this is totally unbelievable. The sense of adventure and anticipation has returned and I am well and truly buzzing.

Cambodia is a country still in major recovery from recent war and resulting chaos, lasting from 1970 and way beyond 1985. Landmines and unexploded bombs mean a great percentage of the countryside is unfarmable and a real threat to anyone who steps off the beaten track. Yep, two fifths of the country was carpet bombed you know who![1] Led by Pol Pot, the Khmer Rouge then took over and turned the date back to the 'Year Zero' and so came the 'Killing Fields'. The figures are not set but it's reckoned that about three million were killed at their hands, mostly tortured and executed. After they fled the country they continued to fight a guerrilla war allegedly financed by the CIA.

27th December: Four hours sleep and away by 7.30, the old trolley bag loaded precariously onto the front of a small boat to leave Don Det. Georgina and I split leaving the gang, though Ev and Matt said they would be ending up in Cambodia some time soon. Across the Mekong and a tuk-tuk to the Strung Treng border where you pick up your Cambodian visa. Then it was a three hour journey to Kratie, the first town in Cambodia. Culture shock or what! The countryside is rougher and a lot of the forest has been removed and sold to neighbouring countries leaving bare and ill-looking vegetation, with a few lonely old tree trunks snaking upwards.

Time to say hello to the first strange phenomenon in Cambodia. Upon arrival to Kratie, the bus strategically stops opposite a desperate row of dilapidated shops and restaurants filled with Westerners unable to go anywhere that is unless they succumb to the relentless pressure of the touts. There is a bus station somewhere in the town, but the combination of the intense roasting early afternoon heat and the aggressive attitude of the locals seems to keep the tourists pinned into this one area under cover.

The most in your face thing about Kratie is how hard you have to negotiate for absolutely everything. We spend two hours trying to get transport to Siem Reap (second largest city). The banter just goes on and on and it becomes increasingly frustrating as the day gets

---

[1] Around 600,000 died in America's secret war.

139

shorter. Though we appear to have developed some kind of connection with one guy who Georgina persistently negotiates with, things seem to be going nowhere.

"Siem Reap too far. It's too late now. If you want to go, you must stay in a hotel in Kampon Chan" (a half way town about seven hours away) is the line. No doubt this is his mates place, one of the most common blags you will hear on the road. Not only that but the prices of the journey being bantered around are all ridiculously over the limit. I mean the bus is just ten dollars, but these guys are asking well in excess of that with a complete take it or leave it angle of attack.

"Thirty dollars to go all the way for one person. Only two people in my car and it is a log journey. Maybe twelve hours". Our steely-eyed 'friend' will just not budge and the look on his face gives away nothing except he is a veteran at this, pure and simple! I also notice that compared to Laos, everything is immediately being done in dollars instead of the local currency of Riel, another easy way to make a profit.

"Sod this!" complains Georgina, "I'm so frigging hungry I need to sit down" joining the thirty or so others also unable to get a ride.

It's definitely worth sitting back and observing the scene though. After the hospitality of Laos, the almost hostile manner of these most hardened of sharks has left a bemused and vulnerable look across everyone's faces. Occasionally one of them will walk past resulting in a swift and abrupt interaction leaving the poor traveller looking even more pissed off.

Scam after scam is shoved under our noses while we sit there and to be honest it's quite overwhelming. The trouble is, not only is it uncomfortably hot outside on the road, neither of us can stomach another bus ride, especially one that will most likely be a totally uncomfortable twelve hour nightmare.

Time to introduce Georgina here. Georgina is quite something. Already travelling with her has become a bit different. She, until very recently, used to be a reporter for the World Service. It's always interesting hanging out with her and she naturally digs out some amazing stuff about what's going on wherever we are. Do not bother arguing with Georgina as you will never win. Here is one person who never gives up and she's like some secret weapon that can suddenly be unleashed in any troublesome situation. Whenever we have to negotiate with someone, the pained look that quickly develops across their face after the first ten minutes is an unforgettable picture. Sit back and enjoy!

Back at the restaurant and having finished eating we attempt to pay. After waiting for ten minutes, no one comes back with the bill. Twenty minutes later, we manage to get the attention of one of the strangely unconcerned waiters. "Yes yes, wait a minute" is the predictable reply. After a half an hour no show on the waiter-front Georgina suddenly catches sight of our 'friend' again. "Hang on" she says jumping out of her chair, making a b-line between the tables in order to intercept him.

"How about the bill?" I ask

"F*ck the bill!" she blasts. "Hey, forty dollars both of us" she shouts over, trying to get his attention before he leaves.

"You again!" our friend moans who, by now is clearly becoming sick of the sight of Georgina. Whether it's this persistence or that somehow a strange kind of rapport has occurred, within minutes we are standing in front of his car having agreed on the insane price of twenty five dollars a shot to go all the way.

"You pay now!" he orders before opening the trunk for our bags.

"Half now!" barks back Georgina, and at that the driver gives a huge sigh of exasperation and continues packing our stuff.

Unable to fight waves of travel tiredness as we speed into the early evening, the ride becomes a pure mix of zoning in and out of consciousness and absorbing the view. Old bomb casings line the way like decorations along another bad road with large sections under repair, our favourite!

At some point during the night, the driver pulls up outside a hotel in the middle of nowhere then proceeds to take our bags out before we have much time to react.

"We are here! You can stay here tonight!" and he drives off. At the same time, someone is already taking our bags inside. In the dining room, the owner pours us a beer each and invites us to sit down.

"Welcome to my hotel. The rooms are all very good. Siem Reap tomorrow ok?"

"You mean this isn't Siem Reap?" breaks Georgina in disbelief.

"Noooooo" laughs the man, "Near Kampon!"

"No WAY! We agreed Kratie to Siem Reap tonight."

"How much for the room?" I enquire begrudgingly, assuming that this was it for the night.

"For a room and car to Siem Reap twenty dollars one person. You also didn't pay for your food at Kratie. That was my cousin's restaurant." Holy shit! Stitched up or what!

"Oh come oooooooon" This is Georgina's favourite opener to any argument and she employs it regularly. When you hear this you

141

know its game on. Unflustered by the owner's unexpected bargaining tool, like a trooper, worn out and without a leg to stand on, Georgina persists for almost an hour. In the end the owner gives in completely and gets us a ride to go the rest of the way. I actually think he just wants to get rid of us as by this time he just looks like he had had enough. As we get in the car, his halfhearted attempts to get us to pay for the beer also go nowhere. Scams aside, I actually kinda feel sorry for the guy as we pull off.

Driving along into the darkness I remember thinking that this is only the first day in yet another country I know absolutely nothing about. Outside, the empty blackness without stars or lights in the distance leave no means to gain any sense of perspective. We reach Siem Reap at 2.30am after eighteen hours on the go, once again covered in road grime from head to foot. I can't seem to be able to keep my clothes clean for two minutes these days. This is also mozzie central and it's hard to ignore the bites anymore.

Bastard! I am woken by a shagging couple at five in the morning and then again at seven. This woman, a total minger, has the worst and most disgusting wailing orgasm voice known to mankind. It just goes on and on and on. Talk about sleep dep'!

'Waking up' the next day was really something. Hanging so badly from no sleep, travel tiredness and shit it's hot here. Trying not to use the air-conditioning in a bid to get accustomed to it but that's a hard one. You just keep drinking water all day. It's like your body is leaking or something. Also Georgina drunk the driver's water by accident so immediately got really ill and later I got a dose from some dodgy chicken I ate somewhere. Why I continue to eat chicken out here mystifies me.

One thing that is blatantly obvious is how completely poor this place is. You really feel that this country was rocked a few years ago. There is still tons of aid being sent from all over the world. There are people with no arms or legs covered in shrapnel wounds begging all over the place. There are few people over the age of thirty in fact most people you see are in their early twenties. As per usual the people are very friendly and you can chat to them all day quickly getting into using first names, but in some there is an inescapable hardness in their eyes.

Temples of Angkor: Another dodgy history lesson on Cambodia Part 2, hmmmm! Between the ninth and thirteenth centuries Cambodia rocked. It was extremely powerful and there was loads of dough rolling around. During this time they built huge monuments which were meant to glorify their kings and their deities. Some of these places are massive but in various states of ruin. The symbol of Angkor is everywhere in Cambodia and a sign of when things were really good and how things will one day be great again. It's part of the national flag, on the beer labels and shop signs; you can't get away from it.

The Angkor Temples take up about three hundred square kilometres, occupy woods and jungle and take over three days to get around aided with a map. The most famous and largest is Angkor Wat though Georgina and I hired a tuk tuk for the first trip, looking around some of the other staggeringly awesome places. At the end of the day from the top of the nearby hill, we looked out at our first Cambodian sunset. Admittedly it was with some six hundred million other tourists all going crazy with their cameras; hard work but beautiful all the same.

Angkor Wat: Getting up early so not to waste the day, we cycled out to see it taking on the commotion of rush hour. I forgot my three day pass so had to blag a lift for two dollars on the back of a motorbike to get back to the hotel. Climbing on board wearing sandals, shades and a floppy hat, my lack of protective gear gave way to a rising sense of precariousness. The owner of the bike, a guy called Marge, was very happy to get money for nothing and his wife was animated to say the least. A completely nerve wracking ride then commenced as he tore through town overtaking just about everything at break neck speed, blasting his way through narrow gaps in the traffic.

Anyway, a serious building is old Angkor Wat. Spent the day looking at the most fantastic and intricate stone reliefs, chatting and having a laugh with the monks. Trouble is Angkor Wat is such a famous place that people from all over the world descend including nearby countries such as Japan, China and Korea. When you finally get into the inner part of Angkor Wat there are hundreds all snapping away with their high tech-cameras. The central tower sits proudly above its neighbouring buildings, only reachable via a lengthy well-worn stone step ascent and it's like watching a carpet of squirming bodies climbing up desperate to get to the top. Inside the crowd go crazy taking a zillion photos and then queue to go to the bottom via one enormously long hand railed decent. As I waited people pushed to the front of a five person wide queue and this guy farted in my face with nerves as he climbed down a difficult step, dirty bastard! Just ridiculous; there must have been five hundred people going up and down at anyone time.

New Year's Eve: We cycled again, out to the western area of the temples. Atmospheric or what! The road that cuts through forest is just one long tarmac strip. Riding along, leaves gently fell down from the trees like snowflakes in the heat and humidity while everywhere a high pitched and very loud screeching from a big beetle-like insect pierced your eardrums.

The temples were breathtaking and the best experience out of all three days; no big crowds and in most places there was nobody, just these enormous crumbling edifices built from massive stone slabs hidden away in the jungle. Huge statues gave up their features to erosion as the land slowly reclaimed them, while towering strangler trees ripped apart ancient walls. On the way back we took the long way round down a single straight road surrounded by burnt out and decimated wilderness under a dark sky. Just starting to get a handle on the fact that this is Cambodia!

The evening turned out to be a very different experience to any New Year that you would normally expect; a cello recital by this Swiss guy called Dr Beat Richner. It's funny, the beginning of this entry was all about a sense of adventure but while writing this, time and space has, in the last few days become far more than that. It has grown with a depth to it that's hard to come to terms with.

Dr Richner runs a children's hospital in Siem Reap and two in Phnom Penh. He is a truly remarkable person. His evenings promote his hospital and spread the word about what's going on in Cambodia. He was about when the Khmer Rouge took over Phnom Penh and when they had finished only fifty doctors out of five thousand had survived. He showed us footage of the dengue fever epidemic after the war. Also at this time of writing, sixty five percent of all Cambodian people suffer from tuberculosis. There is also a strain of TB that sends you blind. Encephalitis is also widespread here. Blind people and people with no limbs are everywhere.

New Year's Eve was a weird one. Don't get me wrong, we had a real good time. One restaurant closed early so the staff could all dance with us at 12 o'clock; that was a top moment. Trouble is as the tourists piled out into the streets it became a weird mixture of pissheads, landmine victims and small kids all begging. In the end it was hard to handle seeing; this weird opposition of rich and poor!

In the short time we've been here, Siem Reap has really grown on us. You will never been treated so well with so much regularity. One of the guys who works in the internet cafe Sam Sokphal calls me his "older brother". You can join in with anyone you see playing shuttlecock football[2] without asking. The staff in the local restaurants will quickly start giving you things on the slate if you go there every day. Just how trusting can you get? Anyway, after a day of getting over New Year's Eve, laying in that dark little oven of a hotel room in a pool of sweat, it's off to Phnom Penh but with the plan to return ASAP and give something back to these amazing people.

---

[2] I don't know the name for it in Cambodia, but in China it's called Jianzi. It's a simple and brilliant game where you kick a weighted shuttlecock like object in the air, decorated with bright coloured feathers. Normally you will play with others and pass it too and fro. The object is simply to keep it in the air for as long as possible. It's best if you use your feet, but there are really no rules or winners. People can be seen playing it all over, including outside shops and restaurants when there isn't much to do. All highly entertaining!

## Phnom Penh, Kampot and Ghost Hunting
## 10th January 2006

Right!
What's going on? Where is this? Have I gone mad? One thing I can definitely tell you is that the world has definitely gone totally mind-blowingly insane.

Phnom Penh: For once, experiencing a straightforward little six hour bus journey, there wasn't much to write home about except the bus unfortunately stopped at the worst restaurant known to mankind. The smell was indescribable, making you want to wretch almost immediately. Two big flea ridden mingy dogs ate scraps from the floor, there were flies all over the food and big piles of stinking rubbish everywhere One guy with one dead white eye and the other missing, sat on the floor next to our table with his no-legged mate begging, making the process of chewing and swallowing your dinner a difficult task. It just underlines how totally screwed up this place is. A miserable experience!

Waking up in Phnom Penh. Where do you start? The electricity cut out for the fifth time last night, therefore there was no electric fan. Almost immediately the room turned into another furnace. The power goes off all the time here. In the evening when it happens, if you're out in town it's a totally weird trip. Prepare to be confronted by moaning beggars in all shapes and sizes, while shady characters emerge from darkened back-streets. The traffic lights also seem to go off with the same regularity creating even more pandemonium.

Not so long back, Phnom Penh was quite a well cultivated city. Then the Khmer Rouge entered and marched everyone out, killing over eight thousand of the residents and leaving it empty for three and a half years. When life returned there was anarchy and lawlessness and you will often be told that this is still one of the craziest places in the world. The hotel staff advise you to put all your valuables in a safe and not to go out with a bag over your shoulder; I guess a tourist is an obvious target. The sex industry is massive including child sex. Gary Glitter lived here for a while before being booted out to Vietnam where he awaits the firing squad[1]. HIV is widespread, brought in by the UN can you believe[2].

---

[1] In 2008 he was released and now lives in England.
[2] The United Nations Transitional Authority in Cambodia (UNTAC) was the UN's special peacekeeping force in Cambodia between 1992 and 1995. Aids didn't exist in Cambodia before they arrived and the sex industry was virtually non-existent.

146

People still carry AK47s and last year five people were killed through "guns being fired into the air". You can go to a firing range and shoot an AK47 and also go and fire a grenade launcher and blow up a cow. How f*cking sad is that! By the way a lot of this stuff comes straight out of the local rag. Like there was a story about some Westerners who hit a cow with a jeep. The police show up, put a road diversion sign up and have a barbeque in the middle of the road. The Westerners had to go for 're-education' from the farmer whose cow it was and were fined $300.

This place is total nuts. I met a woman who works in waste management today. She said that this is the coolest part of the year, phew! During the rainy season which is between July and November the sewers flood and tons of rubbish and shit flood the roads. Can you imagine the illnesses going down during this time?

There are different communities from all over the world here. In one ear there is the Islamic call for prayer being pumped out over a tannoy system and in the other, the Chinese practice a dragon dance for Chinese New Year on top of the roof opposite the hotel room. Needless to say they are very loud and also keep getting tangled up with each other. Ahhhh, China! All highly entertaining!

Went to the Russian Market today. It's one massive place, so you can spend the whole afternoon there ambling around, no trouble. Bustling with life, haggling and joking go hand in hand leading to a definitely more laid back and friendly atmosphere. You can get just about everything you want. To get there, catch a ride on the back of a motorbike. The whole bike experience just makes you want to get up in the morning. You get to see and feel like you are a part of everything when your pillion that's for sure. It's also ...cheap!

Down the road, there is also the Sorya Market; a huge yellow domed building with arched terraces leading off. There is a strange feeling of antiquity when you're inside; the ceiling is so high it bears an almost uncomfortable relationship with the tiny stalls below it. Peoples' voices echo within its old stone walls, giving way to a tranquil and calming atmosphere, chilling you right out after the onslaught of aggressive tuk-tuk drivers.

While you're in Phnom Penh head for the Tuol Sleng Concentration Camp or S-21 to pay your respects. This place is definitely not for those who get easily upset though, really! The whole experience leaves you feeling low and in your head for the rest of the day. At one time it was a high school but was speedily turned into a place to torture and kill thousands of men, women and children.

147

Of course this happened only in recent history, so when snooping around on the upper levels, you will come across piles of old dust covered documents by the Khmer Rouge; dossiers, lists of people being held, the lot, just dumped in heaps all over the place. There are fingernail marks in the plaster walls and old KR markings and graffiti. Outside is a list of rules that prisoners had to obey, including the following:

"While getting lashes of electrification you must not cry at all. If you do not obey the rules you may get many lashes of the electric wire. If you disobey any point of my regulations you shall get either ten lashes of five shocks of electric discharge."

Oh man, this is a hard one to write! Just to say that everything that the KR did to those innocent people was absolutely beyond words and it just tears your head off. If there ever was a hell, it was the S-21.

Next day, a three hour taxi ride took us to Kampot; a small town as far south as it gets. $3.00 for the whole ride; not a bad deal really. Only in Cambodia! The landscape is very different down there. It's green and more fertile and the single standing palm trees disappear into the horizon like giant seeding dandelions. Sunsets often turn the sky red and everything on the earth along with them. They're well trippy.

Kampot, 6th January: I woke up in an alcoholic oblivion in some Dutch bird's room that had the build of Geoff Capes (who ran a 400cc dirt bike) then emerged from the darkness into full on 100% UV. My eyes immediately felt like they were melting and my head like it had shrunk to the size and texture of a prune with the heat. A two litre bottle of water bought only ten minutes earlier was already empty. Walking up the road clutching a small map looking like a right wanker, I searched for the bank as all cash was blown the night before.

School had just finished for lunch so the kids cycled by in neat white shirts and black skirts or trousers. All smiled and waved. Having quickly got lost and wandering off the beaten track another dose of culture shock was waiting round the corner. People crammed as much stuff as they could into one vehicle, defying all known laws of physics. Dirt, rubbish, dust, dogs and mad intense energy made your head spin. Ever been smiled at, waved at and said hello too, continually for over an hour? It's strongly recommend! These people have so little though. Do they realise it and put on a brave face every day of their lives I wonder? On the flip side, it's probably us that have too much and take it all for granted. So there I was down the bank taking out $200. Same old shit as Laos I guess but it's still something that always nags away in the back of your mind.

Went cycling out down a straight road out into the countryside. On and on in the heat. So much on my mind. Matt is in Cambodia and plans on living in Phnom Penh but will do a Vipassana[3] retreat for a month first. I'm splitting from Georgina in a few days, off on a mission, having decided to go back up to Siem Reap and look for a teaching job up there. I want to help these people so much, though can't afford to do voluntary work and paid work is hard to find up there so who knows. Just gonna see what happens I guess. Still, am I scared? Yes! Am I happy? Yes! Am I sad? Yes! Am I exited? Yes! Do I feel lonely? Yes! Do I feel complete? Yes! Do I feel insecure and not good enough? Yes! Do I feel more confident and stronger than ever? Yes! I feel like I am everything all at once today......weird thing my head.

On from Kampot, Georgina and I met this guy called Nick from the UK and together we went up the mountain in the Bokor National Park to visit the old hill station on the plateau. Visitors are normally attracted to the park because of the enormous expanse of jungle that engulfs the area. In all it comes to about 1,500 square kilometers of pure paradise filled with rare plants and animals including tigers and jaguars.

Most people just go up for a few hours, take some photos of the spectacular views and go home before it gets dark. Understandable; the hill station only consists of twenty or so ruined buildings that have been empty for years. The only building still in use is a small renovated house used by the rangers. These few local Khmers[4] have been given the difficult task of guarding the wildlife from poachers and the forest from illegal logging operations.

My friends and I however, had an ulterior motive for going. Along the way someone told us that this was "one of the most haunted places in the world". "A bold claim" was my first thought and like most spooky tales I merely assumed that this was yet another exaggerated and overblown story to get you rattled around the table late at night. The next day though after only a few minutes of research, it turned out that the hill station does in fact have a grim and dark history. Built in the 1920s, the French used it as a retreat from the heat down below and also to maintain their decadent lifestyle, even adding a huge casino to blow their cash in. Unfortunately their luck didn't hold out and in the 50s the Vietnamese came and took it over, killing everyone. It then lay empty for some time until the Khmer Rouge used it as a base and a place of torture. Back came the Vietnamese and a long and fierce battle ensued which they eventually won. We also heard that there was a New

---

[3] A form of meditation.
[4] Khmer refers to Cambodian Nationality

Year's Eve party up there, but were glad we didn't make it. The whole thing turned into a car to car shootout with two people killed. Certainly this was not a place for the feint hearted.

Bokor Mountain Hill Station
It's a long way to the top and the road is really a small track full of craters (again), so we get a decent jeep and a great driver called Pip to take us up there. Ascending up the track I think we all must be wondering what we are doing. Fuelled by some strange fascination, the plan is to stay over for the night in the ranger station and check out some of the supposedly most haunted buildings, though as we go further up a sense of unease has really crept in. One chap we met in Kampot warned us that "Something would definitely happen if we went up to the mountain for the night" and that "maybe we shouldn't go". "Are we really going to stay up there tonight?" I ask myself, giving it a fifty-fifty chance that we would be on our way back down in a few hours.

I am quite envious of the rangers. I mean what a job; this family of young Khmers in uniform living out in such a remote environment, hunting poachers and trappers. They let us use their kitchen and I cook my first meal in over four months while they clean their AK-47's on the veranda. Georgina even does the washing up. Oh, before tea we go to our first port of call, the old church overlooking the sea. Looking out from the church that 'miles away from home' feeling creeps back again; this really is the back end of beyond. Further on up there is a really long cliff line. From the top, the jungle just rolls down in a steep curve for miles down to the coast, the trees looking like some immense carpet with autumn colours and a zillion crickets singing their tune. You can look across to see Koh Tonsay Island through the haze in the distance and to the Gulf Of Thailand beyond.

Later the wind really picks up. It howls through the radio station and the clouds become grey green against a bright half-moon as we walk to the casino. Slowing down to a standstill we briefly debate on the reality of our plan.
"So we're really gonna do this?" I ask, now unable to hide my apprehension.
"May as well. We've come all this way" replies Nick, turning his back as a shield against the wind. "Game on then" I think as we continue. Reaching the top of a small rise in the terrain we receive the full force of the elements.

The casino is a massive building and is the biggest on the plateau. It sits on the highest point and in the darkness becomes one big black monolith. Perched on top of the cliff, the wind blasts through its empty hulking skeleton invoking a feeling of the utterly sinister.

Standing in front of it is a gut-wrenching experience causing us to halt for a second time.

"I'm not sure I want to go in there" shouts Georgina over the wind.

After all, this was a place of the most horrific torture by the Khmer Rouge and my mind is running riot by this time. The doorway is more like a huge pitch black abyss with stone steps leading upwards into it and the only way forward is to go into full auto pilot mode. Blanking any thoughts that something may be waiting in the shadows, we enter armed only with our three flashlights.

Walking around inside the bulk of this crazy, black, paint-peeling place is one of the most intimidating things you could imagine. Further on, down into the basement, it gets too dangerous with the possibility of falling masonry. With some animal growling away somewhere and our nerves already frayed, we are more than unanimous in the decision to leave as soon as possible.

On the way down the hill there is a stilted house with a bridge going across to it from the pathway. It's now so windy that you have to get your head down and run across the bridge and straight through the doorway as fast as you can. Some relief to be out of what was now a gale, though inside, the building turns out to be only a mere shell of a place. Flat slabs of concrete and wooden beams pile up into the gloom after the roof has given way and collapsed leaving a gaping hole on the far side.

Checking out a small side room I remove some rubbish that was rattling around in the wind. As I turn and walk away and there is this a sudden terrific deafening bang behind me so we leg it back outside as fast as possible! We had no idea what it was or where it came from and there were no loose objects or doors to slam. Whatever it was it leaves my ears ringing for a long while afterwards, even feeling slightly concussed. The stilted building is definitely layered with an atmosphere that's far more intense than the casino and the experience affects us big time. Nick even says he's just seen a shadow figure moving across the opposite wall.

"Hey guys, I've really had enough now" says Georgina looking clearly shaken by what had just happened.

Deliberating if we should throw in the towel for the night we reach a compromise. The last port of call will be a visit to the hotel which is on the way back to the ranger station. There's no wind down there as the area is in a basin so any noise is clearly audible. As we approach our voices quickly turn to whispers.

The hotel itself is a strange building in that it hardly matches the grandeur of the casino. Instead it's a minimal two storey design with long rectangular walls constructed from now weathered concrete. In the lobby, the only remaining thing still vaguely intact is the sweeping curved counter of the reception area. There's nothing else apart from rubble to contend with so we move mindfully about the building not only to save our ankles but also in an effort to keep our presence undetected.

Entering what must have been the ballroom, a deep expanse of darkness awaits. Its windows are far across the other side, barely illuminated by the outside night light. We had already spoken about doing a proper vigil somewhere and this feels like the perfect place for one, so we sit against the wall for half an hour, remaining silent and for a time with torches switched off. I never see or hear anything, but Georgina and Nick say they both saw light orbs[5] moving across the far wall.

Upstairs we move quietly together in a line down the single corridor with its adjoining bedrooms. As our shoes crunch across broken glass and masonry and our torchlight scans for the unusual, I am sure our being here must have been heard. Solitary travellers have lived here leaving behind bizarre graffiti, some of it telling their sad stories of how they came to be in such a lonely and unforgiving environment. I mean where does your head go when you're living in such a remote and ram shackled place, as high up in Cambodia as it gets? At that same moment I realise that this is precisely the same situation we are in too, only it is two o'clock in the morning.

Around the same time Nick suddenly comes across something most peculiar in one of the rooms.

"F*ck f*ck f*ck. What the f*ck is that?" he whispers in an intense voice.

"Oh my God! What on earth is that?" adds Georgina.

"F*ck knows. Shit! Shit! What the f*ck?" my voice sounding equally as panicked.

Inside is a strange construction of sticks and string stretching from wall to wall and up to the ceiling like some strange spiders web leaving us unable to fathom its purpose or origin, hence we also can't figure what kind of a mind would actually build such a bizarre creation in the first place.

---

[5] Light orbs are flying balls of light that are thought to be the stage before a ghost manifests.

"Shit! F*ck this! I'm out of here" is my swift solution. Trying not to lose it too badly, we leave, really feeling like we've just invaded someone's space. It's as if some demented lunatic from another dimension may return at any moment and jump out on us.
All in all a crazy thing to do. What were we thinking? We must have been off our rockers to be honest. I mean who wants to see a bloody Khmer Rouge ghost anyway? Hmmm, for some reason we hadn't really thought about that one.

Back at the ranger station it's lights out at 9.30 so it's pitch black when we return. This weird bloodied monkey decides to sit outside the room crying out and scratching at the door. After sitting outside doing some star-gazing I hit the sack and get stuck into a really nice dream about hangin' with my mates back in the UK.
At some point though, the dream suddenly transforms into a nightmare, having never before felt such a dark and surreal feeling. In it my hands are being shredded through the mattress by claws and sharp teeth. My fore-arms become sandwiched and crushed between wooden boards that tighten with metal screws beyond endurance.
In the dream I scream out in pain as my arms start to crush. It's so excruciating that it forces me to wake, sitting bolt upright to be confronted by a six foot high grey white figure at the end of the bed. It is a guy, non-Asian, European maybe, not solid in form and moving slowly towards me. His eyes are pure dark shadows and he has a sick and strange smile from ear to ear that look anything but friendly. I sit there speechless at first, wanting my friends to wake up and hit the lights but am unable to find the words. There's a torch somewhere on the floor but my scrabbling hand can't locate it. I've always laughed at people on various paranormal TV programmes who scream when anything slightly unnerving happens, picturing myself instead calmly asking the apparition questions (yeah right!) As it reaches the bed, all I can do is start shouting "Oh shit, Oh f*ck, f*ck me. Oh my God" over and over with some serious urgency, absolutely terrified that it could possibly touch me.
In the end Georgina turns on then the lights and it's gone. We all retreat to the top bunks on the other side of the room. I'm in shock for an hour shaking like a leaf, have four blankets and clutch my torch for the rest of the night. The incident lasted for about two to three minutes, happened at 5.30 in the morning and is something I certainly won't forget.

It turns out that the ranger station is partly converted from one of the old buildings and it's doubtful that any of these places escaped from being used for some terrible act. There is no doubt that what I experienced in my dream was what happened to the unfortunate apparition; a brief window into what really went on back then; to relive the intense pain and fear even for a brief moment allowing the poor soul to manifest itself. Anyway, that was some night or what!

The next day we went back and retraced our steps. The stilted building was absolutely covered in bullet holes including some by heavy arms fire; a last stand maybe! Also one wall had been destroyed. Oh, down the back of the casino there is a sheer drop where it is said that people threw themselves off when they had an unlucky day gambling. It is also reported that the KR would line people up and smash in their heads with spades before pushing them over the edge.

Anyway, finally it was time to cut loose. After going to see the wall of death at a fun fair in Kampot, Georgina, Nick and I said our goodbyes. At last that moment had arrived. On my own at last and for the time being, life was no longer about travelling but looking for a place to hit the brakes.

## Siem Reap: 20<sup>th</sup> January 2006

So!... I've given myself $200 to find work in Siem Reap. If it doesn't happen it'll be over to Bangkok, then catch a plane to Guilin and back to Yangshuo. I've chosen Siem Reap since it's only got a population of 90,000 and countryside is always near, so it's kind of handleable on the old head. Why have I chosen to try and find work in Cambodia? Because these people are fantastic and need people to give 'em a helping hand and a half.

9th Jan: Upon waking up I felt strangely good. By the time my keks[1] were on I was feeling ecstatic. Within minutes the trip to Phnom Penh had been organised and I said goodbye to the people at the Ta- Eng Guesthouse. The owner Mr Laang was so happy when I dumped the bulk of the remaining cold weather gear as apparently its 'winter' at the moment. There's me sweating my arse off in this mad melting heat and he's literally jumping about with joy wearing my balaclava and those Chinese thermal trackies I bought in Chengdu for Tibet. How on earth can these people think that this is cold?

The taxi took me to the 'bus station' which is really just a strip of dirt with loads of different vehicles parked on it. After waiting one hour it became clear that the driver called Varen, needed more passengers in order to continue and I was his only customer so far. He was desperately unassertive and every time a potential victim would show up they would be snapped up by the other taxi drivers. Not only that but the others continually took the piss out of this quiet older guy and his car. So, as a last resort I went off and rounded up three more passengers, did a deal with them and we were off. Varen was clearly very happy about this as he had just made $16. The others on the other hand, looked dumbstruck and clearly envious as this guy had just done the best business of the day. Returning to the Sunday Guesthouse in Phnom Penh and seeing everyone again was a really nice feeling. We were all pleased to see each other and they even carried the trolley bag all the way upstairs. We played shuttlecock footy together in the yard until collapsing with tiredness and had a great evening.

During the last visit to Phnom Penh, I noticed that you can buy bottles of sulphuric acid in the market. In the Phnom Penh Post, it said that there are now jilted women who throw this acid into the faces of their ex's lover and their child. A victim interviewed said that "she could feel her eyes melting in their sockets". Sheeeeet! The newspaper said that

---

[1] Informal British English for underpants.

this was becoming a "problem!"

As for the kids in Phnom Penh, there are now over 30,000 of them on the streets. Most will never go to school as they have to start earning money from the word go. Many work on the numerous rubbish tips all over the city. They work seven days a week for twelve hours a day looking for materials for recycling and basically live in the rubbish. These kids normally don't live past the age of ten as it's so toxic that they get all kinds of skin and internal organ infections. I tell you Phnom Penh's one screwed up city.

I was reading the obituary section in the Phnom Penh Post. It's a big double pager in the middle of the paper. All the deaths were gun related apart from one where a monk cut off his testicles and bled to death. I don't think they bother printing natural deaths here. Maybe there aren't any!

10th Jan: Up at 6.30 and offski again. Rush hour in Phnom Penh. Now that's really something! This old bus dropped me off where? Yeah, at the bloody bus station. I got on another bus and we waited and waited and waited! Why people continually tell you to be early is beyond me. After over an hour the dilapidated mozzie ridden bus grumbled into 'action' and after eight slow and overpoweringly hot hours we reached Siem Reap. On the way we stopped for a break where they sold piles of fried spiders as a light snack, nice!

Weird being back! Not used to backtracking at all and it feels strange being in such a new head space. Matt showed up and it was so great to see him again. The vibe has totally changed now. Both of us need to get serious about our shit. We had a great night though. Oh, apart from when we made the mistake of going into a pick-up bar....yeeech! This great fat Westerner, I mean he was an enormous whale of a man, picked this girl up who must have been all of sixteen, aaaaagh! So she was taken back to his gaff on the back of one moped and him on the back of another. The poor suspension on his little bike looked like it was imminently about to expire! I tell you that was some sight. Lot of that going on in Cambodia!

11th Jan: Woke up feeling seriously uptight. Dollars seem to run through your hands like water in this country, which is a continual worry. You just want to lie in bed every night saying you've done your best and that's the bottom line. Most people here are so poor living in such terrible conditions; I can't go on without helping at least some of them. I rate these guys so much. The thought of failure churns over and over and it won't go away!

156

12th Jan: After a predicable no-show where a Khmer guy was supposed to be to taking me around, I got a bicycle spending the day going all over town looking for schools. Couldn't find the first one called 'The Volunteer Development Poverty Children School'. It's way out by the Siem Reap Killing Field[2]and ended up just going round and round in circles in the sticks.

The next school, the SITC School, said to come back later but an Aussie teacher who worked there gave me some more leads, though saying it would be difficult to get a paid job here as everything is voluntary. Feeling pretty pissed off I went to the BB University and shoved my CV under their noses. They seemed pretty uninterested and even more so at the ACE school of English. I went to several cafes and pulled job ads off of the wall and returned to the SITC to meet a guy called Mr Derek. He said to come back on Tuesday and do "the test". What test? A test on my grammar that's what! Bollocks!

What test? A test on my grammar that's what! Bollocks! I mean that's all I'm really good for right? I mean I can articulate 'bollocks to this, bollocks to you and bollocks to that' no problem but when you're into stuff like future perfect progressive and modal auxiliary verbs you'll find me hiding round the back of the bike sheds mate. My knowledge on grammar has always been hmmm 'sketchy' at the best of times. There will be two interviews after the test. Heading back to the guesthouse after a long and hot day, I felt utterly pissed off and dying to catch up with Matt.

In the evening we went to a restaurant called the Training Restaurant for Disadvantaged Children. Basically, this guy pulls kids off of the streets at an early age and trains them to be top chefs, waiters and waitresses. In the end our table was surrounded by the kids all wanting to learn English. The restaurant is also part of the CVSG or Cambodian Village Support Group. These guys build villages from scratch, take aids sufferers and landmine victims, relocating them so they can make a living and no longer spend their lives begging on the streets. They help them to dig wells and grow their own food. The amount of stuff going on to help these people is staggering. All you have to do is look just a little under the surface to be amazed. So out there somewhere are whole villages populated completely with people with HIV.

13th Jan: Very depressed in the morning. Starting to look at the various escape routes back to China and the safe confines of Yangshuo and the

---

[2] The Killing Fields are where huge numbers of people were brutally executed and buried.

Buffalo Bar. Still, it's back out on the bike spending hours looking for a photocopier that works. It's this kind of thing that does it; struggling to get the smallest of things done. Another unfindable school! Waiting for a lift to that voluntary school and after two hours the guy didn't show. I returned to the SITC to hand in my CV and certificates. Man that f*cking test!

Mind you I have to keep reminding myself that in all this turmoil, this is experiencing Cambodia at face value now every minute of the day. Often you will see daily life as we don't know it. Take any petrol station that's situated on a corner for example. Because of the location it will have become part of the highway, being used as a short cut by everyone instead of waiting at the traffic lights. Often there will be some major traffic congestion going on in the middle of the forecourt around the pumps. Just being out here is more than enough without doing any sightseeing. Every second of every day blows your mind.

14th Jan: Last night was something down at the Training Restaurant. Having mentioned to the kids that I am a teacher, they had a table already prepared to give them a lesson complete with notebooks, pencils, a little blackboard and chalk, I mean in the middle of the restaurant! God these guys are something else! They're even also learning Japanese from a volunteer.

I spoke to this Canadian guy today who works at the SITC School. If you work there, you have to wear a frigging suit and tie every day and get up at five in the morning as classes start at six! The kids are mainly the offspring of every rich corrupt official in town, old bill, politicians and generals so they can stick their test up their arse! It was a shit night's sleep despite all the Angkor Beer in the world. It really is difficult to find paid work in this place and its causing me major unrest. Voluntary? Piece of piss! I just can't afford to do that though. I need a paid job. The bulk of volunteers come straight here with a wedge that they've saved up or are being supported by VSO. Recon that's the only way really! My head is edging rapidly towards China again and the original plan to get the most out of this place before the visa runs out, yeah and stop arseing moaning and worrying. Too right! Those kids are waiting for class down the restaurant tonight and there's loads of other stuff to take in.

They decided to put in new sewage pipes in the centre of Siem Reap. The only problem is they are doing the whole job at once, so every road has two great trenches down it filled with stagnant shitty water. There are planks running across them to get in and out of shops. The bulk of the traffic which consists of mostly motorcycles and bicycles is now channelled along the pavements, past shop doorways and weaving around coffee shop tables. Funny seeing tourists sitting there having lunch outside as if it isn't happening. The result has been a big outbreak of dysentery in town as it's thought that some of the sewage got into to the water supply.

15th Jan: It's funny how things can change in an instant. The internet place also has a small travel agents owned by Mr Luang who said that it would take one week to get a Chinese visa in Bangkok. Sheeeet, who needs to be in Bangkok for a week when you're so completely broke. He also reckoned that he can get one in Siem Reap with absolutely no waiting around, nice! In that instant, days of worry over what should be done suddenly ended and my passport has gone to have a second Chinese visa added. On the 25th it'll be back in Yangshuo, looking for teaching work that is definitely available.

Blinding win for Man City last night. Round the corner over fifty Khmer locals who all wanted United to win turned out to see the game. Great seeing Stuart Pierce going mental and throwing himself into the crowd. Because they're so skint, someone puts a few TV's out on the street and a load of plastic chairs which are all quickly taken up. It's miles better than going anywhere else.

16th Jan: The beggars are now becoming wearing. On the way back to the guesthouse this kid followed me all the way along the river back to the guesthouse swearing and moaning. Too much! In the early hours dogs howled at the moon. That and the constant heat keeps you awake for ages. This place is another noisy hell hole. You're woken up by power tools and hammering at seven in the morning. Is this my curse? Maybe it's the same people who have been following me around Asia the whole time. Oh and I found a great pile of 'matter' behind the toilet, nice!

Today I visited a few other places, one called 'Concern' which manages forty four villages, making sure they are running soundly, and The Physical Rehabilitation Centre. Wanting to talk to the manager to get some more insight into what these people go through, twatter here walks into one of the dorms that they live in. Inside were more than thirty landmine victims all laid out in bed. Some looked over blankly but others clearly were not happy at me barging in on them, giving more of a glare, and "Hello. Good afternoon" in Khmer didn't seem to cut any ice at all.

Finally finding the manager, Mr Sary, he explained that so far five thousand people have come in and out of his doors. They come to have artificial limbs fitted and spend months learning how to use them. They do have to contribute some money though as it's the only way it can stay open, hence the number of guys begging out on the streets. One startling figure was that out of every thousand victims a year, 39% of these are people that have been handling the mines. Some people are so poor that they go hunting mines and unexploded ordinance for scrap to sell. Some just still have no idea what they are playing around with when they find something. Injuries are also caused due to "fishing with explosives", where someone finds some ordinance and tries to remove the detonator and get the explosives out. If successful you can catch up to eight kilos of fish with one explosion.

It's also well worth the short trip out of town to a place run by this guy called Aki Ra who makes it his business to locate, defuse and collect landmines. After fighting for the Khmer Rouge from the age of ten, he was then taken by the Vietnamese army. Finally after laying mines for years, he realised that he could just as easily remove them using nothing more than a wooden stick. He helped clear the whole Siem Reap area and his home built museum/shack boasts thousands of them piled up into every conceivable corner. From grenades, mortar bombs, anti-tank mines to Bouncing Betties which jump up at you going off at head height, he has made safe a staggering amount of explosives without so much as a scratch. Sometimes he was finding up to five mines in one square metre at anyone time there were so many. There are still hundreds of thousands of mines about. The worst ones are these little green ones made out of plastic known as Anti-Personnel Blast Mines. They are water proof, undetectable and can last up to one hundred years. When the monsoon hits they are washed all over the place often being swept into villages and areas already cleared[3].

At last I found the Volunteer Development Poverty Children School located behind the Siem Reap Killing Fields. One million died in the Siem Reap Province and there are the bones of one thousand people outside the school. I was greeted by the head teacher Mr Kim Srosh who showed me in with a beaming smile. The small school was an absolutely wonderful place with the most unbelievably sweet and cute kids you will ever see in your life. Unfortunately it did ruin Mr Srosh's class and eventually it lost all sense of order. After school I was besieged by these kids. They just didn't want me to go and to be honest neither did I.

---

[3] In 2007 Aki Ra was forced to close his museum by the government who said that he brought a bad reputation to the area. He managed to open a second one four miles out of town funded by the Cambodia Landmine Museum Relief Fund, a Canadian NGO.

The next day their Khmer teacher called Mr Nou Seng was taking the class. Unbelievably this guy was ninety five, had been teaching for fifty five years and built like a brick shithouse, standing proudly at almost seven feet tall. A really one hundred percent top bloke, who got into the vaguely irritating habit of pulling my ears from behind as a joke!

Ahh, class humour hey. Talk about painful! A lot of these stunning kids were ill and being treated at the hospital run by Dr Richner. Sadly some may not make it past the age of ten. Filling the basket of my bike with as many shuttlecock footballs as possible, Mr Srosh and I handed them out before leaving. Out on the playing field for the rest of the day with all the kids and staff was one of those unforgettable afternoons. Sure sad to be leaving!

Right, it's time to split! A job in Yangshuo with a two bedroom flat and salary has materialised, but seeing is believing hey. There are a few days left in Cambodia and Siem Reap before that though, so it'll be back teaching those kids down the restaurant, going back to volunteer school, trying to stay sober and out of this bloody heat until leaving. I finish here with mixed emotions about Cambodia, having not got anywhere near the vision of spending more time here to really get under the surface to help some of these kids. I love this place but hate the weird juxtaposition of rich and poor; Western tourists, ex-pats and Khmer who largely have absolutely nothing. Yesterday there was this English guy on his big dirt bike road raging. "Get out of the f*cking way you stupid Cambodian!" he bellowed in the middle of the street. I mean whose f*cking country is it anyway? Back to Yangers then! I just hope to God I don't have to wear a suit that's all!

# 9

# Back to Yangers
# Square Peg in a Round Hole

One glaringly apparent thing I've noticed about myself are my
unconscious attempts to make things the same as they were before. It's
a clearly identifiable personality trait that's so annoyingly ingrained at
times it touches on the obsessive. There is this theory I heard that the
negative things we need to change in ourselves will attract
accompanying situations to mirror them. They keep coming around and
around until we are finally forced to do something about it. If this is the
case, then this surely answers why on earth I returned to Yangshuo to
become 'grounded'.

After all the complaining in England that something has to give and
how completely sick I was of people complaining about almost
everything, especially on Radio5 Live every morning during that samey
journey into work... after all that, there's me trying as hard as possible
to make everything the same as life before only this time in
China........ and complaining about it, aaaaaaaagh......and in
Yangshuo of all places! You're having a laugh mate.

Here are the three golden principles of reoccurring drabness that I tried
to adopt in Yangshuo:

1.  Get a nice quiet little apartment and have a cosy, quiet little
    time. Read in the evenings. Learn Chinese.
2.  Maintain a professional outlook on work. Be well planned, go
    to bed and get up early. Develop a healthy and balanced
    lifestyle. Rise and shine, yooo hooo!
3.  Remain sober in the week and place your job on a pedestal.

And here are the three basic guidelines to a 'normal' existence in
Yangers:

1.  Don't try and fight the noise in Yangshuo. Go with it. Stay out
    all day for as long as possible, the bar is a good place. Chinese
    people are seemingly oblivious to noise, they are brought up

with it. However, we in the West are just not built to withstand such a continual bombardment on our ear drums.
2. As an English teacher, planning for your lessons isn't so important. Have a vague idea and make up your classes as you go along. Just show up on time no matter what state of oblivion you are and that's okay.
3. Go out and get completely shit-faced every night, seven nights a week until around 3am. Start with the local brew and then move on to gin and tonics after 12. Continually smoke.

You know 'on paper' Yangers is an absolutely idyllic place to live. I mean teaching small classes of friendly adults English with stunning landscape outside the window, along with complete exposure to Chinese life at face value. It doesn't get any better than that now does it? With this total immersion, as time passes and you start to establish a rhythm in your life, the real cultural differences then start to emerge. Like some great widening fissure in the earth, I couldn't believe how dissimilar two peoples really could be. You have to live with it, love it or go somewhere else, after all that's what you came for right? I wonder how many people really think about this aspect of spending more than a vacation and to truly be part of a completely different culture. I certainly didn't, considering language and places to visit but barely giving cultural identity a look in before leaving the UK. I mean how can you?

Take your local Western neighbourhood for example. Normally you will have a couple of pubs and something similar to a Co-op nearby. There will be cars parked along the road and generally all will be quiet. If someone comes home and parks their car you will probably notice and hear it as they close their car door. In China, there are so many people that the whole place is continually in a state of movement. There is activity going on all over the place even right outside your doorstep and it starts damned early.

Small stalls selling different snacks such as 'jian bing' a standard pancake with a mild chilli sauce, or small kebabs called 'chwan' pronounced 'chwar' line the streets. Cars and small trucks sell fruit and veg' from their boot or spread out across the pavement, while numerous 'xu li gongs' are there to repair your bicycle for next to nothing. People still practice Tai Chi in the mornings and in the afternoons groups of old boys gather around tables totally absorbed in Mahjong, a time honored board game. There are all-weather ping-pong tables in most places which people really love playing. In China ping-pong is called 'ping pang qiu'. During the summer evenings, older couples romantically dance in groups to traditional Chinese music, one

163

last vestige of time gone by that's rapidly disappearing. People hang their washing up everywhere even between trees or across pavements, cars can be parked almost randomly at times and it seems like there is hardly any space left. All that and its right outside your apartment! From a foreigner's point of view, the reality of Yangers as a fair example of a typical Chinese town is very different though.

Aside from a sea of tourists in and out for a few days and teachers on a singular mission for self-termination, I only met four Western people who really had what can be determined as a 'regular' life the whole time I was there. These guys generally kept themselves to themselves learning Kung Fu down at George Gao's place. They had funded themselves in the pursuit of seven days a week training and rarely if ever did any teaching at all. I secretly envied their single mindedness, blinkered from the other Westerners and doing something amazing with their time.

On the other hand, at school every morning the delicate aroma of beer and gin and tonic would permeate through the office. At break times, each teacher would emerge from their classroom like some maggot, their eyes swiftly retreating to the backs of their heads at the first hint of sunlight and spark up a ciggie. One teacher was grey, such was his lack of exposure to sunlight. You could watch him sway about while he was teaching, still utterly inebriated. His constitution was so poor after years of living in Yangers that he walked his head moved back and forth like a velociraptor.

I passed out a lot in Yangers. On one totally unforgivingly hot afternoon, I woke up shaking, still intoxicated, utterly dehydrated and rasping for water. After collapsing in the street during the early hours, some locals had carried me home. Unable to go out amongst the general public, my ears were then subjected to the Chinese equivalent of 'white noise' in a 360 degree surround cacophony. There were builders standing outside the window and on the roof all day chatting and hammering nails, they were smashing in walls with sledgehammers downstairs, the neighbours were in full-on turn-everything-up mode and there was a school event out the back complete with a tannoy system. You do reach points of near insanity in Yangers and that really was one of them.

Ah, the nuthouse that is Yangers! Mixed bag this one; can't remember much but it certainly engrained itself somewhere inside of me forever. At the end of the day, I realised that there was absolutely no way you can live in Yangers, not without losing your sanity and the use of your liver. The only solution in order to move forwards was by returning to

England. When I got back, people were pissed off at me as all I'd done was get mullered. Blessed relief to have bought a return ticket and give it another go.


## Settling Down: 16th February 2006

Xin nian kuai le[1].

Warning: This diary is the equal to being utterly constipated for one month and suddenly as Mum would say, "I 'ad a good turnout". Last Monday in Cambodia: Goodbye to Mr. Long at the Green Town Guesthouse. Goodbye to the kids down the restaurant, Mr Kim, Sam Sokphal, Mr Luang and my fave waitress Voleak. Voleak is undoubtedly one of the sweetest, cutest and amazing waitresses you will ever meet. She's 19 and works seven days a week, fourteen hours a day and has two jobs. She gets home at 10pm, does her laundry and then spends an hour studying English. She spent two years saving for her motorbike that cost her $1000.

Along the way you meet people with completely different agendas and ways of travelling like our friend Ola; his whole dream was to go and live in a big Chinese city, live by himself in a small room, never go out and feel lonely. Also Sake, who flew from Hong Kong to Kunming. From Kunming, he flew back to Hong Kong, from there to Bangkok and later from Bangkok back to Hong Kong. All that and he never managed to catch one train or bus the whole time he was 'on the road'; off his pickle I reckon!

A couple were going around the world for six months on their honeymoon. They had actually planned for months in advance every single town and guesthouse they would be staying in from their WKTG. They had made reservations in each one and had a set time limit for every place they were going to visit. Unfortunately in Bangkok they had their passports nicked, so it completely blew all their plans out of synchronisation. Trying to keep all their deposits and reschedule the bookings in so many countries looked like a complete nightmare and they looked far from happy.

One girl we met had bought a ticket where you had to go to as many different countries as you could in four months. She was only spending two or three days in each country, crazy hey! One guy proudly announced that he was going to be travelling for ten years, but upon questioning then reluctantly admitted that he was only on his first few weeks since leaving home. Oh, and whereas most people were heading towards South East Asia, these two top Irish geezers with giant

---

[1] Happy New Year in Chinese

beards and big smiles were doing the complete opposite, travelling north on their way to Mongolia for November. Sounds good to me!

It had been a long time since flying. As the sun went down over the clouds, it lit the whole place up like one giant illuminated carpet until only a tiny thread of orange was left across the horizon and then darkness. Always a weird mixture of feelings; this was supposed to be the end of travelling and back to work, yet here were the greatest sensations one could experience; still facing unexpected beauty ; still moving; still so bloody tired; back to that feeling of excitement. Thought it had all gone!

One other thing! As soon as we left and went into Laos, Ev and I agreed that we both immediately missed China. Funny, we could never really figure out why. As the plane entered Chinese airspace it was like something weird going on in my head; pure and total happiness.

At Guilin airport we weren't allowed to get off the plane. Over the tannoy came, "Please stay in your seats while you receive the spray."

"What spray?" I wondered with a fair amount of concern. Immediately after the announcement, the air stewardesses came down the aisle wearing masks and gloves armed with an aerosol in each hand, giving both sides of the plane an ample helping of some (I assumed) anti-bacterial agent.

"How come we don't get to wear masks?" I thought. I also alarmingly noticed that they didn't spray the VIP class. Maybe it's just that if you have more money you're less likely to carry terrible diseases. For one second the possibility of some conspiracy to get rid of economy class ticket holders went through my mind. "Just what is in those cans?"

Customs searched me big time and instantly found the medical pack. They were astonished when they opened it and it took ages explaining what each medication was about. On the way out, they all commented on how rough I looked. In the washroom mirror some sad ghost-like figure gazed back with sunken dark eyes wearing in threadbare clothes and trousers that hadn't been washed in weeks. Some animal had had a good munch on them at some point (must have been really hungry). My Adios hoodie was also completely mullered and as skinny as I am, I knew I've lost weight in Laos and Cambodia. The poor old trolley bag looked thoroughly beaten up as well.

One noticeable thing; as soon as we got into the airport, there was that smell again! Only in China! Its funny how the tiniest of things can trigger off powerful feelings; just standing there for a few minutes

166

taking in that smell of China; absolute and utter bliss. Another thing; after lying under a big ceiling fan sweating my gonads off in Siem Reap, walking out into the cold night air was almost unhandleable. Though my wafer thin clothes weren't doing the trick in any way, this was just mustard mate. I'm telling you.........mustard!

The taxi driver had a big argument with the old bill and they ended up throwing all my stuff out onto the tarmac. A packed little bus to Guilin. Back to the bright lights, the power and energy of a Chinese city at night. Tired but not taking any shit off of any taxi driver anymore and getting to exactly the desired destination. Just a blur now. Someone insisting that it was crazy to go to Yangshuo at that time and there were no buses. Of course her guesthouse was available and it was better to go the next day instead, hmmm seemed to have heard that one before somewhere. Taxi drivers charging 200 kuai. Some argument with an extremely big and loud Chinese woman trying to get me on her bus. This guy falling asleep next to me with his head on my shoulder the whole journey. Non-stop from Cambodia to Yangers in seventeen hours, two sarnies and one Snickers bar.

Mr Derek strangely continued to send e-mails from Cambodia by the way; becoming ever more desperate and blaming various conversations with other teachers at the SITC as the reason for me not taking the post. Checking into the Double Moon Guesthouse again. Fan and Jason Zhang were at the door and we were really pleased to see each other. For the first time ever in China the price of the room was reduced. The streets of Yangshuo were pretty quiet in winter. Something about it; so beautiful in the evening; forgot how good it looked. Falling through the door of the Buffalo Bar and greeted by Alf and his wife Ming Fang. Getting mullered until 2am, only quitting when my eyes just wouldn't stay open any more.

Tuesday: Right then! Let's sort it out! Let's have one job, well done, hold the mayo! Falling out of bed to look for the school, feeling wiped out, putting on the same clothes, including that ridiculously tiny fleece from Chengdu months earlier. Why oh why do I buy clothes that are the wrong size? I mean it was another two days of wearing this miniature fleece before finally buying another that's obviously way too big.

A really bright and sunny crisp spring morning is what you get every day here and it instantly brings you right up. Found the school and met the boss, making an arrangement to return the next day and have a look around. Wrecked my back again playing Jianzi with the locals all day in the street, but well worth it for the sake of a wicked afternoon.

Wednesday: Instead of any sort of interview, the school landed a class on me with no prior warnings thus I had no lesson plan, prep or anything. "Can you teach a class?" asked the girl in reception. "One of our teachers is sick today".

"You mean they got terminally shitfaced last night more like" I thought "Oh? When do you want me to teach? Which age range is it? What material do you want me to use?"

"They are waiting now" she laughed[2] and that was it; another blag had just gone down and there was nothing that could be done about it. After two painful hours of just making up the class as it went along to a load of uninterested kids, travel-tired and worn out, it was more than a relief to be out of there.

"We want you to start today" stated another employee in a flat tone as if everything was already a done-deal. "There are classes this afternoon that we need you to teach."

"Hmmm, I'd like to meet the boss first and talk over money and accommodation before I start" I aired cautiously.

"He is not here right now. Can you teach today?" By now I could feel I was being pressured without any kind of welcome or introduction.

"Can I see my apartment before I start?" I pressed; the need to get into my own space and sort myself out at the forefront of my mind.

"It's not ready yet. Don't worry you can stay somewhere else until then."

Turned out that "somewhere else" was a frigging dorm, full of other people's clothes and underwear strewn all over the place. Along with that it had a 'lived in by loads of other people' lingering odor hanging heavily in the air. Insisting they delivered the promised flat with the fore-said kitchen and bathroom, someone reluctantly took me upstairs to what can only be described as a total shambles of a building that looked like a grand-slam bomb had gone through the roof. All the windows were broken or had no glass at all, there was no furniture, no front door and big pieces of concrete rubble filled two of the rooms.

"When do you think it will be ready?" I asked, feeling my blood surge.

"It will be done as soon as possible I think" he smirked with a slight chuckle. Blaaaaagh, what a blag hey! Not needing to be in such a space whatsoever and sick of being on the move, I felt more than pissed off with them. You just cannot keep getting your stuff in and out of

---

[2] It took me a long time to realise it but Chinese people will laugh when they are nervous uncomfortable or embarrassed. If something is wrong and you complain to someone, their most common reaction is to laugh. Of course to an up-tight Brit it's easy to take it the wrong way and can be more like rubbing salt in the wound.

your pack every three days! Stress to the power of ten to add to the whole thing. I just wanted to go back to bed and forget it wasn't happening.

Back at the Buffalo Bar, as soon as they heard of the schools blag, in a trice this Australian guy John provided a guided tour of some flats and schools in the area.

"You gotta be careful round here mate" warned John in his big Aussie voice. "There are loadsa cowboy schools in Yangers that'll take the piss. You do the work and then they don't pay you. Happens all over! I mean what are you going to do about it hey?"

Entering a quiet shaded area filled with trees, we stopped at a tall white building with dark green gates and matching green window frames. Its peeling paint gave it a definite aged feeling as it pressed itself in against the side of one of the hills. Stepped pathways snaked their way from the school following the contours, up through a small gorge high up to the right. With the refreshing stillness of the area and its aesthetic feel, it was a place that instantly grabbed you.

"Can't stay here. I got the boot from here a month ago. Best they don't see me with you" said John and he was off.

By the end of the afternoon the school called Zuo Yu for adults had taken me on. They even said they would also look for a flat and in the meantime offered somewhere for me to stay for a few days rent free. Jason took me round a few places but we had no luck finding anywhere. Today he was wearing his blue-grey policeman's uniform, immaculately pressed and finished with two bars on his shoulder boards though he insisted it was a low rank. Despite that, with his grey pressed shirt and silver tie, he sure looked the part and it seemed like the whole of Yangers was saying hello to him wherever we went.

Although he's a policeman here and also does 'massage' if you can call it that. When he saw the way I was walking he grabbed me in the foyer of his hotel and started pummeling my bad back, much to the delight of Fan. I mean there I am in this hotel cursing out loud in pain every fifteen seconds, continuing for an excruciating half hour. He just would not stop!

Thursday: This temporary accommodation courtesy of the new school is the worst place you will ever stay in. The Double Moon Guesthouse had no vacancies. Chinese New Year is just around the corner and everywhere will be so expensive that even when Fan knocked 100 kuai a day off for me it was still unaffordable. I totally hate this place; its freezing and the heating looks like it hasn't worked in years. It's really noisy, has no furniture, is so empty it echoes, it's dark, there are holes in the wall and most of the windows have broken panes of glass with newspaper taped across them. An old poster of Chairman Mao half clings to the wall at an angle and old moldy cardboard boxes give up their contents of other peoples' left over possessions across the floor. You can't walk into the bathroom bare foot or with socks on because the floor is a browny yellow and sticky as hell. As a result from all this, the flu has kicked in big time. Nice one! Reckon it's the big change from the dry Cambodian heat to a horribly damp environment that's done it. Still, it's a freebie! Packing and unpacking...again!

Chinese New Year also known as the Spring Festival is hugely important to the people. I mean they're all going nuts. It means far more than it does to our New Year's Eve version by miles. There are decorations everywhere, especially lit orange spherical lanterns that seem to be almost floating when it gets dark. Excited kids throw firecrackers at each other everywhere. Wow! Christmas on Don Det, New Year in Siem Reap and now a real Chinese New Year. Still ongoing; what a trip! When will this stop? Sometimes it's just an overload situation for the old brain cells.

Unable to use that disgusting shower I am minging big stylee. It's a tough one at the moment, feeling like a total bum surrounded by some of the most stunning Chinese women you'll ever see. Just need to get that flat. I mean the job starts soon for Christ's sake, beginning with five classes a day, a talk at the end at 6pm and something called 'The English Corner' twice a week where students can just drop in for a chat for a few hours. It is total involvement from now on with Chinese culture. You even get free Mandarin lessons four times a week (just as well). You can eat for free or at a two kuai stir fry place round the corner and get three kuai beers. The school is set next to one of Yangers' big hills and you can teach on the roof top in the afternoon under the sun, well nice.

Sunday: Oh man! What's going on? I don't know. Who am I? I don't know either mate. Who am I talking to? What did you just say? I have no idea. That bastard freebie accommodation has ripped me to pieces. Last night was the last straw; sat up the whole time in bed fully clothed, after five Li Chuans, (local beer) and the cheapest bottle of baijiu trying to knock myself out. With my hoodie up, tripping out on this flu, someone was beside the bed talking to me in my imagination. Reduced to the state of an animal. Sweating buckets with a fever and wet socks; my odour eaters are twice as thick now and no there is no way to do the laundry. Maybe they could be squeezed out and a nice aromatic tea made from them; full flavour! Didn't expect this; totally in Stig of the Dump mode at the moment. This is definitely not what it said on the tin.

170

At least it's warm in the internet place. Time has no meaning; you just stay up all night every night because it's so bastard cold and damp! Breakfast normally consists of a big bowl of noodle soup with egg, tomato, pork and 'la jiao' (chillies). If the food isn't covered with red chillies it ain't worth eating. By the end of Cambodia eating raw red chillies had become a habit and I'm consuming them big time in order to get well. When all the noodles have gone and you're just left with the soup it's like drinking rocket fuel and the bottom dregs leave you chewing a whole mouthful of chilli and black pepper.

After a bright and sunny morning, you can normally start breathing a sigh of relief and forget about the previous night. By noon, for a couple of hours it's lovely and hot. Sitting there absorbing the sun and drinking pot after pot of black tea and raw ginger is just what the doctor ordered. Funny how many Chinese tourists take photos of the Westerners. One puts her camera right in my face and walks off without so much as a 'ni-hao'. Now I know what it's like!

Suddenly blam! The flu smacks me in the face like a hammer and runs through me like a wave. The only thought is about having to go back to that shithole of an apartment and the decision is made in an instant. Within minutes Jason arrives in the hell hole to help take my stuff back to the Double Moon Guesthouse. They knock 300 kuai off the rent, which should be paid daily. Jason gets some sleeping pills and crashing out in this place is heaven. It's warm and has a TV, though no windows as it's all he's got left. Still, so bloody expensive though; 1500 kuai for the seventeen days leading up to moving in to the new flat.

Oh yeah, in this oblivious state, at last a flat was found with the help of a guy called Jimmy Lu who owns the second hand bookshop down West Street. He took me on a tour all over Yangers and at the end of a long day we came up trumps. Its overlooks the Li River and is really nice. It needs furniture, but there's still two weeks for that. There is so damned much to do. So much rushing around it's hard to cope with! And once again my head is on major overload as there are so many plans and dreams dancing around in it. Just know that these next two weeks are gonna be super intense or what!

Chinese New Year! I remember months ago going on about Chinese Health and Safety, rather the distinct lack of it. If you multiply that by a thousand then you get somewhere close to what it's like here at the moment. At night down the Li River, fireworks reflect across the water. Sometimes photographs just capture enough of what you want. Huge crowds gather all along the river banks standing there holding their own fireworks and letting them off. In an instant it's out of flue mode and

171

into self-preservation. These guys are off their heads. Suddenly you've got rockets and bangers, the lot literally detonating around your head. Their favourite seems to be these long repeater rockets which they buy in the bucket load and let them off, one in each hand. All the family has a go including granny and the youngest kids and they're at it all night, serious! It's not something the people watch, it's something they do. Firework stalls are everywhere not just a grand expensive organised display. It's just multiple explosions everywhere every second. Just amazing and this goes on seven hours a night for six nights.

Also saw my first proper Dragon Dance; two guys inside a traditional gold Chinese dragon costume go into each shop and restaurant. The dragon dances and jumps around while wiggling its arse. It then has to find the gift that the people have left for it, usually money in an envelope or some food. The dragon even has to climb up the side of buildings to get its reward, which is certainly entertaining to watch, especially the two guys trying desperately to coordinate their efforts. An older woman who owned a small corner shop refused to give them any money and stood there defiantly with her arms folded. Eventually she got really angry and shooed the dragon away. Not good for business I guess. This is all done to the sound of incredibly loud drums, going on all day and into the night. Basically New Year here is just an excuse for the Chinese to be louder than ever. While walking to the internet place tonight, my boss-to-be and his wife ran over shouting "ANDEEEE" throwing a load of bangers at me with great smiles on their faces and then ran off! Nuts!

Hello? Is there someone up there deliberately trying to make life just a total pain in the arse or what? Maybe by going through this barrier this will allow the right of passage to a new life? I mean coming back to the hotel the other night, a coach was parked outside with over thirty Chinese tourists in full outdoor gear getting off and filling the foyer up. My room is on the ground floor and seconds from the foyer. It was and still is utter pandemonium in the Double Moon and even earplugs are unable to block out the din. These are the most excited and noisy Chinese people you can imagine. The hotel has turned into a beehive of activity. They are all up at 6.30 making the biggest commotion known to mankind and then by lunchtime another coach has arrived. Multiply that with X number of fireworks and you have a Spinal Tap volume of 11.

Great! The school has sorted out some more temporary accommodation. Fair play, it's saving me 600 kuai, but the most notorious Westerner in Yangshuo also lives there. My flat mate will be a legendary alcoholic with bar tabs as big as Niagara Falls and also incurable gambling debts. He is banned from The Buffalo Bar and Alf sparked him out and threw

172

him out on the street. So far he hasn't said a word to me as he knows that's where I hang out. We work at the same school; he comes in still minging and pissed up, is always late or completely misses lessons. Just why they keep him on is something yet to find out. Got to share a flat with this guy for ten days. Mercy! Just what is it that is making settling down so bloody difficult?

It turns out that Jason has made it his mission in life to sort me out as much as possible, especially as the new apartment is nearly empty. That's really, really handy most of the time. He knows everybody in town it seems. If we walk into the street traffic stops for him. The other day he got me a pretty good second hand mobile phone with 100 kuai knocked off, even choosing the phone number saying that a lot of the digits are lucky.

"Your telephone number must be good for you" he insisted with a look of seriousness in his eyes. "You should always have a six or an eight. They will bring you the best luck. Six is for a long life and good health. Eight will bring you lots of money" he smiled. "Never have a four. This is not a good number. It has the same pronunciation as 'si', the word for death" he explained.

I did wonder what the implications for this would be and if people were less likely to give you a call if you had a four in your number. Turns out that there are a lot of high-rise buildings without the fourth floor. On the flip side you have to pay extra for sixes and eights to be in your phone number but Jason assured me it was worth it. On the opposite end of the scale, having lots of fours therefore is the cheapest one, but then again something bad might happen to you whenever your phone rings. Actually, the whole thing can get pretty obsessive with people paying thousands for a lucky number plate for their car. Guess it pays to be safe on the road and it certainly seems that drivers need it over here. Red is also considered the luckiest thing of all which explains why you see it wherever you look.

Looking for furniture with Jason Zhang
10am and the phone rings "Andy, its Jason. I am outside and we have a bed for you. Are you still asleep?"
Shit! I mean I hit the sack in the early hours and still feel really full of flu. I get outside to find he's there with his mate. They are in full uniform and have this state of the art four wheel drive flatbed police truck.
"We have to collect it now. No other time!" and at that we were off.

Turns out, the bed is on the top floor of the Li River Hotel as they are throwing out some of their stuff. When we get there, unable to move the thing, Jason is on the radio getting even more guys to help him.

From up on the roof, I can see more police literally running across the road from all directions to help out. Two emerged from the park at top speed. It's like he's called for back-up and something big is going down. So there are all these policemen helping Jason with this bed, base, headboard and mattress down all these flights of stairs, making a right old commotion.

On the way back Jason drives right through a road block. As we go past, this squad car bursts into life and goes ahead of us lights and sirens ablaze. I don't think this can be for us, just bizarre timing. I mean there we are taking a bed back to the hotel with full escort and police protection.

"What was it with this bed?" I think, leaning out of the window to see people stopping in the street, heads turning, all wondering what was going on. At this moment there is the strong temptation to shout, "WE HAVE THE BED AND WE'RE COMING THROUGH!" When we get to the Double Moon, the final thing is finding that Jason has a lock up. Like bloody Del Boy[3] or what! That's where my bed's stashed right now.

Still living out of the trolley bag, living in guesthouses and temporary accommodation, it's still difficult to stop feeling like you're travelling and I desperately want to drop out of this way of life. It's really hard trying to feel professional when you can't do any lesson planning and your possessions are so minimal. Still haven't taught any proper classes, though did an introductory 'speech' to the school and they gave me a bloody round of applause, amazing! You also have to do the chat room on the internet to promote the school. It's like being on a radio talk show with people from all over China queuing up to have a conversation with you. Everyone on-line can hear and can type in comments at any time. While you're online, one of the bosses brings in beers continually for the whole two hours. Not bad hey!

Monday: Lying there half asleep in the morning, trying to fit what's happening into one week, there was a sudden realisation that it's not possible to cram so much into such a short space of time. Looking at my visa I saw that it was going to run out in a week or so, sheeeeeet! At that moment I also remembered that I had to move out and into the school's temporary accommodation, bollocks! So within fifteen minutes, the old trolley bag was being lugged back across Yangers again, leaving the warm and friendly confines of the Double Moon. Mind you, it's not a bad place really; reminiscent of student digs, though surprisingly quiet and there's an awesome view of the hills out of the window.

---

[3] Well known character from the British comedy 'Only Fools and Horses'.

Tuesday: Andy's little insertion plan into Hong Kong: And so started the briefest and most intense bit of travelling done to date. Blaaady Hell! In the evening it was another sleeper bus, this time to Shenzhen[4], right on the border to Hong Kong. The plan being was to get the visa sorted during the following day, then in theory catch the same sleeper bus that night back to Yangers. Thirty six hours on the charge! Still, had to be done!

The bed on the Shenzhen sleeper was really really tiny at barely sixteen inches in width. Most of the night was a half-conscious fight with pillows, blankets, the full beam of oncoming traffic plus contorted pain! I had to admit there was now nothing exciting about the trip at all. Funny how what was adventure a few weeks ago had become part of everyday reality; filthy roadside stopovers in the dark, filled with litter, foul toilets that inverted your lungs, noise and the commotion of a hundred or more people. Having no idea about where we were and not caring a monkey's about it. Just get it over with! Still, one of those giant pot noodles sure made you feel ten times better!

Wednesday: Shit, they were bad roads, but did manage to sleep somehow. Supposed to be hitting the train station at sevenish, it was out of the bus station and off to...another bus station by accident; Shenzhen is another huge city so it's easy to get things wrong. I thought it would be a little town on the border, but it's just like Kunming or Chengdu. The border crossing at Lo Wu is confusing to the newcomer to say the least, checking out of China only to find that you had to transfer to another bus then buy your next ticket in Hong Kong dollars and not Chinese RMB. How are you supposed to know that hey? The cost of living is far cheaper in Shenzhen so people have to commute this way in order to get to work. More than half a million people cross the border everyday including well over twelve thousand school kids. If you are one of the unlucky ones then be prepared to get up damned early every day to get to work on time and for many, the alarm clock goes off at 5.30.

After a very stressful half hour it was sorted, the bus went through and there was Hong Kong. Blamm! How unexpected was that? After living in Yangshuo, Hong Kong is probably the most powerful looking place you could imagine; utterly modern, huge shining towers on Hong Kong Island, massive, massive sea ports with huge cargo ships coming in and out and being loaded up. Arrived at the visa place by 10am and by

---

[4] In the latter part of the 70s, Shenzhen was a tiny fishing village. Forty years later it's become one of the busiest ports in China with a population of almost nine million. Amazing hey!

11am after some predictable hassle, it was stage one done! Outside, breakfast was served costing an unbelievable 68HK dollars (that's about four quid)...and it was sooooooo small! Ordered a baguette to put this tiny breakfast in to pad it out but it turned out to be just a quarter of one! Still, only for one day hey!

So, still feeling okay and with seven hours on my hands, rather than sit on my arse, I took the Star Ferry over to the Island from Kowloon. Awesome! Never saw anything like that before! All you can see is pure mirror glass going way up reflecting the sea, sky and sun. On the island, power dressing suits run to somewhere at top speed with their briefcases like they're late and full of stress. The Giorgio Armani building is enormous; affluence, money, all the Westerners look rich and well groomed. Strange to think about the poverty of Cambodia only three weeks ago compared to this.

A tram ride and a cable car up the hill takes you to one of the most stunning views of any modern architecture you'll ever set eyes on. What must it be like to be that filthy rich and own one of your own apartments in one of those skyscrapers? There are thousands of them, all growing up from the ground like cut crystals on a bright clear day. Hundreds of boats and ships sail lazily in every direction through the heat haze.

Walking around the most affluent area you will see killing time; cash, cash and more cash; big rich houses on the side of the hill and me minging like a piece of old Cheddar. Looking down people's driveways unable to make the slightest connection and wondering what it must be like to be able to afford anything like that. Most of my stuff was now shot; the Salamon Boots completely super-glued together and my trouser pockets falling to bits, the pocket camera mullered after all these years, with no memory card and a scratch on the top right hand part of the lens resulting in a black splodge in every photo.

Rush-hour Hong Kong traffic in an open topped bus. Now that's quite a trip, but I do remember getting a wave of tiredness and wishing it was all over. 70 HK dollars for a pizza! Still, despite all the whingy grumbles about everything, it really had been a mind blowing day. So started the maddest dash across town. Got the visa. The visa office was high up in tower B in some big plaza somewhere in the middle of Kowloon. Taxi drivers speaking only in Cantonese but eventually getting to the train station double time. A train that was delayed with only three quarters of an hour 'till the sleeper bus went. Checking out of Hong Kong running to the terminus and checking back into China. Got to the wrong bus station. Argued with this driver who tried to pull a blag and give me an expensive ride before legging it as fast as possible to the next bus station. With five minutes to spare there was the bus. Sense of achievement! Yes, yes! It was the same bus as the previous night, so they showed the same crap low-budget kids film about a dog all over again.

Sleeping? Sod the discomfort; it was my smell that was pissing me off. Anyway...... RESULT! Opening my passport, inside was a brand spanking new one year multi entry F visa. It felt like a noose being removed, leaving me with a completely different head space; here to stay! It took us two and a half hours to drive out of Shenzhen, all lit up at night, wicked! That night was just a hazy memory and really cold. Some of those road stops were truly terrible. Someone tucked me in and this woman next to me was a major snorer.

I was talking in my sleep so someone woke me up. Suddenly the bus went round a blind corner going too fast in the wet and up the arse of another stationary sleeper. The driver steered wildly out of the way and that great hulk of a bus went careering up the verge into some trees. Okay though, though it did plunge everyone on board into complete panic there for a while. Pulling into the bus station at the crack of dawn, we were woken by the driver shouting "Yangshuo Yangshuo" at the top of his voice. Job done!

Some other day: Well that time has nearly arrived. Two days 'till the job starts proper, two days till moving into the flat. I want it so bad I'm drooling. A few doors down, lives this woman whose dog barks continually. The neighbours have complained enough times. The last time they said that if she didn't control it from then on they would eat it!

This morning the alcoholic flat mate burst into the room with just his white keks on and three days stubble on his face, swaying around wildly. He looked terrible and still utterly pissed from the night before.

"You couldn't teach my classes for me today mate could you?" he croaked.

"Like hell" I thought. Mainly as I gave my liver a good beating the night before too. Not covering his lessons he went back to bed. About two hours later Ray, one of the bosses phoned to say he was coming round! Within minutes he was sitting on the end of the bed discussing hours and contract terms while surrounded by beer bottles and a heaving ash tray (the lot cost me the equivalent of one pound sixty). Ray then proceeded to bang on my flat mates door for ten minutes until he begrudgingly let him in. In one hour amazingly he managed to talk his way back into a job.

Went with Gary, a great bloke from the UK and his missus furniture shopping today. Jesus. What a hassle! Why does the slightest little thing you want to buy turn into a major argument? It's all about saving face between you and the salesperson and yeah, so I wanted buy a duvet and they sell duvets by the frigging kilo (no really), so negotiations over a bloody duvet go on for hours. And there's Jason at the end of the day (just when I'd had enough), explaining to me in detail the different weight ratios of duvets and how these can vary according to how they are made...waaaaa!

And finally, last Monday the job started and I also moved into the flat. Phew, what a trip that turned out to be. Funny how so many things can happen in such a short time. It's only been twenty two weeks or something since splitting from the UK. Just to think what was going on before then and how different it is now; quite a bit really.

Matt is out of Phnom Penh this weekend and is on his way to Yangshuo which is totally brilliant. The Chinese New Year seems to drag on and on with more fireworks every night outside the flat. I thought it was supposed to be over a week ago. Putting this to a Chinese friend, they said that it was because it was Lantern Day. On Tuesday the explosions just bloody well carried on, keeping me awake for hours. Asking the same friend the same question, they replied "Oh, it's because it was Dumpling Day!" What's it tomorrow?" I thought, "Frigging Biscuit Day or something?"

## A Healthy and Balanced Lifestyle
## 17<sup>th</sup> July 2006

To Mum and Big Andy thank you both so much for spending so much time sending all that stuff in the post. It's not just the time taken to do this, but the expense of sending so many boxes of Nicorette Inhalers. You guys ain't made of money so it's a big deal for me. While writing, this is day seven since quitting smoking. I really have to give up. It's not only the twenty three years of smoking that's freaked me out, but the nature of what I've been smoking since being away. Asian ciggies are the absolute pits of the universe. They are total rubbish. I mean after changing brands so many times in an attempt to find something half decent, I've lost count. Having smoked Tibetan, Lao and Cambodian ciggies, Baisha, Chunghwa, Zhenlong, Hongqiqu, herb blend charcoal filters from China and cheap imitation Marlboro lights from Vietnam, the verdict is that they're all shite! They're all the same! They absolutely rip your lungs to ribbons, especially a heavy night down the bar. Mum has also sent me two boxes of the best ear plugs you could imagine and boy are they needed at the moment.

My Flat: I love my place. It's mine all mine; my own space; a place to go nuts in and do absolutely whatever I like. Being next to the Li River, this is a beautiful spot and certainly one of the nicest places anyone could live. It's getting into spring here now; the peach blossom trees outside the window are a rich pink and the birds' unfamiliar songs always a wake up call before the alarm. At 7.50 in the morning, go across the road and along the river to the first port of call, Johnny Lu's bookshop, for a bowl of his finest noodle soup.

On the way, groups of old geezers hang together in groups, chain-smoking ciggies before work. School kids flock around the Chinese hamburger stall and on the water the cormorant fishermen make steady progress. People are always doing martial arts along the river, including this sorted guy in black doing Kung Fu on the corner and a group of well handy looking women practicing with swords. Going down West Street for breakfast so early means the streets are wonderfully empty. Just sitting there watching the place slowly waking up is a chill-out in itself. Next, it's fifteen minutes through a network of back streets and alleyways to get to school. At night this area of Yangshuo is something totally out of heaven; it really is incredible. Just opposite there is a wicked kebab stall. Very handy! For only six kuai you can get five chicken stomach kebabs with chilli powder in naan bread. A bit chewy mind!

The trouble is it's also the worst for, yes, you guessed it, total noise pollution! Sometimes on a bad day you can feel like you're under siege by the neighbourhood as the din is so bad. So far the only solution is just not to be in for long periods of time. It's okay after 11pm and to be honest you get used to the Chinese noise levels after a while. The trouble is this is more than difficult to handle at the moment; it's a total nightmare, really! The neighbours have their TV on full whack every day. Jason has written in my book "Can you please turn your TV down" in Mandarin. I have to knock on their door every day and show them the message. They have the child from hell who has this toy that plays 'Twinkle Twinkle Little Star' over and over again. She also likes to blow a whistle continually that is awesomely annoying. There is a car alarm that continually goes off nearby. When it goes it lasts for four minutes at a time with the distinct possibility of it starting all over again adding to the stress. There are groups of people that hang out outside in the evenings making loads of racket. One of them has a set of bongos and is the worst drummer you will ever hear.

Out the back is a middle school populated by the worst behaved kids in the world. I've been out the back brushing my teeth in the morning watching them as they run around all over the place in their little yellow caps getting the bins and throwing rubbish all over the school. Chinese kids learn at school how to be noisy very early on. The whole area is also overrun with giant rats, I swear some as big as cats. One day I'd parked myself outside the back door overlooking the school yard to smoke a ciggie, when one huge rat stood bolt upright and stared me out!

On the river boats continually blow their horns and so does every car and motorbike that drives past. As per usual there is Chinese building work going on everywhere and last Saturday it sounded like an airstrike was coming down all round. The flat shook violently all day from 8am to 11pm as three shops below me got their walls put through with sledge-hammers and got converted into one space. The neighbours replied by turning up their TV to max volume.

This morning I got out of bed to see half a ton of bamboo scaffolding going up outside the window. Shite! More building work! A heavy banging immediately started against the back door. Opening it, there was a guy tying some scaffolding onto the outside security gate. I uttering something like "What the f*ck are you doing?" and he shouted something similar back at me. Knowing that soon the door would be completely stuck, I simply booted the bamboo out of his hands and pulled the door to. The flat now is covered with huge lengths of bamboo for some reason and now looks like some weird tree house. The worry is that some major construction is about to take place right next door.

The landlord and his wife, Mr and Mrs Li, speak no English. They phone when a bill is due and squawk unintelligibly down the line in a dialect that bears no resemblance to Mandarin. The other day Mr Li appeared at the door. He just walked past into the flat, picked up the best plants in the big pots over by the window and started taking them away. So there we were trying to wrestle this big plant out of each other's grasp in the middle of the flat with no way of comprehending what was going on. In the end I let go, only to find out that he had some bulbs and cuttings he wanted to plant. He planted them, watered them, put the plants back where they came from and disappeared!

Back to work at last. The school is the most unbelievable place you can possibly imagine. It's the source of much of the craziness running through my soul at the moment. It's run by a local Chinese guy and his word is absolute and final. He is also an incredibly good bloke, filled with mad energy and the desire to see his school do well. It's the best English language school in Yangshuo and the students, about fifty at the moment, save up or are wealthy enough to leave their jobs and come from all parts of China to study there.

There are dorms, a canteen and they all live together studying and playing. Classes are from 9am till 11.30 and 2pm till 4.30 and teachers have to give lectures in the evenings for an hour. The students work harder than anything I've ever seen in all my days as a teacher. They get into school an hour early, walking around the three-storey flat roof building, relentlessly reciting English out loud. It's a weird thing to hear, like monks chanting prayer in a Buddhist monastery or something. They study in the evenings and attend a grammar class from 8 till 10! Their intense desire to learn English is phenomenal. In a few weeks the improvement is astounding; a total transformation from hardly speaking any English to being nearly fluent.

You get to know your class intimately and my level 3A class is now like my second family. They all have their own Western names, the closest being Sunny, Kevin, Carol, Melanie, Jessie, Simon, Linda. These days, it's common for many Chinese people to adopt a Western name. Unfortunately many have absolutely no idea what they doing when choosing their new name. So far I have got to know a Doreen, Doris, Bonus, Better, Mable, Bo-Bo a Bi-Bi, a guy called Thunderbird and one called Apollo......hmmmmm!

From a Westerners perspective, to be honest though, I much prefer Chinese names. They're often far more interesting than plain old Steve or Jane. If you ask someone about their name, often you will find that it may have some special meaning, for example, my friend Lei Lei's comes from 'hua lei' which translates to 'flower bud', nice hey!

One of my neighbours is called Guo Lan which means the mist you see between mountains. Wei Zhuo, well his name means 'outstanding' or 'stronger' and his friend Jian Man comes from 'lang man de' which means 'romantic'.

3A will do absolutely anything for me and I love 'em to bits, helping to help pay my first leccy bill, to replace the empty gas cylinders and Jessie was even doing my washing at one point. At lunch times they teach me Mandarin in their dormitory (still crap at it by the way). My bag bust and one of 'em stitched it back together. Sunny, Linda and Kevin took me for a shopping day in Guilin; that was full-on. Nothing like a Chinese city to utterly run your batteries dry. When I was ill they all came round, bringing some really nice get well presents. If you're unwell in any way they are always there to rush off to the chemists to get you a double dose of Chinese medicine, mercy!

The teaching team is fantastic! They are all English and total party animals! At weekends there are trips out to the countryside, normally it's cycling and there will be a big pack of us, usually thirty students with some on tandems. One Saturday the outing was to an incredible old village called Jui Xian and there was a quite brilliant party up in the hills near the school last week. Gary did the sounds, there was a big fire and everyone, especially the teachers totally lost the plot.

Teaching the students is both a unique experience and a real laugh. Its great putting absolutely every bit of energy back into classes again. The students keep coming up with all kinds of eccentricities. Like one guy called Kami; I asked, "Where are your notes?" He pointed to his head and said "In here!" I set some homework where they had to write about their ideal romantic candle lit dinner for two with their partner. Carol's was a large fish head in a white soup. Jessie's main ingredient was monosodium glutamate. Oh, and another assignment was about an activity they could do on Valentine's Day. One student wrote that she would like to go to the countryside with their boyfriend "camping and fisting." I guess it doesn't get any more loving than that does it!

    Back on the subject of food, one of the students reckons that her favourite is harvest mouse and also the moth pupa which are apparently very tasty. Indeed if you're doing a topic based on food, asking anyone to list ten types of meat is always an experience and a half; "beef, pork, goat, chicken, duck, pigeon, fish, turtle, snake and dog" is normally how it goes. After a while you realise that even the most straight forward questions or activities don't go how you envisage them. We were doing a lesson on cooking when I asked for some similar verbs to the word 'cut' expecting to hear 'chop, slice and dice'. The problem is, Chinese students love to have their heads buried in their electronic dictionaries which, although can be quite handy, often bear no thread on the language we use in daily life. Instead of the predicted answer, one of the students comes out with the word 'slash'. So there I am trying to explain why we wouldn't use the word slash in this instance and when we normally use it, showing them the difference between cutting and slashing using my board marker instead of a knife. Of course they delighted in this new word and it was in use for days after.

Nearing the end of class it was time to put all the new vocab into practice and they were given five minutes to work out the recipe for making a chicken and salad sandwich in English. "Easy" I thought.

"First you need to buy a chicken" explained the first student. "Take it home and slash it with a knife in your kitchen until its dead. Put your hand inside and pull out its stomach." At that point I quickly stopped them, guiding them onto the 'putting everything between the bread' stage before it got even more grizzly.

We were discussing various jobs today. One that came up was that of a life guard. I asked what they thought a life guard was. One student guessed that as you move through life it was someone sent to protect you against danger. While doing a class on various warning signs from the text book, we discussed the one with a picture of a hard hat. One of them put his hand up and said that you would normally find it when 'destroying caves.' He explained that it is normal in China to rip the guts out of any cave and sell all the stalagmites and stalactites.

During a talk on the most important inventions in history the compass and paper were of course the first to get a mention. After all China was the first place to start using both way back near the beginning of its five thousand year old history. One guy however put his hand up with an excited look on his face; "guns" he said.

"Why are guns the greatest invention?" I asked. "Surely they are the worst."

"Yes but they are more convenient" he explained.

The canteen food is something else! You always really have to check what's been served up in front of you from the other students. Like a lot of it is offal, such as heart mashed up with all the valves sticking out or a very nasty and skinny chicken with everything still attached. These guys love their freshwater snails. Jessie last night told me the translated name for them is 'dirty water grazers' and said that the dirty water adds to the flavour. Yes they live on all the sewage from the bottom of the Li River! Nice!

The students wonder why Father Christmas never visits China. They reckon it's because if he did come over they would eat the deer.

The Matt Phenomena: From the moment Matt said that he was legging it from Phnom Penh to Yangshuo, it was certain that we were all in for a crazy time and he was going to make a big impact. Some understatement though! He showed up looking like a sad little cat that just spent a night in a hedge at the side of the road in the cold and rain. Once again, the change from the heat of Cambodia to the cold and wet of Chinese springtime had taken its toll and he sat in my classroom shivering his arse off. At lunch we went back to the flat and I sorted him out with some warm gear. Man he looked funny in those huge woolen green Chinese army surplus long johns. I mean the moment he arrived he had us all in absolute stitches! He now teaches in the classroom next door and it just doubles the crazy factor! It's a blast! Who'd have thought it when meeting this guy on the slow boat to Luang Prabang last year.

Dog & Chips
One evening I take Matt to the Cloud 9 Restaurant. It's the best restaurant in town with good service, great atmosphere and superb views from the windows complete with balcony tables.
"I'll have dog and chips please" requests Matt.
"Dog and chips?" I ask with a raised voice, as usual immediately breaking into laughter. "Do you want it wrapped in paper with a couple of pickled onions as well?"
"It's not that I want it. I've just always wanted to ask that question, that's all".
Pointing to the pictures on the menu, the waitress writes down the order but Matt can't find the chips. "Xiang tudou" is the nearest I can say at this time, meaning 'want potato'.
"Dun gou rou he tudou ci shenme?" replies the waitress standing there waiting for our response.
"That's fine" goes Matt as if he understands, "Hao hao hao" (good good good) waving her off in an effort to get rid of her.
After fifteen minutes of expectantly waiting, the waitress finally appears with the "dun gou rou" or 'braised dog' in a steaming pot. She places it in front of him and removes the lid. A plume of steam rises up in his face and the woman simply says
"Dog!"
before walking off. The mixed look of disappointment and bewilderment on Matt's face as she lifts that lid is unforgettable. Basically the meat you will find on the menu is from a special dog that is bred just for the table. It's called a 'vegetable dog' as that's what it's been fed on, so never eating scraps or left-overs and rubbish from the floor. After it's killed it's smashed up into little bits and cooked in a big pan. The first thing we see is a paw sticking out over the lip of the bowl.

I try some but I can't get on with it. A bit gamey I would say. Matt can't bring himself to eat it either!

The 'tudou ci' isn't much better, though it is one of the normal ways for Chinese people to eat potato. It's just finely shredded potato fried for a few minutes in peanut oil and served with lashings of vinegar. If you are hoping for something reminding you of home, you certainly won't find it ordering tudou ci that's for sure.

Just returned from the most amazing hike so far in Yangshuo; walking and walking until just winding up in the back end of absolutely nowhere....proper! Moving through bamboo forests, through swarms of giant dragon flies and huge black and red butterflies down to the river; what a place to live!

I've now lost count of the number of festivals they have here now. The other day it was Sister's Day, so lots of fireworks were once again going off the whole time. Then it was Tomb Sweeping Day, It's relentless! One afternoon these awesome and deafening explosions went off for about ten minutes leaving us unable to continue class. All we could do was stop and wait. You couldn't even shout over it. Chinese folk are especially wary of any ghosts or spooks and the fireworks are meant to scare any evil spirits away from your family's graves. So anyway, I'm out in the countryside today. It's only bloody Ancestors Day isn't it! Even right out into the countryside you can't escape it, as the sound of detonations resonate through the valleys from miles away. More fireworks and fake money, fake paper mobile phones, the lot all gets burnt and sent to the other side to your dead relatives

Other stuff, oddments and other unusual observations in no particular order:

Cloud 9 Chinese medicine soup menu: Pig lung soup (good for breathing and stomach), Fried bee larva and cashew soup, grilled ducks tongue soup, cuttlefish and peanut soup, (regenerates the skin and "perverts aping") and pigs brain soup, (relieves stress and improves the memory).

While looking through the DVDs in a shop down West Street, there was one about Prince Harry called "To be a Prine."

It's been raining hard every night here in Yangers lately. Every morning this thick black sludge appears all over the pavement and roads from the sewers. Lovely!

Ate donkey last night! Actually not bad; better than the dog I can tell you and it's a lot cheaper.

Now China may not have qualified for the World Cup but they sure made a point of going on and on about how they won the world cheese sandwich eating competition on the sports channel last night. They also had a special feature on the police car formation squad. They looked so damned cute in their little cars. I mean can you imagine how hard the police in the UK would have the piss ripped out of them if they did that. They could even drive backwards in a straight line together and form triangles at high speed. Useful on the way to a callout I should imagine!

Chinese people are generally a great bunch. You can spark up a conversation and make friends at will. If you are on a good one you can go home and walk through the doorway having just made a heap of new friends. Just up my alley Yangshuo is! It's crap being a Westerner at times though. If you buy something from anywhere that you haven't been to before, be careful; the seller may well try and shred every last single kuai out of you just like the touts at the bus station.

When Gary went into the hardwear shop to buy ten feet of rubber tubing (as you do), the woman under measured each foot of tubing by two inches. Gary noticed this but when he pointed it out she went completely nuts. You can't comprehend what it's like watching a Chinese woman when she loses her temper. Its something to behold I can tell you. A Chinese catfight really is something special to watch and will last for ages. Anyway, Gary finally got his bit of tubing. The next day he went back to get something else. He handed her a fifty kuai note to pay. She turned round and did something out of sight and then handed back the note saying she couldn't change it. Gary got home to see that she'd gone and swapped his note with a fake (there are tons of fakes in China). The police said they couldn't do anything as Gary went home with the note. This led to another huge commotion in the shop. All that because he spotted her trying to pull a fast one on him the day before.

One fine Saturday I joined a school cycling trip to Moon Hill. All was going well until about ten minutes down the main road when this guy came running out shouting that one of the students called Lisa had damaged an (already broken) wing mirror on his moped. It seemed that he'd deliberately left it out in the bike lane rather than parking it out of the way with all the others. The whole thing went on for over an hour with the guy and his friends charging into us aggressively, trying to be as intimidating as possible. He then tried to attack Lisa, so Gary came steaming in wielding a big piece of bamboo to fend him off. Just crazy! The police arrived and after much deliberation announced that the guy was a cheat as there wasn't even any broken glass on the floor.

Even after the old bill had reached their verdict the argument continued. In China it's all about saving face over everything and seeing as this guy had just lost an argument with a short girl in a cute pink puffer jacket in front of all his mates, he waited for us on the way back. Leaping out in front of her, the whole thing started all over again. The guy even started crying. All that over something that he had created in the first place!

Saving face or 'mianzi' is one of the more negative things that can happen here. If someone is in the wrong, you may get blanked as if it's your fault. In extreme cases you will get blamed as if it was you that made the mistake. This can creep into personal interactions even with good friends or at work. If you're doing business, really check this out before you commit to anything. On the most superficial levels, you can upset someone and they will suddenly not be talking with you, for example if you say no thanks to something no matter how politely or important the reason.

It now appears that the building work going on under the flat is not going to be a supermarket as I had stupidly assumed. Yes, you guessed it, in a few weeks ready for the May Festival, (yawn and big groan), it's gonna be a frigging karaoke bar. Talking of noise, the middle school round the back now has a new tannoy system for the playground which resonates around the block. Some bastard has been selling bird whistles to the kids too.

The weather is pretty hot now. If the sun isn't shining, it rains like crazy all night and it's normally really muggy. The Li River is bustin' its banks today reaching a dangerously high level widening dramatically. The current is furious and you can see rubbish and tree limbs moving past at a rapid rate[5]. It's been absolutely arseing it down for days now as we move into the 'wet zone'. The school flooded the other day with a torrent of water sweeping into the office and submerging all the plug sockets. Bars and shops are still open though so people have to get used to playing pool submerged up to their knees.

The flat is continually damp and the bread board has gone orange and green with fluffy mould. Life is a fight to keep everything dry. A typical place has dark tiles on the floor and white ones on the walls. It means that you can wipe all the moisture off of everything and combat mould big time. Books and paper are always damp, which is a

---

[5] China is notorious for its flooding. Every year the south gets a total hammering effecting hundreds of thousands of people. The worst flood ever recorded was in 1931 where three of the major rivers which span across China flooded from end to end. It is reported that the death toll was as high as 4 million including those from disease and starvation.

right pain. It also explains why there are absolutely no carpets here and therefore no vacuum cleaners.

At school the classrooms are also the same. Flooding aside, the floors are always wet anyway and so are the white boards that the teacher uses to write on. I have an electric mozzie killer that looks like a tennis racket bought in Cambodia, (220 volts) and you can kill over a hundred of the bastards each day in class but it still doesn't stop you getting bitten to pieces. One of the teachers passed out leaving his window open the other night. He finally stirred to discover they'd had a right old royal banquette on him from head to foot across the whole of his right side; looked excruciating!

After being in Yangers for sometime really you start to realise with how totally impoverished this place is. On Sunday morning, I was standing out the back and looking down over the old school yard when I noticed, crouching down formed into a virtual ball, an old woman with a big flat hat on picking up seeds from the floor. The seeds had fallen from the trees, most of them too old and rotten, but she stayed there all day mindfully choosing the best ones until she had a little carpet of them drying in the sun.

Been using as many back streets as possible these days, so it's easy to keep away from the noise of the main drag. The squalor and deprivation is pretty stunning at times. Roaming around old Chinese tenement blocks, many of them are dark and foreboding places. It's amazing how people live like this all their lives, but that's only the view through the eyes of a middle class Westerner. To the locals, it's just a normal way of life. Of course there are many worse off places in the world. I mean look at Laos and Cambodia for a start, but there's something about this place that can really smack you right in the face at times; the smells; the colours; the dark; the rubbish; the decaying architecture; everything is so run-down around here. It's only the bright lights of West Street that makes this place seem comfortable. Then you get the backpackers who just say that Yangshuo is "too touristy!" If only they would get away from West Street down one alley for thirty seconds they would be transported into another dimension!

I'm totally gutted that my great friends Jez and Niki have had to leave for England. Most mornings Jez and I would go running along the banks of the Li River, to that amazing village previously mentioned last year called Shi Ban Qiao. I mean wow! What a great way to start the day! A few days after they left and I stopped jogging, my ankles turned into two balls of swollen pain. It went on and on for days with the locals all laughing at my hobbling around.

In the end I succumbed to going to the hospital. Believe you me, you don't want to spend any time in Yangshuo hospital. Come back Bristol Royal Infirmary, all is forgiven. They took me to the 'body fluids' unit. What a dark and decrepit little bag of germs that place is. I mean absolutely foul! Flies regularly buzz around your head and a stale smell of sickness lingers in the air to mix with the sticky humidity. A woman in high heels, tiny denim hot pants and a miniature pink t-shirt with a silver love heart over her chest, examined me, who, very unsurprisingly had no idea what she was doing. I ended up having "physiotherapy" of sorts in the end. This consisted of the worst massage ever, where the doctor dug his fingers into every sore part of my ankles in order to "increase circulation." Following this he immersed my legs in this bucket of rank water for a very long half an hour sitting in a rancid insect ridden toilet. A truly miserable experience all in all.

Finally someone advised me to see Dr Li Li, reputedly to be the best doctor in Yangshuo. Down one of the side streets look for the burgundy shop front with gold Chinese characters and a row of people sitting outside against the window waiting to be seen. Inside you are met with the distinct smell of Chinese Traditional medicine, something that's familiar in most chemists. The foyer is packed full of shelves with bottles and potions pushed into every space. There are large demi-johns filled with amber to deep sienna liquids sealed with red muslin cloths. Each one has some extra ingredient stewing away at the bottom like various seed pods, plant material or snakes. Dark brown jars of homemade pills wrapped in purple paper labeled with calligraphy are there to be taken home. Raw ingredients such as dried plants, fungi and sponges are at hand.

Dr Li-Li is especially known for her 'cupping' techniques. This is used to treat a variety of ailments and involves heating up to thirty bamboo 'jars' then placing them on your back. When they are heated it creates a vacuum thus "stimulating the blood flow and drawing out toxins". Afterwards, the patient will be covered with circular red bruises; the darker the colour means the more toxins. Luckily for me she quickly diagnosed that torn tendons were to blame and a stiff massage was all that was required. After session upon session of torturous pain and three times daily applications of some burning hot Chinese skin cream she seems to have done the trick. At least it kept the mozzies at bay.

The building work under the flat has nearly finished. Thankfully it turns out that it's actually only going to be a wedding photo shop and the distinct lack of banging is now noticeable, especially power tools and nail guns not going off anymore. It's such a relief after six weeks of continual deafening noise and people climbing about in front of the bedroom windows. One thing though. I was lucky enough to see a complete building job done from start to finish. Screws and raw plugs do not exist here. Instead the whole thing is constructed out of untreated plaster board and held together with thousands of nails. Nail guns were in continual use for weeks and there's no doubt that the apartment will be above the greatest fire hazard ever when the weather starts to dry itself out. At the moment however, such is the humidity, there's no way that plaster board will get through even one year. The ants are going to have a field day that's for sure. Only in China mate!


Onwards

A few weeks down the line and even with the good news of the Wedding photo shop, life is still as difficult as ever. The continual noise levels driving any Westerner over the threshold of insanity and the alcoholic self-embalming lifestyle has brought me to one conclusion. Shit I need a holiday! Yangers is just too much for me and certainly not any place you could seriously settle down. The plan was to change my life for the better, not create an Asian replica of how things were in the UK and that's all there is to it.

Such a shame; the decision to split hasn't been an easy one. Yangers is an absolutely stunning place to live in so many ways. It's a pain in the arse conclusion that's been heading gradually in this direction ever since arriving. Hand on heart if I'm honest with myself, since the first visit last year I never really thought it was possible. Maybe it's all about going through your options and hoping you'll be successful rather than any form of realism. If this is the case it seems like the options have all but run out.

I can't think straight anymore no matter how hard I try and focus. With a return ticket in my hand, I think I'll just head back to the UK and try to get my head together, regroup and make fresh plans. It does feel like I'm running back home with my tail between my legs though. Damn it! I've had it with Yangers

# 10

# The UK – No Fixed Abode

Saturday 1st of July: Just three days left to go before leaving this crazy 'island' called Yangshuo. Like yesterday in Kelly's restaurant, Mei, a local martial-arts expert sits down at the table next to me.
I say, "What's in the case?" pointing at this bag she has with her.
"Sword!" is her simple reply.
Kelly and her staff are eating these boiled eggs with clear blue whites and brown yolks. She tells me that they are duck eggs dipped in alkaline. Only in Yangers mate! You can never take this place for granted.

It's been a long time since I slept in the oven-like bedroom having been forced to move into the living room. It's so hot that the only option is now trying to sleep on the rock hard Chinese wooden sofa under the fan which is continually on full whack Cambodia stylee. The extreme buzzing sound of these big brown insects called 'zhi liang' on the trees outside and the sound of the fan fill the room, but my head is filled with so many things that it doesn't make a dent.

The last day at school for a start! The class wanted to know about the journey back to the UK, so I put it all up on the white board. The end result filled me with dread and over 5.5 thousand miles and there's me worrying about getting a bloody National Express ride to Bristol after getting off the plane; a poxy two hour journey away. I mean in China no probs but in England? I actually seem to becoming nervous about going back. I also learnt that after all this time my student Lily's nickname, Mantou, translates to 'steamed bread'. Oh, and when I came in that morning, there was Kami Lee singing "the referees a wonker" (must have been one of Tom's lessons).

Forcing myself up and out of the flat, down the street in the heat on a mission for water and milk, shades on, my flip flops slap against the souls of my feet. I pass some guys that are doing Tai Chi in the park. "Why couldn't I have got into something like that?" I ask myself. It's a simple answer really. I was a teacher at Zuo Yu!

There is that end of an era feeling big time, like the end of term before the summer holidays, like something really special is coming to an end but the next installment is about to take place. Many people have said that going back to your home country is the hardest part when travelling merely adding to this rising sense of anxiety.

Its still a really good time in Yangshuo though, it always is. My now ex-student Linda and I have been hanging out together. She's so funny and her advice is always the best. Also my best mate Yvonne from Laos last year is here having now become a tour guide, wicked! Dreamy and funny days, lying around together in coffee shops like lazy cats.

Shenzhen: After weeks of worry I find I can hardly contain myself I'm so excited. Feeling great to be on the move again. The first thing noticeable thing is that this isn't the only sleeper bus on the road. There is a column of them mixed in with lorries, snaking off into the darkness. From above it must look like a line of ants, a reminder of what is happening here. A massive workforce is forever moving into and filling Shenzhen. This kind of movement is going on all over China. In this corner of the country many people you meet either live in, or are moving to Shenzhen. People will leave their families and go off in search work in the big cities where the money is. Everyone from here and the surrounding provinces goes to Shenzhen for this reason. As we get to the outskirts all you can see are industrial estates and road expansion, building and more building. It's insane! For the longest time, there are nothing but chimneys bilging smoke out, going at it twenty four hours a day. From the outskirts of the city it takes hours to drive into its heart. This place is massive and growing ferociously.

In the morning I say goodbye to my mate Elsa who has been travelling with me. She really helped me out, taking me all the way across town to meet my old mates Gary and his missus who moved from Yangshuo. First it's over to Gary's school, squeaky clean with loads of earning potential and then to his flat (also very squeaky). You could easily forget you are in China in this place if it wasn't for the terrific view from the tenth floor and the chicken's feet stew brewing away in the kitchen.
    Contrary to the previous experience of being here, with more time on my hands to take it in, Shenzhen is awesome. Looking out from the balcony across the Nanshan district, this is unlike any place I've set eyes on before. Its flyover central, but the buildings are modern and no expense has been spared to bring a great sense of aesthetics to it. Trees, artificial landscaping, small parks and raised gardens fill every available space.

192

In the Hua Qiang Bei shopping district you can buy just about anything under the sun for next to nothing like digital cameras, camcorders and laptops....hmm now there's an idea! In fact loads of ideas seem to be popping up. It really feels like this is the land of opportunity. In the nearby market you can buy any decent quality thing you want, even tasers that can deliver an 800 kilovolt charge at your attacker for only 20 quid. There are fast food joints everywhere, the best one is the popular Japanese chain, Ajisen Ramen, where the super spicy beef noodles rip both your face and arse off with a vengeance.

Thursday 6th 00.45am: Twelve hours to go before the plane takes off. Everyone has gone to bed and I'm clock watching big-time. The second hand on the clock is loud and pronounced and the same apprehensive feelings as the night before leaving England have surfaced.

At Hong Kong airport, I fought back some big emotions, like a big part of me was now being left behind in this amazing place. In Yangers, Nikki's advice was to get a return ticket in case it was difficult readjusting to England. Sound advice there for sure! Approaching the check-in counter, the decision to come back as soon as possible was made almost as instantly to saying yes to just one more pint before closing time.

Friday 7th 4.00am, Doha airport, Qatar: Interesting headspace this; like you are on autopilot and you enter a complete sense of timelessness. I realise that travelling by plane is now my least favourite aspect of being on the road; you rarely talk to anyone and you stare blankly at people with their family, friends and loved ones for hours, all conversing and sometimes embracing. It's also always really expensive in airports and I'm always skint. Why is it that no one else ever has carrier bags? People stare as my crisp sarnys drop broken crisps and crumbs on the floor.

My attempts at quitting smoking in Yangers failed abysmally after only two weeks and each ciggie I spark up is met with an accompanying sense of disappointment. The airport smoking rooms are always the absolute arsehole of the universe and you always feel like some kind of sad outcast while you're in there. Though your clothes and hair stink like an ash tray after a few minutes, it still doesn't prevent you from reaching for a second one even if it makes you late for your flight.

The staff looked quite pissed off and were waiting for me as I ran into the departure lounge, having held the connecting flight back. The window seat turned out to be next to a large emergency exit and as we took off my mind conjured images of it blowing open and being the first passenger to be sucked into outer space. It was also right the toilet. After ten minutes of slamming doors and people queuing up next to me, the staff managed to relocate me to two empty spaces further back. Hours of discomfort followed as my body tried to mold itself over that unmovable arm rest dividing the two seats. Propped up by pillows, folded blankets and spare clothing, the whole lot would irritatingly keep falling out of position every two minutes. That disgusting plane food went right through me and the sensation was quite upsetting really. I even had a dream where someone was force-feeding me the stuff. It was all over my face and I cried out "Oh God help me. No more, aaaaagh!!"

The final hours of semi consciousness; dreading breakfast as the next dose of gut rot made its way on the trolley down the aisle; watching our progress on the moving in-board map system as we slowly approached the coast. Not long now

## Reverse Culture Shock: 2<sup>nd</sup> August 2006

In all of my diary writing this has been without a shadow of a doubt the strangest one to do. I guess it's because it's all about observing how things are different in the UK compared to all the other countries crossed off the list so far and how your perspective changes while being away. Of course, still being on the road and not living in the UK anymore also has a lot to do with it. Combine that whole lot together and it's one of the most unusual and trippy feelings you'll get; I mean coming back to a place that you used to call home and to merely to be travelling from A to B, having no job or place to call your own space and then leaving again! BEEEEZARRO! Another thing! Without involving some heavy shelling out for bus and train tickets and having no car anymore, the realisation is, the whole trip will be virtually dependent on lifts with very little control over destinations. Nothing like being random hey!

Flying over the coast and finally over London, I'd forgotten how green everything is. Even over suburban areas it's green. In Asia a lot of the terrain is actually brown. In Beijing the surrounding mountains are black so you really notice the difference when you return. In the built up areas this colour comes from there being so many gardens. Yes, the UK has gardens. Generally Asia doesn't! This was the first observation of this mad country and it took me quite by surprise. I didn't think I would be seeing it in terms of a series of observations, but that's how this experience turned out. From above it looked like thousands of individual little squares separated from each other with blocks of green. I'll never forget that unexpected moment before we landed and I still use it in class when explaining to students some of the basics of our culture.

We like our 'space'. We have a strong need to have a distance from other people. We erect fences to mark our boundaries, keep out the rubbish out and dogs from crapping on the lawn. In China seeing as there are so many people crowded together in high rise blocks, they have to use the space outside communally. Even before the high-rise families had to share their space they shared everything even down to their kitchens. Personal space isn't something that's top of the bill in the East that's for sure.

And what about lawns? You can't beat lying out on your lawn at any time right? The feeling of lying on your lawn in the summer; top! Of course with every lawn comes the necessity to mow it; a strange little activity really; pushing your hover mower backwards and forwards over the grass or in sweeping arcs, especially when there are a couple of neighbours also doing it at the same time. Nothing like a good mow hey!

I don't know about other Western countries but we Brits have a definite zone surrounding each of us that only our nearest and dearest can enter. This other aspect of our boundaries can only be a result of such a huge difference in population. It's an invisible area that extends to about 15 cm's around us. If someone gets too close we can feel immediately uncomfortable or even annoyed if we don't know them. 'You're in my space' is a concept that does not exist in China and I've never got used to it. You can be walking down the road and someone will walk into or really close to you rather than around you. Don't stare at anyone from the UK or you could find yourself in trouble really quickly. Across the water, everyone stares at anyone or anything that's out of the ordinary. It just doesn't matter.

At London Heathrow bus terminal I made my first purchase on home soil. Amazingly one of those crappy sandwiches drenched in mayonnaise, a carton of Ribena and a packet of cheese and onion' came to almost a fiver. I mean that's about sixty kuai when it's at home; enough to last you a week. Holy shit! The thought of being immediately skint sent a shiver down my spine even before I'd got moving. Mind you, those crisps[1] were damned good!

The bus journey was not bad at all really. Ok, so it was predictably late but who gives a monkey's about that. All I can remember was that the bus was just so quiet; no loud TV or crap pop songs on a continual loop, no one talking mega loud into their mobile phone, no one shouting across to their friend and no one greffing on the floor. No one spoke! I guess we were all in the land of the undead on that ride. The oncoming traffic seemed staggeringly fast but also incredibly quiet as it whooshed past. The clouds were stunning! I was sure they weren't like that before.

Quite weird carting the trolley bag across Bristol City Centre! Shouldn't I be doing this in some far flung region of the world? After finally catching the Badger line bus to Long Ashton, I arrived at my old place that Big Andy had taken over. Great to see him again and time for a few down the local; the first decent pint in such a long time had that Ice Cold in Alex feeling to it (check out the end of the film).

Saturday 8th: Is this real? Reality? Is that you reality? Waking up in what used to be the study; a small box room I used to do all of my paper work in, was not the greatest of starts to any day. The first sight that met my tired eyes was the final remnants of an old life. All of my stuff that never got thrown away before leaving had been pushed out of

---

[1] British English for 'potato chips'

the way and stacked up against the walls to make room for the sleeping bag. "Your life here is now gone!" were the first words that immediately sprung to mind.

A Nightmare in the Aisles
Finding myself in the Tesco down in Nailsea in the afternoon, AAAAAAAAGH! This should be a pleasurable experience but under these strange circumstances it's more of a nightmare. As it happens, what's left of my poor brain goes on total shut down into a tight knot of inanimate matter and I end up buying a load of twank, such is the sheer indecision and panic of the moment.

And what's happened to England? The sound has been turned down and it's on 33 instead of 45. Everything is in slow motion. Even town seems quiet. Have the buildings got smaller? Where has everyone gone? Why are there empty spaces? Maybe all the people have been disappearing while I was away and no one's noticed like in the Twilight Zone. Jet lag? This is more than jet lag! I didn't understand what was going on at the time, but since then discovered it must have been 'reverse culture shock'. Removal from your old life sure allows you to see things with new eyes but re-adjusting to your old world is harder than it sounds. It's like things have changed but you don't know how or what.

Everything is the same but slightly different. I mean if you go on holiday for even a few weeks you get that 'been away feeling' upon your return. You can't describe it, but you sure can feel it. Multiply that by a year or two and you're definitely out to lunch mate!
Not only is my uncooperative brain feeling like a pile of undercooked scrambled eggs, but the trolley is misbehaving. The front wheel seems to have locked itself in a sideways position which is highly irritating. I grumble to myself that I've paid a pound deposit to encourage people not to steal it but who's going to run away with this old thing anyway? After pulling a few items off of the shelf though, the trolley suddenly becomes revitalised and the shopping experience starts to become far more enjoyable. I can push it and let it coast out ahead of me, even doing one handed turns.

At the opposite end of the store, I reach over to buy some pasta sauce only to realise that I already had some. Puzzled by this strange occurrence the penny suddenly drops that my head is so shot away, I've walked away with someone else's trolley.
Guiltily I quickly remove everything and dump it on the nearest shelf in an attempt to cover my tracks, then head back to look for the original trolley with my shopping. Arriving at the scene of the

crime, I position myself on the other side of the aisle until the coast is clear.

"I just can't understand it" says this woman to her friend sounding completely mystified. "I am sure I left it here."

"Well it must be somewhere. Where did you go last?"

"Over there to get some sauce for tonight's spag-bol" she replies "but I'm sure I brought it over with me. I must be going mad" and at that they head off unknowingly towards all the evidence. As soon as they are gone I seize the opportunity, dash over to my old trolley and immediately go in the opposite direction at lightning speed. Oh dear. How messed up can someone's brain possibly get?

Recovering from my self-inflicted mini drama it's back to the usual hum-drum of shopping. "Don't eat that, high in this, low in that, rich in vitamins" I forgot how ridiculous some of the instructions on the packaging were. Even the vegetables are wrapped up complete with information on what to do with them, like cabbage for example:

"Remove packaging, place in boiling water" and "drain before serving" Really? I never realised. I guess if the instructions weren't there no doubt I'd pour the whole lot out on to the plate in one go, water, plastic and all; a disaster! No wonder my romantic candlelit dinners for two never go well. It was the cabbage draining technique all along!

In China of course there are no such warnings, merely statements on how amazing the product is no matter how disgusting. Generally they far more entertaining though,[2] like the one I saw for preserved vanilla olives in Shenzhen:

"We like the new taste. We need the quality and when we eat the best food here you will find what you want in cool fashion need the cool taste. You are the new man. We do not forget the special taste. Return pure flavour taste. You are the mineral feeling."

Supermarkets in the UK really are astonishing places though and as I push my new free flowing trolley gently along, it is like I have entered some food nirvana or something. It's comforting to know that where ever you are, there is always some huge outlet nearby to come to the rescue when you're in need of your luxury dessert. Do people realise how well off they are in terms of what goes down their neck in Blighty

---

[2] Chinese translations into English are legendary for being inaccurate and are often hilarious. People have created websites dedicated to what has now been termed as 'Chinglish'. If you find some good Chinglish it will leave you absolutely crying with laughter. When you're in China watch out for street signs, food packaging, your menu, you name it, it's everywhere!

I wonder? I certainly never did when I lived here and the stark comparison to a Chinese supermarket feels huge.

I know people say that these days they are too busy to spend time in the kitchen, but really let's be honest about it. Surely the word 'busy' should be replaced at least ninety percent of the time with the words 'can't be arsed'. I can't believe the number of ready meals that are on offer with posh sounding names, for example 'Sicilian chicken, carbonara and bacon with an arabiatta filling and a side dish of Moroccan cuscus' or if your bored with that tired old number then best stick to the 'beef chianti' right? The last straw has to be the sight of ready chopped vegetables in plastic packaging. Mercy!

The variety and sheer overwhelming luxury confined to one small area on the earth is a simply staggering phenomenon. Rounding the corner of the aisle, I encounter the cake section. This endless wall of comfort eating extravagance surely wins the pure gluttony award hands-down. Apple pies in a multitude of sizes and flavours, Jaffa cakes, Mr Kipling's, various apple crumbles with added extra anything, Victoria sponge cakes, flap jacks, shortcakes, Swiss rolls, jumbo Swiss rolls, McVities lemon, ginger or chocolate pound cake, (pure gut expanding indulgence), walnut loaf cake, sultana and cherry fruit cake, carrot cake, chocolate mini-rolls (phew, I'd forgotten all about those ultimate little temptations), iced ringed doughnuts and jumbo monster jam doughnuts 55p for a five pack and two packets for a quid, (so bad), cheesecake in sticky toffee or with a blackcurrant topping and black forest trifle; it was all there in one go. Holy smoke! No wonder people seem to have become bigger while I was away and that's no joke. It's not surprising when you see what is placed under the noses of every British citizen when they go for their weekly shop.

Amazingly about half of the food in supermarkets and over ninety percent of all fruit and veg is imported; after all you just have to have your kiwi fruits from Israel right? I did work on a fruit farm for a few years near Bath. The produce was really good quality and it was a great place to be every day. The owner had to sell the farm in the end though, as the local supermarkets would only buy French fruit. How totally crap is that hey!

A Taste of Paradise
Strange place this, the UK! Supermarkets aspire to help the poor helpless customer and their appetites with organic and vegetarian choices. Green packages tell us that this product is slightly healthier than another. People claim to worry over what they eat yet all the time but simultaneously eating the unhealthiest food on the planet.

A few days later I have my first chicken and chips in a year down at the chippy in Hucclecote near Gloucester. Big Andy drives me over there to visit the folks and it's the best one in the area. Mum and

Dad used to go down there all the time and Friday night was always 'chip night' in our household. As we pull up in the car I can smell those chips a mile off leaving my senses going into complete overdrive. I've never been so excited at being in a queue for anything in my life. Reaching the front, the girl behind the counter looks up with a smile, her face covered in spots; clearly a sacrifice made for the greater good.

"Leg of chicken and double chips. Two pickled onions in the same bag please" I fire off in my best fluent English; for some reason I've been rehearsing it in my mind over and over beforehand. At that she removes the leg from behind the glass I've been coveting since coming in; the big one between the battered sausages and the fish. The guy before me had also asked for a leg of chicken but he'd got the smaller one that had seen better days next to the pile of savaloys. I could almost see a look of disappointment in his face, but he was too polite to ask for the other one. The moment her tongs grasped that leg I knew the big one was mine.

As she serves me, the chicken almost disappears under the most enormous pile of chips before attempting to balance my pickled onions on the top.

"D'you want salt and vinegar?" she asks in a broad Gloucester accent.

"Just salt please" then she applies a coating thick enough to give anyone whiplash.

"That's three pound ten please" and that's another fiver I've instantly killed. Still, worth it though! The weight and heat of the oversized white paper package is an enjoyable feeling. Outside, Big Andy, Mhairi and I sit on the grass next to the funeral directors as the fat on the chips glistens against the setting sun. All this time dreaming about that moment and my guts just can't take it. Still, delicious is an understatement of the decade and anyway, a quick trip to the off-license[3] next door soon dispels any worries of gut rot.

I must say I was tempted to go for a Pukka Pie as it's always been enjoyable making a hole in the side of one and dunking in my chips. The best are of course the steak and kidney ones, though to be honest it's difficult trying to dispel the knowledge of the foul contents that lurks inside. I mean what steak is that we're talking about? Its zero steak and mostly kidney right? And what do kidneys do? Of course we all know that kidneys produce urine so it's a wonder that anyone actually eats them. One chef I worked with used to fry them up for his breakfast, yeeeech! What a stench and a half that was.

---

[3] Off Licenses are shops which specialize in all types of alcohol in the UK. Also referred to as 'the Offy' they also sell ciggies and snacks to go with a late night binge. They are everywhere in the UK.

In the UK people love these pies and their contents; mashed kidney in an aromatic sauce. I mean there's me in China, contorting at the sight of a length of duck's throat but not giving a Pukka Pie a second thought. I guess we're just good at covering up the grim truth of what it really is and where it came from. In a similar vain, we shouldn't forget the pork pie here. Though this is less popular now, it's still easy to enjoy the special delicate texture of cold aspic jelly on a hot summer's afternoon. Oooooo loovely!

Further Displacement

Back in Bristol, the next day I spend my time wandering about the old favourite haunts. The first port of call is and always will be the Falafel King stall next to the Watershed Arts Center. If you want to get as full as your stomach can possibly expand and on the cheap then this is the place to do it. It also has the best chilli sauce in town and is a super healthy meal. The trouble is, as wonderful as it all sounds, the sense of dislocation from the surrounding world is showing no signs of diminishing.

"That's two pound fifty please" says the woman handing me my falafel.

Unfortunately I'm miles away and don't hear a word she says. When she speaks it's like being underwater or something. Worse is to come when displaying a terrible habit I've unknowingly picked up in China. Chinese people have no equivalent of 'Pardon, Sorry what was that? Sorry I didn't quite catch that' or anything similar. Very occasionally someone may say 'duibuqui' which does mean 'sorry' or 'excuse me' but that's as far as it goes. Instead try this. Say 'Huuuu?' with a steeply inclined upward tone as a tonal substitute for 'What?' Now say it really loudly and take away the letter 'h' which softens it. This is the most common way for people convey 'What did you just say?' in China and it's how I instinctively answer the poor woman at Falafel King.

"Uuuuuu?" The instant look of complete disgust she gives me and my complete loss for words will stick with me forever. At that point I have three choices. One: to give her an explanation in full, Two: tell her that I've forgotten how to say 'Sorry, what was that?' and Three: to get away from there as fast as possible, leaving her with the impression that I am some arsehole with no manners.

"THAT'S TWO POUNDS FIFTY!" she storms.

I hear it that time and "Cheers" doesn't seem to matter as she snatches the money out of my hand. I choose to eat my Falafel elsewhere, my head completely zapped after that one minute interaction.

On from there I amble over to St Nick's Market, an amazing old place that's been around for hundreds of years. Inside are stalls that sell everything from local farm produce, art, to books and there are some great gift shops. The best place to be is the organic café in the centre and I absolutely love getting a brew in and watch the world go by from there. On my way out I see a woman who seems strangely familiar.

"Oh hiiiii, Andeeee" she beams excitedly. "How are you? Your back then?"

"I'm really sorry" I stammer, "but I can't remember who you are."

"It's Thelmaaaaa"

Oh my Lord. Thelma! I worked with Thelma for years in that place the boss did a runner on. Thelma is a really nice person and certainly someone you wouldn't forget. At this point my body decides it's going to have a complete panic attack and I totally forget everything that I would normally say.

"You went to China didn't you?"

"Yes" I reply bluntly.

"How was it?"

"Great" is all I can think of. "I went to Tibet!"

"Oh wow, that must have been amazing."

"Yes it was" and we stand there for a painful few seconds in silence without making eye contact.

"Well it was great seeing you again. Have to dash" she says looking fairly confused and that's it! Poor Thelma must have wondered what on earth had happened and to this day I hope that I'll bump into her again to explain my unusually uninterested and rude behaviour.

Wales: And just when you thought it couldn't get any quieter! Well, it's Sunday the 16th and I'm at my old mate Nige's place outside Presteigne. Nige has sorted out his van and it's an amazing space to get my head together. I love sleeping in vans and Nige's is a good one. Inside there is sheepskin everywhere and candles are used at night. No noise except the wind blowing through the corn fields, insects buzzing and the sound of dovecotes; the sound of pen to paper and the turning pages of this diary even seem pronounced against the stillness. This truly is a place to get rid of the travel-tiredness and culture shock in order to get into decision making mode again.

The view would be quite breathtaking if it wasn't for Old Radnor Hill. Two weeks ago this was a beautiful looking place with a traditional village at the bottom. The old church can be seen for miles. Then Tarmac turned up and in fourteen days reduced the whole hill into a crater, attractively called Gore Quarry. Dave the farmer next door is quite sure that they are paving the way for a disaster

"They don't know what they're doin'. They're openin' up a volcanic pug they are" he worried. "It could go off at any moment and then we'll all be f*cked."

It's amazing that something that has been there for thousands of years can be destroyed forever. So there I am chillin' out under the sun in the complete silence one afternoon and there's this siren that screeches out from the hillside some five miles away. Then boom, two huge explosions rip through the hill and the whole thing is engulfed in dust and smoke. As it clears the profile of the hill has dramatically changed as another piece of the landscape has gone forever[4].

One notable time in Wales, we all jumped in the car and visited this place called the Spaceguard Centre in nearby Knighton. What a total eye opener that turned out to be. Basically it's a tracking station with a giant telescope looking out for any giant asteroid or comet that's roughly on its way to destroy the earth. These are referred to as 'Near Earth Objects'. We were lucky enough to have the founder of the observatory there that day, a chap called Jay Tate. He told us that in the early days the government said that they would only fund the centre if all discoveries were withheld from the public. Since then it's been a privately run operation with all donations gladly accepted.

As the tour progressed Jay explained that we had one 'global killer' that missed us by the distance of the moon not so long back. In the great scheme of things that was an incredibly close shave.
    "There is a very real threat that something at least a kilometer across may impact the planet" said Jay.

Turns out that there could be up to a thousand of them floating around out there that are capable of 'an extinction level event' and we left feeling somewhat alarmed by the whole thing. Since then I've done some poking around into our lovely blue planets chances of holding it together as we know it and to be honest the odds don't look very good. If an asteroid doesn't get us, or the Yellowstone Park super-volcano doesn't blow, NASA has warned that there is a big chance of a solar flare knocking us for six sometime and if that doesn't do the trick the oil should be running out soon anyway, just to make sure.

Later, in Leominster that evening Nige treated me to one of the local delicacies it had to offer; a giant 'mixed kebab'; three pound fifty, very reasonable! Just the trick to forget the paranoia of a world catastrophe. A nice 'doner' can be one of the greasiest things in existence and this

---

[4] Old Radnor Hill has now gone.

one was no exception. It's said that an average doner contains over one thousand calories so this one must have been well up there in the fifteen hundred region. So there we are in Nige's car wolfing it back. They were so big that we couldn't eat them so wrapping mine back up I opened the car door and leant over to get out.

"Hey, where are you going?" asked Nige.

"Going to bin it mate. I just can't possibly eat it all."

"Oh no, don't bin it. Save it for tomorrow's breakfast. That's what I always do".

So there I am waking up looking for the Nurofen in the morning while Nige reopens the paper and starts eating his kebab all over again.

"Good value for money!" he declared heartily before sparking up the first ciggie of the day.

## A Few Other Handy Little Observations about the UK
## 3rd September 2006

The next stage of this little excursion led me from Wales back once again to my hometown of Gloucester. Just doing some painting and decorating with Nige in a school during the summer vacation but I forgot how much fun that can be even if it is a graft. Managing to blag somewhere to stay on someone's garage floor, I must admit I was beginning to realise that its hard work sleeping at other peoples' places all the time. In some ways this one was even harder than usual; the sleeping arrangement consisted of a single mattress surrounded by traffic cones. Maybe it was so no one could run me over when backing in with their car. To cap it all, the ceiling was so wafer thin, at night the grim discovery came that our mate Mark, who was crashing-out upstairs, not only snored loud enough to be heard in the Outer Hebrides, he also ground his teeth. I've never heard anyone grind their teeth before and it took me a long time to get used to this excruciating noise and get some shut-eye.

Another thing that became apparent when dossing-down at someone else's space was the continual reminder that I had nowhere to live or life of my own anymore. It was like looking at others' dramas through a window or something. Although the decorating job gave some kind of rest-bite from it, generally, it was difficult to escape the feeling that you were merely observing other people, all thoroughly immersed in life's details. In contrast, the most meaningful thing I would be doing was going out for a bit of a walk to buy a Ginster's giant sausage roll and a packet of dry-roasted.

Often the view through that window left me jealous and wondering of I'd ever reach a point of stability like that again. Sometimes though, the view wasn't a good one. The woman who had kindly let me stay on her garage floor was living an existence of pure stress. Having split-up with her partner who had thoroughly taken the piss, she had been left with debts up to her eye-balls and was forced to put her house on the market. It was a beautiful place with lovely gardens and had been in the family for generations. People in China have an impression that the UK is a rich country. I have to explain to them that though on the surface a lot of people may look well-off, it's actually only a veneer constructed by credit cards. Many people dread the unnecessary expenditure of Christmas and for some, January is the worst month of the year.

On a lighter note, something that stuck out like a sore thumb and really struck me at this time, was how everyone seems to specialise in drinking. Mark and Nige would drink Stella in the evenings, even freezing it first and drinking the leftovers with lime cordial, yeeech! For some strange reason people drink a lot of Stella in the UK and it has the effect of changing even the most passive of best buddies into the worst antisocial life form known to creation. You certainly don't want to end up in Accident and Emergency on either a Friday or Saturday night in Blighty I can tell you.

You name it and we will drink it. Indeed the drinking culture in the UK is unique to the world. We do it good, oh yeah! We have shops that sell nothing but booze and often the worst most liver-pickling and 'whitey' inducing drinks known to mankind[1].

And we have cider! Oh yes, we have cider! Cider is one of the great traditional drinks made from apples and has been available for a long time as strong as 7.5% in strength, loaded with chemicals and in economy three or four litre bottles (after all we need that extra bit that goes flat for the morning right?). The best or maybe the worst stuff you can lay your hands on is called Scrumpy which is normally local organic farm produce. When I lived in Bath I used to go over to a village called High Littleton on the motorbike to buy it. I could just-about fit six one gallon containers into my panniers and for three-fifty a pop, that's what I call a bargain. The strongest was called Kingston Black, something guaranteed to get you slurring within the hour. The problem with scrumpy is although it brings you closer to nature, when they make it, the apple seeds are left in it leaving tiny traces of cyanide. You don't get any old hangover with scrumpy. It's more like driving a six inch nail through your forehead.

On a similar note, our lager can be just as offensive with the word 'super' often being slapped on the end of a brand name to encourage the by now salivating alcoholic. A well known combination of these two is known as 'the snakebite' where people like to combine cider and lager together and produce a delightfully invigorating beverage, guaranteed to make you pass out with your head in the toilet by 9pm.

Without a shadow of a doubt the UK is home to the biggest load of alcoholics on the planet. At the very heart of our culture is drinking. If you look back in history, people weren't just getting drunk they were often getting completely ripped. Nowadays the term 'binge drinking'

---

[1] To 'pull a whitey' is British spoken English for the physical effects of mixing your drinks. This also happens when drinking alcohol and smoking strong weed.

has been created to describe anyone who A: drinks fast and hard, and B: drinks continually over a long period of time, so that accounts for at least half of the country right? Amazingly in 2005, the government created a new law so that pubs and bars can stay open all night, thus sanctioning this love of defilement. We will drink absolutely anything that's shoved under our noses and down it super quick.

In Europe a few glasses of red wine is seen as a healthy way to enjoy a meal and is great for the digestion. Across the Channel, their neighbours will happily down the whole bottle in less than ten minutes when they come back from the pub and then go hunting for that bottle of cheap supermarket brand sherry that no one else would drink. People even do 'booze runs' to France, filling vans up to the max saying that "it's cheaper this way" then drinking as much of it as possible as soon as they get through the door![2]

One bizarre thing I noticed was that smokers can no longer smoke in pubs. What an oddment that was. I noticed something was missing almost as soon as I went into my first pub. At first I couldn't quite put my finger on it. It had an empty feeling to it. Then I realised that even though it was pretty cold out, every smoker was forced to stand outside shivering their arses off in order to get their ciggie in like some leper.

Can't complain too much though; in China, people will spark one up just about anywhere and even as a smoker it can piss you off. Someone may leave a ciggie burning in the ash-tray right under your nose in the internet café. People will often completely ignore 'no-smoking' signs in restaurants and you can cause quite a scene if you ask them to put it out. I was waiting for an elevator in Shenzhen when this guy started smoking while leaning against one such sign, "jinzhi xi yan". I pointed to the sign and he laughed. As he entered the lift he continued smoking despite a second sign clearly visible inside.

Parental Quirks
Being back in Gloucester of course meant that I could at last spend at least a few days with Mum and Dad. Great being looked after especially being able to get off that garage floor and not having to listen to Mark's teeth all night. Quite incredible really; I mean I have no job, nowhere to live, no girlfriend, wearing the same clothes for months and now harbouring a deep feeling of lack of achievement, yet my parents seem to love me as much as anything. It also gives Mum an excuse to

---

[2] Since writing this, some local council have introduced 'SOS buses' in an effort to ease pressure on A&E from the huge number of piss-heads that need patching up. Run by volunteers during the weekends throughout the night, they are meant as a drop-in to for people up who are so pissed they have smashed themselves up or may have poisoned themselves.

go into full 'action stations' mode and run around doing as much stuff for me as she possibly can. Within seconds she's doing all my laundry, a bath is being run and dinner is on the go. Ah Mums hey!

Talk about opposites; while Dad is more content for the quiet life watching TV these days, Mum still rushes everywhere displaying all her eccentricities in fine style. After dinner we sit together and watch TV.

"That film 'Coat Hanger' is on tonight" she goes enthusiastically. Turns out she means 'Cliff Hanger' with Sylvester Stallone.

As master of the house, lately Dad has taken over use of the remote controller and if you want to change channels you have to run it by him first. He then bends right over, holding the controller up to his face before pressing the wrong button and going to the wrong channel or going over to the blank screen for playing DVD's. After a painful five minutes we get there just before the film is about to start.

For the show, Dad gets given one small can of Heineken. Recently he's not been allowed to drink anything stronger and I gloomily hope it's not the shape of things to come for me.

Instead Mum hands me a huge pitcher of Woodpecker Cider shandy[3] and whispers in my ear

"Andrew! Don't get drunk tonight will you".

"No chance of that" I think. Aside from the negligible amount of alcohol it's also a hard graft doing more than a pint of that stuff before it turns to warm syrup.

Funny how Mums still talk to you like you're a kid and it seems to rub my nose in the heightened sense of nothingness I am experiencing. She's also the only person who calls me Andrew.

Time to hit the hay and encounter another one of the household quirks. That bed has always been mega soft and I wonder why anyone makes something that is so completely uncomfortable. Not only that but Mum hasn't discovered duvets yet and still uses an unnecessarily large number of layered blankets firmly tucked in. With being sandwiched between a mattress like a marshmallow and sheets like plywood, this has to be one of the most fitful night's sleep you will get. Lying on my back, the bed clothes are so tight that it spreads my feet apart like a penguin and I react like Houdini trying to get out of a straightjacket throughout the whole night.

8am and Mum is already in the bedroom with a brew made with half a pint of full-fat milk to wake me up and I slowly emerge giving my back a chance to repair itself. Though it's too early for my stomach to take

---

[3] Shandy is a mixture of lager or cider and lemonade. Yeeeech!

breakfast, the kitchen is already in full swing. From the vantage point of the table, I watch Mum in action as she throws together her own unique version of cheese on toast. This consists of sliced white bread with a thick layer of extra mature cheddar followed by an ample helping of salt; certainly something to jolt you out of your slumber that's for sure.

After breakfast, Mum and I take a trip into town. While I was away, they got rid of Dad's oversized Saab and replaced it with a much smaller shiny blue Fiat. It's always been quite an experience with Mum when she's driving and for some reason she leans over the steering wheel in an effort to get as close to the windscreen as possible. At the same time we are doing less than the 30mph speed limit and within minutes we have a string of cars all following us itching to get past for the whole journey

Parking up behind the Co-op, it's the exact same route that we've always used as far back as my school days. Talk about a trip down memory lane. Out past Boots and up to the Cathedral to have a wander, we stop and buy two jumbo Cornish pasties from the bakery; well nice! A pasty is basically a baked savoury pastry with the edges crimped and filled with beef, potato though sometimes they may have onions or carrot. It is protected by law so no other country can copy it and is one of the UK's most traditional of foods[4]. Just mustard; sitting there on a bench with Mum eating giant pasties for lunch out of brown paper bags.

After doing our fair share of wandering we head back to the car park only to find that Mum's car key fob doesn't work.

"Andrew, I don't know what to do" she says with an immediate panic in her voice, "It's always worked before"

In an instant, there's Mum shouting over to the car park attendant, "Hello, helloooo. Can you help us please? I can't open my door".

At that the elderly guy with graying hair in his yellow day-glow coat comes over and has a go. "Don't know what's wrong with it. You had better call the break-down service. You can use my phone if you like."

---

[4] Since writing this the government tried to introduce 'the Pasty Tax' a story became known as 'Pastygate'. According to the Chancellor any food sold "above ambient air temperature" was to be subject to 20% tax. In an effort to calm people down and show that he was 'in touch' with the nation, the Prime Minister announced that he "buys a pasty every year when he's on holiday" with ensuing newspaper reports titled "David Cameron remembers his last pasty". Unfortunately the papers found out that the shop had closed down long before his alleged purchase. It seems he may have been telling porky pies instead. So what's new?

So there's Mum on the blower getting all in a panic. We are even joined by two other guys walking past who had heard Mum's worried voice from the pavement. As the four of us try to calm her down waiting for help to arrive, she suddenly spots that this is the wrong car and hers is some way to the left of us,

    "Oh my God. This isn't my car. That's mine over there!"
Phew, I guess they were identical though.

Onwards with the trip, this time moving west to the county of Somerset. Previously in Wales I managed to get a freebie into the Big Green Gathering but on one condition, to do a talk in the Green Talk Tent on China! This is a festival held on the Mendip Hills[5]. It promotes ecology, environmental issues and peace. People make friends and have big time fun. Highly recommended! The organiser phoned up and grilled me with some serious questions on a level that I found hard to handle. He said that I would be on stage with a mic and there could be up to one hundred people there, deciding that it would be called 'China, Rising Giant!' OH SHIT! At that moment I was completely filled with dread. Never thought I would be challenged on my return trip, help!

    Luckily only three people turned up for the talk. As it was the first one of the festival, everyone was annihilated the night before and there were empty beer cans everywhere. Phew all that dry retching in my tent at seven in the morning for nothing. Fantastic time though, and what better place could there be to spend your 40th birthday. Camping next to Alcoholics Anonymous; I don't think they were best pleased with the cart load of beer I failed noisily to sneak into my tent. Amongst other things, I stayed in a giant double bed with sixteen other people, two policemen with feathers stuck in their helmets pretended to arrest me for a joke and a giant white angel cycled past on a bicycle.

The festival scene in the UK has to be one of its most interesting phenomena. We pride ourselves on our freedom and this surely is freedom at its most expressive and creative. People who genuinely care for the world join from all across the country at these events. The biggest 'Greenfield' festival in the world is the Glastonbury Festival of Performing Arts. Fantastic to have such a thing going on in your own back yard. The Glastonbury line up has always been amazing. You name it, from T-Rex headlining the first ever one in 1970 to David Bowie, to New Order and to that most awesome of Saturday nights when the Prodigy set the place alight. Let's not forget Shakin' Stevens and Rolf Harris who also drew massive crowds.

---

[5] The BGG was shut down by the police at the last minute and more than 15,000 people had to be turned away creating pandemonium. Nice one guys! The festival is now called the Green Gathering having moved to Chepstow in Wales.

For me from 1995 to the year 2000 were the Glastonbury years where we had the most fun. In '95 the fence came down and people spilled in without paying. It was the festivals 25th anniversary and the atmosphere was awesome, rounded off with Page and Plant and an Egyptian Orchestra with a rendition of 'Kashmir' and 'In the Light' on the pyramid stage. '97 was the first 'Year of the Mud' a common pattern in Glastonbury history. Often it would rain so hard the place flooded then quickly turn into a quagmire. Not only that, but in one famous incident over at the dance tent, one of the trucks that cleans the crap out of the porta-loos sprayed its entire load across the floor rendering the area totally unusable.

The next year, my friends and I went armed with wellies and full waterproofs and our foresight paid off. It rained so hard that tables and chairs could be seen solidified at different angles in the ground. In some places it got so deep that tents disappeared. Much to our entertainment, a couple shagged in the slurry in front of us while we sat outside a beer tent. That year it was the World Cup and they laid-on a giant screen away from the site to watch England play Columbia. Quite surreal seeing Desmond Lynam's huge mug lit up against the pitch blackness. Though it arsed it down that night, thousands turned out for it with the red cross over white painted proudly on their faces and after winning the game our celebrations went into overdrive.

The next day our hangovers were so bad that my friend Barry was unable to move. To cap it all, the rain had stopped and the sun mercilessly opened up on us with a searing heat. In an effort to go and look for some pain killers I stumbled down the hill clutching my head trying not to throw up. After about five minutes though, a nearby stage started up with some terminally bad free-form jazz with a bass line plus accompanying trumpet that was so loud it seemed to penetrate the very fibre of my body. Shocked by this immediate bodily reaction I headed for the nearest toilet without a second thought.

Glastonbury toilets were always terrible and on a hot day you just didn't wanna know. By now my head was pulsating like an octopus as the vocalist put her finishing touches to the din with a wailing Cleo Laine like voice. Why anyone likes this kind of music is beyond me and I've always hated it with a passion. At that moment in that tiny stinking blue plastic furnace, unable to escape from the fierce grip of free-form jazz resonating through me and wretching myself inside out, I thought I'd surely gone to Hell for my sins.

The amazing thing about festivals is that no matter what state you get in, you always leave utterly transformed forever. I can't quite say what it is, but you feel fantastic for weeks afterwards. Years ago when I was a full time teacher, half of my Year 10 class wanted to go to Glastonbury.

It became a big issue in school with full staff meetings and letters going home to parents to deal with this serious matter. Irrespective of this, about eight of the class bunked off and went for it. One lad Danny Clark came into school with his rucksack before leaving complete with pots and pans. I remember watching him with total envy as he walked across the playing fields, pausing only to spark up a ciggie before jumping over the fence. On Monday, despite being in some major trouble, they were all back in class with huge uncontrollable smiles and some hilarious stories under their belts.

The last full week of the trip was spent down in Cornwall at my mate Duncan's place; at last a comfortable bed with a real duvet; total bliss-out. I forgot how utterly amazing the countryside is down there. Mind you, most of it is in the UK. Admittedly, the countryside isn't for everyone; my sister is a proud Londoner, has always lived there and finds the countryside utterly tedious (until we get a pint in that is). To me though, slowly walking down a Cornish foot path in the summer, insects buzzing, taking in the smell of the earth, plants and the pollen as the air becomes alive with the heat is truly energizing. Turquoise blue to aquamarine, turquoise green to cobalt, from ultramarine blue to violet and to purple in shimmering iridescence; these are the colours of the sea down in Cornwall. Warm feelings of sadness that the time in this place is short-lived, the ephemeral nature of our lives and what will happen next; these are all feelings you experience looking out from the cliffs at Zennor to the horizon. Best get down the pub as soon as possible then hey!

Back on the road and down to Brighton I am bowled over at how expensive the train ticket is. Maybe I'm just used to China travel prices now but ninety five quid for a train ticket? Serious! That's almost a thousand kuai and to cap it all the train was delayed! Some things just never change now do they! Notice how in the station the word 'late' is naturally replaced by the word 'delayed'. Of course you are far more likely to blow a gasket if your train is announced to be late for the third morning this week.

"Good morning. This is an announcement! The 7.45 from Brighton to London Victoria is late! We apologise for it being late and have no real idea when it will arrive or even where it has gone. Please stay calm and wait in that rancid little flea-pit of a waiting room with super-uncomfortable, cold, hemorrhoid inducing plastic seats and no heating for an hour, then pray the 8.45 is at least aimed in the right direction."

Of course there would be a riot every morning, regular as clockwork. Briefcases would become banned in train stations and classed as weapons unless carrying a license. Riot police would be on patrol on the platforms and passengers would have to carry 'Commuter IDs.

As a commuter in the UK you should set off at least an hour earlier before you would normally go or risk being late and even then that may not be enough. The most popular reason for train delays is because of 'leaves on the line' and efforts are being made to produce a 'leaf fall timetable'. Ahhh sweet blame hey! I am sure trains are kinda heavy but even so apparently leaves make the trains go slower. Now don't get me wrong, but until the age of about thirty five I had never heard one word of blame on leaves for the continual lateness of the British rail service. Maybe someone in the government had to come up with a 'blame list' sharpish and they thought that one was the best; "Hmm, stubborn cows with an attitude that can climb the fence wandering onto the line? Heavy head winds? Strange weather conditions producing optical illusions, spatial distortions and dancing lights confusing the driver?" Actually when you think about it, blaming something for a train being continually late is kinda difficult. Leaves indeed! Maybe it's a particular type of leaf that is the nemesis of train? Maybe the sycamore?

The most extreme example of lateness I have ever experienced was on a three hour trip to Wrexham. After changing at Birmingham, the train just stopped in the middle of nowhere and there it stayed for at least half an hour. Must have been a big pile of leaves I guess. Despite the nice view of some fields to take our minds off of things, it got harder and harder to breathe. Those narrow rectangular windows just above head height just wouldn't budge and all the ticket officer would do was just look vaguely irritated by my questioning when he finally showed up. We moved forwards, a bit. We moved backwards, a bit. Finally the driver coaxed the train into Crewe Alexandra where an announcement was made.

"Can all passengers please leave the train and proceed across the bridge to Platform 2. From the exit you will see a bus which has been provided for your connection to the next station. Thank you."

Off we happily went, across the walkway with all our bags, out of the station and onto the coach. After all the bags were squared away and we had found a seat, we waited in anticipation of some form of movement but after ten minutes an inspector boarded the vehicle

"We are very sorry, but can all passengers return to the train which appears to have been fixed."

With one giant harmonious groan, we all reluctantly picked ourselves up and backtracked to our original seats.

The train stopped again quite soon after leaving Crewe. Though we were clearly getting our money's worth, we were by now well over two hours late. Again, to say it was getting hot and stuffy in that carriage is a complete understatement. Like trying to take a beached whale back into the water the train went painfully forward until we finally reached a small station.

As the doors opened two paramedics suddenly ran on board and immediately went to work on this old boy sitting in front of me. I hadn't ever seen a defibrillator before then, but the penny really dropped when the machine fully charged and I heard the word "Clear!" As they zapped him it seemed like he was jolted right up out of the chair. They must have zapped him three times before giving up and wheeling him past everyone down the aisle on a stretcher. Poor guy, I'm sure it was the lack of air and the complete stress of being so late that was just too much for him, that and carting his bags about all over the place. What really blew my mind was that someone got on at the next station and sat in his seat right after. No one had the heart to tell them!

Other stuff, oddments and other unusual observations in no particular order:

Chinese food never tastes the same in the UK as it does in China. In Bristol, one Chinese restaurant displayed a big day glow sign that proudly announced it sold 'Beijing traditional spare ribs'. There is no such recipe in Beijing let alone 'traditional' and it pissed the woman behind the counter off something rotten when I asked her about it.

In the UK people like to buy ready cooked food from 'takeaways' and then return home with it in small foil containers to eat rather than sit in a restaurant. Of course it's cheaper, but from an outsider's perspective, it sure is bizarre behaviour.

People watch an awful lot of telly in the UK. This could be unconsciously linked to why people eat so many takeaways, such is the need to watch and eat at the same time.

People drive on the wrong side of the road. I always thought that everyone else in the world drives in the same way and that the French were the only ones to be different. It turns out that Japan and Hong Kong are the only other places in the world to drive on the left hand side.

People from the UK are world experts in using bad language. No matter how far they are up the IQ chain they are, or from which social background, in the right circumstances, a Brit can freely articulate the greatest rainbow like display of expletives in the world. It's ingrained in us. We suddenly become experts, with perfect intonation, balance and dynamic tensions, working harmoniously like the embodiment of nature itself. Where do we learn this hidden talent from I wonder? No matter where I've been so far no one else has been able to copy it or get near it.

You know Beijing has six ring roads? Of course there are three times as many people, but there's London with the poor old M25! Also if your unlucky enough to be on the M1 or M6 in the morning going to work good luck mate. Like two huge clogged arteries, the enormous tail backs in the UK are something that would make a great photo in the National Geographic. It's easy to come across newspaper articles condemning China for its pollution, especially the number of cars in its big cities like Beijing. Actually we are lucky the way things have panned out around the world. Most Chinese families only own one car and hundreds of millions use bicycles. In the UK a family may have two cars and rarely cycle anywhere. If we traded populations and you had 1.3 billion Brits and 60 million Chinese people it would be an environmental disaster. Lord knows what would happen if the same figures were swapped with America!

With roads being as static as the size of a giro cheque[6], it's no wonder people go crazy during rush hour; a strange term to be used under these circumstances really. Road rage is another special phenomenon in the UK that you rarely see in Asia even though people there weave in and out all over the place and never indicate. It's easy to see people snarling and gnashing their teeth at each other in the mornings as traffic gets slower and grinds to a halt. That's a poor excuse though, we do it anyway! Sometimes you can even see people chasing each other at high speed. For sure we aspire to be polite and gentile creatures. We say "cheers" and "thanks" at least three times after we have bought something, but if someone doesn't wave to say thank you when you let them pass first in a narrow street though, they instantly become a f*ckin arsehole.

It's easy to encounter road rage in England, especially down south. During my last few days before leaving, I misjudged a red van that was going faster than I thought as I crossed the road. It had to slow right down in front of me and you could see the driver calling me a "f*cking wanker" at the top of his voice. He revved his engine then aggressively sped off, throwing hand gestures behind him as he went. Continuing on my way, I went down an alley-way and onto the next street only to see the van turning the corner and coming down towards me. At that moment a set of traffic lights went from amber to red. Oh the joy! We all have our finest moments in life and this was clearly one of them.

---

[6] British English for 'welfare cheque'. Also called 'Income Support'

As the driver stopped at the lights I bent over and gave a gentle tap on the side of his window

"Open the window then mate. What did you just say to me?" Incredibly, he just sat there staring forward in a bid to totally ignore me with a visible look of discomfort on his face. No matter how loud I got and how heavily I rapped on his window, he just would not get out and as the lights changed he sped off double time. Gutless piece of sh*it!

Upon reaching Brighton, the final port of call, I realised how utterly super tired I was. It was like being in some kind of haze or something. After so much travelling, normally you would just go home, eat and chill-out for a few days before going back to work right? No chance of that here! The first place I stayed at was with one of my best mates, Dave, who let me stay in his daughter's room as she was away for the weekend. Weeks ago, I'd started to wonder about the possibility that each place I stayed in may have some cosmic message for me reflecting a part of my life. With kids' brightly coloured stuff littering the room, mobiles and Mickey Mouse pictures, if there really was someone looking down on me from above, they were clearly laughing their arses off by now.

The last person I caught up with was one of my oldest mates from school, Hanna, who came to see me off. Hanna is an established singer-song writer who has been recording and performing in Brighton for years and it was amazing to see her. Of course it's always fantastic catching up with old friends. Truth-be-told though, after seeing everyone with their lives in full-swing, settled and involved, by this time all I could think about was getting back on the plane and continuing with the quest to get my life back; that and still coaxing my trousers into holding together for yet another month, With an overpowering need to sort it out, the UK was the kick up the arse that was needed to get serious about getting my shit together.

Right! Time to hit the road again, though this time with sleeves rolled up. Worry keeps creeping in as I board the plane though. This is undoubtedly about having absolutely no real plan about anything. Before, at least I had a rough direction but simply having a plane ticket, no cash and a few vague ideas does anything but steady your nerves. At the moment there are two options. The first is to head back and get my head down in Shenzhen.

Gary did an amazing job of hooking me right into the place and there is a realistic chance of making a go of it there and I can't wait to get back. The second came in the form of a bomb shell e-mail from my friend Briony in South Korea. It's an almost irresistible temptation that's hard to put down. A teaching job where you can save a grand a month, the boss gives you a car, pays for your apartment and your computer plus there is no contract sure does sound like a sweet deal.

Mixed in with all this, there is also a sense of relief; to be back on the road again proper into new and unexplored territory, like some fix of a drug needed to feel normal and returning meaning back to life. Guess that's freedom for you!

## Decisions: 1st October 2006

Heathrow was a nightmare! Not as bad as I thought, but over two hundred people trying to get through the baggage check was no joke. There were some people going over the barriers in a mad panic at their delay who jumped the queue. My toothpaste, lighters and emergency Chinese Snickers bars were taken off me. They also check your shoes. What a crap job that must be, doing that all day. Think about how many thousands of minging shoes someone has to check, yeeech! Maybe after all this time though Security has secretly gotten into it;

"Hey Bob, check out the athlete's foot on this one! I think we will have to confiscate these and do a more thorough search in the office with the blinds down."

An endless check-in with everyone streamlining their bags at the last minute. Delayed flights and planes queuing up down the runway, crazy. No food was allowed on board so it was a pure diet of plane food, yum!

After arriving, next was a four-hour blur of a journey across Hong Kong. I refused to get the ridiculously overpriced 'Airport Express' train, instead doing the bus which just missed a full-on pile up in the tunnel by about half an hour. Three coaches, a lorry and a load of cars were in the accident, filmed by the news live just minutes after it happened. Anyway, joy of joys; going back through Chinese customs again. And there it is. That smell of China as soon as you walk over that yellow line, weird! Hooray!

My friend Kami Lee had invited me to his neck of the woods and said he would send someone to pick me up. He couldn't make it though, so I took a taxi which, for some unknown reason stopped after fifteen minutes, the driver unloaded all my stuff into an unmarked car and then that was it. I mean the car just kept going on and on for well over an hour into the night right out of Shenzhen. To be honest, I was too gone to care and just succumbed to that who gives a monkeys feeling.

I had no idea where I was. Apparently it was the Bao An District in Long Hua Town, a suburb in the east of Shenzhen. Kami got me into a hotel which had a terrific view of the vicinity; a huge industrial area where the sound of factories could be heard twenty four hours a day; a sprawl and a half that went on for miles and miles. As the only Westerner in a city of millions, it was easy to be filled with dread and amazement at the same time. This is what happens when you travel with absolutely no idea about what you're doing. It was also seriously hot, really muggy and the atmosphere like walking through treacle

Kami took me out for a few drinks. He invited some friends and then more friends "Gambei!" This is what you say when you raise your glass and it's down in one. Save me please! These guys made it their mission to get the Westerner as annihilated on Tsingtao as possible. Jet lagged to ribbons, the last thing my stomach digested twelve hours previously was half a warm omelette on the plane, very tasty. After a serious and lengthy session, it was with great relief when they decided to call it a night and we parted company well into the early hours.

The next day I woke up at 3.00pm. Dinner was just awful. It smelt like bile so I ate a little bit and went out with Kami into the night. He was totally freaked when I walked straight into a gambling house down one of the narrow back streets by mistake. From then on he banned me from going out with my wallet in my pocket unescorted. Kami was done over by five guys last Friday and they nicked 5000 kuai off of him. I mean this had to be definitely one the hardest places so far.

There was stinking rubbish dumped everywhere. It seemed to overflow from every side street or spew out across the pavement. This was the real deal here it really was. I mean shit, where was I? Downstairs people collected rubbish for a living. There was a small freshwater distribution point round the corner. At night the whole place became an awesome warren of darkened buildings that you could easily get lost in. Toxic fumes billowed out from vents of sweat shops which filled the area. People looked up and cast a hardened stare as we walked by and I was glad to have my escort at my side.

On the flip side, Kami and his friends were absolutely the total dog's dinner[1]. They insisted on paying for absolutely everything. I mean everything; the taxi fare that cost over 100 kuai; the hotel; the food; even when you were buying something from the shop. Having a meal with these guys was really something. They spat and cleared their noses out on the floor, they wouldn't let you leave until all the beer had been polished off, raising their glasses to gambei relentlessly. They chain-smoked and loved trying to make roll-ups out of my Golden Virginia. They would do just about anything for you! My lungs took an instant dislike to the place. It's not surprising when looking out and seeing what was being pumped into the atmosphere. An ex-student and good friend Willy Wong from Hong Kong came to visit. Really great to see him again! He was stunned at where I'd been living. His first question was "Why are you here?"

---

[1] Informal British English for something that is very good.

Friday something: Finally I managed to get in contact with Gary and his missus in central Shenzhen. Phew, sense of relief or what! Turned out to be a major effort getting away from Bao An and a real test of patience though. Talk about wearing! Kami had sorted out a lift into Shenzhen, so I waited and waited but nothing happened. In the end it turned out that the driver decided he had other things to do but neglected to tell anyone about this. By this time it had been five hours since checking out of the hotel room and it was all becoming hard work. Kami then, on the busiest day of the month, managed to beg his boss to give him the rest of the afternoon off, catching the bus to the hotel and went off to find a taxi. About an hour later he showed up with a van.

The lifts in the hotel were not working so another hour was spent searching for a porter to carry the bags down the stairs, aaaaaagh! Kami insisted that I should not carry my own bags and to be honest, my energy levels by this time were so low, I was more than happy to let someone else do it. I mean what was it about that place? It felt like I was doomed to stay forever. It took a total of seven and a half hours to get going. In the end we got to Shenzhen. Kami drove all the way with me there and back, such hospitality I won't forget!

What a contrast! Arriving on Gary's birthday, from being in such a rundown area, he took us to one of the most upmarket restaurants in Shenzhen. We ate posh food by the bucket load on huge plates. The table was next to a small stage with live music; an elegant woman in a long light pink dress singing sleepy downtown jazz songs to the piano. After, we went next door, getting a place next to a stage that had Chinese pop, rock and rap bands playing; some experience that was. No power chords though! The next day we had chicken and chips while watching the Grand Prix down this Irish Bar that sells Guinness. Shenzhen's so awesome that it just has everything in large amounts. There is even a ship that's been brought inland some 200 meters and turned into a super high class restaurant. Why they just didn't leave it in the water I seriously don't know!

Shenzhen is not bad at all as Chinese cities go. There is a big ex-pat community and life is good. It has everything you would ever want and it's fully understandable of Gary's disbelief at my decision to go to South Korea. For a start it means binning any experience and understanding I have about China including those small inroads into the lingo. At least I've been to Shenzhen a couple of times and experience counts for absolutely everything. The trouble is after such a long time on the road, when you're tired, burned out and it's hard to think.

Tempted by great money and being able to save for another trip is what it's about and that's all there is to it. The cash flow or rather lack of it is now on urgent level with the bank account falling way below zero. Having started using the credit card to get around, the bold promise of South Korea has been an irresistible temptation.

Still, it feels like a really strange move to be making though, like something's not quite right!

South Korea.............hmmmmmm!

# 11

# South Korea
# Staring at the Calendar

Those first few days in South Korea will stick with me forever. It wasn't just culture shock all over again and that somehow I would have to summon up the energy to make yet another fresh start (I was really burnt out from being continually on the road for months), it was the realisation that I had chosen the blandest place to live you could possibly imagine. There isn't one place in the UK that you could say would be any blander; now that's really saying something. I mean even Coventry bus station on a Sunday afternoon has got more character.

There was one predominant feeling myself and many of my friends had in South Korea. If it was ever brought up in discussion although we agreed something wasn't right, we couldn't quite put our finger on what it was. It was like a sick feeling or something unharmonious lurking just under the surface. At the end of the day it can only be described it as continual emptiness.

The detail of South Korea is a vivid memory which serves to remind me to enjoy every second of what I'm doing now. We were at a party when one of our coolest friends broke down in tears. Another friend said they cried in bed in the mornings. There were certain places on various routes to work which seemed so horribly drab that they surely must have been close to some portal that led to directly to hell.

I stared at my calendar a lot. I have never stared at a calendar like that before, counting the days down and envious beyond description when anyone was leaving. To think, they had made it and they were out of there. Each day seemed like an eternity. I quickly became an insomniac and discovered that Korean sleeping tablets are amazing. They are so strong that I still carry them on big trips as painkillers and have used them as such for several emergencies. I discovered they took that empty feeling away and became easily addicted to them.

I found myself smoking like crazy. I would have three in bed in the morning just to put off getting up for as long as possible. After breakfast I would smoke another couple before going out. I stank of ciggies and my mouth was like a walking ash tray. It killed my appetite and as I disliked the food intensely anyway, my energy levels were always low. After a month of this the only possible course of self-preservation and survival of living in South Korea was to quit smoking completely.

I had one failed attempt ending up with chain smoking in bed, spilling a full ash tray all over the bedclothes at 3am. That was the last straw! I haven't smoked since. At least I got something positive out of living there.

Although I only had a spoken contract with my boss (and so worked completely illegally), a contract is a contract all the same. In order to do the honourable thing, stick it out and keep from going quickly insane, I pulled out the map of China to look for a solution. Realising that Beijing was in close proximity to South Korea, in a second it became my new target and obsession, leading to three visits there while I was away. In the end, my time in the land of the bland turned out to be some strange and bizarre patchwork of confusion. Whist living in a wholly disagreeable culture, hanging with some great Western friends and dreaming of the next escape was what life became about.

Of course every place has its good points and there were some people who really liked it. A lot of the Westerners were college graduates who were paying off their student loans from lucrative wages as English teachers having never been abroad before. Maybe if a place is your first country to experience away from home, then that's the one you fall in love with and remember for the rest of your life, who knows. If you've already been on the road though, having experienced a richness in different cultures and had adventures, living in South Korea is more like pulling a sicky on a grey Monday and watching daytime TV all day.

# Continual Study Land: 13<sup>th</sup> October 2006

Anyong Haseyo[1], (as they say!)

Thursday August 31st: What a mad, mad trip life is. I mean it must have been only about a week and a half ago since leaving England. Found that you can just get a ferry from Shenzhen to Hong Kong airport and avoid the four hour hassle of going via the border at Lo Wu, cool as you like! I mean a forty minute journey across Shenzhen Bay and you're there; what a total bliss out way to travel.

Ever get the feeling that you're doing the wrong thing though? At the check-in with half an hour to go they said flatly that you can't go into South Korea with a one way ticket. Luckily Gary and his missus had come along, who immediately went to work on sorting things out. Within two hours I was back in business and it was really offski this time. Still, I was left a nervous wreck after the experience, really thinking that leaving China was a bad move. China! Oh no, what am I doing? The wait for the plane was great though. Sitting there eating noodle soup in Hong Kong airport. Watching the planes was yet another great buzz, like this is still an adventure and its all still happening.

Got into Incheon National Airport well late. Briony from Devon, who arranged the job came and picked me up in one of the company cars. The first night in South Korea! Unfortunately, the boss, let's call him Mr A, was away but at least I got to speak to him on Bri's phone. I call him Mr A as after a month or so, his teaching agency turned out to be run wholly illegally with many top officials turning a blind eye to his operation. Best keep his identity a secret I rekon.
        "I am not here" were his very first and somewhat strange words. "In a few days I'll return and then we can have a meeting. You can stay in a hotel until then."
        Great! Back to waiting and being as patient as possible. With no accommodation, it came down to the usual routine of trying to find a cheap guesthouse to doss down in. Hmm, easier said than done here. At night, the neighbourhood was a mass of flashing neon lights filling every conceivable space in a completely new language; nothing but symbols that look like they come from another planet.

---

[1] 'Hello' in Korean. Also 'Kamsa Hamnida' is 'thanks' and 'Makju hana juseyo' means 'I'll have one beer please.'

Unfortunately and unbeknown to me, the only hotels in the area were called 'Love Motels'. As I checked in with Briony's help, the staff were all sniggering at us. They must have thought we were going for a quick portion or something! The whole place turned into a warren of small and dimly illuminated corridors and my room geared towards one thing and one thing only and that's shagging! Big hearts were all over the walls and boxes of cleanex and spare condoms were left in handy places. It did have a TV but when surfing the channels, the only thing you could find was porn!

The next day was a complete reality check. Waking up in the love motel with really bad guts, totally dehydrated and in a completely alien environment, I made myself get up and go and get something to eat. Outside I was confronted by a mass of grey, samey and characterless buildings. In the restaurant that Briony had recommended, I was unable to communicate with the staff in any way, not having a clue what to order. All I knew was that despite everything, I had to eat. So, pointing to various Korean food in my little phrase book and finally managing to find something that they had, I sat back wondering what was going to be served up. A large black bowl of ice, some cold green noodles and vegetables in it plus some kind of weird vaguely unpleasant smelling sauce was deposited at the table. The chopsticks are hard to use here. They are much longer than Chinese ones and made of metal. It's kinda like using knitting needles as embarrassingly the food keeps slipping off of them all the time. It was a dreadful meal, just dreadful but I couldn't just leave it. At least I had a go.

Returning to the love motel I could feel myself sinking into some sort of immediate depression. Stuck in that place for how long? What is there to do here? Everything looks the same. What do I know? Bloody nothing that's what! Friday night was a bad night. With couples coming in and out for a quick one, the staff couldn't figure out what I was doing there. I mean 35,000 won is what you pay for one hour per room, yet there I was with bags unpacked just living in there. In the end the manager came up and demanded more money. Not a good vibe to add to the whole situation.

On Saturday I found Briony and explained the need to get the hell out of there sharpish, so she very kindly let me crash on her sofa. Still, someone's space is there space and by Sunday it really felt like I should be somewhere else. Walking around the area desperately trying to find a park or something with something green in it, in the end I found a bench and just sat there trying to come to terms with everything. I mean just high-rise after high-rise, soulless, nothing, a terrible empty feeling. What the hell am I doing in this place? Truly awful!

Once again I spoke to Mr A on the phone. "You can stay in the office until we find you an apartment. There's a bed in it and you can do your lesson planning in the morning" he joked. Oh, very funny! Having no choice I reluctantly moved in, a relief of some sorts. At least this gave me some headspace and a view of the place from the 11th floor, but still the most major unshakable feeling was that 'what the hell am I doing here?' vibe.

Monday 4th: There's a big hill they call Gyeyang 'Mountain' nearby. It's really the only thing worth looking at and is about 1000m above sea level. That was it! Head for the hills! It was such a boost to find the way up, like some salvation in the only bit of countryside around here. Time to reflect on all of this! Too many thoughts, doubt and worry. On the way up there were numerous bunkers, a reminder that this place was at war and of the continual state of tension between countries. From top of the hill you could see North Korea, hmmm, so near to this new home. Maybe not so good! The immediate view was of yet another sprawling mass of concrete with planes lifting off from the airport in the distance.

As I sat there this woman beckoned for me to come over and ended up teaching me my first Korean. Shit this language is difficult. I mean 'I don't understand' is 'anio- moodaradurossoyo'. It all sounds like everyone is talking backwards. What a nice lady though, Kim Chee Xue. We were then joined by two pastors Lee Yi Kwon and Lee Sang Jin who led me back down the other side of the hill and bought me dinner, cool hey. Definitely put a smile back on my face!

The next day I wanted a lie-in (as usual) but it's hard staying in bed when there are people you don't know doing lesson planning round you and using the photocopier! Still, wondering what on earth to do with the day, I found the metro line, worked out the route and went to Seoul (as you do). Chuffed is an understatement. By 2pm I was in the capital of South Korea, cool as you like. There are so many places to visit, with great shopping and market areas and it's even got its own national park. It's truly an amazing place.

Still in limbo though! It's just hard establishing yourself and starting from scratch over and over again, living in the office with nothing much to do. Friday night was awesome. Wild Bills (also called Number 10) is the bar that all the teachers go to, as it's literally over the road. I've never seen so many Canadians and Yanks in one place. There are only three English people here aside from me; Briony; Lara from Leeds who loves thrash metal and Janna from Bristol. I can safely say that I will have an American accent by the time I leave here.

15th September: Well at last I met Mr A and we sat and discussed things over a coffee in the morning.

"At the moment there is no work but don't worry, you can stay in the office until then. We should have an apartment for you in a week or so, maybe next Monday. You can be on holiday until then" he smiled.

"Next Monday." I mean, really! Who wants to live in the office for a week? In another down moment, that night I had my mate Flora in China on the phone. Flora works in a travel agents in Shenzhen and she immediately went to task sorting out a plane ticket. At this point, with bags packed and the airport just an hour away, doing a runner was looking highly likely.

Needless to say that never occurred, deciding instead to stick it out and spend my time exploring and getting to know the place. On one occasion, noticing a tiny hint of tradition, there were some rooftops that were kinda curved upwards oriental style amidst the grey sprawl. Guess most of this area got completely flattened in the war so you can't be critical.

Well a week on and Mr A shows up to say that there is no work for another three weeks until the frigging 9th of October after the Autumn Festival known as Chuseok.

"Once Chuseok is over then you will have some classes" he promised in his by now familiar tone.

This took the form of sounding vaguely irritated every time we met or spoke on the phone and over the months it really started to grind. I must admit that I could never quite fathom out Mr A. It always felt that he was trying to project a feeling that our interactions were just some great inconvenience to him, that or I'd made some kind of royal mistake. Layered on top of this, he looked continually red eyed and I was sure he'd had a good smoke before he left his place every morning.

After hearing the words "three weeks" I ended up having another fitful night with the bags packed once again, thinking about an immediate 3.00am departure to the airport. At least he'd sorted a flat out for me. It's kinda like living in a squat as there's no furniture, but it's pretty quiet so it's immediately better than any place in China. Oh, having said that, there's only a bleedin' tannoy system in it; at times you can be woken up to some guy's bland voice whittering away that goes on and on and on about God knows what. I think I'm gonna smash it up with a hammer. It's all slow going at the moment and really about summoning maximum staying power.

Still, mad things keep happening. The Westerners as per usual have their groups that they all hang out with and that's fine by me! In that case I'm hanging with three Brits, four Canadians, four Americans, one Aussie and an Irish guy. They're the coolest of cool! If there's nothing to do, then people hang just outside at the Ministop, a 24hr convenience store which has four white plastic tables outside, umbrellas and white plastic chairs. One night we were sitting there when we got chatting to this guy, Johnny from Montenegro. He's a striker playing for FC Incheon, a really good bloke who lives in the opposite apartment block. So he invited us all to see his team playing Seoul FC on the following Saturday.

Well I didn't think much about it really. I just assumed it would be in a little pitch in a park somewhere, kinda like lower division stuff. Turns out that it was in the Munhak World Cup Stadium, his team's home ground. How unexpected was that hey? Wow! A full on professional derby with the Incheon supporters going nuts, waving huge blue banners and lighting these huge flares. Incheon scored in the first thirty seconds and there was Johnny doing his stuff. Although there were no more goals to be had it was a great game and when we got back he sorted out a table in the Galbi restaurant for us all (a traditional Korean barbeque). Too much hey! By the way! Johnny is not just a great bloke but he's hilarious. He can't stop winning things in competitions (as if he needs them). The last thing he won was a bloody washing machine![2]

The Westerners have their own space so it's easy to meet new people here and watch all of it going on. The Koreans behave so differently from the Chinese; they don't stare at all, maybe the occasional glance but generally you feel like your being blanked. If you do engage you will always be greeted with a pronounced bow and an "anyong haseyo", so the interaction can change instantly. I met this Korean couple who had lived in Blackpool for five years. They said that the Koreans are a shy people. Either way, I'm still yet to find out about what makes them really tick. I was talking to my hiking mate Kathryn from New Zealand. She's been here for ages.

"I know what you mean about this place" she agreed. "Why don't you try seeing them as the Italians of Asia? That's the way I look at things" she suggested, putting all this head-scratching about the South Koreans into a different light.

---

[2] Johnny AKA Dženan Radončić was a founder member of Incheon FC in 2004. He left the club in 2009 for Seongnam Ilhwa Chunma and won the Asia Champions League with them in 2010. He now plays with the Suwon Samsung Bluewings.

Wow! Revelation! I mean not only do these people spend ages on their appearance with suits, high heels and flash cars everywhere, they are also the most highly-strung people in existence. The fear of failure is enormous and cannot be at all understated. This is the most in-your-face thing you will notice here. If someone thinks that there is even the slightest chance of failure, they won't do it unless they really have to.

The pressure of success in South Korean Schools: Full-on this! At the moment most sixteen year olds are revising and taking their CSAT tests (College Scholastic Ability Tests). These kids have been prepping for their tests for nearly their whole lives. I mean kids in South Korea rarely spend any time doing anything else apart from studying. In their spare time parents will have arranged extra classes for them after school and at the weekends. Every parent's dream is for their kids to get into one of the top universities. Getting into one of the best colleges is felt to be one of the greatest achievements in anyone's life.

The stress that get placed on these kids shoulders is absolutely enormous. I'm teaching kids who are doing their CSATs now and they are literally falling asleep at the desk, bleary-eyed. The worry some of them go through if they can't answer correctly in English seems to tear them to ribbons, just crazy! It is a national obsession here for parents to see their kids get a near perfect grade. When the tests are taking place the military stop test- firing and motorists are not allowed to honk their horns. There is a level of intensity in the air, even people on demos and protests agree to put it all off for another day. On the day of the CSATs parents may visit temples or churches and pray for their kids to be successful.

The demands on them have become so bad that in the past few years the suicide rate has been on a rapid increase. Like last year one father torched himself, his daughter and his wife outside the school because he was dishonored through bad grades. Statistics vary on how bad it's getting but generally they are similar. In one report it says that 462 kids killed themselves in the past five years leading up to or taking the tests. Another says that at least 50% of them seriously contemplate it.

Let's not forget the long term psychological problems it also causes. I mean these kids dedicate their whole lives to doing well in these exams and afterwards they find only a great empty space and sense of nothing, phew! Just think what these kids miss out on; a whole childhood that's what! Making dens, wearing wellington boots and catching eels and frogs in the stream under the M5, cherry knocking, garden creeping, collecting bird's eggs and playing in the old air raid shelter up on Nut Hill; I couldn't imagine what growing up would have been like with no fun. I mean its Chuseok now and what do you think these kids are doing? Their parents have arranged their whole holiday for extra study. Very nice!

Bad Play: There is a teacher's day here where it's traditional for families to give their kid's teachers gifts of appreciation. Now it's turned into a form of bribery with some cash 'gifts' being totally OTT. Cheating in exams is full-on now. Honour and all that stuff is out of the window these days. There are security checks in schools including the use of metal detectors now. If anyone is caught cheating they have to retake their tests the following year and do forty hours character training.

The job finally kicked into gear. Phew, it took long enough. Without a shadow of doubt this is the most unusual job on the CV. I feel like some scum bag that's merely taking advantage of these kids' misfortunes. I drive from academy to academy, from apartment to apartment, teaching them in their spare time when they should be out learning to rollerblade or something. I teach really young kids over and over, so they practice English all of the time. On the other hand it's great driving around and it's better than teaching at just one school. You also get to meet the parents who only want the best for their kids and family. Teaching thirteen hours a week in peoples' homes is a truly wonderful experience, getting to see how the South Koreans live and how complex these guys are. All of the students lead the same lives, like Lina and Cindy. They study thirteen subjects and take another two as extras in their 'spare time'. They do three extra classes after school at home and study all weekend which includes accounting, aaaaaaaaaaaaagh!

One afternoon I stumbled across a teachers' demo, just outside the government buildings in Seoul. The police were there in mass, looking hardcore, armed with kendo sticks, black riot uniforms and gold rectangular shields just waiting for the word go. On the other side of the road, the protesters did choreographed disco dancing for the whole day wearing red; all very peaceful and loving. The message is simply that there aren't enough teachers on the payroll. There are lots of jobless teachers with all the qualifications but no one will employ them. Classrooms are terribly overcrowded and employed teachers are under enormous pressure. I guess it's just another reason why the likes of me get a job, so the parents can ensure their kids will get those top marks!

It's hard to put your finger on it but this is just one of the oddest places I've ever been to. I mean there is an undercurrent here of...well I just don't know. Firstly, the Korean people care about their appearance way too much. Guy or girl, they are the most image conscious people you will ever come across. There are mirrors everywhere. You'll see people frequently stopping to check that a hair is not out of place. Mr A keeps a big reel of that shiny brown tape in his glove box. Before we knock on anyone's door, he gives himself a good 5-10 minute going over with the tape in order to remove ANY fluff off his clothes. He even does his crotch with the stuff! Women paint their faces white, wear red lipstick big time and they spend a lot of time on their eyes. You should go hiking here. Not only do people really dress up for the part but the make-up the women wear to get to the top of a hill is astonishing. Plastic surgery is well in! There are places to go under the knife everywhere. It's really big to have an eyelid job; women are obsessed with making their eyes rounder. And check this out. The biggest kind of plastic surgery here is to buy your daughter hymen reconstruction...sheeeeeet!

At the same time there is an underlying lunacy that goes on here in the evenings around tower block central. Koreans like to drink! Boy do they like to drink. On the street at night, everyone sits outside getting annihilated. You see mad Korean guys in suits fighting, stumbling and pissing everywhere. Outside the flat yesterday, a huge pool of blood came from the lift with finger marks raked through it. The blood continued inside the lift and down onto the floor of level one.

The apartment is in one of four blocks tightly bunched together on level 6: flat 618! It's above a brothel and quite often you'll be in the lift along with a couple of minging hookers plastered with make-up. On the bottom level of the complex is a 'sexy bar.' They are everywhere here, I mean everywhere! There are also hundreds of massage parlours only recognisable by these twirly signs outside. Haircut and hand job kinda thing! To balance this out, the church is also really big; at night a similarly massive number of red or blue neon crosses are lit high up above every night. Maybe people think they can be saved after all their bad behaviour! Extra-marital relationships are common here.

Other stuff, oddments and other unusual observations in no particular order:

Firstly, I cannot stand South Korean food. It's horrible! There is nothing that can do about this. Most of it is pickled and there's a lot of seafood here. Most of the time your table will have many small side dishes of pickled and spicy vegetables which you kind of pick at. The most popular food here is the national dish called Kimchi; a pickled cabbage in a red spicy sauce served cold. 'Galbi' is ok though; BBQ beef and rice. Most people think it's just the case of a Brit moaning that "it's not like at home", but I always leave the restaurant hungry and miss Chinese food big time. The other day at the footie we had this stuff called 'gimbap', yeeech! It's like a sausage of rice, with an outer shell of seaweed and a stuffing of something from hell that makes your guts instantly turn inside out. Oh well it was gimbap or that two foot dried squid they all go for..... and at the footie! I suppose it's their equivalent of a meat pie. There are piles of dried squid everywhere and they love the stuff. Squid, squid and more squid! Oh and at the top of a mountain all the outdoor people love to down whole cucumbers. Not a bad idea that actually!

Recycling is compulsory. If you get caught mixing up your rubbish you can get fined big time. You have to separate your stuff all the time and put the unusable garbage in special bags you can buy downstairs. Also, the amount of discarded furniture you can find is really something.

There's a florists downstairs that also has a meat section! Or is it a butcher's with a huge selection of flowers?

There is only one channel in English on TV. It's an American military channel for the armed forces and it's both tedious and hilarious at the same time. Of course it does remind you of what a lot of this place is about; the hundreds of thousands of soldiers placed over here.[3]

Strange! The Koreans love to wear T-shirts with English writing on them. Maybe they think this is cool or something. I don't know! The trouble is, for sure they have absolutely no idea what's written on their T-shirt. Some of them are so OTT that the Canadians and I are keeping a record of the best ones. Here's a few pulled off of the list:
"Pull my finger, Equal number of blueberries in every muffin, Get the f*ck out of my face, Your holiday will be happier with a book, Best hand job in town, Don't crying sunshine may the forest be with you, Behold my Roundness, Face down arse up that's the way I like it"!

Other places visited since September 1st:
China Town in Incheon. Hoping that it would take me back somehow, this turned out to be one of the lowest days so far; a mere shell of a place run by Koreans and one or two Chinese people merely made me miss the land of the greff even more.

---

[3] There is still a massive show of strength in South Korea. There are almost 30,000 US troops and 5,000 South Korean troops working along side them known as KATUSA, over 600,000 active Korean troops and 3 million in reserve. The Korean armed forces hold a huge and highly modern firepower. Don't Mess!

Namsan Park in Seoul: From its famous Seoul Tower there are awesome views of the river and city. On one occasion though, on the way to the Botanical Gardens, I was taken by surprise by a squad of well 'ard looking soldiers with assault rifles who must have been doing some training. They suddenly emerged from the bushes with one even brandishing what looked like an M60 heavy machine gun. I even got mixed up with them as they formed up, much to their amusement. Oh the embarrassment!

Insadong shopping centre: You can spend all day exploring this maze of different lanes and alleyways with small tea and antique shops. Myeongdong district is a non-stop shopping experience for the day! Also Namdaemun market, which is one of those in-your-face Asian markets with thousands of stalls and everything you ever wanted but also including all of the food you never wanted! In Seoul, you can also see the Changdeok-gung Royal Palace; a beautiful place that was built about 700 years ago set in well-kept woodlands and shaded gardens. Mind out for the huge tour groups though!

Bukhan-san National Park is breathtaking. I mean you can see these mountains from virtually everywhere for miles. This huge park sits just north of Seoul with suburbs hugging it from all sides. As you get closer to it, it becomes a truly striking sight. I've done a number of day walks round there. It's autumn full on here at the moment and the colours in the forests are beautiful. Within its valleys are numerous temples, monuments and old buildings. The old wall and its battlements can be walked in a day from the west to the south of the park.

Over Chuseok some friends and I went to this amazing place called Muuido Island for a couple of days. With a big old full moon, bonfires, fireworks and Soju on the beach (local brew like embalming fluid), what a fantastic few days of partying to have before winter sets in. Made friends with the coast guards too, who let me and Benny from Australia to check out their hovercraft. Wicked!

Total insanity and driving in South Korea: One really annoying habit that Mr A has is that he is always late, I mean ALWAYS! I admit that we are all human and sometimes it happens to the best of us but still, I just can't stand lateness. So I'm waiting for Mr A to drive us out to meet some parents who want me to teach their kids two days a week. The phone rings and its Mr A in a complete panic, saying he will be there in ten minutes. After half an hour, he screeches up and shouts through the window, "GET IN!" and we speed off breaking the sound barrier.

"You are late!" he tells me as if it's my fault. "You will have to apologise to the parents and make an excuse".

We race out to the estate and finally arrive where he takes down his mountain bike attached to the back of the motor. From the other side of the vehicle he then proceeds to put on his lycra cycling gear on, complete with gloves, wrap around shades and stream-lined multi-coloured helmet.

"Here are the keys and here is the address" he goes, slapping both into my hand. "You can drive home!"

"But aren't you going to introduce us?"

"You can do it! You should go now. The have been waiting for you all afternoon and I think you should teach a class to make up for it".

"Your f*cking joking" I snapped in a rare moment of annoyance in front of the boss, after all, I hadn't planned for any classes. And that was it! Off he cycled as if he hadn't heard me and I was left with this Korean brand new 4x4 Super Cherokee Land Patrol Cruiser or whatever it's called. It's automatic with left-hand drive. When I came out it was dark and the attempts to find the lights sparked the windscreen wipers on max power. My god I can look so uncool at times!

Going back was probably the biggest white knuckle ride you can experience with right hand lanes, lunatic South Korean driving and the fact that I haven't driven anything in well over a year...aaaaaaaaagh! You have to have 360 degree eyes here mate, with people weaving in and out with absolutely no signaling. Some of the roads are four lanes wide. When you park you have to go nose in. I can't park nose in to save my life, having always reversed. And check this out. When you park, often there is zero space, leaving you with no choice but to box people in. When leaving the car, you have to keep the handbrake off and the gears in neutral, then put a block of wood or something behind the wheels. Often you will return to find your car has been moved down to the end of the road, which is a total pain in the arse as all the cars look the damned same.

About half way home I scuffed the front end against a crash barrier, an easy blunder to make on your first excursion into left hand drive I rekon. It's hard judging the distance from where you're sitting to the right hand side of the car, your senses just aren't used to it. "Bollocks, now I have to phone Mr A" were my only thoughts, not that I care a rats arse about his car, but the fact that I'd made a mistake. When he heard, he was round in an instant to look at the damage. With relief, it didn't seem to bother him and after only a couple of minutes he left.

"How long have you been driving?" he asked in an excruciating tone loaded with sarcasm. "I'd better get another one for you as soon as possible".

At last things are becoming a bit more stable (it certainly took its time). I have my own motor now, so can really get out into other, hopefully, nicer parts of this country. Also there's the DMZ to check out. I mean all this missile testing over the border and the North has been sending troops out into 'no man's land' recently so it's all a bit tense over there.........hmmm! Life's on the up at last. Taekwondo and quitting smoking goes a long way over here, the autumn is amazing and a total bliss out.

## Pei: 26th February 2007

Two days a week I teach at a place called the Kimpo estate about half an hour out of town. It's quiet here! Outside during break time, the sound of playing children resonates between the apartment blocks. The towers are higher than twenty stories and in varying shades of light sandy browns, with huge numbers painted on each. Funny, these buildings are far from drab. There is something harmonious about the way they reach up so high into the late October sunshine. Even though there are so many people living here bunched up together, this area still feels really peaceful.

I like my Tuesdays and Thursdays; there is always time to reflect. In the afternoon when you walk around the perimeter, the view is across miles of farmland broken up by a few small buildings. The local croquet team in their matching kit just seems to add to the sense of tranquillity. The distinctive sound of the balls cracking together reverberates between the flats, briefly disturbing the calm autumn afternoon. Far away, the expressway is reminiscent of Portishead (romantic hey) and in the other direction is the airport.

At night this place is like Blade Runner. The blocks are lit up and it seems to hum with energy. It's directly on the flight path from every plane taking off from the airport and the roar of the jet engines fills the air as each one starts to accelerate down the runway. It's fun waiting for one to suddenly appear. As they snap into sight above the trees lit up by winking landing lights, it's a wonder something so big can make it off the tarmac. Climbing so fast, each one somehow manages to gain just enough height to clear the buildings and then turn sharply, disappearing into the darkness.

### South Korea to China - Beijing Part 1:
Saturday 25th November: A winter weekend in Beijing.
Well at 5.00am I am out of bed like shit off a shovel. It's the day that I've been dreaming of for so long. Riding the 111 bus to the airport, it's a struggle to be in the moment with the whole thing. Deliberately leaving some of my most important documents behind, the option to do a runner and not return has been erased. Somewhere in my subconscious I have been readying myself mentally for the return trip and it's something I dread having to deal with. A high pitched warning sound from the rev counter hurts my ears and keeps us all awake as the bus rattles through the chilly darkness. Watching the sun rise over Incheon Airport, it's a beautiful morning; a reminder that moments like these are truly what life is about.

Forgetting we are travelling with Air China, before take-off we are greeted by an announcement in Chinese. The woman's voice is just music to my ears and it immediately pushes all of my emotion buttons. Upon arrival, stepping out of the plane I briefly pause at the top of the steps and take a long and deep breathe of the cold Beijing air. It's snowing and I savour the moment. This is total seventh heaven! I've never been met by anyone at an airport before and today Pei Li Peng and her good friend Wen Ti are waiting for me. Pei is an old Yangshuo connection who is 'an office worker in sales' somewhere in the North East of the city. Wen Ti is a taxi driver and takes Pei all over the place for next to nothing.

Do you know that feeling when a day is really feels like the day it is supposed to be? We go to a small diner for lunch. Other than having the sports section of the Daily Mirror to read and listening to the footie with my mate Barry, it couldn't feel more like a Saturday. Oh, and that first Chinese noodle soup in such a long time went down so well.

Pei is taking her driving test today. She failed the last go so it's a nervous time. Wen Ti drives us to the test centre in the north of the city, past old buildings and along bad roads with battered cars. Such a contrast to the slickness of South Korea! Parking outside the centre on the side of the highway, we wait for Pei for hours. Here, as part of this wintery scene, it gives my head time to really start to accept that, even for a short time this is China; proper mate! From the relative warmth of Wen Ti's little car, we watch people who live and work outside in the freezing cold all day go about their daily lives. Security guards, litter pickers, people sweeping snow, riding rickety bicycles or old motorcycles all seem to be wearing less than adequate clothing. Big old lorries thunder by down the tree-lined highway that disappears into the wintry distance.

Saturday evening is just great. Pei passed her test and we celebrate with Beijing hot pot, similar to the Sichuan one only without any chilli peppers. All the shops and restaurants have these great heavy hanging padded canvasses in the doorway. They are designed to keep out both the cold and the sandstorms from Inner Mongolia. Are people really spitting their food out onto the floor? Pei is one of the most adventurous people you will meet. She has just returned from living in the Xinjiang Province north of Tibet and along the Kazakh border, just hanging out in the countryside and horse riding. Next year she wants us to go together, though maybe Annapurna or anywhere in Mongolia are also options, great!

So I'm woken up in the morning with "Do you want to go hiking along the Great Wall today?" It's amazing. I mean I never really thought much about going to the Great Wall but at this moment I am so excited I don't know what to do with myself. Wen Ti picks us up and we drive north through flat farmlands, old villages and communities for hours. At one point Wen Ti gets lost so stops the car to ask for directions. To our great amusement we realise he must be saying something like "Excuse me! Do you know where the Great Wall of China is?"

Our luck is in today; there are few people as we are firmly in the strong icy grip of winter and the whole area is frozen. For once I am spared the onslaught of a zillion tourists at a famous place and get a chance to experience somewhere amazing without getting pissed off (makes a change hey!) The wall itself is really something special. It consists of long sections separated by guard towers. Since each section is curved, it hugs the contour of the land resembling a giant ancient snake. Looking out from the battlements, the stark black icy veined mountains rear up far off in the distance as a strong breeze whips in with a real bite.

It's hard to start taking in the significance that The Great Wall has to the people of China. Just to say that it was built between the 5th and 17th centuries and from soldiers, to labourers, to political prisoners, it is said that the number of people that lost their lives building it runs into the millions. I always assumed that the Great Wall is just one long wall, but it's actually lots of sections which stretch out over a really wide area. If you see it on a map it's more like looking at spaghetti. No one can really say how long the wall is as there are so many segmented areas and also a lot of it is being eroded by desert storms. Some guess it's longer than 5000 miles though. It extends far west towards Xinjiang and north towards Russia and east to North Korea. Contrary to what some say, there is absolutely no way you can see it from outer-space as its only 30m at its widest point. Oh, by the way, there is a great sign on the way up to the Great Wall that reads,

"Former American President Bill Clinton visited here on June 28, 1998 and said that: The Great Wall here is very beautiful, very grand, more beautiful and grander than what I imagined". Yeah right my son! I always knew he was a bit of a geezer.

On the way back we are talking about various pastimes in the UK, in particular my old motorcycling days including accidents, broken bones and near misses.

"I've never had any accidents" says Pei. "There is this though" and she pointed to a scar she had on her chin just below her bottom lip.

"My Grandmother did that with a stick when I was very young" she tells me without a second thought.

"Wow, what did you do to deserve that?"

"Oh, nothing special. It was common to be beaten if you did anything wrong when you're a child in China. These days things are much better. It doesn't happen so much anymore."

I exclaim that we don't do that kind of thing in the UK and you'll even get into the local newspapers if you raise your hand against a minor.

"Yes, but I was brought up in countryside and there aren't many laws there. It's such a big place lots of terrible things used to happen. Because I was a girl, my Mother wanted to throw me into the river. She took me to the water and just before, my Auntie came and saved me. She took me away and I grew up with her instead."

"What was wrong with being a girl then? Didn't your Mother love you?"

"You don't understand how poor it is in the countryside. If you are a girl then you have no chance of getting a good enough job to help the family. You are an extra person that they need to look after. People will always hope that they will have a boy. It wasn't just my Mother who did this. Years ago it was just normal for a family to reject their daughter in this way".

Lost for words, the rest of the journey is spent in silence while I contemplate this sudden learning experience leaving Pei to chat to Wen Ti instead.

In the evening we go out into the Hou Hai area in Beijing. It's like the shops, bars and restaurants of Lijiang and Yangshuo rolled into one. Hugging the edges of a lake, it is lit up beautifully with coloured lights and lanterns reflecting right across to the other bank. Giant willow trees gently reach downwards, breaking the water's surface and forming archways over the path. As we make our way around, it feels like nothing other than being transported to complete paradise.

Monday: Certainly one never to forget. So Pei goes off for a job interview and I take off for a wander. Pei lives in the Changping District, a northern suburb of Beijing; a strangely quiet place. Each district has its own central power plant for heating with big-fenced off areas and check points so people going in and out can be monitored. A security guard follows me who doesn't seem to like people taking photos, so when I get lost and come back the other way, it must look fairly suspect. In an effort to avoid any further contact with him, I jump over a wall, walk across a rubbish covered wasteland and out into a muddy road with some seriously run-down buildings. It's amazing how many things can be said in just one simple look. The locals stop what they were doing, some even standing up to get a better view. Pei would have been freaking if she saw me right now. With no other option, the only thing to do is to get over the nearest wall and leg it! On the other side, at the end of the street, suddenly there is this twenty foot high picture of Steve Davis hanging from a tall building completely dominating the area. Ok, so it's the local snooker club, but quite a surreal moment went down there for sure.

In the evening I say my goodbyes to Pei and Wen Ti. A lot happened between Pei and I and I am sure I'll be seeing her again as soon as I can possibly arrange my next escape. Walking up to the check-in I'm taken aback. Of course, this flight goes to South Korea! All the people there are South Koreans. At Gate 7, a large group of South Korean men get absolutely annihilated on at least four bottles of Red Label vodka from the duty free shop, stuffing their faces with chocolates while their wives sit in a separate group nearby. On the plane the air hostesses are clearly exasperated by them, their complete lack of manners and disregard for anyone around. There's a great commotion as they try to find their seats and put their baggage away. The simplest of tasks becomes a great problem as if there is some emergency going on.

December 9th: Phew, was that really two weeks ago? So here I am at 6pm, still in bed, on the sixth cup of Tetley tea with this laptop. Lately things have either been either really good or really grey. Again life is so intense that something just has to be written about this mad place.

Firstly, I now know some really nice, great wonderful Korean people. To be honest I can't say that they are my 'friends' in the truest sense of the word. I mean I don't know them like the brothers and sisters back in the UK. I just really like them that's all. The person that instantly stands out from the crowd is Sabonim, our Taekwondo master. He's such a top bloke. The class got invited for a meal at the Grand Master's house on Christmas Eve; a true honour. One of my students Jun Hun Lee insists that are lessons are done in two different restaurants every week and he picks up the bill every time. Some of the Korean teachers paid for lunch one day. Ganaan Duck was on the menu, the best grub in town served on a platter with roast vegetables. I mean there are friendly and kindhearted people everywhere.

Also, my total respect and complete over-the-top liking for many of the Westerners here is too much at times. It's the one thing that keeps your head together and if it wasn't for these great people, I would have legged it a long time ago. And yeah, people do. Some people just can't handle it. The other week there was this guy from the

US we went to see the footie with. In the evening we went down Number 10 for a few beers and the next day he was just gone and so was all his stuff. No goodbyes or anything! He must have planned it for some time and that's the only way to do it. You just can't tell anyone.

When I got back from Beijing the first person to phone on Tuesday morning was Mr A to check up on me.

"Are you back?" were his only words.

"Of course I'm frigging back" I thought in response to this stupid question but I guess he was right to be paranoid.

So what is it about this place that makes me stare so longingly at every plane I see taking off from Kimpo Airport? I mean on paper this lifestyle is incredibly cushty, I mean really cushty. You start work at 2.30 and the teaching team are the only bunch of Westerners who get to drive to work and have the use of a car at the weekends. There are some serious lie-ins every day and you get to bed in the early hours. You are online in your own apartment all the time for free. You get to cook ridiculously large breakfasts and evening meals. The money is great. There's nothing better than hanging with Briony and the girls plus the Number 10 crew and the weekends are wicked.

All the same, there is always the feeling that it's really people trying to make the most of things in a dull place; always looking for things to do to make life a bit more bearable I guess. A few years ago my mate Barry and I made up a parody of a new-age book called the Celestine Prophecy calling it 'The Art of Repetitive Blandness. The Steps and Pathway to Sameness'. Well congratulations and here it is; a place so dull and nondescript condensed into one area that it ceases to be just plain old ordinary. Everything looks the same! It really does. All the cars are the same. Everyone tries so hard to be the same. Yesterday that familiar sinking feeling paid the first of its many daily visits while on the way to work. To be honest it's always there lurking away, only this particular wave of negativity was so overwhelming it felt like a massive wave driving itself downwards from head to foot. It's always there ticking away.

Aside from that, at the moment most students are studying over twelve hours a day for their exams, some over fifteen. I mean can you believe that. I made the stupid mistake of telling one student's mother that her daughter was just too exhausted to work. You just knew that she was on for a beating from Mum the moment class was over. You see students falling asleep everywhere at the moment. Normally they sleep in the classrooms at break time.

My Car: I just have to write something about my car here. It's a white Hyundai Avante and looks pretty much the same as any other. I don't think they have MOT's in South Korea which means its ok to drive around with one headlight down and a crack right across the windshield. It's a total death-trap and there is absolutely no way that it would be allowed on the road in the UK. The only way you can get out of the car is by lowering down the painfully slow side window and opening the door from the outside. Shit! I should have travel insurance! I love it though. It has the growliest engine on the road and it seems like it's got the only manual gear box in town so you can burn everyone else off at the lights, oh yes! When you are getting in and out of it, it normally gives you an electric shock as you touch the body work. Talk about a car with personality or what!

January 6th and it's the first Saturday of the year. Its grey and snowing and my doss bag and duvet are my second skin. It's hard to remember much about December in South Korea, just driving like a lunatic, hard work and plotting another escape from this place. Taekwondo has kept me alive. You never know what's going to happen so it keeps you in the moment all of the time. Example: like it's a bright sunny Monday morning and Sabonim has us running in pairs outside around the block in our 'Doboks' (Taekwondo uniforms). There's one Scot, one Alaskan, two Yanks and me looking like a right wanker with my white belt about to have a seizure waiting for the traffic lights to change. The Taekwondo people are really something else and it's helped me survive here big time, especially repeatedly kicking that great big hanging punch bag.

Before each session starts we have to warm up. This consists of fifteen minutes of excruciating stretching exercises. The worst is where you have to sit on the floor with your legs outstretched as far apart as they will go, (that's not far) with your arms together. One of the black belt guys then sits in front of you, grabs your arms forward and pulls you over. At the same time they place their feet inside yours and push your legs open even wider. This is absolute mind blowing agony, causing you to shout out more expletives than you ever did the whole of last year. Talk about being in the moment!

Aside from various routines which are usually practiced they throw in other more unusual activities. One time they had us punching candles out without going near the flame and punching free hanging newspaper in half. This really isn't as easy as it sounds, especially with everyone watching you; pressure big time. All in all Taekwondo is ingrained into the culture and something that's hard to avoid in South Korea. It's taught all over the country and most people learn it from an early age so be careful when your down the bar and get into an argument with a local.

I guess it's all a blur really, mixed thoughts about coping in this place. Black puddings are really squid ink sausages. Green tea is really made from seaweed. I wear fluffy bear slippers at one academy. Meditating in the winter sunshine with heavy machine gun fire in the background.

Going for a walk with twelve helicopters in formation, hugging the hills near the border like Apocalypse Now. Homeless people fill Seoul station underground in this ridiculous minus fifteen degrees centigrade temperature. Christmas is intense and brief. There are no holidays here, just mass shopping and then it's over in one day. If only the UK could be like that hey! Christmas itself was excellent. On Christmas Eve there was a great party at Hazel's apartment. Briony led the way for all, shaking her thing up in front of the big plate glass window in full view of every passerby down below. The next day Angela and Wendy knocked up a terrific Christmas Dinner including real mashed potatoes and a wicked gravy. I think at that time we all felt together, it was truly a brilliant time. They're all fantastic!

## South Korea to China - Beijing Part 2:
The next bit I wrote on bits of paper last week so have to copy everything down. This is New Year's Eve weekend 2006: This is my second trip to Beijing now, I just couldn't help myself and I'm enjoying it thoroughly before even getting off the plane. The plane was delayed by an hour and as we descend through thick cloud with visibility only to the wing tips I can see why. It feels like we really are just a little blip on some traffic controllers console and I hope they haven't been on a baijiu binge the night before. The windows overlooking the wings are the best seats to grab. They're amazing things really the wings. The whole thing is just a complex system of lightweight aluminum flaps that form one flat surface when airborne. Somehow we emerge from the weather right on the nose to Beijing airport in mid-winter. What a stunning sight; the snow coming down hard; planes being towed back to the concourse; emergency vehicles working in packs all in this wintery whiteness of Northern China. Proper mate!

After an exhausting few weeks in South Korea and another 5.30am start to the day, all I can think of is a chilled-out and mellow time in the quietness of the Changping District, but Pei has other plans today. First it's the long drive up to her place followed by a taxi ride and two subway train rides to arrive at Beijing central train station by 6.00pm. Never a dull moment hey! The station itself is a remarkable place. In the freezing cold evening, hundreds of people barge, shove and push to the front of numerous ticket booths. The building itself is huge, dimly lit, reminiscent of something from the 50s, all highly atmospheric. When the gates open for the train, the pushing is overwhelming and the pandemonium continues when we are on board the train; a two story ageing dinosaur snaking off into the smoggy darkness, with a guard wearing a long coat standing at outside each carriage. Inside it's also poorly lit and we fight for some standing room, anywhere, as we couldn't get a ticket for a sleeper compartment or a seat. Amongst the mass of people and boxes packed into every possible space, the prospect of a five hour journey to Qinhuangdao seems just too hectic for my poor head to contemplate. Eventually and much to my relief, Pei manages to blag two beds in a ticket inspectors compartment. I learn to say

"Mashang gei wo piao kuai yi dian" (tickets please, at once), winding a few people up as they file past and Pei delights on wearing the inspector's hat.

"I'm so happy I feel like I'm dreaming" beams Pei from her bottom bunk.

Once again, though completely cream-crackered a state of complete and utter contentedness consumes me. From the dusty window of this darkened carriage, wintry China goes by, while the distinct 'clack clack' of the train wheels sends us both off to sleep.

I had never heard of Qinhuangdao before today. Who would have thought it when leaving the apartment in South Korea at 5.30 this morning? But here we are at midnight in this strange town on the east coast. We are met by Pei's friend Yen Chin who is a police woman and takes us to eat barbeque pigeon. At 2.00am I finally hit the sack in another Chinese hotel in a place I know nothing about. I absolutely love Chinese hotels. They are all the same, they even smell the same! Bliss!

Sunday! AAAAAAAAAAGH! No time for a lie in! AAAAAAAAAAGH! It seems that the day has been completely arranged and I'm kicked out of bed way too early. We are met by Yen Chin and her 'Chief' Xiao Ming in a big black expensive car who drives us to the seafront for brunch. This consists of a huge spread of seafood that they all choose live from two walls of fish tanks. The restaurant has a real run down feel to it. In fact the whole town has a feeling of being pretty rough around the edges.

After, we go to Yen Chins flat in the sticks, down back streets and past frozen lakes with people skating on the ice. For over an hour I wearily experience the biggest cat fight you will ever see. Pei and Yen Chin have a fierce argument with the landlady who is supposed to fix the heating and it's so cold inside you can easily see your breath. Looking out of the window, it really feels like you are in the back of beyond. Opposite in a decaying grey tenement block, an old man just sits on his bed motionless in an empty room doing nothing apart from staring out of the window.

Next, another officer Gao Yu Lin drives us out to the beginning of the Great Wall. My friends tell me of its meaning and significance but Mr Grumpy here can't help but think that it has to start somewhere and surely the middle of the Great Wall is equally as important. Anyway after visiting a temple called The First Pass Under Heaven we are on our way back. Or so I thought! I am then taken on the most incredible detour of my life to the biggest port in Northern China.

Gao Yu Lin has security clearance to the whole place so he gives us the grand tour. First we go to the train yards. A vast proportion of China's coal comes through these yards from the Shanxi Province, home to some of the most dangerous mines in the country. After finally reaching their destination, the incredibly long trains come through a monster of a machine; it's over thirty feet high and rotates five of the carriages at a time upside down, dumping the coal with an enormous and ear deafening crash. You really have a feeling that this coal has been on a serious journey to get here and it's an awesome sight. There are endless mountains of coal that disappear from view far off into the dimming winter light; millions of tons piled up as far as the eye can see. Next we go to see the supertankers. I mean this is just the absolute heartbeat of China. This is what makes it tick and just an unforgettable once in a lifetime experience filling me with excitement. All these ships take the coal to southern ports and they are like nothing I've seen before. In the fading light the supertankers seem more like black sleeping giants as we proceed along the harbour's edge. Close up, we come to one called the Dong Fang Sheng, its name written in white characters, standing out against the weathered terracotta and black paint work high above us. Waiting to be loaded, its big bulbous bow stands proud out of the water and I wonder how many thousands of tons it could carry in one go.

The Chinese get ten out of ten for hospitality every time, but this is getting ridiculous. Our escorts leave us at the "most expensive restaurant in town" to find that the bill has already been paid and we can eat anything on the menu. It's called the International Seaman's Club; a large, cold and strangely empty place, feeling more like something fixed in the past. Pei and Yen Chin have a big plate of jellyfish. To be honest I find the food hard work in this town and can feel my energy levels dropping rapidly. After dinner we all go to the "best massage parlour" in town and this stunning woman called Liu Chang gives me a two hour going over (though unfortunately with the hairiest legs you will ever see on a woman). My God, did that massage hurt! Wrists like cast iron or what!

245

The next day we have to check-out of the hotel early. Aaaagh! It's New Year's Day and also Pei's birthday. The queues for train tickets are massive, so we get the bus back to Beijing. I reckon that lorries outnumber cars twenty to one on this highway. Petrol stations are heaving with heavy transport. It's just another sight that sticks in your mind forever as the bus weaves in and out between lorry after lorry, after lorry. You see it all on this road; livestock is so squashed together that the animals can't move, coal, coal and more coal, animal skins, boxes, heavy machinery, wood piles, just the lot going to Beijing. Such a good journey! I admit it's also been a serious one. I mean I'm shafted, but it's been an amazing experience. It really feels like I'm hanging for the right woman for once. Pei is so where it's at; every moment with her feels like an adventure.

Well I stopped writing at that time. Pei took me to a great restaurant and she was delighted to win twenty kuai on the lottery. From the bus we took a further three taxis and two train rides on a bitterly cold night, maybe the coldest I have ever experienced. Back at her place we sat chatting about the future and then I went for a quick shower before bed. Upon returning to the bedroom, I noticed that Pei was no longer in her white dressing gown. She had her clothes on, her coat and scarf and looked at me coldly,

"I forgot to tell you I have a friend coming tonight so one of us has to stay in a hotel."
"A hotel?" I repeated, unable to believe my ears. "Why don't they sleep in the living room?"

Pei was having none of it though. I asked for some reason whether her friend was a girl or a guy, I don't know why. "Girl!" was all she said. It was already past midnight and I had to be up at 5.30 again to get the plane, not only that but I was absolutely knackered. All I wanted to do was to be in bed with Pei and sleep with her in my arms for the last few hours but something had changed.

"I'm going out now and there's a taxi coming in two minutes. Be in it!" And then she left.

Blown away is the understatement of the decade. I mean one minute I'm in the shower and the next I'm putting my clothes back on, packing my bag and getting my coat on at 12.30am. Still in disbelief and shock I decided to wait until she returned and get an explanation but the taxi driver came to the door and looked to be getting impatient. With major reluctance I took my bag outside, shaking my head and repeating

"What's going on? What the f*ck's happening?" again and again. A car pulled up across the road. Pei got out and walked straight towards me.

"Go now!" she simply said, refusing to give any sort of explanation. No hug or kiss goodbye, nothing! She turned and got back into the car. At that moment a man got out of the driver's side. In the darkness he glared at me and started shouting in Chinese. He walked towards me shaking in rage but stopped half way, threw some more curses and returned to the car and that was it. I was off sharpish.

The next few hours were just a blur. Some taxi ride to a hotel. I have no idea what part of Beijing it was in, still trying to figure out what had just happened. The staff in
the hotel spoke no English at all, but I managed to get a wake-up call, pay for the room and order a taxi to the airport. I did not sleep that night; it was awful. With great relief I got to the airport but absolutely stuffed from another 5.30am start. I was driving to work in South Korea by 2.00pm, my head in utter oblivion. It took me the best part of a week to get over the whole experience physically.
To this day I have never heard from Pei. I have never seen Pei again. She has made no attempts to contact me in anyway and I will always wonder what on earth happened on the evening of the 1st of January 2007. She is divorced so maybe that was her ex-husband? Maybe it was a family member who hates Westerners? Maybe she had another guy? Who knows?

Life is an open book. The future is a clear sea with a strong current and limitless horizon. The apartment is nothing but somewhere to contemplate this. I took my calendar apart, sticking its individual pages up in front of the bed. The walls are covered with maps and bits of paper, where I unload my cluttered head that fails to be in the moment. I have my China map, a map of Mongolia and a beautiful map of Tibet, Nepal and Bhutan. There isn't a moment that goes by when I don't think about getting away from here and starting again. It's an all-consuming feeling, full-on and relentless. Bollocks to it!

# DMZ and North Korea: 24<sup>th</sup> March 2007

When I came over here I didn't think too much about anything other than it was something different to do, giving no thought whatsoever to the small fact that North Korea would be next door. The army presence here is always in the background so you are well aware of something going on, but what can you do hey? Instead you quickly put it to the back of your mind and just get on with your business.

Yesterday put a completely different perspective on things though, as some friends and I got about as close as you can get to North Korea from here. So, from a blurred 4.30am start we left Seoul by bus to Camp Boniface, the nearest military base to us on the DMZ or Demilitarized Zone. This 2.5 mile wide bit of land separates South Korea from what has got to be one of the most secretive and compelling countries in the world.

Soon after we start driving, the traffic noticeably thins out. I don't think it's just down to the fact we are out of Seoul. Along the river bank suddenly there are now guard towers and barbed wire fences everywhere and we've only been out of town for ten minutes. Up on a hill is an observation post. I think we were all stunned when we are told that the town just across the water is in fact a 'fake' North Korean town. This place has been built so it looks like North Korea is modernised. In reality the white tower blocks are empty and we are looking at a ghost town.

At Camp Boniface everyone was ushered into a briefing room where a sergeant gives us a run-down of what is going to happen. I actually thought we would be going to a hill where we would just look at North Korea and that would be it. Instead we are to be taken deep inside the DMZ to the Military Demarcation Line (MDL) which is the actual border. We sign a waiver in case anything happens out there, show our passports and get onto another bus. It's mad. We are being driven out into No Man's Land. The bus starts to move out and there is no doubt that this vehicle is the most looked at object for miles. Past countless observation posts and check points and out into open space, we pass the anti-tank walls and go through mine fields. You really feel that you are on a thread out here and you do exactly what you are told; quite a buzz I must say.

The first place we are taken to is a place called Panmunjeom. This is the only area where the UN and North Korea ever meet for talks and the MDL goes right through the middle, marked with white signs, posts and raised concrete lines. There are two big buildings on the south side, Freedom and also Peace House, both quite flash, built for conferences and the like. We are led through Freedom House to the other side where we look across to the North Korean equivalent called Panmungak. This is about as far as it goes out here; between the buildings is the MDL and built directly over the line are small sky-blue huts where the actual talks between the two sides take place. What a trip! We are escorted to the central hut where two totally menacing South Korean guards stand motionless. There is a central table which is placed directly on the border and two booths either side where the conferences are recorded. At one time for at least five minutes I am on the other side of the table and am therefore standing in North Korea.

Something more amazing than that happens outside though. Waiting to leave, we stand together to get a group photo and turn to see a North Korean guard appear from the Panmungak building. Now this is a rare thing. I mean how often do you see a North Korean hey? Another joins him and then more until about ten North Korean soldiers are standing next to the MDL. One's got a camera and they proceed to pose away in front of us having their photos taken. The American soldier that is with us tells us that they are most likely taking photos of us. It's a very strange feeling to think that at some point in the very near future, someone in North Korea will be either developing or downloading my mug. How weird is that hey!

After Panmunjeom we are driven to an observation point which has a staggering view across the DMZ. The border is just below us so everything we look at is pretty much North Korean. The whole area is just a vast network of towers, fences and guard posts. An empty highway goes from our side and connects with a 'propaganda town'; another fake. It has a massive 160-metre flagpole which proudly boasts one of the biggest flags in the world, purely so it can be bigger than the one being flown by the South. The wildlife in this area has flourished and at least twenty buzzards circle lazily above and the whole place may as well be a nature reserve. In contrast North Korea is a barren wasteland of nothing and deforestation is now a big problem.

Nearby on the side of the highway is a memorial to two US army captains. They were trying to cut down a tree that was obscuring the view of a North Korean guard post. The North Koreans sent over a truck full of soldiers who axed the two captains to death. There is also the 'Bridge of No Return' where the last prisoners of the war chose which side they wanted to be on.

The last part of the day is spent at the Third Tunnel. The North Koreans spent a lot of time and effort digging tunnels under the DMZ in attempts to invade the South. We walk down the 'interception' tunnel first, which is 78m long and at a 12 degree angle and finally join the tunnel proper. This was discovered in 1978, is 1,600 metres long, took them five years to dig, is deep enough to avoid detection from above and carved out of granite. Some piece of work I can tell you. The guys that did the digging worked in terrible conditions and could only manage to dynamite and move forward one metre a day. When discovered it was only 48 km from Seoul and is easily big enough for a whole division of troops to pass through in one hour.

There is also a museum with a chronological list of even the smallest events that have taken place on the DMZ across the wall and there are a lot! All in all an unforgettable day, more so as now I know how ridiculously close we really are to North Korea. What would the people over there do if they knew what life was like over here just a few miles away from them. To take a trip around Seoul would blow their minds. They have nothing and the South Koreans have got it all. Satellite views at night of Korea show two very different halves; South Korea is lit up like a Christmas tree and the North is just a black void.

## Pingyao: 11<sup>th</sup> April 2007

Hiveras: From the top of Gyeyang Mountain the tower blocks seem endless. Space is precious here! The Daewoo plant's chimneys discharge smoke 24hours a day and the smog is really something; just this great thick barrier of gas that separates grey and blue. Even on a good day you may still not be able to climb above it on the mountain. Some days the taste and smell of the smog penetrates right into the back of your sinuses. And there in the middle of it is Hiveras.

Hiveras stands apart from the other buildings. Actually Hiveras is four identical square high rises that fit tightly together, forming just one enormous monolith. It looks completely different from the other high rises which are slim and pencil-like in pastel colours. Its four blocks are named A, B, C and D block. It has a three level underground parking system and has a life of its own. The view out of my B block window is of...A Block! Up, down and left and right this is what you see. Actually, tell a lie, you see a bit of C block if you look out of the window to the left! You never really pull the blinds back in case someone from the opposite block looks in and with the other buildings so close, no bright natural light ever penetrates the apartment. If the sun is shining you will have absolutely no idea of it.

Hiveras is more like a phenomenon in Incheon than a place. Every time I'm driving back and it looms into view, I shake my head and laugh, "Do I really live in that place?" On the other end of the scale, I was walking down this back street round the corner the other day and there was one of the most beautiful old temples you'll ever see. The moment you are inside all you want to do is be still; such a nice vibe there; a complete blessing!

My friends are more like a family these days. Briony is going next week. That's gonna be another tough one. She found something called 'D-Day Counter' on her mobile phone so she can count the days til she returns to England. We sure are gonna miss her that's for sure. Parties, road trips and hiking in the national parks keep us all alive. Benny, the mad Australian, who used to work at Buckingham Palace. They gave him a Christmas pudding which he put on eBay and then sold the story to the Daily Mirror for 3.5 grand. This sure is a great place to meet new people.

Other stuff, oddments and other unusual observations in no particular order:

The car won't stop when you turn off the ignition. You have to wait for a few minutes first and then it turns off on its own accord. When you go to get petrol they fill up while the engine is running, amazing hey! A fireball waiting to happen!

Eagle FM are doing a regular slot on weapons of war. Yesterday on the way to work they did one on the history of the grenade. Hmmmm, very nice, in fact almost sentimental I would say. Ah, what would we do without the good old grenade hey?

Some great things continue to happen at school. Like last week the principal had got me some new slippers! Gone are the days of the fluffy bear ones, now I have some slick new rabbit slippers! The kids I teach and the staff are all great. Parents are always giving me presents. I got a ginger tea box set today and last week a Pantene Pro Vitamin shampoo set; just my thing you know, been scrubbing my hair vigorously ever since.

The Police have showed up a few times while I've been teaching, but Mr A phoned and gave a few minutes of advanced warning. Indeed his prior knowledge seems strange to say the least.

"You should move your class next door as soon as possible. There is a calligraphy school you can use. The owner is a friend of mine. Do not leave there until someone from the school comes and gets you."

It's bizarre relocating your class in order to evade the bad guys and I wondered what would happen if they found us. Certainly a time to keep your head down.

Things are still pretty tough on the psyche these days, well that's an understatement. One Monday morning my head was so mashed from being in this place that I turned around a few minutes from my destination, pulling a ridiculous U-turn in the road and went all the way back, convinced I needed to look for my Wednesday academy. Upon the discovery that I'd driven to the wrong place I did another U-turn and went back the way I'd already been. Shot away mate I can tell you! By the time I got there I was in a right old mess! Sometimes my soul is wracked with such a deep depression that I feel like tearing my face off. It's an unbearable feeling that's hard to deal with at times and the line that one day I'll be out of here is the only driving force behind this existence.

Strangely, to cap it all, in some painful cosmic coincidence there's now a single called 'Snow Hey Oh' by the Red Hot Chili Peppers continually being played again and again over the air waves. Being as it's all about starting over and wiping the slate clean, (in my dreams mate) its lyrics are therefore loaded with meaning. No sooner than you've jumped in the car and turned on the radio, there it is, once more ramming this crap state of affairs home like a nail in the head. An odd combination of "God this is good" and "Oh no not this one again!" is the immediate reaction.

"The more I see the less I know, The more I like to let it go...... Running through the field where all my tracks will be concealed and there's nowhere to go" are the unstoppable words which thoroughly ingrain themselves into your mind, whirling around and around inside for the rest of the day.

Luckily I've met this guy from New Jersey called Daz who is totally uncaring about hiding his true feelings about South Korea and we've become brothers in despair. "F*ck this place!" he would often boom. "And f*ck everyone in it!"
This fearless guy used to be a teacher in the notorious city of Camden where he tells me they installed metal detectors in his school so no one could bring a gun or a knife into class with them. His outspokenness about South Korea has in fact alienated him big time from the other teachers and often he refuses to travel with them on the yellow bus to work in the morning.

"Right, I'm going over to No10 to kick the shit out of those c*nts" and like some soju fuelled Exocet I'd watch him walk across the road to vent some serious anger and destroy the bar yet again.


### South Korea to China - Beijing & Pingyao Part 3:
March 3rd: 7.30-9.30am waiting. 10.30 plane delayed! 12.45 plane delayed again and
then again as thick fog and drizzle keeps everything on shut down. My hard earned week's holiday and planning will be down the toilet if it doesn't happen. The good old CA138 to Beijing is now delayed until 1.45. I don't know why but I have clearly identified an obsession with Beijing. With sleep dep from the Soju heads that kept me awake all last night hammering and banging doors, it's dead brain time. Everyone waits; staff and passengers. There is nothing to do. Our departure gates are changed a couple of times and we end up next to a restaurant. Some of the South Korean guys take full advantage of this, whacking neat Soju down at lunch time until there are bodies stretched out everywhere, passed out on the seats.

Nothing to contemplate this time really, nothing! Oh, except this totally annoying pair of boxer shorts I am wearing. Why oh why I keep wearing them, I do not know. Yvonne bought them for me to go swimming in the Li River last year and since then they haven't really had a look in. Lately though I've been getting too worried about going commando stylee, you know, flying low and all (must be getting forgetful in my old age), so I'm playing it safe. Anyway, I realized one afternoon that they have a nasty habit of working their way upwards until they reach the bottom of my rib cage. Now that's a pretty weird sensation anytime let alone when you're teaching in class. I feel like they must have invisible braces pulling them up kinda like the Germans' lederhosen or something. The worst part about them though is that the crutch has gone on them. Now put two and two together and ask yourself, do you really want that image in your head? I am just glad they can't see it all in their x-ray machines here at the airport! Why I keep wearing these strange boxers from another dimension is beyond me. But hey! I'm not the only one who suffers from gravity inverting underwear. Ask Briony anytime about her tights.

As you can see there is clearly sweet FA to do in this airport. It's hard not to start laughing to yourself really as you contemplate underwear of times gone by (I think people are staring). Repressing laughter becomes almost painful especially when remembering those gigantic white Y-fronts Mum bought for me when I was 11 years old.

The worst and most embarrassing example though, was the silver and grey suit I bought second hand from Oxfam as a student teacher at the extravagant price of eleven quid. Wearing them every day, my girlfriend eventually protested that the trousers were so grimy that she just had to wash them. No worries! On Monday morning I simply took out my reserve trousers from the closet only to find that they were five sizes too small (I'd never tried them on in the shop). I mean these trousers were absolutely miniscule. Now I am skinny but even for me it was hard to breathe in them. They were also a totally unmatching light blue and so short that you found yourself putting your hands in those tiny pockets to push them down as far as they would go. In fact, so small were they that when you sat down, the trouser legs would lift two inches above my ankles sexily revealing short socks and hairy white legs, very nice! So paranoid about them was I, that I decided to wear a pair of white long johns to cover up. They were so bad that at break time one teacher even came up to me in the canteen leant over and quietly said, "Andy! Don't EVER wear those trousers again!"

In the afternoon it was getting hot so I took off my jacket and hung it over the chair. At this time, about ten of the girls in the class who clearly had some private joke started to become more than irritating. In the end they were having shrieking laughing fits and crying til' it hurt. Eventually, one of them managed to point to my trousers before collapsing into more hysterical fits. Sexily, I had unknowingly tucked my tie into the long johns. In turn the long johns had successfully inverted gravity, escaping from my trousers, travelling upwards to above my stomach. To the class it looked like my tie was tucked into an enormous pair of white underpants. Mercy!

Around this time I had no briefcase, so instead carried my teacher's notes in a stylish Waitrose carrier bag. Not only that, but the totally uncomfortable second-hand shoes that came with the suit, had been quickly replaced by a pair of hiking boots. How I got away with teaching in this strange get up I have no idea, but somehow managed to wear it every day throughout the whole second teaching practice. One morning, while waiting for my usual lift from one of the teachers, a vivid purple sports car with silver flecks pulled up. It had tinted windows and on the side had "Chris Eubank. Simply the Best!" written in red italics[1]. As the driver's window came down, there was the man himself looking me up and down with a mixture of total disbelief and contempt before blasting away down the road. I don't know what was worse, the suit or his car!

Descending with only 15-20 foot visibility, weird! As the vapour jets across the wings, the plane changes colour from green to yellow, to red then blue. The clouds seem to open for us and the first thing that you see from above are endless piles of rubbish, ahhh sweet China! It's pouring with rain and as we splash down, once again I am amazed at how these planes can operate in such harsh conditions. This time I am met at the airport by a woman called Feng Xiao Lei who is a tour group leader. I know this sounds really hmmmm, unadventurous, but after my last experience in Beijing I am taking no chances.

Beijing is so vast it's impossible to contemplate. With its six ring roads and the Olympics coming, the construction industry is on express mode everywhere. I mean where do you start in a place like this? Well you start off with the Chinese guts from hell of course. Within twelve hours my arse has turned into the equivalent of a howitzer. Through a crazy fever that accompanies everything, Feng is there the whole time as some nursemaid from heaven or perhaps from hell, as she subjects me to the worst Chinese medicines known to mankind including numerous foul tasting teas.

---

[1] Chris Eubank was a middleweight and super middleweight champion boxer in the UK during the 1990's. Also arrested three times for his anti-war protests.

Monday: A freezing blue sky day! I missed the snow while I was out for lunch. Two days up the swanny! Nothing ever goes to plan. I look out from a high-rise across as I later find out is Tong Zhou County, way out east past the fourth ring road, phew! Venturing out trying to take in even a little of this place puts you in awe of its vastness. It's a mixture of flash new apartments with perimeter fences, run down hutong areas, building sites and wasteland right next door. In the evening Feng and I have hotpot. We choose between three types of meat; cow's tongue; cow's head or back. Hmmm, decisions decisions!

Tuesday: Let's get on with this vacation then. Tiananmen Square; obviously a highly significant place to the Chinese people. I mean there's the place Mao is laid to rest. I couldn't get to see him. He's being restored at the moment. There's the monolithic Great Hall of the People where the Peoples' Congress has its meetings and the Gate of Heavenly Peace leading to the Forbidden City. It must really be something for the Chinese people to see, especially after coming a long way during on hard saved money. It's a once in a lifetime trip for most. Once again though, Mr Grumpy returns. For me it's just a lot of paving slabs in one place and lots of people taking photos (including myself). I try to imagine the passion and history that's gone on in this place (and not all good of course) as red flags fly brightly against the crystal blue February sky, but how can you?

Beijing Hutong: There's one main thing that sticks out like waving a flag in your face here. It's the feeling of depth that I haven't experienced in any other city in China so far. It's not just a load of shiny new high-rise offices in a variety of interesting and way out shapes. A great deal of Beijing's heritage is still intact and certainly not just the palaces, temples and tourist attractions. Imagine a small old single-storey house with a courtyard. It may have a wood burner. It may have animals. There may be washing stretched out to dry on the line, maybe a few bikes leaning against the wall. Outside is a small alleyway that links up to more alleyways and then more again. Somewhere in the centre of this maybe a crossroads with a few small shops and open spaces, creating a strong sense of community. Multiply this warren to the power of a thousand and you have some idea of what the hutong in Beijing is like. Maybe twenty five percent of the population of Beijing still lives in the hutong and it's been this way for centuries, as far back as 1300.

Exploring these places is both fascinating and a bit nerve-wracking though, especially when it's time to take the camera out. An article in a local English written magazine recently had an article where Westerners set out to find the answer to the question "What is the real

China?" Hmmmm! Well without going to extremes all you really do is just sit here and be still for a moment. You don't have to be some great expert. Just sitting in an area central to one of the hutongs and just watching life going on as per usual is enough. Keep it simple hey! Unfortunately these wanderings also fell upon a lot of areas which are being knocked down and used for development. Maybe the Olympics have had something to do with it, or maybe China's need for continued growth where nothing will stand in its path, not even to preserve its past in some ways. All in all the hutong of Beijing is being torn down at an alarming rate.

Near the lake at Hou Hai you can get an amazing view of the local hutong from two old 13th Century towers which stand opposite each other. There is the Drum Tower that has twenty huge drums that are beaten on the hour and then the Bell Tower. The Bell Tower has a massive 63 ton, 2 foot thick bell that when struck could be heard across Beijing as a means of keeping time. Can you imagine what would happen if the bell ringer was a bit late one day? I guess heads would roll!

Pingyao: I am taken aback as the bus approaches Beijing's West Station. I remember having the same feeling about the Central Station with Pei but this place is bloody enormous. Feng tells me that on a busy day over 400,000 people can come through. She also warns me to watch my pockets and bag as it's not a safe place. There is a different vibe here. Hundreds of people are crashed out on the floor. Various darkened departure lounges are heaving. Families are waiting for how long, sitting on bits of cardboard with their carrier bags, boxes of food and belongings, the security guards moving people along and the stare of white eyes seems to follow you everywhere. The restaurant is empty; people sit on the floor in the dark all over, just outside looking in as we have our noodle soup.

The departure hall, one of many in the station, is a vast sea of thousands of people. Hundreds form two separate queues for two trains and the noise is a cacophony of the highest level. In order to compete with this, the tannoy system blasts out hurting your ears. It's so simply deafening that your head instinctively ducks downwards into your shoulders. When the first train arrives and the gates open to let the passengers through, it's more like a stampede.

As our train approaches people start to push forward, slowly at first but as the minutes tick by, the noise becomes louder and people start to become more squashed together. While your body is carried along by this pulsing current you have to watch your step and climb over people's bags.

And they're off! Like dogs coming out of the gates at the races chasing the rabbit, the next few minutes are a test of asserting yourself and giving out as much as comes your way. Finally Feng and I get through the gates and literally join the pack running to the train; madness! "I don't know why" I naively thought, "Everyone's got a ticket with their seat number after all."

We get to the train to find that for every five carriages, there are only two open door ways to let two thousand people on. Its pure pandemonium and after finally boarding the train we find that we're in completely the wrong carriage. I guess that's what happens when six people are trying to get on board at the same time. The aisle is so maxed out that I wonder if we're ever going to get to our lovely sleeper compartment at all. Amazingly after ten minutes of climbing round people and over luggage we encounter a woman with a trolley coming the other way selling food and drinks thus creating an explosion of activity ahead of her. I'm forced to sit on half on an arm rest and half on someone's lap while a girl unknowingly presses her arse into my face in order to give the trolley room. Eventually we find our carriage and throw out two people who have already fallen asleep on our beds with no ticket.

By 8.00pm the hard sleeper to Pingyao finally starts moving. This small town is in the north of the Shanxi Province and I'm well excited. The Shanxi Province is in fact the most polluted and utterly contaminated place in China. About a third of the country's coal comes from Shanxi and it's widely used to keep warm and create power. The ground is so bad they hardly grow rice at all so Shanxi has become famous for its noodles. I am told about a city nearby called Datong, where the mining has been so extensive that parts of it have started sinking. Apparently Datong is described as an "accident waiting to happen" so the tip of the day is don't buy an apartment there. Guess they must be pretty cheap. As the train goes south from Beijing and leaves the Hebei Province, the night air noticeably changes to smog and you can taste the soot, even within the protection of the train carriage.

A hard sleeper has six bunks in each open compartment. People walk past, stopping to check me out. The occupants of the bottom two bunks, Mr Zhang who is seventy five years old and his son invite us to sit with them. Mr Zhang tells us of his experiences during the Cultural Revolution and when he saw Chairman Mao while he was eighteen years old in the army. He tells us of the Vice Chairman's efforts to get rid of Mao and his famous attempt to escape upon his failure. Apparently he died accidentally during his plane flight to Mongolia. He also tells us about the 1976 Tangshan earthquake in the Hebei Province; the largest one ever recorded in China where over 250,000 people lost their lives.

All in all, the experience is everything I always hoped a sleeper train journey should be about, just brilliant! Even the two guys snoring in stereo loudly on either side of our compartment don't detract. One guy snores so loud the only way it can be described is that he sounds like he's farting out of his face. At 5.00am we arrive at Pingyao. Unfortunately Feng's rucksack drops on Mr Zhang's head from the middle bunk. Also, I am so used to sleeping on the bottom bunk that as I sleepily get my shit together I reach out in the dark to get what I think is my bag without looking. Oh dear, I grab young Mr Zhangs leg and virtually drag him out of bed. Poor guy lets out a yelp as he is woken up and wonders what is going on. I apologise profusely in Chinese but he sits there looking worried and disorientated curled up in a ball at the back of the compartment and I can't say I blame him!

Ah the wonders of hangin' with a tour guide. If I wasn't with Feng none of this would be happening. A car is waiting to pick us up and her friend Mrs Chung greets us and takes us to her hotel, cushty! Waking up, I find myself in the most amazing beautiful and certainly the oldest bedroom I've ever slept in. Its thick beams of darkened heavy wood and white panelling encourage a sense of antiquity and just sitting up and looking around the room makes you just go "Wow!" Not a bad start to a day hey? This place is called the Yide Hotel and was built in the 18th Century. All the rooms surround courtyards laid with old worn tiles and the dining room is simply the most aesthetically pleasing place you could ever have your breakfast in. Outside, there are even the original stone pillars and steps where people would tie up their horses all those years ago.

Pingyao itself is encircled by one giant wall with moat and drawbridge which was originally built in 1370 and has been continually rebuilt and repaired ever since. Known as the 'Turtle City' its name comes from the shape the wall makes as seen from the air. It's done a good job, not just protecting the town from invaders but also from change. The town outside is completely different from the one inside. So much of the original Pingyao remains and you can get a rare look into what it was like hundreds of years ago. I mean welcome to the world where women had tiny bound five inch feet so they could hardly walk. It is also known for having the world's first bank.

There's the old police house complete with the prison cells. If you were caught breaking the law then you were taken to the first house. If it was a particularly bad crime then you were taken to the inner house. There you could get a damned good thrashing with these huge wooden paddles. You could also get given the Tiger's Chair which basically had you tied down and your legs pulled up over and past your head until you're back broke. Either that or it was a beheading or for more serious crimes you would get 'Lingchi' which came from the phrase 'going up the mountain slowly'. Also known as 'Slow Slicing' the condemned person would be taken out to the courtyard, tied to a post and have their arms and legs cut off. Sometimes they would be given opium to keep them conscious so they could see what was happening to the last. Finally after decapitation, all the parts would be placed in a basket and taken away.

Dark histories aside, of course there are some beautiful temples and many other sights to see. The best experience by far though, was walking around the town via the top of the surrounding wall. From the wall you look down for a perfect view of the streets, blackened single storey homes and back yards where daily life continues untouched. Just before leaving, we ate at the restaurant with the oddest translated menu you will see. You can have "glue pudding"(yummy), "precious ingredients gruel, shit ache mushroom diced egg gruel" (a personal favourite of mine), "you the surface, you the surface rubbed hands on fish, element soup, fried cat ear and orchid zhuo knife cut face". Hard to choose from it all really hey!

Well, that was the Saturday. Amazing really. From South Korea to Tong Zhou, having explosive artillery barrages for bowel movements to snooping around the hutong and sightseeing around Tiananmen Square, to Pingyao/Shanxi on the train, a second plane ride to Beijing and a third the next day to get back to South Korea, that was the weeks holiday over and back to work on Monday. It was just a brilliant brilliant time made all the more amazing with my new friend Feng who is a total nutter and true extrovert.

Since returning to South Korea, I set my D-Day counter and it's on fifty eight days then I'm out of here. Bring it on! The summer is comin', the world is out there waiting and the boxers are still chaffing. Once again I have absolutely no idea what to do next. There is an advert on the TV for bomb disposal expert with high rates of pay and excellent opportunities for promotion, who knows hey!

# 12

# Mongolia
# Where the Eagle Hunters Live

You won't get a bigger contrast between two countries in Asia as between China and Mongolia. Although they're neighbours, the distance between any place of note is vast thus explaining why they are so different in almost every characteristic.

Mongolian people are particularly hardcore. The majority of the population lives out in the countryside, where winters up north near Russia can easily drop below minus 40, or down south in the Gobi Desert to a rosy little minus 50. Mongolians are tough rugged people who are brought up taking what we see as a hardship as part of their everyday life. You can see the youngest kids racing each other at top speed on horseback or helping when the goats get slaughtered; its just common place.

Chinese people in contrast quite simply are like fluffy panda bears and are almost unable to manage the slightest of confrontation. Of course you do see the occasional display of anger at times, but generally if you even slightly lose your temper in China, most will look like they are about to have an instant on-the-spot cardiac arrest. Generally Chinese folk are extremely friendly. They will go out of their way to the power of one hundred to help you and show more hospitality than you can possibly imagine. You can instantly be invited into someone's home or to a restaurant for dinner and exchange of telephone numbers can be swift. In any big town you will often see a Western person accompanied by their new Chinese friend, who will be, I am sure, offering them maximum assistance to almost anything.

On the other hand, Mongolian people seem definitely more laid back about meeting Western people, almost to the point of not being arsed. Of course they are friendly bunch, but it takes more time to get to know them, same as the rest of us I guess. Maybe it's that there are too many other far more important things to think about, like finding a new starter motor for the bike, or that another winter is imminent, but often a Westerner can be more like a vague curiosity.

Having said all of that, if you do end up staying off the beaten track then word of your arrival will spread fairly quickly. You can be laying in your ger dozing off, when someone can just come in and sit next to you, staring down at you in utter amazement for a few minutes before leaving. It's quite a surreal experience when it happens I can tell you. Maybe they heard from a neighbour there are foreigners staying around the next mountain, second ger from the left by the stream and they've just popped in to have a quick look.

If the door is open, you can just go up to any ger and just walk in and sit down, really! You will then be offered tea and cheese! If you leave your ger door open it's kinda like an invitation saying 'come on in' to anyone. Of course if you get into trouble then you'll get plenty of people that will suddenly help and ask nothing in return. If you do get invited in then watch out for the vodka coming your way in hideous quantities.

Gers: Well generally speaking, Mongolian culture is based on herding, whether its horses, sheep or cattle. In order to keep up with where the good grass is, they can move anytime anywhere and are a truly nomadic people. I guess this becomes especially apparent in winter when necessity comes knocking at their door. Most people live in a ger, which is a white circular construction of wooden ribs with conical roof, normally about 18 feet in diameter and about 10 feet high, but can be a lot bigger for large families. In winter they can keep you really warm and in the summer are excellent for keeping you cool. It takes less than two hours to erect a ger and about half that taking it down. These days, families can move their ger and possessions by truck though also still by traditional methods such as pack horse or camel. You do see a lot of gers being put up when you are on the road and one night my friends and I had the unforgettable experience of putting up a ger with a family near the Kazakh border.

From the ground up, first floor boards are laid down and then around that a circular wooden flexible lattice work forms the wall. The roof is supported by over thirty struts that locate into the wall and then project diagonally upwards converging to the central 'crown'; a circular wooden frame. The whole thing fits together rock solid and is covered by a thick tarpaulin that can take any weather, tied down with string made from super strong woven horse hair. With a central wood burner, chimney and surrounding beds you won't find a more relaxing place. Often families will make their ger extremely colourful inside and if you find yourself staying in one it's always hard to leave.

Unlike any other country I visited while on the road, whether in the countryside or in town, it's still commonplace for Mongolians to wear their traditional clothing. Although you see daily life becoming more modern, Mongolia has really kept a sense of timelessness. There's no secret to this or special attempt to preserve national identity. The climate is often so hardcore that anything else apart from the tried and tested simply will not do. Normally, people choose to wear a long gown going down to the ankles that can be thickly padded known as a 'deel'. If you try one on you instantly feel and enjoy its weight and won't want to take it off. Riding boots are commonly worn. In the cold weather, a really thick super warm pair of horse hair or felt socks will fit neatly inside, toasty! Clothing is also bright, extremely colourful and made of silk. Maybe it's to balance this simple nomadic way of life, who knows! Anyway, against a clear sky and vibrant landscape, when someone thunders by on horseback in their deel, it instantly paints one of those pictures you never want to forget.

Life on the road: Firstly, tarmac only exists in the biggest towns and normally ends as soon as you leave. Most of Mongolia has 'tracks' in the earth which for some unfathomable reason are marked as roads on any map you can buy. Often these will split up into as many as twenty smaller ones and then converge in a few miles. Tracks will have deep ruts or cracks in them in the dry seasons and become huge impassable mires in the wet. I really have no idea why people even bother to stick to the roads. The best thing to do is use a compass and go 'off-road'. Be prepared to continually change your tyres.

One of the absolute delights of the trip was cooking in the evening in the Steppe, the name given to the Mongolian grasslands. Every evening it would be a case of methodically getting the gear out and knocking up some top grub out in the open. In every big town there would be an open-air market, so you could stock up on what veg you found and buy a whole load of sausage to keep the cold out in the evenings. One time we bought a side of goat jerky which although it looked completely inedible, really did the trick. As the trip went on more and more dried food got hung up inside the vehicle; goat, cheese and fish, all swinging around leaving it seriously minging.

Days are long on the road in Mongolia but twelve hours seems to just flash by no problem. Perhaps it's because you're so in love with the whole thing or just because absolutely nothing matters. Time really loses its meaning out in the Steppe and you begin to see why Mongolian people have a completely different reality from the way we live, think and breathe in the Western world.

## Exit South Korea

June 1<sup>st</sup>: Well words can't describe how I feel today. Tonight is the last night in South Korea and tomorrow I'll be decked out somewhere in Beijing. Once again, this is the end of a journey and it sure has been long one. Subtracting time spent in China it's been 260 days. Does that seem like a lot? I dunno, but it does seem like I've lived a whole chapter of life here, to be honest an eternity. I can't believe I'm finally out of here; I thought it would never end. The last few weeks have been everything rolled into one and I'm going kinda confused about how I feel about things now. The one thing I'm gonna miss are my friends. I rekon I'm going to be able to hear their voices clearly in my head for a long time after splitting.

Anyway, here's a general unloading of anything that's gone on in the last few weeks in, as usual, no particular order: Visiting the Traditional Korean Village in Yong-in City, which turned into a riotous time in the car with Rache, Germaine (Rache's Mum), Daz, and I. There was also The White Lantern Festival in Seoul with my ace Korean friend Misia; a totally mesmerizing display of paper sculptures beautifully decorated and lit up in a huge procession that lasted the night. There's an English academy called 'Toss English' and a car company called 'Kolon Motors'. Watching Cobra gunships circle our neighbourhood from above on the mountain. Hangin out downstairs at the Ministop drinking cheap beer, volleyball in the park on Sundays, followed my more hangin out at the ministop!

I was warned of the Yellow Dust the one day but as per usual didn't think too much of it. A friend told me it's pretty harmful stuff that comes over from the Gobi Desert, so ignoring everything I went up Gyeyang Mountain. On the way it became quickly apparent that the city was unusually quiet. From the top, you could see that the area had become enveloped in a weird yellow cloud as far as the eye could see. One of the oddest sights you will ever look upon; the whole place looked like it had been hit with a mustard gas attack. Down below, bizarrely, the view through the dust cloud remained crystal clear with the colours of the buildings seemingly magnified. In the distance, mountains emerged from the mist, silhouetted black as far as North Korea. People stay in when they can if the yellow dust descends. It's really trippy! People take it as seriously as any other dangerous weather phenomenon so if they have to go out they will always wear masks. There's even a US military website which issues warnings if it gets too bad. When it rains, something similar to glue falls from the sky and if you leave your car parked outside it will become sticky overnight. Only a professional car valet will be able to clean it off.

I had to judge five English speaking competitions. "Don't worry" Mr A assured me before the first one, "It will be easy. Just go there and listen to some students talking in English. At the end you should decide who one is the best speaker". After all this time you would think I'd have wised up to it when Mr A used the words "don't worry" and "easy" but instead I went there feeling pretty cool about a quick earner.

Upon arriving though, outside a huge banner said "Welcome to the 18th National Schools Speech Contest" while hundreds of people filed their way in.........hmmm. Inside a packed auditorium eagerly awaited the beginning of the competition while a technician did some last minute microphone checks on the stage. Someone led me to the front and introduced me to a warm applause and then someone whispered,
       "Can I see your speech?"
       "What speech? No one told me anything about a speech."
       "You have no speech?" they replied looking shocked.
My assumption that having no speech had just gotten me off the hook was short lived. A few minutes after things had got going they signalled for me to get on the stage. Focusing on not having a heart attack, there I was making the speech up as I went along, telling everyone what a wonderful time I was having and what a wonderful event it was blah blah blah. All this was being translated for me while simultaneously wishing that the ground would open and swallow me up. When the ordeal was over all I could think of was locating Mr A immediately and strangling him until he begged for mercy.

A brief stop-over in Beijing
11th June. Some Monday's are just too good to be true and this is clearly one of them as I'm on that big train to Mongolia. It's 12.30 in the afternoon and there's little air in this compartment, so it's hard to get any shut eye. This Mongolian kid keeps playing the flute and all I can think about is where to ram it! Still, you certainly get your money's worth on this one and we just pass the roughest and most expansive Chinese industry you can imagine, through vast orchards and long tunnels through mountains. I wonder if we actually went under the Great Wall? As the train snakes northwards away from Beijing I can only look back on the last week with great memories and total excitement about the future.

The Red Lantern Guesthouse: Certainly one of the nicest places to stay in if you end up spending any time in Beijing. If you're in town then definitely check it out. Located in one of the central hutong areas north of the Forbidden City, the area is one great hive of activity. In fact it was so overloading that you only needed to photograph the view from the front door and that was enough. The guesthouse is stunningly beautiful, especially at night. I tell you, there's nothing better than sitting there at night in a traditional hutong courtyard, especially after living in Incheon for nine months; its just total bliss.

The staff are fantastic and Wei Ni, one of the girls who worked there, bought me an ice lolly made from mushy peas, a really popular flavour. The local supermarket was quite interesting selling all the old favourites like vacuum packed chicken's feet, chicken's necks and edible alkali (yummy). Zhongheyuan described their cashews as "Foods, best quality and good taste. It will captivate with relish. Have it! You'll have the world. Give endless pleasure. The natural fresh vogue delicacy is each the farmers master is refined." You know I knew there was something missing from my English lessons.

Yvonne showed up on Day 1, so I had three days of hanging with my crazy Dutch friend again. My card got eaten by a Chinese ATM on Sunday, aaaagh! Now you try going into a Chinese bank and try to communicate what had happened, where the ATM is and how it can be returned! Anyway we did find someone who can speak English and in true Chinese style, there were four members of staff waiting by the ATM at 9.00am on the Monday morning to retrieve it. Relief!

Made three trips across town on different mornings to the Mongolian Embassy, a sadly run down and knackered looking place compared to its neighbours. On the way you go down the central drag, past Tiananmen Square and the Central Business District. I tell you, I've never seen buildings like that before. Unlike the normal gravity defying skyscrapers that you might see, say in Hong Kong, the ones in Beijing are monolithic. They are heavy and definite with a clear message, "Hey! We are the Chinese and we are here to stay. We are the best and we are awesome!" I mean when someone gets the world cup or something that may just build some more stadiums or do up their public transport system. But for the Chinese it's an excuse to light the touch papers and go all out to do as much building work as possible.

Beijing duck in Beijing with Yvonne, nice! Over to the Lama Temple to see the Maitreya Buddha figure; 18m high by 8m below the ground, carved out of a single trunk of sandalwood and beautifully decorated. We also took a trip to The Silk Market, an insane place where people actually grab you by the arm and pull you into their shop.
"Hey Sir, you wanna buy pants? Wanna buy t-shirt? Best quality!"

You could buy scorpion, silkworm and cockroach kebabs, also sparrows and duck hearts on a stick.

I met these two nutty extrovert American pianists called Nathan and Ryan who had been learning the piano since the age of three, on a return trip from a competition in Chengdu. We visited the Summer Palace and also the Old Summer Palace called Yuanmingyuan. After ten kuai, a rip-off rickshaw ride and two hours wandering around we concluded that the Old Summer Palace wasn't there anymore, just an empty soulless space and a lake known as 'The Sea of Happiness' the only things remaining.

Actually there's a big reason why it's not there anymore. In 1860 Lord Elgin and the British forces teamed up with the French and burnt it down, stealing loads of valuable relics. Some are still in the British Museum to this day with no signs of returning anything. Before it was destroyed Yuanmingyuan was said to be one of the most beautiful buildings and gardens in the world. Nice one on that guys!

This all came about as a direct consequence of the Opium Wars which began in 1839. While Britain's dependency on laudanum was in full swing (it was cheaper than gin), its first multinational corporation known as the East India Company was selling huge amounts of opium in the south of China getting all the locals thoroughly addicted, thus becoming one of the largest drug dealers of all time.

Talk about bad sports though. The Emperor Daoguang sent his best man Lin Zexu to deal with the problem. Within a short time, he had effectively kicked the door down and busted the British big style, seizing well over a thousand tons of opium. Amazing hey! I mean when do you ever hear about a million keys of any drug being stashed around the corner right?

Nearby Yuanmingyuan's replacement, The Summer Palace itself is a breathtaking sight; its magnificent colourful pavilions following a single set of wide stone steps to the top of Longevity Hill. From the top there is an amazing view of Kunming Lake and its famous Seventeen Arch Bridge reaching over to Nanhu Island. You also get a 'clear' view of Beijing and the surrounding mountains.

Beer is cheaper than water. We had mutton vertebrae in a Mongolian restaurant that night. Apparently the spinal cord is the best bit (mouthwatering) and you eat it wearing plastic gloves so you can rip the bones apart before sucking the insides out. The sign of things to come I think. Oh dear!

The Train to Ulaanbaatar

The train reaches the last big city in China, Datong. Every town in China we go through from now on has an emptiness and harshness about it. Past gangs of track workers labouring on the line and dusty villages made of mud bricks; mud, mud and more dry mud. Eventually after twelve hours we are in Inner Mongolia and I am instantly aware of a growing fear inside of me about the whole trip. This place is.....well...everyone warns you that there's nothing in Mongolia but then you think to yourself "Yeah well, I love the countryside. The countryside is such a wonderful place. I'm so harmonious in the countryside", blah, blah, blah.

So there I am staring at Inner Mongolia at endless nothing thinking, "Shit! There's nothing here, just nothing! Why am I here? Why have I done this to myself?"

There's absolutely nothing but flat planes and a few hills far away in the distance.

Erlian is the last town in China before the border and the train tracks between the two countries do not match up. The Mongolian's did this deliberately in case China decided to invade. The train stops and is literally lifted up carriage by carriage while they change the wheels. This is certainly a most unique experience. Each carriage is then placed on the separate Mongolian lines. It takes six hours to exit China then into Mongolia and we are kept in our compartment for way too long.

The lack of air in this tiny space is kinda like being on a train in the UK all over again. I am sharing my compartment with two American brothers, Shawn, who can read and speak Mandarin fluently and Kevin, who paid to come over on a cargo freighter. There is also a Mongolian guy called Tulga on the top bunk, who teaches us our first Mongolian words. Oh, there's a young Pastor called Josh with a huge ginger beard, who is going as a missionary to help the disadvantaged children.

In the morning the train goes through the tail end of the Gobi Desert, the source of all that shitty yellow dust over South Korea. Two things happen. Firstly, everything I have been bottling up about the trip immediately jumps to the surface in a mad wave of apprehension. I wonder how often this feeling will come around and how intense this will get in the weeks ahead. Secondly, how woefully prepared I am for any kind of trip into Mongolia. Maybe I'll just go for a bit of a walk and generally stay in bed the whole time. Still, I'm here now and that's all there is to it.

We stop at Choyr just four hours from Ulaanbaatar. The air is so deliciously fresh. The sky is so blue. It's so bright and I reckon we've gained 1-2000m in altitude. Space, space and more space; as we get closer to Ulaanbaatar there are guys herding horses at speed across the Steppe. The carriage in comparison looks like a bombs gone off in it and stinks of bad breath, farts, feet and BO from four guys in a small space with no ventilation for thirty hours.

Ulaanbaatar (UB)
Well it's the capital of Mongolia. Mongolia has 3.5 million people and UB has 2.5 million; hard to believe as it's such a small city and you can see mountains surrounding it everywhere. In theory then, that leaves only one million in this absolutely vast country....hmmm! It's well-rough around the edges and consists largely of old Russian tenement buildings with paint peeling off everywhere. No all-weather paint in Mongolia! It's reminiscent of Tibet big time with 4x4's everywhere. There is the smell of Yak here, but there aren't that many. It's kinda difficult typing in this internet café. There are five people squatting around a skinned cow in the next room hacking off one of its legs.

A lot of the people look like they live very rough with blackened, ripped clothes and dirty, darkened faces. I guess living out in Mongolia doesn't come any harder than this. There are packs of homeless kids everywhere and there are some holes in the ground leading to the heating ducts they live in during the winter. As per usual though, there are people who look very well-off and great looking Mongolian women in high heels. The guys look well 'ard here, with scars, cuts, bandages and they really like to fight.

I got a cheap deal in my guesthouse from my new friend Nagi who I met at the station. From then on she's helped with everything and we've been hanging out a fair bit. The room is an L shaped space on the top floor. With two different views looking out from each end, you can see a lot of what is going on around here. It's down by the train station so you can see the mountains but more importantly all the piss-heads in the area, oh and also the car park attendant woman; a strapping lass that wears a floral carrier bag on her head when it's raining.

Being a bit worried about taking the camera out in UB. It's off to the market tomorrow and you definitely can't start snapping away around there. Last week some people got rocks thrown at them for taking photos but it's having your camera stolen that you should be careful about. I've already had two attempts at someone trying to half-inch my stuff. One guy brushed past in the street, his intention so obvious he had no chance.

Another time, on my way back to the hotel though, I felt something pulling me backwards stopping me in my tracks. Looking back, there was this enormous filthy alkie swaying around with both arms in my rucksack. I turned round with a loud "What the f*ck?" and he replied with a "Yaaaaaargh" and fell over on the street unconscious as he was so pissed. Guess I was lucky on that one.

The plan now is to go as west as west can be in Mongolia where it borders Russia and China. Spent the day putting adverts up in café's and guesthouses in order to find others who might want to come. Most people come here and do one week trips to the north or down south to the Gobi and aren't interested in going that distance. It seems really ambitious and so far no one's shown even a spark of enthusiasm. It's easy to be completely tunnel-visioned at the moment about the whole thing though. There are these Kazakh Eagle hunters who live in the Altay Mountains near Olgii. They train golden eagles to hunt for them, launching them to attack at high speed while on horseback. I mean can you imagine hanging out with those guys. It's just gotta happen mate hey! So it looks like its time for an extension on the old visa for a start.

How to get a visa extension in Ulaanbaatar
Locate immigration office. Go to the first counter and pay 1,500 tugrik (T) for a form. Go to the second counter and get a photocopy of your passport for 100T and a stamp on your form. Fill out the form and write a letter in Mongolian (Nagi did that one) saying why you want an extension. Take these to the first counter and have your passport photo stuck down and sign the letter. Go to a third counter and submit everything and have the form checked. Go to a fourth counter in another part of the building and pay 15 dollars and 100T to get a payment slip/ticket. Go back to the third counter and hand in the ticket. The guy then sticks the ticket to the letter. Go back to the fourth counter and pay 10 dollars and 100T for a same day payment slip. Go back to the third counter and collect your passport with extension. Ah, so simple! If only getting Housing Benefit could be that straight forward hey!

## Way out West: 3rd August 2007

Sitting in a cafe watching the rain come down, I wondered what the hell to do. The guys who were supposed to be joining me on the trip had vanished into thin air and I was clueless as to what my next move was. It all started to seem really too long, too difficult and just plain out of reach. So there I was in a right old mess unable to come make any decisions when this guy came in and started reading the notices on the board paying special attention to mine. I remember sitting there going "Come on, come on" England stylee under my breath as he read it.

After chatting about it, he really seemed like he wanted to go but thought it too ambitious due to various time limitations. After five minutes though, I managed to sell my idea and it was game on. Two emotions occurred at that moment, relief and a mega rush of nerves and excitement. You don't get that too often in life and when it does though it only lasts for seconds, you sure do remember it.

My new travelling partner was called Aaron from Providence, the capital of Rhode Island in the States, about three hours from New York and a thoroughly nice guy. He is a 'health care data analyst' specialising in disease treatment (all a bit over my head really), with an insane laugh and can knock up a wicked stir-fry. At the outdoor shop around the corner we started looking for warm gear. While we were chatting, this woman suddenly turned around upon hearing our conversation.

"You're not going to the West are you? Can I come?" and we were met with this great smile; good old Mando!

Her mate Ken joined us later and that was it! Mando is a dance performer and teacher living in Montpellier, France, although she was American born (great accent!). She also likes duct tape! Ken was from Dublin having just finished engineering in the Philippines as voluntary work building new houses in poverty areas. He also lived above a pub in Basingstoke for a year (as you do).

The next two days were intense. Planning, meetings, shopping and building supplies left us all completely knackered. Leaving Ulaanbaatar, the jeep maxed-out with gear, it seemed weird being so exhausted at the beginning of a big trip, but the job was done and we were off. Kinda mad really driving off into nowhere, not really knowing where your going to end up and what's going to happen, past worrying that our gear was most likely woefully inadequate and trying to stay awake as the jeep passed through the ger suburbs.

The Route: Firstly Mongolia is so big it's split up into provinces called 'Aimags'. Each aimag has its own unique character and you can really feel the changes as you move from one to the other. Check out the map. Start at Ulaanbaatar in the centre and work your way down south west to Bayankhongor. Move clockwise to the west then north for a bit, and then go east, simple! Yeah right!

Another thing is that when a town is marked on a map, it often is the smallest place in existence. It's marked on the map purely because there isn't anything else for miles around. 'Cities' are really small towns consisting of a few Russian brick buildings surrounded by wooden shacks and gers. They are pounded by the severest of winters and are generally in the worst state of disrepair. Most people live in the countryside and have no desire to live in town, just occasionally coming in to get supplies.

Tov Aimag
Saturday 9th of June: One week since South Korea, that picturesque view of A Block from my apartment window to this. How time flies and things change hey. Dreams definitely do come true, you just have to work extremely hard, be super patient to make them happen and keep yourself from going mad in the meantime.

Delicacies of Mongolia, Part 1: Right! I heard long before the trip that the Mongolians aren't too big on vegetables. One thing they are big on is goat! Goat, goat and more goat followed by a double, quadruple, supersized portion of goat! That and noodles. On the first afternoon of the trip we pulled over and grabbed our first taste of real Mongolian food. Our driver Tushik ordered us all a bowl of 'tsuivan' (pronounced soban) and Mongolian tea called 'tsai'. My friends had already done their fair share of travelling so waited in anticipation to see what Mongolian food is really like when you're on the road.

"Here it comes" Aaron noticed as the food came out of the kitchen, our first tsuivan of the trip. Basically it's just goat and noodles and later we found that occasionally if you're lucky you'll get some spuds in it. Although we were super ravenous after about five minutes our pace visibly slowed.

"Kinda hard going" commented Aaron, his chewing motions becoming more pronounced.

"I know what you mean" I replied while Mando promptly went into trying to repress a laughing fit while still eating.

"That's what the tomato ketchup's for I guess" noted Ken.
"Still, you have to finish it" he added wisely, "You'll be hungry later." Tsuivan is a truly serious meal. It's so completely heavy that the most immediate effect it has can only be described as tsuivan inertia, where

it knocks you out for about an hour. No one spoke in the jeep after our first tsuivan and our heads lolled around while we drifted in and out of consciousness. After a few days of eating this for brunch every day it really started to become an ordeal. Yes....here it comes.....another big steaming bowl of tsuivan. Hard to eat! Hard to swallow! You can go for a run of days without being able to take a dump as it bungs you up big time. After three days it really starts to become an issue. It can really get hmmm.....uncomfortable to say the least. Your arse cheeks start feeling more like a combination of two tectonic plates grinding together with something similar to Yellowstone Park about to explode beneath. Still, get it down yer neck! Days are long in Mongolia. You would be driven out of your tent at 7am by intense UV, like you're sleeping in a microwave oven or something then on the road for twelve hours or more. In the end you were glad for your tsuivan and you really start to appreciate why the food is the way it is.

From Ulaanbaatar we drove through the day to the Khongo Khan Mountain and camped for the first time in the Mongolian countryside or 'The Steppe', what a hit! I mean I've always liked camping, but camping in Mongolia! You're having a laugh aren't you!

Ovorkhangai Aimag
After a reluctant 7am start (get used to it mate), we arrived at the Erdene Zuu Temple near Kharkhorin, a fantastic place that instanteously brought your mood right up. They say that this is the land of the big sky and wow did it feel expansive. The temple itself is beautiful, resembling those in Tibet, but what really struck you were the huge white four hundred metre square surrounding walls creating an incredible sense of space. Colours became more vibrant and your emotions seemed to become magnified. Funny how something so simple could do so much.

Another Monday! A crazy morning of river crossings in the jeep, down the Orhon River Valley to the Hangayn Naruu National Park. River crossings are just completely wicked by the way. A hike up the sacred mountain of Khairkhan Uul to the Tuukhen Monastery. Not a bad way to start the week hey! So peaceful high up in the mountains; eagles circling closely both above and below with thick endless forests and hills surrounding us somewhere in the middle of Mongolia. If only all Mondays could be this stress free we'd live a lot longer.

Twats in sleeping bags

After only two days we get completely lost in the jeep. We drive and drive through endless valleys, through mountain passes, stopping at gers and asking people directions. Along the way, there's even a ger that has a solar powered washing machine outside chugging away. We keep going until it gets dark. The Khangai Nuruu Mountain range is massive so we are quite relieved when Tushik blags our first stay with a Mongolian family in their ger.

So he pulls up in the jeep has a quick word with this woman and we were in. She introduces herself as Ertensek and she has two daughters Anna who is six and Doya four years old who are immediately shooed off to the ger next door. It's just out of this world being here. To the other side of the Ger, opposite the doorway are Ertensek's family photos on display in frames and a beautifully decorated set of cupboards. In the centre is the stove and cooking equipment and there are sturdy metal framed beds either side with thick purple and yellow blankets.

I think it's a bit much for Ertensek to be honest, five strange people in this small ger but she rushes around making space and sorting out something to eat, kindly offering us an assortment of butter, thick cream and fried doe. She also gives us a bowl of 'oron' a yak milk yoghurt and gestures that we are not allowed any tea afterwards. Tushik laughs and points to his stomach and his arse and we all get the message not to drink anything.

After an hour all anyone can think about was crashing out. So there we are, the three of us all lined up on the floor in our doss rolls, Mando having strategically blagged a bed. We're all starting to nod off when the door bursts open. In come three big guys who are clearly stunned at our unexpected appearance in their ger. I don't think they've seen many Westerners in the first place, let alone as their guests.

So there we are lying on the floor in our sleeping bags in a line looking like a right bunch of f*cking idiots as the three guys come over and sit right next to us looking down with total curiosity. Reaching into my trouser pocket once more my friendly little Mongolian phrasebook comes to the rescue.

"Minii ner Andy" (My name's Andy) followed by "Minii ner Aaron. Minii ner Ken. Tany ner khnen be?" (What's your name?)

"Tomotichol" replies the closest who I guess is the man of the house. Leaning over to his friends he says something and they all break out into laughter.

"I think they're taking the piss out of you" offers Mando smugly from the safety of her bed. Helplessly immobilised in our Lowe-Alpine polyester cocoons and smiling along with the whole thing, we have to suffer their private jokes for a painfully long hour before they get bored and leave.

Shaking like a leaf throughout the night; their last gesture is to remove the tarp from the top of the ger letting all the heat out so the temperature drops well below freezing. Nice one! To top it all those frigging howling wolves keep us awake all night.

Bayankhongor Aimag
Finally finding a way out of the mountains we reached the city of Bayankhongor. It roughly has a population of 22,000 and is the 9th biggest in Mongolia. As we repacked our gear into the jeep, people kept coming up trying to buy our stuff like it was a car boot sale. They seemed particularly interested in buying our pink washing up bowl. It's also one of the few towns with a spa. I think there are three or four in the whole country. Get used to never washing in Mongolia; you can go for weeks without getting a shower in. Most people don't look like they ever bother and you quickly get used to high grime levels when you are on the road. Sometimes it actually feels like you have another set of clothes on. Within seconds of arriving at the spa in Bayankhongor, we were diving out of the jeep and running for those antiquated old showers at top speed.

Delicacies of Mongolia, Part 2: Dairy products are a big one in Mongolia and it takes a long while for your guts to become accustomed to it. You are offered tsai everywhere which is basically warm milk and salt with the merest trace of tea. Normally two cups are all your guts can handle before they start burbling away. While we were hanging our clothes out to dry outside the spa, this woman came up and gave me some cheese (as you do) called 'arun'. Its rock hard and it's the strongest of strong with the sharpest taste you'll experience cheese-wise. It exploded up my nostrils and down my throat making me cough and wretch uncontrollably much to the amusement of the locals. There is also a similar one called 'byaslag' which is really popular and often offered when you enter someone's ger. After tasting byaslag for the first time, there is certainly no desire to give it a second try, so you will normally end up carrying it around instead of eating it. Keep it though, as you can give it back to other Mongolians along the way when you say hello. This always goes down really well when you meet someone for the first time.

Off into the nothing of the northern Gobi Desert, heading west on the way to Altay. Never been in a desert before let alone camping in one! Serious! Not one vehicle passed on that road the whole time we were camped there...and that was the main 'highway' between two major towns! One thing about that area of desert was there were vodka bottles everywhere, I mean everywhere! It's hard to quantify but they completely litter the roadside. Most people drove completely wankered. As the trip progressed across the rocky plain, we saw what looked like a pile of diamonds in the mountains shimmering and gleaming in the sun on the horizon. Getting closer, it turned out to be a huge heap of thousands of vodka bottles. I don't think anyone has a hang-up about drinking too much in Mongolia mate, even when you're driving! I guess there's nothing to hit. I think if you combined the genes of someone from the UK with someone from Mongolia we would create the super alcoholic.

## Gobi Altay Aimag

From the desert we arrived in Altay, the friendliest town on the trip. Altay had one street in particular where everyone just stopped and said hello, so it was really great just hanging out outside and watching the world go by. Altay has a population of about 17,000 and is the 16th largest city in Mongolia. Instead of just passing through we decided to treat ourselves and go for a wild night out on the town, staying overnight in the Altay Hotel.

You really felt like Altay takes a shellacking in the winter, with damaged and abandoned buildings all over. Wandering down the weathered pot holed roads, a guy in a black cardigan came over and shook our hands enthusiastically before gesturing for us to follow. He introduced himself as Armarasehen, the manager of the Altay Dance Ensemble and showed us around the place; an aged worn out looking building filled with a strong feeling of the past. He proudly showed us his picture mounted high up amongst many others; old black and white portraits of other no doubt successful dancers from times gone by. We got to meet the whole crew including his top performers were called Munkchummock and an elegant woman called Mungentugus. No hangin' around with names around Altay!

They had strange ways of doing things in Altay. One time Mando tried to send some postcards. She marked them to France and Germany but then they said that they had given her the wrong stamps and she needed to pay more. It went on for over half an hour and somehow became an enormous problem. The people working there even ended up on the phone trying to sort it out.

Eccentric old place the Altay Hotel. Aaron asked for the menu in the restaurant and got given a roll of toilet paper. You have to pay extra to have water in your room and fair play to Ken and his super persistence in getting it.

'Halon uus' means hot water in Mongolian and Ken continually followed the maids Ichma and Atarra wherever they went hassling for halon uus doing their nuts in. "Uus Uus Uus! We want Halon Uus."

Our big night out was next door at the worlds oddest disco. With just ten cans of beer behind the counter, the only time people danced was for the last song of the night, all very self-consciously in a big circle.

At 6am after our night out there was a loud banging on the door and it was the girls shouting "UUs, UUs Haaaaalon Uus" and that it was only going to last for fifteen minutes. Not wanting to waste this rare window of opportunity, I jumped under the shower to find only a trickle of freezing water would come out.

Khovd Aimag
More desert; unforgiving nowhere and seriously hot. You just don't wanna break down out there I can tell you. Onwards we drove, through the Dariviyn Nuruu Mountains into Khovd Aimag where we camped at Khar Lake.

Khovd: Really in the way out west of Mongolia now. Khovd has a population of 26,000 and is the 7th largest city though it really has the feeling of being a lot smaller, ready to be engulfed by the surrounding mountains. Tushik got smashed the night before with some of his mates in town, so we ended up hanging out in his mate's ger for the morning while he slept off some of the vodka. A great place! They even had a solar powered PC so all we could download all our photos for them.

As soon as Tushik started to sober up though (it took long enough, grumpy old git), we blitzed back into the wilderness to the Burateen Davaa Pass. Camping high up by a river round the back of a small diner, we proceeded to have one of the best times of the trip. The people who lived there not only helped put all our tents up, but invited us in to their little living room for the evening. In the warm and dark, there was no choice but to instantly fall asleep, packed against everyone else like sardines to the sound of Russian Karaoke on the TV. Often out there where you ate is where you slept so Tushik crashed spark-out right in the middle of the restaurant still nursing his hangover.

While we dozed, the girls continued to work all night while jeep and lorry loads of people came in and ordered buzz and tsuivan. You'll never see anyone work so hard in a kitchen as they did and this was their routine twenty four hours a day. Buzz (pronounced Bazz) are goat dumplings normally served with a wicked jar of chilli sauce and are made from scratch every order.

The next morning, I was getting the first brew together round the back of the jeep, when one of the girls Bolitzika (about twelve years old), walked by clutching a fresh goats head, threw it into a box, then greeted me with "Ugluuniimend" (good morning) and the biggest smile. We watched as the girls hung up various bits of goat on a big pole to dry out. All round the living room in the diner there were bits of goat everywhere. There was even a leg balanced on top of the TV.

A bit later, while standing there with a tea taking in the scenery, this guy with a camel rode up. "Can I have a go?" I called out. Camels are really tall and you feel really high when you're on up one. Not only that but they are fast and this one took off like a rocket at the speed of light. As a Brit, you swear a lot at the top of your voice when this happens. Still, a good awakener and hangover cure. Other highlights of the morning included Ken hilariously shepherding a flock of goats away from our tents in the wrong direction, much to the shock of the herder. We played volleyball together and Mando managed to smash a window. I guess we all felt pretty guilty about that one, as for sure there aren't really any shops that sell panes of glass out there.

Bayan Olgii Aimag
From the diner up the pass, our Saturday was spent in the tiny town of Tolbo. You're really 'out there' in Tolbo. People are no longer Mongolian. You're in Bayan Olgii Aimag which is populated largely by Kazakhs. Tolbo has around two hundred people, a tiny shop that looks like it is continually closed and shed loads of bones everywhere you walk. There is also a small mosque with pink walls, white towers and a light blue domed roof topped with the crescent and star of Islam. It's certainly a quiet place, dusty with tumbleweed blowing down its empty streets.

To be honest, we were all feeling a bit apprehensive about how the people out there would receive us, so when this huge guy with a big black beard came out at the other end of town heading straight for us down the middle of the road, we became somewhat on edge. I guess with no one else around, it would have looked pretty odd walking off in the opposite direction, so with no other choice we proceeded towards each other.

"This is like some spaghetti western" commented Mando as we walked nervously side by side down the street. As we got closer, much to our relief he stretched out his arm to shake our hands, giving us the warmest of greetings,

"Asalamalakum. (the Islamic greeting meaning 'peace be upon you') Welcome Welcome. Welcome to our town." He introduced himself as Khumar, the Town Secretary, with a voice as hearty and loud as Brian Blessed.

Delicacies of Mongolia, Part 3:

"I am very happy to have you here in Tolbo. Please come this way and join me and my wife for dinner" insisted Khumar.

Inside his wife Banksh was already setting the table and getting the food ready. Once again this consisted of nearly all dairy products. We were given 'hort' which was hard white chunks of cow's milk, 'illimichic', similar but sharper tasting, 'kazlamchk' similar again but yellow, 'mie' a salty butter, unpasteurised milk served from a light blue bucket and 'Iren' a yoghurt that had a real zing to it and was actually really delicious. The only non-dairy product was called 'balsak' a puffed fried dough. Quite often you'll be invited in to someone's place in Mongolia and this is the kind of hospitality you'll get every time.

Embarrassingly I forgot my manners. Leaning over to my ear "You can only use your right hand to eat and drink" whispered Mando. It is said that your right hand should be used for clean things especially when eating and is important etiquette in these parts. Your left hand should be used for cleaning and doing all the dirty work.

Khumar was especially fond of his picture of Arnold Schwarzenegger as Terminator which took the centre space of his living room wall. It was certainly an unusual sight to see all the way out in Tolbo, looking strangely out of place. "He is a symbol of America and freedom" he boomed proudly. Hmmm, best not get into that one right now I rekon.

All in all prepare yourself for a diet based almost entirely on dairy products and goat when you're in Mongolia. You will hardly ever get offered any vegetables and as for fruit, maybe you'll find the odd apple if you're lucky down the market. It's amazing how in the UK we fuss about what we eat and how important it is to maintain a balanced diet and yet in Mongolia people are the healthiest looking people you will come across, hardly eat any fruit and veg and get ripped on vodka on a regular basis. I mean how they can really live without essential fatty acids as part of their daily nutritional intake is a mystery. How does a Mongolian live without aloe vera when considering dry skin and damaged hair? How do they live without labels on everything and how do they live without those safety warnings? How, how, how?

The following afternoon upon finally arriving in Olgii, (8th largest city, population 28,000) the best choice seemed to stay overnight in the Bastau Hotel. What was it about the Bastau Hotel? It was, the staff boasted "the most up-market hotel in town". Our room, decorated in faded emerald green and pink also had pink flower net curtains plus nouveau lightshades in green, pink and gold to match.

Down the centre, between the beds and barely above head height, a great big green pipe was a continual annoyance, but at least you could hang up your towels somewhere.

Negotiating and planning for the following stage of the trip came next. This was with the main aim of going as far west as possible, looking for the Eagle Hunters on horseback in the Altai Tavan Bodg National Park. Here the Chinese, Russian and Mongolian Borders meet. There are eagles everywhere in the west. They easily outnumber any other type of birds and to the locals they are more like pests there are so many. They hangout on rooftops in the market and swoop down and grab any spare scraps when they can.

Another perfect Monday: From Olgii to the village of Tsengel, camping nearby in an amazing green oasis. High up in the mountains the river split up into many smaller tributaries and streams forming lush curved islands of flat green with a protective canopy of deciduous trees you don't often see in Mongolia. A nomadic family of herders had already established themselves on one of the larger areas of land in two large gers positioned comfortably between the trees. Outside, a horse had been tied to a makeshift post. In its blue blanket with ochre and violet star designs, it must have been a most valued and well looked after animal. Their huge six wheel Russian flat-bed sat heavily towards the far bank ready to transport them through high water levels or across any difficulty, though a black jeep was also parked up close at hand. There were even two spare tyres for both vehicles propped up against the trees. Clearly they were very well organized with all eventualities covered. Piles of wood suggested that they were there for some duration having already found their spot for the summer. The sound of the surrounding cattle contentedly grazing in the late afternoon sunshine was dampened by the trees immersing the area in stillness; a perfect place to be.

An older woman came out and carrying a kettle between gers. Her vivid pink head scarf and long yellow and purple dress below her knees were matched by a black quilt jacket and sturdy boots lending to life's practicalities. Two boys ran to the water's edge to fill up a milk churn while their dog jumped around their legs. They then carried it back between them, leaning outwards to distribute the weight while water spilled out down the sides. For these people it was just business as usual without batting so much as an eyelid at the spectators setting their tents up across the way. The wish to be transported to the other side of the river and be a part of it was by now buzzing around my head like a swarm of angry bees.

280

Strangely though, the usual warm welcome we had become used to was absent. Perhaps it was something to do with moving into the west, but even Tushik kept his distance this time, just going over for a brief moment, no doubt to fill them in on who the visitors were.

The next day, across from the border pass, we stayed overnight in our first ger camp. A ger camp is basically a group of gers complete with wood burners and beds that you can hire out for the night; kinda like a ger drive in. Normally you cook your own food, but often it's easy to blag something from nearby if the need arises. At the camp everyone played volleyball including the whole family who lived there. Surrounded by mountains and lakes, we played until it got dark and even Tushik got stuck in. When you're on the road you certainly get your highs and lows and that game of volleyball was truly one of those greatest and most unforgettable of times. The kids Uynga, the eldest, Solongo, Ornaa and Ivelee were always helping out and the older sisters, Mandah and Naraa were just brilliant.

That night, while stoking up the old wood burner (wicked wood burners in Mongolia by the way) there was a sudden disturbance outside. These pissed-up Kazakh guys had ridden into camp and were hassling for somewhere to crash, shouting and cussing at the tops of their voices while their horses went nuts. Mandah tried her best to get rid of them but they were completely arseholed and are having none of it. Out came Naraa, a big girl in traditional Mongolian dress wielding a great big tree branch. Waving it around her head she eventually chased them away. As they rode off into the dimming light one of the guys turned around, charged back into camp and shouted some obscenities at the top of his voice, clutching a half empty bottle of vodka. His horse reared up and then he was off into the darkness!

Well the guides Ertinbatt and Normonchan showed up with the horses, amazingly on time. The trouble was the horses were clearly pissed off with the whole thing. One of them definitely was not going to be ridden and broke free going crazy. Normonchan got hold of its reins, but then was dragged off into the distance at the speed of light. Like a trooper though, he didn't let go, later returning with one very reluctant horse. I'm sure everyone was thinking the same thing at that moment; "that is definitely not gonna be mine!" Luckily, it turned out that it was in bad condition and saddle sore, hence the short temper so the guys had to go off to find a replacement.

On horseback we continued north alongside the snowcapped mountains of the Chinese border and camped at Hurgan Nurr Lake. There were two ways to remember this part of the trip. Firstly, utterly amazing! A dream come true, to think of actually riding in the Steppe, across rivers and alongside mountain ranges hugging Xinjiang on the other side. There is another element to this though. Apart from Mando, none of us had ridden a horse before. It seemed that horse riding over any speed other than walking was utterly ball-busting. As soon as we went even into a canter a blind panic set in as my testicles were given a thorough pounding against the saddle. How anyone rides a horse fast is utterly beyond me. Oh, one other thing. I didn't realise this, but horses will fart and crap all day and all night, even when you're on the move.

If someone is riding up ahead, when their horse rips another one off, you immediately associate it with them, it's hilarious! This of course immediately dispels any romantic thoughts you may have had about majestically journeying through the wilderness. You never get that in the movies now do you!

The Eagle Hunter
Onwards and we're sitting in this ger near the lake. Beautiful colourful hangings are everywhere. The lady of the house Gudnass lays on byaslag, salted mei, tzai and biscuits for us. Her husband Uluphaan, a strong stocky looking man in a blue denim jacket comes and sits next to us quietly playing tunes on his dombaa, a bit like a two stringed lute. He has a slight smile and knowing look in his eyes as if he is studying the four visitors sitting in his ger. The guides had mentioned that this family hunt with eagles so we came over to visit them early in the morning as soon as we broke camp filled with excitement. They also said that it was important to bring presents and that a sharp kitchen knife and some butter always goes down well. Mando hands them over to Gudnass who receives them with a big smile. For sure this family feels really welcoming, having a relaxed and open demeanor about them.
      At that Uluphaan puts down the dombaa and gestures for us to follow him back outside. The family has two gers side by side perched on the side of a hill that look out across the valley with the lake shining like a mirror down below. Donning his black leather cap, he mounts his horse and leads us down to the water's edge where the eagle is kept. He puts a super thick pale animal hide gauntlet on which comes up to his elbow, kneels down, unties the eagle (no cages around here I guess) and it obediently jumps onto his forearm without a second thought. Amazing to see this huge beautiful bird close up; its wingspan from tip to tip must have been well over a metre allowing it to soar to over a thousand feet and dive at 200mph; its curved beak and razor talons allowing it to tear to pieces its prey; its call carrying for miles between the mountains. In the winter Uluphaan will hunt with the eagle, launching it at high speeds from his horse to catch small game but even foxes and small deer if he's lucky. Not a bad way to get your dinner in!

It can even have a go with wolves if necessity bites. Uluphaan then jumps on his horse with the eagle and does a few circuits for us and he effortlessly charges around at breakneck speed.

It's a truly moving experience, especially so far out in the wild. As we leave though, I can't help but feeling a bit disappointed by the whole thing. The experience with Mr Eagle Hunter is cut way too short and its already time to move on. Having come all this way and put so much effort into making it happen, staying at least one night to get to know them better instead of just passing by would have been at least some sort of medicine. At that moment I vow that I'll be back to have another lash at this one day, to really try and find a Mongolian family that I can really hang out with and experience their way of life. This time it's the journey and the getting there that's more important, not the final result. Final results never turn out the way you want them to be anyway! We continue as far as we can; the border police wouldn't let us go much further. We ride for a few more hours to the mountains of the White River which has vibrant almost pink drinkable glacial water!

On the return journey, we got back to Olgii in one day. Phew, some serious distance! Back to the Hotel Bastau! A strange place was the Bastau; the people were really weird. There was an odd woman called Goldan and an even weirder guy called Gwambik who had a strong resemblance to the flying dwarf out of 'The Singing Ringing Tree' an old children's TV programme from the 60s. As a child I found it utterly terrifying, causing many a sleepless and tearful night. 'Gwambik!' Now there's an attractive name to call your child in any country right? Gwanbik wore the same multi-coloured jumper every day that looked and smelt like he never washed it or took it off. It had a delicious looking brown stain from the chest downwards, presumably from years of spilt dinners and wiped his nose on his sleeve. He also slept downstairs in the hallway on the same chair every night and at times you could feel his eyes following your movements about the hotel including breakfast time.

Everything smelt of mutton by this time. To be honest it was getting a bit wearing; your piss, sweat everything smelt of mutton. Even the usual cup of Tetley tea had a delicate mutton aroma about it. Rice porridge with goat's milk for breakfast and tsuivan for lunch. Said goodbye to Ken and Aaron so that was a tough one. They had deadlines to make so flew back to UB. A pleasant and mild mannered chap called Nicholi from France joined us and as we were shopping in the market, Ken and Aaron's plane blasted over us at low level; an old looking twin propeller driven thing looking like a WW2 Mitchell Bomber.

From Olgii we pushed on to the north-west, camping at Uureg Nurr Lake in Uvs Aimag. The sound of a zillion mozzies was the dawn greeting from outside the wafer thin protective skin of the tent. All wanted to say good morning; a continual high-pitched shrill warning you of what was waiting. Getting out of the tent, the only option was to run as fast as possible while completely engulfed in a black buzzing cloud of insects. Breakfast had a new organic favour about it and camp was struck in record speed, not even allowing time to brush your teeth. They found their way into everything and everywhere; in your breakfast, down your back, in your ears, eyes, nose and mouth causing your head to twitch profusely as if possessed by some nervous tick.

UVS Aimag:
Monday: Reached Ulaangom, the 12th largest place in Mongolia with a bursting population of over 20,000, then headed south to camp in Kharra Valley near the village of Tarialan. Nice spot. Mando taught me the art of rock balancing! I was instantly hooked! Just find a rock with smooth edges about the size of your forearm from any river bed or beach. Get it to stand upright on its axis on another rock or bolder without it falling over. Talk about a mindful activity or what!

That afternoon Tushik took us to buy some 'airag' which is fermented mare's milk, a common homemade Mongolian drink. As a Mongolian countryside equivalent of a bar, instead of the normal family type of ger, this one was empty except for thick dirty floor boards to sit on. To one side, in a large open twenty gallon plastic blue drum there was the airag brewing away. You could either sit and drink in the ger or fill up any plastic container you cared to bring with you as a take away. Tushik ordered us the first round with a smile and the proprietor went to work over at the drum. As he stirred it with a long stick, it was apparent that it was fairly thick in consistency and my stomach was already preparing itself for another dairy based ordeal. The penny then dropped that the horse just outside was the aforesaid mare, a reminder of what was about to go down your neck. Actually, considering it must have been stewing away for some time, it wasn't that bad really; strangely fizzy and sharp with a bit of a kick. Apparently it gets stronger as the summer gets hotter...aaaaaaagh! Just imagine necking five pints of that down the local!

We got mega lost the following day; driving through the desert again, past the same abandoned Russian factory again and again, across the same dry river beds which did their best to destroy the jeeps suspension. Finally, at the end of a long hard day, we ended up staying somewhere in the Khan Khokhiy Nuruu Mountains. Now the tip of the day is you really don't want to camp in the top of a mountain range in Mongolia when you are surrounded by thunderstorms. Mando and I sat there watching the main storm slowly coming our way with trepidation until it got too late. We took a real pounding that night but amazingly the cheapo tent survived. Another little tip is also not to go for a stroll by yourself. There was nothing there! Alone! Just prickly bushes, rocks, bones from horizon to horizon and occasional bits of now useless rusted metal to show that humans were there at one time. You could get lost in a second if you weren't careful, seriously!

Tushik: Well before the trip comes to its finish, it just wouldn't be the same without a few words for yet another mad jeep driver. He is married with two daughters, Zeeman and Tenman. His wife is called Natsodu. He is an experienced driver having clocked up a huge mileage across Mongolia. He sucks the marrow out of bones after a meal and has lots of sugar in his tea.

The first noticeable thing about Tushik was that he would just veer off the road and into absolutely nowhere. Often we would get completely lost and were saved only by Ken's GPS. We had a hard time after Ken left spending a long time aimlessly going around in circles in the desert. I mean it would be like, well here's the map, that's the road and it's all really simple, but no! Off goes Tushik in completely the wrong direction followed by stopping at every ger and asking for help. He would go wildly chasing animals at top speed and when arriving at Olgii would deliberately aim at people walking down the street to make them jump out of the way then go "Blaaaaaagh! Kazakh!" Mongolians and Kazakhs don't really get on with each other really it seems.

We were baptised early on in the trip when Tushik really wanted us to get to the top of Khairkhan Uul and the Tuukhen Monastery. Almost as soon as we began hiking it started to rain and then hail...hmmm, was someone from up above saying that we really shouldn't be going up there or something? Anyway, suddenly Tushik pulled up in the jeep and everyone jumped in thinking he'd just come to get us out of the bad weather. Oh no! Onward he blasted up this sacred mountain along the track which was rapidly turning into mire. The jeep didn't even get halfway before completely losing all traction and were forced to slowly turn round and ride a white knuckle out of control descent that left us bogged down with a flat tyre. Twisting and sliding in all directions narrowly avoiding trees I think we were all clenching quite hard that afternoon!

Khovsgol Aimag:
Some Other Day: Still lost, the friendliest biker ger gang in the country gave us directions and invited us into their ger for lunchtime vodka, yeeeech! Camping on the Ulaangom-Moron highway (yes, there really is a place called Moron). As we got some food together, this guy and

his missus rode up on these big horses, dismounted and sat there checking us out for a while. They never spoke to Tushik, merely leaning over and exchanging whispers in each other's ears, no doubt passing comments. After dark their mates arrived and speedily came to a noisy and dusty halt. The two jumped back onto their horses then the pack thundered off into the night. That was really something! You get plenty of timeless moments in Mongolia and this was one of them. Somethings really feel as if they are unchanged across the years out in the Steppe for sure.

Arriving in Moron, (5th largest city, population 35,700) there was the choice of staying either at the Dul Hotel or the Turt! We chose the Turt! On the menu for the evening was 'Potato Shack, Capital Salad and Round Meat' very nice. Next door the 'disco club' boasted that it also sold cheese but apart from that there wasn't too much going on in town.

From Moron, Tushik drove at the speed of light up the west bank of Lake Khovsgol Nurr and got immediately bored after only a few miles. It was more than frustrating as the plan was to be going a lot further to visit Nagi's family, but Tushik wasn't having any of it, not budging another inch. He could be a crotchety old pile of pants at times for sure! On the flip side, we blagged a stay in the most amazing ger. Inside it had the brightest and most colourful wall hangings imaginable, three beds and a car battery with crocodile clipped cables to supply electricity during the evening.

The lake itself is the centre of one huge nature reserve and is a staggering eighty miles long and twenty miles wide crossing over into Russia. It is one of the most tranquil places you will go to. I mean, imagine going to some nice chill-out spot for the day. At least sometimes you will be disturbed by something like a car in the background or someone walking by. At Khovsgol there is just a continual uninterrupted calm twenty four hours a day. The water slowly laps against the shore line, a bird calls out or the wind blows gently into your ears; this is about as noisy as it gets! You can even drink straight from the lake it's so clean. Be careful though! There is a legend that a monster similar to Loch Ness lives in the lake. The locals call it 'the underwater deer' and a diving party with sonar even picked up a huge shape moving deep below the waters at one time.

Monday 29th: This was the last day on the road stopping to camp at the Amarbayasgalant Khiid Temple. Not a bad way to wake up on your last morning though. The temple is the second largest in Mongolia and a seriously beautiful sight to open your eyes to before hitting the road for the last time. Sitting below some hills and looking out across the flat grassland, its silent terracotta walls perhaps give a less than realistic representation of what it used to be like in the past. At one time the monastery had over 2000 monks living there and by the early 1890s Amarbayasgalant was one of the greatest pilgrimage destinations in Mongolia. Taking a few minutes to sit back and take in the area, you could only start to imagine the busy collection of gers, people and animals not to mention countless other smaller temples that must have filled this now empty spot outside.

These days the building is a mere shell of what used to be. In 1937 the communists under Stalin came and sacked it as they did many other monasteries across the country. They took out most of the books, artwork and burnt the lot; the smoke could be seen for billowing away for miles and lasted for days. Figures seem to vary but well over ten thousand monks were killed in Mongolia at that time many were also taken off to perish in Siberia.

Today at Amarbayasgalant, sadly only around thirty monks remain, some of them children and teenagers and they help in the restoration of the building. Their numbers are so few that though the central buildings are well taken care of, the rest of the place has fallen into dilapidation and it's easy to wander around for hours exploring the old buildings which are in the process of being reclaimed by the earth. Seeding weeds push paving slabs aside and even grow high up between the earthen tiles on the rooftops, while murals fade away under the sunlight. Carved smiling Buddhas poke their faces out from the undergrowth. Doors hang open, their peeling paint work finally surrendering to the elements exposing decaying wooden panels and frames underneath. Inside, most outhouses are now left empty or have become places to dump old relics out of the way, which, by now have become covered by a thick carpet of grey and white pigeon shit. Clearly the pigeons moved in a long time ago and they give their presence away with gentle cooing from up in the rafters adding to the whole feeling of tranquillity on a warm still day.

Our kit was by this time totally knackered; not surprising really. A bit sad to see it so mullered, but it did well under the circumstances. Finally, the jeep sped into Ulaanbaatar though the unexpected sight of huge traffic jams soon dispelled any thoughts that the trip was over. The Naadam Festival was about to begin. Talk about good timing!

The Naadam Festival is Mongolia's biggest festival. It is a national holiday and takes place between the 11th and 13th of June every year. Although the biggest celebrations are held in UB, many smaller ones also happen all over Mongolia. Upon our arrival, Ulaanbaatar seemed like a completely different town. I mean it was seriously heaving. After being on the road for so long and being so burnt out, the need to chill and do nothing for a few days was all consuming. Tough luck mate! The main events of the Festival are held in the main stadium just outside of town, which of course was totally maxed-out to capacity. The biggest event is always the wrestling. 512 enormous guys try to bring each other to the ground over two days of contests until only two are left in the final. Wearing tiny red or blue pants called 'shuudag' and traditional style Mongolian boots with upturned toes known as 'gutal' this is a sight you certainly don't see very often. They also wear a 'jodag' which is a long sleeved jacket with the front removed so that the wrestler's chest is exposed. After the match, they perform the 'eagle dance' where the loser must 'fly' under the outstretched arms of the victor. The final went on for ages leaving both competitors looked absolutely exhausted but after three-quarters of an hour the two times champion and favourite won and the crowd went absolutely nuts.

There is also the archery event, a sport that originates from before the days of Genghis Khan and is the weapon that allowed the empire to become so successful. Quite something to see, especially the richness in colour of the traditional Mongolian costume. Twenty archers line up and get to shoot forty arrows in the men's event and twenty for women. Talk about a dangerous job though; the judges have to stand right next to the target without flinching and shout out each score. I guess you get paid treble time for that one.

A painfully hot and extremely dust ridden journey had to be endured to see the horse racing. Of course no one will ever be more in tune with their horses than the Mongolian people who show no signs of ever changing this aspect of their daily life. Over two thousand horses will also be there, though around one thousand will be actually raced so this is a must see part of the festival. Unfortunately the trip was as part of a tour group (grrrrrr). By now weeks of travel tiredness had become all-consuming and the ability to make polite small talk suddenly vacated the premises. Packed in like sardines, the minibus joined a surreal convoy of assorted vehicles all going to the racetrack, only just making it in time to see the end of the day. It was the youngster's race though quite a remarkable sight. Unbelievably the kids are between four and eight years old and on that really hot day they rode the crap out of their horses over a thirty two kilometre field. At the finish line one horse keeled over and three guys kicked it repeatedly trying to make it get up again. Many just walked across the finish line as they were so completely done in. In the evening a thousand vehicles left all at the same time creating the greatest man-made dust cloud ever. Quite a day!

I still can't believe the trip we did and it's easy to miss the intense feeling of freedom you feel in the Steppe. Last year on a brief trip to England, the plane flew over UB and then Lake Khovsgol Nurr and the immediate need to be there returned; completely carefree in that amazing ger, cooking dinner on the wood burner. At that moment I made a wish to be back there again. We flew on for four hours over Western Siberia on a clear day at 40,000 feet; scary and compelling with straight roads ploughing into the horizon and a single building here and there; white, blue and silver and great frozen circular lakes with vast cracks in straight lines as the ice expands in the morning and contracts at night.

Right……..Back to Beijing….Oh the madness!

# 13 China: The Olympics are Coming

# 2008

From the freedom, space and stress-free existence of a summer in Mongolia to the high energy of Beijing, 2007 and 2008 turned out to be one of the most intense years you could experience. Setting foot back in Beijing, this was never going to be an easy passage into a stable life off the road. Indeed, even though it was easy to find work and an apartment, it quickly became apparent that continuing to view things as a phenomenon was the only possible way of making sense of the world.

Of course starting afresh always requires that you summon up energy and staying power, but as a single soul setting off in a metropolis of over twenty million, you sure do have to use up every bit of your mental fortitude. Somehow every morning I would have to draw on all of my energy reserves to resume a multi-tasking process tapped into every aspect of a new way of doing things. At the same time, this was one of the loneliest moments of the journey, proceeding through a long, cold winter. Strange how that happens in big cities where there are the most people. Sometimes in life you're surrounded with mates and other times it's just the opposite and that's all there is to it I guess. At least if you move to another city in your own country you can jump in the car and visit your friends or family for the weekend right? No chance of that in Beijing!

In the first few days of job hunting, I came across Ritan Park, a small oasis of calm in the middle of the cacophony where I could sit on a bench and try and keep my head together, preventing myself from feeling like nothing. Quiet, beautiful and traditional, you can see old geezers flying their kites so high as to become specks in the sky and old women walking backwards all over the place in a bizarre form of exercise (no, really!). The only solace to be taken was that at least this wasn't South Korea anymore and holding onto that thought really made a big difference, hooray!

As China marched its way towards 2008 and the Olympics, its people had absolutely no idea of the extraordinary and terrible chain of events that awaited it. One thing after another, it just never seemed to stop. It was hard to believe what was going on and my woes quickly became buried into insignificance. Here's the road leading to the Olympics month by month during what quickly became known as 'China's year'. January: 2008 kicked off with the worst snow storms the country had experienced in fifty years. Half of the country was affected, amazingly though it happened in the south of China and not the north. The north which borders Siberia, Mongolia and North Korea usually has temperatures dropping to around minus forty in winter. Indeed Harbin, the biggest city of Heilongjiang Province is famous for its ice festivals. The South on the other hand is known for just the opposite. Palm trees and a relaxed way of life, even the diet is different down south to accommodate warmer conditions, so it came as a complete surprise when it snowed, especially in places like Guizhou, Guangxi, Fujian and

Guangdong. Most people had never seen snow in their lives, let alone being snowed in for weeks on end.

Now don't get me wrong, but if you look at a map, Guangxi and Guangdong are in fact on a parallel with Vietnam. Actually it got so cold in Vietnam it was reported that over 50,000 water buffalo died. There's got to be something wrong with that right? If you don't think there is anything even mildly insane with it then pull the other one! As the north of China enjoyed a normal winter, the south was of course completely unprepared for what the weather was about to dump on it. Around 2 million people were evacuated over a fortnight with immense damage to livestock and property. Fuzhou, a city of almost 4 million was without power for three weeks and Chenzhou with over 4.5 million was cut off for at least a fortnight. Although 129 people were reported dead, it could have been far worse considering the total devastation over such a long period of time.

February: The storms continued on relentlessly and conditions refused to get any better as Chinese New Year got closer. During this month more than 300 million people normally travel to their families, mostly by train. It's not just that, it's really the only long holiday in the Chinese calendar (usually two weeks) and a tradition that is older and far deeper than we can imagine. Though the storms were clearly going to make travel virtually impossible, still train stations all over the country became packed with tens of thousands of people creating pandemonium in each city. You do have the option to go to an agent to buy a train ticket and these days even buy online, but back then normally people would mainly choose go and wait all day at the station. In some cities people in their hundreds of thousands descended on the station. The worst was in Guangzhou where over 200,000 passengers got stranded.

March: The time of the infamous March 10<sup>th</sup> protests in Tibet leading to riots and death in the most sacred of places. News quickly travelled around the world and suddenly it seemed that it was all anyone was talking about. As the Olympic torch relay started its longest journey in history, what better way to protest against China's occupation of Tibet and its human rights record can you get? I mean instant world media coverage lasting for a whole month.

April: As the Olympic torch made its way around the world, protesters in their thousands came out to demonstrate. If it wasn't before, the eyes of the world were now fixed firmly on China. Most people in China didn't get to see the protests in London on TV, but amazingly CCTV9 showed those in Paris where demonstrators actually put out the flame itself.

Late April saw one of the country's worst train crashes where 72 people died and almost 500 were injured. A high speed train going to Shandong from Beijing derailed and another train going in the opposite direction collided with it. Although this only made it onto the world news for one day, once again China was being remembered for all the wrong reasons.

May saw the ascent of Mt Everest by a team of Chinese and Tibetan climbers on the 8<sup>th</sup> with the Olympic torch. Aimed at demonstrating harmony between China and Tibet it merely seemed to give critics more fuel to their arguments. All in all it seemed a strange and unnecessary gesture to be making.

On May 12<sup>th</sup> 2.38 in the afternoon Beijing time, a ferocious earthquake ripped through the Wenchuan area north east of Chengdu. Not only was the loss of life catastrophic but the devastation and suffering that followed on after the immediate shock was so complete that to this day its damage has still not been undone. The area largely hit people living in rural mountainous areas living in poor conditions so rescue operations were extremely difficult and dangerous. Over 11 million people became homeless with over 68,000 deaths. The worst of it was that at least 7,000 school buildings collapsed. The official figures for this say that 5,335 students died in the tragedy. China became instantly mobilised with volunteers and donations pouring in from every part of the country and China's critics kept their heads down for a while.

One week later, a three minute silence was held across the country to remember the earthquake victims. I was on my way to Tiananmen Square with my friend Carol at the time. She was on a month's visit from England and going there was on her must do list. For some reason neither of us thought there would be anything going on in the square; the idea was just to have a slow wander around, take some photos and have a lovely day out, that sort of thing. Emerging from the relative quiet of the subway, we were met by instant pandemonium. Thousands had come to the square to vent their grief and for a few hours the authorities allowed this exception to their strict rules in the most sacred ground in China. At the same time, all traffic in Beijing ground quickly to a halt. As Carol and I made our way to the square, the noise became louder and louder. Eventually we managed to get into the square where people locked arms and formed tight groups crying out

"Zhongguo, Zhongguo"

"China, China"

Red flags and banners were held high, people sobbed and cried uncontrollably as their feelings poured out. Some people instinctively grabbed us and took us into their circle protectively as things had gotten so intense that it all felt way over our heads. During this crazy time an increasingly awareness that there were no other Western looking faces at all in the crowd dawned. The realisation that this was clearly not our place grew and grew until it felt so uncomfortable that with relief we managed to slowly inch our way to the sidelines.

These people weren't just grieving for the earthquake victims though. They were venting some serious emotion about everything that had happened to China since Christmas including taking a bellyful of criticism of just about everything you can think of from so many other countries. Weeks of protesting about Tibet had also inadvertently pissed 1.3 billion people off as generally Chinese people have no idea what's going on over there. With Chinese news rarely reporting disturbances or demonstrations and the country being so vast, instead the protests were taken in the wrong way than intended. To most it was more like the West was sticking a giant middle finger up in their direction.

Around that time many of my classes turned into strong-felt debates about the situation. Along with all this came underlying feeling that Chinese people were being demonised and even some Western friends had written "I do not like China" (well, words to that effect) somewhere on the internet. People used the term 'the Chinese' like you use salt and vinegar on your chips. Like the earthquake, something major had to happen in order to shut everyone up again and this role was happily taken up by good old Sharon Stone. As a great authority on spiritualism she announced that the earthquake was karma for all the terrible things China has done to Tibet and embarrassed apologies instantly flooded in from all directions.

As the countdown for the Olympics got shorter, the feeling of foreboding that something terrible was going to happen was turning into more of a certainty. Perhaps a giant super wave was somehow going to travel inland from the east coast, or the ground was going to open up and swallow the Bird's Nest live on TV in front of the world. Thankfully of course, nothing of the sort happened and years of hard work and planning paid off. We saw one of the best Olympics ever and things went off without a hitch. Well I say 'we' but that really means everyone except yours truly. Unfortunately, after all this time in China, I missed all of it, never getting to see one second of it either in real life or even TV! Amazing hey! For any Westerner in China, the worst time of the year is always renewing your visa and of course this special time joyously fell just one month before the Olympics. Even with weeks of doing everything possible of to get my visa sorted (my company only used a travel agent to help out their foreign teachers), once again it was bye bye China!

Leapfrogging majestically onwards past the Olympics, 2008 then lazily plodded on without too much of an incident. Actually there were still many things that happened, from the terrible mudslide in the Shanxi Province[1] to the tainted milk scandal[2], to China's first space-walk, from three other earthquakes and a total of four typhoons. Relentless! I guess it must have been a kind of comedown or something though, but compared to the first half of the year news wise things became a lot quieter.

Before moving on, one can't finish without a mention of one of the largest robberies in the world. Without a doubt, if it didn't have such a tragic ending, it would make a great comedy that really could have only taken place in China. The story starts in 2006, when the manager of a branch of the Agricultural Bank of China in the Hebei Province called Ren Xiaofeng 'borrowed' 200,000 kuai from the bank (that's about 20 grand in the UK and 30,000 dollars) and played the whole lot on the

---

[1] On the 8th September in Linfen, Xiangfen County, an unlicensed landfill mine collapsed killing at least 267 people. A huge operation was mobilised to recover those buried but some were never found. There are many mines still operating illegally in China.

[2] On the 9th September news broke that a well known brand of milk powder for babies had been contaminated with melamine. This gave the appearance that the milk had a normal protein level whereas in reality the babies were becoming malnourished. As usual it's hard to give the figures, but around 300,000 under 2 year olds were hospitalised. Six babies died of kidney problems and 13 simply starved to death. The scandal had been brewing for well over a year before the shit hit the fan and it dragged on for a long time after. People were arrested left, right and centre. Two men were executed for their part; Zhang Yujun, a dairy farmer who added 600 tons of fake milk to bulk out his product and Geng Jinping, for selling 'toxic food'.

lottery with the idea of paying it back after he won. We all know the chances of winning any lottery. I reckon you're more likely to be hit in the face by Elton John's toupee during a hurricane (fight it off) than winning the big one, so it amazes me that Xiaofeng even considered his idea to be even remotely feasible. Against all the odds he won and was able to pay all the money back on the sly without anyone knowing.

Talk about not quitting while you're ahead though. The following year, Xiaofeng teamed up with another manager called Ma Xiangjing. Together, over two months, they removed 33 million kuai from the vaults and blew the lot on lottery tickets (that's over 3 million pounds). Now at this point you really have to picture these guys in your mind and imagine the scene. The most expensive Chinese note you can get is a 100 kuai bill, so this amount of cash would have weighed about two tons. I doubt if they would have had it all in one go, but what on earth did they do with all the lottery tickets? Their homes must have been absolutely full of cash and useless tickets. Imagine their desperation when the money started to run out and they still hadn't won anything. In fact they got so out of control that in one day they went back and ripped off another 18 million, spending it in one day, thus accounting for over half of all lottery sales in Hebei. After hardly winning anything, they were caught after a few days of being on the run both were somewhat ironically executed on April 1st 2008[3].

2008 in China! Madness!

---

[3] China is one of 58 countries that retain the death penalty, though it is at the top of the pile by a long way.
If you are going to receive the big one, then you may either be given the firing squad or a lethal injection. If you are shot, you are driven to a secret location with two perimeters and hollow point bullet from an assault rifle is delivered to the back of the neck. If you get an injection you are taken for a last drive in an unmarked 'execution van'. An execution van has no windows, cameras to record your last moments and they simply just drive around anywhere while it happens. A strange thought, being driven around in public and past the supermarket as its time to meet your maker.

## Subway Pandemonium: July 2008

### Living in Beijing

July 2007: Well, you won't get more of a contrast of environment than flying for a couple of hours from Mongolia and Ulaanbaatar to Beijing, that's for sure. Phew! The holidays over mate! Welcome to another dimension! You're moving to Beijing! Amazing!

'Someday in Beijing' I scrawled on a scrap of paper while waiting in the blazing heat outside some crap McDonalds somewhere, for another letting agent and their grand tour.
"There's one thing about Beijing; you have to be all about it here. You have to have your shit completely nailed together and be one hundred percent focused on exactly what you want and what you need to do in order to get there.
Day in, day out, hitting the subway and going to a new place for an interview, demo class or to look at an apartment. Quite often I've caught the wrong bus then another wrong bus in order to get back to where I started, followed by a taxi ride where the driver gets lost. The subway is full-on as are the buses; packed to capacity with people pushing and shoving with absolutely no space. Standing on the bus is a complete endurance test. A journey can just go on and on forever. Sometimes when you're walking along, you can get caught out if someone barges into you and your blood immediately starts to boil.
Living in a hotel and then moving to another, re-packing and moving back to the previous space for a while. Living in the equivalent of a shed in the hutong and then putting on a shirt and smart trousers, carrying a briefcase before hitting the central business area of Beijing trying to land a decent job. It's seriously hot here and day after day of trying to start from scratch all over again in such high temperatures is wearing beyond belief."

February 2008: Well, six months later and what's been going on? Well unlike the south of China which is completely snowed in, though it's now ridiculously cold, Beijing is as dry as a bone, I mean really dry. The back of your throat really takes a pounding and is sore a lot of the time. There is no water. Fruit and veg have lowered in quality and prices have gone out of the roof. When you're sick, you try cycling into a below minus-ten Beijing headwind, it's no joke I can tell you. Not only that but actually there's a major drought that's been unbroken for years. All the northern water reserves are dry. Businesses are closed and hundreds of thousands are without water as it's diverted to keep the capital going.

The 'powers that be' have been firing chemical rockets into the atmosphere to make it rain. Quite stunning to hear that one! Beijing is notorious for its lack of water and they've been doing this for some years now, doesn't seem to be working though does it! Needless to say that if it does rain, it's so dirty that you sure as hell don't want to go out in it.

Though temperatures will vary between seasons, Beijing has a predictable single weather pattern throughout the year. Week in week out, the weather always seems to be the same. Normally you will have a week of crystal blue skies and then the smog will build up. The pollution levels will continue to rise until the air quality is quite unbearable. The sky will then clear itself again and the process repeated. With millions of cars in use every day and a high pressure front keeping all the fumes in one area, the government is doing everything it can to keep the pollution in check[1]. In an effort to manage the situation, the latest idea is that you can now only drive your car on certain days of the week. Which days you can drive on now depends on your number plate.

When the thick blanket of emissions envelops the city, weather forecasts choose to refer to it as 'fog' rather than 'smog'. This is therefore an unusual natural occurrence, as of course fog is water vapour and therefore uncharacteristic of the local environment. Where does this mystery fog come from? Surely this should be attracting meteorologists from around the world to solve this puzzling oddment of science.

It seems that most of the students at school have never heard of the word smog before and in class you have to explain to them that the grey chemical soup that hangs between the buildings on a daily basis is hardly a natural phenomenon. Whether it's London, Paris or Seoul we all know that in any major city, pollution is a problem. One must say though, in Beijing it's so bad that you can see the physical effects first hand on the population. People feel continually drowsy and fall asleep everywhere no doubt because of the lack of oxygen and high toxicity. It's no joke. Everyone in the office complains about it, as do friends in other companies across the board. Seems like an odd place to be having the Olympics in that's for sure.

---

[1] Since writing this, the government has come up with a remarkable system to manage the traffic problem in the city. From now on, all non-Beijing number plates can only be used at weekends and after 8pm on weekdays. This has meant that Beijing number plates have become more like gold dust. Whereas Beijing ren are immediately entitled to a local number plate, all outsiders need to enter into a lottery if they want to obtain one and therefore be eligible to drive. This policy will be in place for at least three years.

The winter also brings another strange happening. The authorities actually decide when it's time to start the heating in everyone's homes. It gets turned on simultaneously in every place! You also have no control over the temperature in your apartment and often it's unbearably hot. As a result millions of people leave their window open which is normally just above their heater. An absolutely mind-blowing waste of energy when you consider the size of the population, in a country that says it's hard-up for natural resources. Down south, homes have no central heating, relying purely on air-con' or electric fan heaters to keep the place warm in winter.

My place: I live in a space called Ping Guo She Qu which translates as Apple Community in the Central Business District (CBD). The word 'community' refers to the hundreds of thousands of apartment complexes that are built side by side. This is the same all across the city stretching way out into the suburbs. In the city centre most are new but this quickly changes as you move outwards to the older red brick constructions that were mainly built in the 90's. A strange combination of building is Beijing; you will normally see a flash new high rise slap bang next to some crumbling darkened pile of bricks with bars across the windows, washing hung out to dry from the windows and rubbish everywhere. Old or new, each complex has its own surrounding perimeter fence plus a central gate and the more modern ones will be manned by security guards.

Inside will be one or two small shops, parking and a landscape garden with an exercise area for everyone to share in the centre. In the summer months families will be seen hanging out together here, especially during the day when Gran or Granddad will be charged to look after the youngest while their son or daughter is out at work.

From the protection your complex you can at once start to unwind from the commotion that is heaving away outside. Ping Guo She Qu is a nice space and generally quiet.....amazing! It may be one of the more modern places around but it's just what you want to come back to at the end of the day especially during a minus ten winter and you're cream-crackered. Once again, the apartment has hardly any furniture and is virtually an empty space with a distinct dull echo to it. At this point I still have the same trousers bought in South Korea and wore all over Mongolia. The menders downstairs are getting increasingly exasperated as their task of repairing them gets tougher and tougher. The only shoes by the door are the ones that Matt borrowed for a while in Yangshuo (also mended twice) and the razor Gary gave me in Shenzhen in 06 just got binned. Recently nature forced me to change my odour eaters as after a year and a half they just started falling apart....sad days indeed!

298

So this place is pretty expensive but as ever quality often goes out of the window in China. It's all about how something looks with no one ever giving a monkey's about quality. Everything's built so quick around here. I mean take this apartment for example. Quite often nothing works, the lights are continually blowing as the power fluctuates all the time. The bulbs are these weird ones you can't buy anywhere so it actually took three months and ten people to change them. Isn't there a joke about that somewhere? Also, alarmingly the block directly opposite really looks like it was built at a slight angle.

If you buy clothes watch out for what you are paying for. Often what you buy will not last a few weeks let alone a year unless you go to one of the super expensive department stores inside the third ring-road. Things can shrink into really strange shapes or lose all their colour in the wash. A friend Zhang Jing bought a pair of high heels only to discover that after two days they started bowing inwards heavily making her walk like a chicken; very sexy. One day I'd just opened the door to go out when my belt suddenly broke causing my trousers to fall straight down around my ankles, even sexier!

If you think by buying a brand name and you're safe then think again. Because there are no real laws concerning fake products and most people's incomes are so incredibly low, cheap imitation goods have been knocked out for years in China. I mean why buy a hugely expensive unaffordable imported Gucci bag or Rolex when you can buy an imitation from a catalogue kept under the counter in the nearest market right?

The trouble is there is a very big difference between making your own choice and trickery and at the end of the day the only ones to be suffering from it all are the 1.3 billion. It's this fraudulent aspect of the whole thing that gives the notion of cheap products its bad name. Most people find it exasperating and are more than pissed off with being continually on the receiving end of this shit state of affairs. If you're a teacher doing a lesson on social problems this will always be in the top five of complaints that the students will name. Indeed they can rant on about it for hours making your job a very easy one. When world consumer day comes around on March 15th the number of complaints about dodgy goods hits the roof and there is a hotline that people can call if you come across something fake. There are even numerous websites now for people to post their grievances though in reality they rarely lift a finger to respond to the consumer. Instead, these days, March 15th has become huge business for the websites, who now pick out the most well known companies, contact them and charge vast amounts to remove the various complaints. Some websites can make a fortune in one day, amazing hey?

Fake products can be unearthed with regularity and in the most taken for granted areas of daily life. Having heard that the tap water wasn't the greatest, the next logical step was to therefore start using the large half gallon containers of Nongfu Spring instead. After buying one that had the aftertaste similar to the discharge from Sellafield though, the idea that I'd been cooking with luxury water went straight out the window. It was even more than shocking to learn that almost half of all bottled water on the shelves is fake. With the cloud of nonstop scams that flood the market, stuff that passes as real can often be dangerous. This includes fake water filters, fake toothpaste, fake medicine, fake hospital drips and fake cooking oil known as gutter-oil. Gutter oil literally means that it's removed from the drains round the back of the restaurant and recycled, yeeeech![23]

Round the corner: If you want to get out and about, turn right at the gate and go past a great big art gallery with the worst sculpture outside you could possibly imagine. There were these giant metallic-silver turds on plinths outside for a time. Now there is just one big one pointing skyward. Does that mean that someone actually bought one? Where would they have put it? Maybe management thought that the small ones somehow detracted from the overall feeling, creating an inappropriateness of spatial relationship and therefore dynamic tension. Also a giant plastic matt-red dinosaur in a brown plastic cage is strangely suspended above the doorway. It's all beyond me. Years of art college didn't teach me anything I guess!

Next, turn left and there's a brief taste of the real world as the road is a well-known 'eat all you can' for three kuai street used by the taxi drivers. Taxis line the way on both sides and are often double parked. The 'si-ji' (drivers) will always be seen leaning against their vehicles sharing their time with their mates while chuffing on another ciggie. Many form into animated groups around the various ramshackled

---

[2] Since writing this the string of dodgy goods has continued to expand including some absolutely mind blowing ones. Referred to by at least one newspaper as 'Chinese Fakeaway', the list now includes fake Apple computers and Apple shops, fake non sanitised condoms lubed up with vegetable oil, fake organic produce and replica hand made eggs. There are even 'schools' set up to teach people how to make them with a single egg ten times cheaper than a real one. You can also buy fake pigs ears!
[3] You will also find fake certificate ads randomly stuck all over the place around residential areas including the stair wells of apartment blocks. Forgeries can be made for anything if your CV isn't up to scratch.
Disturbingly, it has been recently revealed that Shenzhen Airlines took on 200 employees with fake pilots certificates in 2008. Aircraft parts can often be fake!

diners choosing lunch from a wide selection of gut exploding food. Aside from the normal rice or noodles, boiled kebabs of different ingredients are incredibly popular and can be bought everywhere. Be careful though, they use the same water all day in the kebab production line, so whatever you choose will have a variety of delicate after-tastes including spam and seafood; it definitely takes a while to get used to the street food in China.

While the drivers attack their cheap meal with gusto they are surrounded by rubbish which spreads across the street. Down the far end towards the junction there are piles of garbage that spew out of the broken bins and around the radioactive red brick outside toilets. As its winter, the leaves have left the trees being replaced by old weathered and torn carrier bags in a variety of colours. Having become attached to the branches, they flutter in the 'Beijing da feng' (big wind) reminiscent of Tibetan prayer flags as if making some offering to the god of rubbish.

Turn right and you come to the Soho area. Yes you're suddenly into yuppie territory now for sure. Hundreds of similar white tower blocks with matching boutiques and coffee shops full of people trying so hard to appear middle-classed. There is a three storey Starbucks and similar places full of people wearing black, glued to their laptops with jazz-muzak being played in the background. There are also loads of the fittest looking airhead bimbos who do nothing all day but go shopping and walk around carrying expensive looking Dior bags. Interestingly the word 'bimbo' translates into 'hua ping' which means 'vase'. The idea is that something can be beautiful but you can't use it for anything else.

Walking around central Beijing, sometimes it's easy to forget that two thirds of China live in complete poverty. The fashion world seems to have got a fierce grip to such an extent that often I can hardly believe my eyes. The Korean style high heels have now become out so OTT you can see woman literally swaying around as they try to maintain their balance with calf muscles twitching under the tension. When the winter comes it gives women an excuse to don their favourite boots with thigh lengths being a measurement of how well-off you are. Thigh lengths are not seen as smutty or inappropriate. They can be worn in any place including meetings, important dinners, in the office, even students and teachers can be seen sporting their boots. Can you imagine the stir it would create in school if Mrs Johnson showed up in her favourite thigh lengths to teach Year 10 maths back home? No one bats an eyelid about it around here.

301

Fake leopard skin seems to be the most popular design at the moment, especially leopard-skin scarves, though jackets, leggings and shoes are also really 'in'.

During the winter, fur is also now in big time in Beijing and worn without a second thought. I'm not sure how much of it is real or not, but if you go into a shop and ask, the shop assistant will always say it's genuine. Of course no one wants to buy fake fur right? Perish the thought of it!

There is also a strange new trend where people wear glasses with no lenses, just the frames! Some have great vision and some will still have to wear contact lenses which seems even weirder; certainly hard to get your head round that one.

As for the guys, well like all men, all we have to do is throw on a t-shirt, jeans and a jacket and that's it. Same in most places around the world I rekon. There is though, one very popular style that belongs solely to the men known as 'the comb-over'. In China, the thought of baldness is out of the question. Men would much rather expend their time and energy on desperately trying to glue those last spider like tendrils of hair across their gleaming bonce. As Beijing's notorious wind blows across from the west, you can often see that well placed hair freeing itself and raising up in an almost welcoming gesture. Maybe it's just another of nature's many ways of attraction in initiating the mating ritual.

The most noticeable thing about the Beijing CBD is the amount of building work going on. It's fast, furious and non-stop. There are a vast number of new big buildings being built. Above the lot are the CCTV tower and the China World Tower dominating the skyline. Everything seems like a race and building work continues ceaselessly twenty four hours a day. Each night the highest levels of the World Tower are lit up with the flashes of the welders at work. Night after night they are always up there, grafting away and exposed to the elements.

During the day in some areas there is no other option but to create makeshift pathways through the building work for the suits and high heels. It really is an odd sight as sometimes there are absolutely no boundaries between the ongoing construction and pedestrian areas. Once again health and safety goes right out the window. It just becomes just a huge mixture of labourers with hard hats and office people walking through it shouting on their mobile phones. At the same time, great window panes get hoisted up on huge ropes by hand high above their heads, and heavy machinery thunders away all around.

New places are built so quickly it's like their thrown up or something. Down the road in the embassy area was a small restaurant. With its red paper lanterns hanging up outside against its black brick exterior, the curved Chinese style tiled gable above the doorway was always a welcoming sight. Tucked away in a shaded area alongside the tree lined road, it was a nice escape from Guomao and its modern tower blocks. A really friendly place; the boss and staff would always say hello and would even remember what you would normally order. Then one day it was closed. Even the windows were boarded up. The next day it had been flattened along with about a blocks worth of other places. In one week a wall had been put up around the whole area along with the labourers' accommodation. A few months later virtually a whole apartment complex had been built and they were just adding the finishing touches, creating landscape gardens and the perimeter gates.

The most worrying thing about all of is the distinct lack of safety and forethought that's going down[4]. Beijing could be in for a real disaster here. I mean the Japanese invest in huge mega shock absorbers in all of their high-rises for the worst case scenario. Of course Japan is unlucky enough to be smack next to four active tectonic plates so it really needs this kind of protection, but let's not forget about Tangshan and the earthquake that pulverised it in 1973 leaving 250,000 dead. Alarmingly, though Tangshan is only a one hour bus journey down the road from Beijing, absolutely no precautions have been taken into consideration with all the new building work whatsoever.

At the moment most Chinese people are scratching their heads in confusion. The most important thing to anyone is to buy somewhere to live for their family, yet if you ask them what the most serious problem is in this town, one hundred percent will say it's the crazy house prices. The Olympics are the most immediate driving force behind this, but once it's all over, the building will continue as will the wealth gap. The well-off invest in new apartment blocks and continue become even richer. One of the topics in our schools text book is called 'Rent or Buy' and of course this issue is always the first thing to come up. One of the students Jiang Wei is a home owner.

"When I bought my home in 2004 it cost me 600,000 RMB. These days if I wanted to buy it, it would be over 1.5 million and mine

---

[4] In 2009 the reality of China's cowboy building became clear when Beijing saw its first major blaze. The Television Cultural Centre next to the new CCTV tower caught fire from a nearby fireworks display during the Spring Festival celebrations. The building, standing at 34 floors high, costing a friendly little 730 million dollars went up like a torch in just over ten minutes. Not surprisingly it was described as the greatest pyrotechnic in Chinese history.

is a cheap place. Most people can't afford the new apartments. They cost up to 4 million. Only people with a Beijing hukou can afford them so they will always have an advantage."

Your hukou is the province in which you were born and therefore registered and it was evident that Jiang Wei was becoming angry.

"If you have a Beijing hukou you will get many advantages compared to people from other places. Beijing ren[5] can buy apartments for less than half the price as other people in some areas."

Out of pure interest, the following day I opened it up as a discussion in class to see what would happen. Talk about lighting the touch papers though. You don't often see Chinese people getting annoyed over anything, so it was more than surprising when people started shouting at each other. Within seconds the debate had exploded into heated exchanged between the local Beijingers and the other students.

"Everyone knows Beijing people need lower scores to get into college" shouted one guy, "Even if I get good scores Beijing ren will always get chosen.....and the fees are always lower." Well at least they were speaking fluently. Phew, I felt like jumping for cover behind the desk. Clearly people walk around with a lot bottled up inside regarding this and it's never been mentioned in class since.

Another astounding thing that emerges from all of this is that if you buy an apartment in China, you only own it for seventy years (no really!) After that it will belong to the government. If you buy a house, you won't own the land underneath it thus completely redefining the meaning of the word 'buy'. Since seventy years still hasn't passed since the birth of this law, no one quite knows what will happen. Watch this space!

To accommodate the rapid growth of Beijing and a bid to reduce the number of cars, the subway system is also expanding. A good friend Wang Chun Guang who is a professor at the University of Mining and Technology invited me down to see the latest work being done on line 10. This is one of the new subway lines which will mean that a lot of the really congested stations can thankfully be avoided in the future.

I have to say that the whole thing was pretty exciting. I mean going underground is a buzz any day of the week let alone under China's capital city. As we drove to the building site we started chatting in more detail about the afternoon ahead.

---

[5] Beijing ren are people who are born and brought up in Beijing.

"You are about to see the largest tunnelling machine in the world" said Chun Guang proudly as he handed over a white protective hard-hat over and ID badge.

"You must stay with me at all times because we are going into a restricted area. Also we don't want you to get lost when you are down there" he added with a smile.

The site itself covered a wide area, with pipes and all sorts being laid down into the ground via a giant crane spanning between two rail tracks. Finally we reached the pit where the drilling was being done and could look down and Tunnel Boring Machine (TBM) some sixty or seventy feet below. The smell of welding, earth and cement hung heavily in the air.

"Don't worry about anything. This is a skilled team who have been working together for years" assured Chun Guang already starting to descend down the metal stairwell. "You are quite safe."

Quite amazing being down there, though the TBM wasn't working that day. Instead a crew of ten guys were installing a new drill head which is basically a huge circular set of metal teeth.

"The cutting head weighs seventy tons and costs 4 million RMB" he managed to shout over the noise. "The problem is that Beijing is so dry that the soil is very hard. There are also lots of rocks and pebbles. Each cutting head will last about nine months and it takes a month to replace."

On the way out we stood next to a large picture of what the station will look like when it is finished and my friend rounded the day off.

"If you're lucky enough to have a subway station built near your apartment then it's like winning the lottery. It will instantly double in value. Any new apartment block around here was sold even before it was built. Some companies will know where the lines will be built years before anyone else and buy the rights to build on the land in advance."

Chinese New Year 08: The Chinese Spring Festival in Beijing is a strange occurrence really. The most noticeable thing is that over two thirds of the people leave for their hometowns to see their loved ones. The city becomes strangely yet blissfully quiet and still for nine days. You can sit down on the subway or bus and at rush hour even get a choice of seats.

Traditionally, people buy huge boxes of fireworks from stalls on the corner of the street. The reason for this is to drive away a huge monster known as the 'Nian' which stays under the sea for most of the year but comes to the surface to eat people and their livestock. As the big day draws closer the peaceful ambience starts to be replaced with the sound of detonations. It gets steadily noisier and more intense until at 12 o'clock on New Year's Eve Armageddon is here again. Louder and more intense that Yangshuo in 2006, It could easily be mistaken for an air raid if you were in another part of the world. Rockets go off continually right outside apartment blocks, clearing their fifteen storey windows and continuing until about 2am. People let them off long roadsides and on junctions. If you choose to go out, you need to have eyes on the back of your head especially when things get overpowering for long periods of time. It restarts annoyingly at about 8am the next day. And then....nothing! For two days Beijing seems to be so quiet its like some virus has escaped and everyone mysteriously died. Trippy! Occasionally one big blast will go off in the distance resonating between the tower blocks.

On New Year's Day everyone descends on the nearest temple and there are a still quite a few about in Beijing still well-preserved and beautiful. In Ditan Park and the Lama Temple thousands of people go nuts delighting in the festival and praying for good fortune for the oncoming year.


**Working in Beijing**

Work kicked off when I blagged two part-time jobs and nailed the hours together. Kinda ok really; no contracts, flexible hours and absolutely no meetings (hooray!) The first place was in the Soho area. Sitting outside after a duff interview, it was so hot and things had become so stressful, I wondered what on earth to do next. In some mad flash of anger, turning round and walking back into the building, I took the first likely looking business from the company list in the foyer, went into the office and asked for a job.

Through the glass walls of his office, the secretary could be seen handing my CV to the boss who gave it a quick read. After introducing himself as Mikel from the States followed by a no bullshit interview, he quickly became one of the then most helpful people you could hope to meet. Mikel would find you all kinds of interesting corporate jobs in big flash buildings like Microsoft and IBM and I started making some well handy contacts there.

Of course as per usual lesson plans printable from the main database were often appalling or non-existent. One time they called me in to cover someone's lessons in the Chinese Ministry of Commerce for an evening; a huge building with a foyer made from black polished granite. Upon hitting the computer to print off the lesson plans, alarmingly, the topic turned out to be two hours on UFO sightings. To add to it all, the material was absolutely the worst and most minimal load of rubbish you'll ever read.

Quite surreal really; teaching top executives about flying saucers and ET in a huge board room next door to Tiananmen Square. Admittedly they did look slightly confused about the whole thing. A strange lesson that was for sure!

As an EFL teacher from a native English speaking country, life is seriously cushty in China and if you work for a decent company then you're laughing really. Welcome to a life void of any stress or worry about how you're going to keep those frigging bills at bay this month. Welcome to a world where once you're established and settled in, waking up becomes a pleasurable experience, especially when you open your curtains and it's China outside the window.

Actually there aren't any bills! Amazing hey? You have to pay for your water, gas and electricity meters using a card. It's really cheap and lasts for a long time, paying the equivalent of twenty quid for gas and electricity every three months and about four or five for your water. The phone line costs about fifteen quid a month and that's as pricey as it comes. Most people use their mobile phone as credit is also really cheap. Landlines are virtually redundant at home these days. All in all as a Westerner, life's pretty comfortable and if you were worrying about how to make ends meet for year after year back home, it's more like floating in a sea of bliss.

You don't have to have much of a skill level to earn a reasonable wage either. To many companies, they just want a few foreign looking faces to have sprinkled around as window dressing. There are English language schools all over the place in Beijing and often a school will have the most talentless and bone idle Western teachers in their classroom getting away with blue murder. A standard starting wage for any English teacher in Beijing starts at 150 kuai an hour which is huge compared to what most people Chinese people will earn. Normally this is twice as much as any skilled and qualified Chinese-English teacher can achieve and it's a topic no one cares to talk about. Full-time is considered 80 hours....a month!

Like many places in the country, there are the men and women who are extremely poor and do all the physical jobs. If you're a builder, electrician or engineer you may get paid next to nothing and work all hours. There are the shop and restaurant workers who also earn an incredibly small amount, and then Beijing's finest! Yes, the white collar worker! These guys make up about one third of Beijing's population and their time is divided up into three parts and three parts only; work, eating and shopping. Firstly, they work hard. I mean they work their arses off. People will often be seen camping in the office surrounded by half eaten takeaways and half-drunk flat 3 litre bottles of coke after a weekend stint of pure anxiety.

There are no supervisions to monitor an employee's performance and certainly no system of discipline anywhere to be seen. There are also no verbal or written warnings and when you're out its sudden. End of story! Because it's always been so tough looking for work here, people really feel the pressure of keeping their job and so therefore usually lose any benefits that we would normally expect to see in a contract. You can't complain about anything and you'll get what you are given. If you're told to work on Sunday at 8.30am then you had better be there or be in serious trouble.

It's also common to see people sleeping in the office during the day (no, really!) This is perfectly acceptable in any establishment and it's normal to see staff sound asleep, using their arms as pillows across their desk. If there are sofas or any comfy chairs this will of course be the first choice. Lunch times and mid afternoon are good times to crash out. People will continue working as per normal around sleeping people.

Office folk are usually too busy, too tired and may have no kitchen if they are on a low pay scale, the average wage being between two and three 3000 kuai per month. As a result they may eat every day at one of the thousands upon thousands of restaurants that Beijing has to offer. Indeed, whether they are man or woman, boiling up a pot of instant noodles is often the only thing they can make. In terms of the kitchen most of them are utterly useless. Even their parents dissuade their child not to learn as it is seen to be a waste of time, detracting from the more important work of studying at college. People are amazed when they learn that we all learn how to do basic cooking at school and most people cook nearly every day for themselves back in the UK. In terms of them doing any
DIY and mechanics you've got no hope. Actually there are only few DIY stores as we know it in Beijing; it's cheaper and less time consuming to get someone else to paint your walls for you.

In some effort to get a deeper insight into what it must be like for a Chinese person to live and work in this vast city, my colleagues were more than happy to help.
A good friend Han Dou Dou who does the schedule for the foreign teachers comes from Yili, a county in the north western corner of the Xinjiang Province.
        "I grew up in the small town of Zi Ke Tai. When I was at school we had fifty students to one teacher. Later, there were so few teachers that they had to join two classes together so there were over ninety students at one time. Even these days this is a common number for any class. It was so difficult for the teacher to control the kids that

in those days, if you were badly behaved the teacher would beat you across the hands with a bamboo stick."

By this time Han's words had become more than absorbing. "As you can imagine it's difficult getting out of Xinjiang and being accepted at college in Beijing. Universities have the legal right to offer 'Regional Protection' so they will recruit most students from their own province. This means there will be fewer places for people outside of Beijing."

Luckily, Han had studied English for her degree so her level of detail really painted a clear picture.

"At college I would get up at 6.30 every day and we would do exercise before breakfast, then classes started at 8am. You would have a 'physical card' which you had to get stamped fifty times each semester." Phew, talk about worlds apart. It's hard to imagine any student in the UK surfacing that early for anything, especially after a good night out down the local.

"For the four years I studied, I shared a dormitory room with five other students. When it finished I was lucky to rent a space in a dorm until I found a job and earnt some money."

"Lucky? I thought you couldn't wait to get out of that dormitory into your own place." I posed.

"You don't understand how difficult it is for a college graduate looking for work. Most have no money and there are so many people that they have to get the cheapest places to live possible. If you haven't got work by the time the winter comes, life can be really bad. Many people have to live in the underground hotels that are all over the city."

"I've never heard of those before. Where are they?" I asked naively.

"They are everywhere. I guess you can't read the signs and walk past them. The government doesn't allow this kind of place anymore, but they are still here. They say that they are too dangerous; if there was a fire you couldn't escape. People get their belongings stolen, bad people can come in during the night and you can't get a signal on your phone to call for help. I looked at a few when I finished college but they looked like an underground jail with no windows. It was like being in a nightmare.

A lot of landlords will put ten beds in their apartment and rent it out for 700 kuai a month. That's good money and many of my colleagues have lived like that. In the end you can save up and share an apartment with two or three work mates".

I remember we all moaned about the DHSS back in the UK but I guess any welfare system is better than no welfare system. I have friends in England who still get their rent paid for them and as I listened to Han, the gap between China and my own world just seemed to have widened like a vast crevasse.

"So what are the hardest things about living in Beijing?" I asked, pushing the boat out as far as possible.

"Getting a job" she laughed. "Just having a degree isn't enough. You have to have a master's to improve your chances of getting a good job. Even then, it looks a lot better if you've gone abroad to get it. Millions of students look for work every year. I went to a lot of job fairs and so many people went they couldn't close the doors at the end of the day[6]. There is even competition for the low paid jobs. It's a serious problem.

The other thing is that sometimes you have to take a job that may be a long way from your apartment. You can travel for hours every day on the bus. That's the worst thing! I can't bear standing on the bus for so long."

Besides the monthly effort of trying to locate two schedules together, when Mikel sadly left all interest in the corporate work quickly vacated the premises. Business English is a pain in the arse anyway and definitely overrated. You spend hours trying to find the right place which you aren't paid for and when you arrive half your students don't turn up because their busy. Many are only there because its part of a training program or because their boss told them to go, spending half the time on their phones or looking at their watches. Instead of focusing on the work at hand, you can normally tell that some are really only thinking about the mountain of work that's piling up on their desk while they are away, doubling in size upon the hour like some life form that's getting out of control.

As the second job moved full time mode it was time to say adieu to the 'ye olde corporate work' and follow the real demand for English teaching. These days the big money is to be made with the rapidly expanding 'training centers' which help students get placed overseas. Indeed some are so huge it's more like being in a crowded supermarket when you walk in, buzzing with a thousand staff and students with one united purpose. Many schools have now become so massive they also incorporate lucrative agency work into the business. They can help with advice on which country to go to and which colleges offer the most suitable masters degree, accommodation and travel. You name it they will sort it for you, all wrapped in a tidy package with an astronomic price tag that is seen as an investment by the parents that have to fork

---

[6] Normally 60,000 people will visit a job fair in one day. They will be competing for between 7 and 10,000 jobs. Around 7 million students will graduate each year adding to the already huge unemployment figures.

out for it. Most importantly they will sort your visa application out and also find colleges by ranking. Of course the higher the ranking the better chances of landing a decent job when you come back.

Inside the classroom students are there because they want to be and have a high level of self-motivation. Most need to take an IELTS or TOEFL[7] tests to be accepted into a university abroad and at least 3 million a year will sit the exams. People will travel from as far as Guangzhou or Xinjiang to Beijing to give themselves the best chance of getting a high score in the test. They work their arses off and from the teacher's point of view, life has never been easier. The days of spending eighty percent of your energy keeping OFSTED[8] happy are long gone. Lessons are alive with a cheerful energy and it's easy to fall in love with your class. Their work ethic is completely different from that back at home. If there's a holiday, students will always show up instead of doing anything else, that or go down the library to review their notes.

## Getting around Beijing

If are going to be part of the 6 million that use the subway every day, then prepare yourself! What insanity the Beijing subway system is. Rush hour in the morning or evening is outrageous. Like some heaving mass of ants bottlenecked in and out of their tunnels, the commuters form one giant moving carpet as they head for the escalators. There are guards that actually push people into each carriage until everyone is tightly packed together. I tell you, being squashed in with so many people is no joke. If someone has bad breath you know all about it. On a bad day all you may be able to see is that back of someone's head covered in dandruff. Someone sneezed into a friend's face at point blank range last week and they were going down with something almost immediately. Because of the higher risk of transmission of different bugs and viruses it's common to see passengers wearing masks covering their nose and mouth; quite a surreal sight if you're a newcomer. On top of that, there will be limbless beggars who go from carriage to carriage being pushed on a cart, blind people singing or these guys who are terribly burnt. That's kinda hardcore first thing in the morning, well anytime really.

---

[7] IELTS: International English Language Testing System. TOEFL: Test of English as a Foreign Language.

[8] OFSTED is the UK's wonderful system of inspecting schools. Once a year the suits and briefcases arrive with a high level of seriousness, combining classroom observations with meticulously going through every scrap of admin with a fine tooth-comb. Preparations before an OFSTED visit are a nightmare, with meeting after meeting trying to get things right. An OFSTED visit is always the most stressful time of a schools year.

When the doors open people spill out onto the platform, especially at transfer stations and proceed at top speed to try and beat everyone else to the next stair well. For some reason often people can't wait for their fellow commuters to disembark, pushing past in the opposite direction in an effort to get on first creating ten seconds of mayhem before the doors close; a particularly annoying habit in any lifetime.

My colleague Han, already mentioned the wonderful buses. You don't wanna be on one really. You rarely get to sit down and once again people are tightly packed in. Journeys are so slow since the traffic is so bad. Sometimes you can't see out of the window and you'll miss your stop. Sometimes it's hard to actually get out of the bus as it's so packed. If you're waiting for the bus and finally see it coming in the distance it can be so slow it's more reminiscent of a canal boat that's broken its mooring on the Norfolk Broads. When it finally reaches the bus stop, the crowd mob the door as everyone tries to get in all at once[9]. There is one bus numbered the 300 in the centre of town that's so bad, it's become famous to all residents. If you are waiting near the 300 bus stop, so many people will surge towards it when it arrives, you can get caught up with the crowd and actually become an unwilling passenger. Still, it's only one kuai for a ticket and the subway costs two kuai to go anywhere. If you buy a travel card it lasts for ages so you can't complain really hey!

Cycling, now that's a trip! Although the number of cars being used is on the up and up, at least 10 million still use bicycles and if not choose to go by electric bikes which are also really common. There are big places put aside to lock your bike up next to subway stations, department stores, colleges, offices and housing complexes for 5 mao a day. In many places you will see huge piles of old blackened bikes still chained up that people left and never returned to claim.

One evening after work I was unlocking my bike when I knocked over the one next to me. This produced a domino effect as nearly every bike for about thirty feet went down one after the other finally ending in the last one crashing down on the attendant sitting by the gate who was not best pleased. The unfortunate old woman who was at that time sitting on a stool reading a newspaper jumped up and gave me a right earful.

---

[9] I have to be frank about this one. Chinese people aren't very good at queuing up, especially down south and that's all there is to it. If someone tries to lean across you when you are buying a ticket you may have to push them out of the way to regain your space. If you're waiting for a taxi, someone may well stand in front of you and try to pinch your lift. If you flag a taxi down, other people will run to it even if you were waiting first.

Cycling everyday can be one of the few dangerous ways of travelling as Beijing's flat so you can cycle fast. You have to have a 360 degree awareness at all times. I mean people just do not look out for anything or anyone else. People will just pull out or step out in front of you. Drivers will open their car doors without looking. I've hit a few people full on so far and the other day my mate Nathan got his foot squashed and broken by a taxi poor bastard! I hit a motorbike the other day. Generally, cycling around is a great feeling though; truly amazing going around Tiananmen Square for exercise every Sunday I can tell you.

Commuting: Here's a little tip. Always get a place to live near to where you work. If you don't then you will definitely be hitting the bus or subway two times a day so watch out. Joining the millions who start their day using public transport, my day normally starts in the same way. First, cycle to Guomao for 8am and leave the bike in an underground parking area (three kuai ticket for one month). Guomao subway line 1, change at Jianguomen Line 2 and up to Xizhimen station and walk to line 13 (Xizhimen is particularly vicious at rush hour). From Line 13, stop at Dazhongsi and catch a taxi to the first class of the day at Nongkeyuan. Normally this will take about an hour and a half. Before lunchtime, walk back to the subway and go to Wudaokou for the second and third classes of the day. Repeat the subway journey to get back, normally staggering in at 10ish. It's easy to become exhausted here. I call it Beijing Exhaustion, or BE for short. At least two thirds of it is from travelling. Recently I realised that I have been sleep walking during the day. In ten minute bursts of nothing there will be no recollection of where I've just been walking or anything; simply asleep and moving at the same time.

### Dating and Romance in Beijing

At long last it seemed that for better or for worse, I'd finally found a place I could truly get to grips with and settle down in. With a job and apartment tucked firmly under my belt it was time to find that all elusive missing piece to the magic puzzle of life. Surrounded by talent of the highest order and fuelled by months of zero activity going on in the love department I shifted myself uncontrollably into top gear, spending every conceivable bit of time and energy on getting sorted.

As a foreigner, you will find that within a couple of weeks your phone will effortlessly packed full of numbers of potential dates. It's quite remarkable how much interest you get. Be careful though. From the out, if you start applying a Western approach to this you're in for a nightmare, really! Was I in for a steep education or what! Of course this is written from a man's perspective, so if you're a woman reading this please excuse me. The same rules generally apply though.

Right, here we go. If you're a guy, holding back on how often you call her and send messages on your mobile, will confuse a Chinese girl incredibly. If you're only sending a message or calling her every other day she will get mixed signals big time. If you drop her a line every few days, then this is a total disaster. Instead you should be sending lots of messages every day from the moment you get her number. If you're a woman, expect a Chinese guy to immediately start sending you a river of text messages in order to show his interest. Amazing hey! I mean in the West, if we guys send messages and phone everyday most women will think we're some kind of needy sad loser desperate for a shag;

"Oh shit, it's him again!"

Her interest levels will plummet instantly and we become nothing but a highly amusing topic she will enjoy sharing with her friends.

If a Chinese person says they 'like you' it means they fancy you. It actually means more than that. It means okay, you now have the go-ahead to see me as often as possible and it is highly likely that we are going to be seriously girlfriend and boyfriend. Generally casual dating doesn't happen in China. When you start seeing someone it is normally heading in one direction with one agenda, so watch out. 'I like you' can happen after a few weeks or even a few days. From the beginning, you really should be seeing each other at least two or three times a week, even if it's to nowhere special. The notion of 'hard to get' is non-existent here in China. It's very hard to explain to a Chinese person and most don't understand this concept.

It's okay to buy her gifts, I mean even if it's early days. Of course you want to show how much you like her and you are thinking about her. Do that in the West and the death knell is already sounding. You are quickly compartmentalised into the 'good friends' section and maybe even thought to be 'a bit weird.'

If you go on a date, the guy will pay for 99.9% of everything every time, I mean taxis, tickets to anything, the restaurant bill, the coffees, you name it. If she insists on paying for things normally you have been relegated to good friends.

In China, it's okay to say this is my girlfriend or boyfriend and not be having sex. It's still pretty traditional here and a lot of people below their mid-twenties are still virgins as 'sex before marriage' can still be a

314

taboo. You might be dating someone and suddenly the penny drops that there is a ninety nine percent chance that they haven't ever got their kit off. If so your work's cut out mate, especially if they're still living with Mum and Dad. In the West you're having a laugh right? If you are having above average sex THEN you may start thinking about long term, I mean you're not gonna ask a crap shag to go out with you right? At the end of the day in China, cash, the ability to bring up a stable family, followed by personality are the most important things. To us shag level is far more important.

If you're a guy and you start seeing a local Beijing girl then be prepared to have the following resources in large quantities: patience and money. Your date will go home to the parents every evening at the crack of nine and rarely venture forth to your apartment. Their folks may have no idea about your existence and if by some miracle they are told and it's ok, you will then be invited to meet them to establish their approval for marriage. During this time there it's also highly probable that you won't have slept together. If you have enough to buy a car and an apartment then you may be in with a chance. If you're a guy and you do get married but don't make quick and steady upward progress up the money tree, it may mean a total disaster. Your wife's family may pressurize her into early divorce; a common story in these parts.

Check out from the beginning that Mum approves of their son or daughter dating a Westerner. Normally, what Mum says goes and that's the bottom line! Often they will say No! Westerners, well Western men should I say, have a 'love em and leave em' reputation amongst Chinese parents.

People here normally want to be married well before they are thirty and will be looking to start a family as soon as possible after that. It is very unusual for someone to have had more than two partners in their life. A Chinese woman will always stay with her man so if you're a Western guy and you disappear, then you're going to break someone's heart. If she's still single at the age of thirty then alarm bells are ringing. After thirty, it is widely accepted that a woman's body isn't fit to have a child, amazing hey!

As the years tick on, the family's expectancy that their child should be married leads to a high burden on their shoulders. If someone is still single past twenty five, it is now common to hire a fake boyfriend or girlfriend to take home to meet the parents to keep them happy. You can hire someone from an agency found on the internet for less than 1000 kuai a day to do a thoroughly professional job if parental nagging gets too much.

You see lots of foreign guys going out with Chinese woman but you don't see many Western women walking around with Chinese men. There are a couple of definite reasons for this. The first is that Chinese guys have absolutely no idea about the dating game in the West. If you even start to talk about this subject in class, the notebooks immediately come out of every guy's bag and they start writing everything down, it's hilarious. Secondly, Chinese guys are far too nice! They are also a bit shy and intimidated. Lastly, Chinese guys are often shorter! That sounds harsh, but ask anyone from any place to imagine going out with a taller girlfriend or a smaller boyfriend and see what they say.

Watch out if your date is an only child. The single child policy of 1977 has changed the dynamics of any family completely. The child will always be the centre of the family, especially if they have a boy. In a still fairly unequal society having a boy is still more desirable; eventually he will be the one maintaining the bank balance, looking after the parents and paying the mortgage. If they have a girl, she may well be spoilt rotten and have many things done for her. This is often seen as essential education in a girl's upbringing though has had the knock-on effect of creating millions of virtually ungettable prima donnas who soak up attention like a super-black hole.

I had the misfortune of taking out a few girls who were 'only children' and you could really tell. For a short spell I was seeing the only child of a high ranking officer in the army. In the beginning all went well and we had some great moments together. The first time we went out, was for a walk around Bei Hai Lake. It was one of those beautiful effortless days that could have lasted forever. We even fed the wild white cats that live on the southern side of the shore and then took a boat ride in the late afternoon.

After only a week however, it became apparent that she had been keeping an explosive temper at bay. Like some kind of loaded gun, she could go off at any time in anyplace over the tiniest of things if she didn't get her way! The first time it happened we were on the subway after spending a great day at the 798 Art District. I'd asked her how to say something in Chinese, a common thing to ask anyone and certainly nothing to lose your rag over.

"DON'T YOU TAKE ADVANTAGE OF ME" she suddenly shouted at full volume stunning the nearby passengers.

As the train pulled up at the next stop she jumped out of the door barking "NEVER ASK ME FOR ANYTHING. DO YOU UNDERSTAND?" before the doors closed. Holy shit! After a final rip roaring detonation in a crowded coffee shop the decision to throw in the towel became the only option. I'd been waiting for her for two hours and despite sending a few messages and calling her there was still no reply. Having become unimaginably bored I put on my coat and made my way to the subway line. On the way the phone rang.

"Oh dear, I wonder who that could be?" I pained.

Predictably it was Madame, "WHERE ARE YOU?"

With great reluctance I u-turned and went back. Through the window there was Madame, her face screwed up like a dried cow-pat with arms folded, already primed to go.

"THANK YOU FOR GIVING ME THE F*CKING SHIT" were her warm greetings. Back to the drawing board then!

One of the more (or less) memorable of times, was a blind date arranged by some friends. Here's a single bit of advice if you are going out on a blind date: phone up, cancel and avoid the pain of hours of inward contorted agony as you spend time with someone you pray your mates won't see you with.

The initial few seconds went very well actually with the "Hi, nice to meet you" and "You look great!" formalities, plus a big smile.

After that it was all one way traffic and that was downhill like a rocket propelled toboggan. First we went to a quiet coffee shop as it was still too early to get food. Here I quickly learnt two things; firstly, we had absolutely nothing in common with each other and therefore nothing to talk about; secondly that we would have to endure each other's company for at least two hours until dinner was over allowing escape.

"So what do you like to do for fun when you go out?" was my first attempt at breaking the ice.

"I stay at home!" was the quick and 'to the point' reply.

"Oh! What do you like to do in your spare time then?" was my second attempt with a painted smile the size of a canoe.

"I play games on my computer and do online shopping!" was the monotone response. Now don't get me wrong, but that doesn't give you much scope for conversation right? It turned out, that she never ever went out, never had a job and studied English from textbooks. Oh the pain!

"Do you like travelling?" I sparked, scouring the bottom of the barrel heavily, looking for some common interest of some kind.

"No. I stay in Beijing" was the ultimate conversation killer. In the restaurant, the menu became the center of attention, even after we had ordered. While she continued to look at the menu, I would gaze out of the window and pretend to have an interested look on my face. At this point time really started to feel like time was slowing down. I could see people outside and started to feel envious of their freedom, especially those immersed in happy every day conversation.

317

As I took my turn at looking at the menu for a second time, she quickly used her mobile phone as a distraction before going to the bathroom. Her return was also my cue to disappear to the loo, where I could briefly summon up the energy to keep things together, propping my smile up until enough time had passed to ask for the bill!

Aside from that one, I went out with a woman called Dong Dong, had an internet date that turned out to be the living barrage balloon from hell (I never learn), a girl that decided to go hiking with the highest heals available, one that wanted marriage after only a week and another girl who insisted that I should continually buy gifts for her as well as giving her full access to my bank account, hmmmmmmm! Seeing is my balance is as barren as the surface of the moon, needless to say, that one didn't last too long either. There was also a woman that annoyingly never ate, even if you had just bought a really great meal in a superb restaurant, and a woman who never spoke and just ate everything within a ten mile radius very loudly. Quite a sight when you just ordered the extra large thick crust pepperoni that was supposed to be for two, I can tell you!

## Sights around Beijing

So far the Great Wall, the start of the Great Wall, the Summer Palace, the hutong, the Drum and Bell Towers, Tiananmen Square, Hou Hai and Bei Hai lakes have got a mention; all wicked. There's shedloads to do in Beijing. Although the new buildings are going up really fast, it's still easy to get away from it and see the old traditional stuff.

One fascinating place to spend an afternoon is the Dongyue Temple. It's one of the few Taoist temples remaining in the north of China and was built way back in the early fourteenth century. It is named in reverence of the God of the sacred mountain in Shandong called Tai-Shan, 'Dongyue' meaning 'East Peak'. Taoism is to do with the balance of nature, the flow of energy between all things, the positive and negative forces which balance the universe and where the black and white ying-yang symbol originates from. For many years Taoism stood side by side with Buddhism, though in the end it was the latter that became most widely practiced.

When people go to Dongyue they will buy red good luck tokens and offer them to one of the deities represented in the many 'departments'. Each one is represented with a large statue surrounded by those of mortals frozen in varying states of turmoil and anguish. One of the most frequently visited is the 'Department for implementing fifteen kinds of violent death' where if you kill someone via

318

"Starvation, clubbing, revengeful murder, stabbing, death caused by fierce animals, snakes, burning fire or flood, poisoning, outbreak of madness, tricks of an evil person, incurable diseases or falling into an abyss" then exactly the same thing may happen to you. I guess it paid to be nice in those days.

There is also the the 'Department of official morality', where you pray for your boss to be nice to you. It's absolutely covered in good luck charms.

DO NOT go to the Chinese War Museum. There are so many people there it is totally pointless. You get angry within two minutes. Mind you a great selection of weapons to choose from, maybe you could borrow a tank to get home in.

The Natural History Museum seems to be sadly lacking. It's more for kids and is full of plastic dinosaurs. Strange and kinda disturbing; on the way out next to the exit is a hall full of embalmed human body parts. It's all quite stomach-churningly weird. I mean can you imagine being placed in a glass box for all time with various bits of you removed on public display. There are kids running around all over totally delighting in these gruesome sights including a box with someone's cock and ball sack floating around....hmmmm....Don't bother with your sandwiches at this point!

Outside of Beijing is the Fragrant Mountain and the Botanical Gardens; beautiful with real fresh air; they say that these gardens are the 'lungs of Beijing'. There are pathways leading up to the mountains and it has the Temple of the Reclining Buddha at its centre.

Huo Hai Lake in the winter is an amazing site. Despite the numerous signs saying 'Keep off the Ice', hundreds of people go skating and riding around on chairs with skis, some in tandem. Whole families skate around in random directions for the afternoon until the temperature becomes unbearable. My friend Xu Jing said that people frequently break through the ice near the edges and fall in. There are also ice swimmers; one guy singing at the top of his voice before taking the plunge.

Nathan and I had the misfortune of going to Beijing zoo the other day. To be honest it's a fairly miserable place. As we left I asked Nathe what was up as he seemed pretty blue. "The zoo sucked away all my happiness" he replied.

The Beijing Guoan experience: You gotta check the footy out right. So we went to see Beijing Guoan FC play Shaanxi Zhongxin at the Fengtai

Stadium. The total crapness of standard is totally made up for with bad tempers and number or cards displayed. Also, the fans in their green and white use the worst language possible projected in unison at the opposition; highly entertaining. Their language by the way, is surprisingly far worse than anything you will hear in England, serious! All in all a brilliant experience, though definitely something you wouldn't take your kids to see.

Other stuff: Oddments and other unusual observations in no particular order:

The local Carrefour is the biggest nightmare in the world. Queues can be more than twenty people deep. They turn the heating up full whack so you want to get in and out of there at top speed. Don't go there at the weekend as the lines at the check-out are enormous. The other day they were playing AC/DC's Highway to Hell and David Bowie's Heroes in the background (a bit trippy that one). You can get all your required vitamins there including essence of yak's penis (essential), essence of kangaroo (for energy I guess), super placenta tablets, lung cleansing pills and child flavoured tablets, yummy!

One of our company's offices has no toilet, instead you have to go to the Mariot next door; a five star luxury hotel and use the loo on the fourth floor. The porters hold the front door open for you, welcome you and call the lift down for you. This is the most expensive public toilet I have ever used.

The chemist downstairs also has a large section that sells cigarettes, in fact it's commonplace here.

If you want to call someone 'stupid' you can call them "Er bai wu" which means two hundred and fifty. You can shorten this to "Ni shi er", or "You are two". It is totally mind-blowing for any Chinese person to be called this.

At the moment a tree similar to a willow tree called 'liu hua' is seeding. It's well weird, feeling like a cross between Silent Hill and a snow storm as you go down the street. The white fluffy seeds float around and fill the air all over Beijing for weeks. If you have hayfever or allergies just don't bother being here as it's so easy to breathe the seeds in, oh and don't walk or cycle for too long with your mouth open.

Beijing ren are a unique bunch by any standards. True Beijingers will speak 'Beijing hua' which is the local dialect. This is unlike any other way of speaking in China and if you have a Beijing accent, in other parts of the country people will not be able to understand you. It can be likened to Chinese with a West Country accent from Somerset; highly rounded, for example 'bi ji ben' or 'notebook' becomes 'bi ji burr' with Beijing hua. I'm sure the Wurzels[10] have ancestors over here.

Actually China is so big that it's easy for two people from different places to be unable to communicate with each other. Because of this, every TV programme on every channel will have subtitles at the bottom of the screen.

Jiang Wei tells me that the hardest dialects to understand are down south on the East Coast where most people speak variations of Cantonese. If you go down that way it's definitely time to throw away your years of learning Mandarin. In the Fujian Province, Fuzhou hua bears absolutely no similarities to Mandarin at all. People there openly reject it as 'rubbish'.

"Worse" said Jiang Wei "is Wenzhou Hua, which is spoken by Fuzhou's neighbour in the north. This is famous as being the most difficult dialect to understand in the whole country. It is so difficult that in the Second World War, Wenzhou Hua was combined with Morse code so the Japanese couldn't read it. Unfortunately, though they were unable to work out the code, often even the Chinese couldn't read it either".

Because of the Olympics they've really gone to town on sorting out many of their legendary 'bad English' signs in Chinglish. Unfortunately they haven't done a very good job of it. Why people don't employ a Westerner to translate things is beyond me. In Ritan Park next to the pond there is a big sign saying

"Notice for Angling. To avoid possible death of the caught fish regardless of their size should not be returned to the water. Those who violate this will be fined 50 Yuan per fish. Participants who avoid or escape from paying for the fish caught or given to another person will be fined 200 Yuan. Participants are not allowed to use fishing gear supplied by themselves. Practices like concealment, steal and transference are forbidden. Escapers will be fined 50 Yuan. A fine of 10 Yuan will be exercised for each fish. Three pieces of fish caught within half an hour can be taken free of charge".

In the lift in Block A of the Soho area is a sign saying "No jumping up and down or behaving in a silly way". At Guloudajie Station there is a sign saying that if you catch fire while on the train you should "roll around on the floor and not run around in circles".

The best can be found in the driving test theory manual provided by the government. Here you will find ninety pages of pure joy if you're ever feeling pissed-off. Doctors should prescribe it if you're depressed

---

[10] Well known country band from Somerset in the UK. Somerset is a county in the south west of England.

instead of drugs. Here are a few examples:

*Blowing the horn in an area where horn blowing is prohibited is not permitted. True or False?

*Travelling on a road perilously close to a mountain the driver should be very prudent. In case the brakes suddenly go out of service he should A: shift to a lower gear, B: Turn off the engine, or C: jump out of the car?

*To deal with the surface of burned we should A: treat it with medical oil, B: prick the blisters, or C: not put medicine arbitrarily, treat with oil or prick the blisters?

*For an open abdominal wound, such as protrusion of the small intestine tube, we should A: put it back, B: no treatment, or C: not put it back, but cover it with a bowl or jar and cover it with a cloth or belt?

*In the summer when a driver drives he can, A: wear slippers, B: not wear slippers since it's unsafe and not polite to wear them, or C: wear any shoes including slippers?

*When a driver encounters a traffic accident scene that requires help he should, A: continue driving, B: offer some assistance, or C: negotiate with the party concerned for a reward available ok?

*What should a driver do when he needs to spit while driving? A: spit out the window, B: spit into a piece of waste paper, or C spit on the floor of the vehicle?

Continuing on that line, greffing is still as popular as ever here, but nose picking is also a common thing to see in Beijing. You can be on the subway and there will be someone with their finger right up there like they've lost something. One day while stuck in traffic in a taxi with a friend, we noticed this really stunning woman in a BMW behind us. She was glamorous and well-dressed but was clearly in a world of her own, obviously really enjoying having a nice long nose pick, switching from nostril to nostril at her leisure. She only stopped when catching sight of us crying with laughter at her out of the back window. I wonder if she stuck it on the dash board and saved it for later.

**Visas:**

May 7th 08: Phew! My mind is just a blur with this. As the Olympics draw closer it's getting harder and harder to get a visa. I've also been trying to get my driving test sorted so with that and the visa thing combined, it leaves you kinda numb. Going from one office to another and then going back to the office you started at, to be told that you need to do something else and should return again another day and so on; you can get knackered on your day off very easily. Westerners are having to leave in their droves as they can't get a visa. Even if you are working and have a job it's frigging difficult.

My company guaranteed me a visa (yeah right) but time is now so tight that it's just got silly. There are rumors flying around about some magical Z work-visa for only 8,000 kuai. Just send off your passport and see what happens and hope for the best ...hmmm I think not! These days life is about dedicating all of your free time into providing the relevant documentation in order to stay here. This includes a health check which takes two weeks to be processed, 800 kuai, a nice dose of radiation and then joining the end of a long queue of worried looking foreigners for a blood test where the nurse doesn't wear gloves, yeeech! You also need a complete translation of your CV into mandarin, along with all of your certificates and a further 200 kuai.

Phew, a week later and they are now are saying that you have to do a visa run out of the country if your one of the unfortunates like me who has a business F-visa. After that you have to then turn it into a tourist L-visa. You should then submit it in Beijing to turn that into a working Z-visa totalling about 10,000 kuai. So far the options are a train journey from Beijing to Hong Kong (and that's a long trip), Mongolia, Korea or Thailand. The former is the most likely trip. Who knows, but it has to be done in order to stay in this country. Rules and regulations change on a daily basis though. It's now impossible to keep up with anything. If you arrange to travel somewhere to get a visa, requirements may well have changed by the time you get there. The next time you can get a one year visa is in October that is unless you get married.

Another week later and now they are saying if you go to Hong Kong, you also need the contract of your apartment and certificate of temporary residence. This meant four hours waiting in the police station; my agent neglected to register me when I moved in so have been living in China illegally for nine months. Since apartment prices will rocket when the Olympics are on its most likely I'll have to leave my lovely apartment in Ping Guo She Qu anyway hence making a visa impossible. Oh my poor head! Watch this space!

Early June 08: Well I've never finished a diary where I started before but in a month it's looking 95% like its Mongolia again, heading back to Khovsgol in the north close to the Russian border with Nagi and her family. At the moment it's the best option to sit it out and wait until the Olympics are over, then get a new visa. I'm in need of a holiday big time but I'd give anything to be here for the Olympics. I even had a ticket to see the women's footy! This place is going to be incredible. I have to say that at night all lit up, the Bird's Nest is one of the most beautiful modern structures you will see. Photos don't show this off, you have to be there. I can't believe I'm moving out of another apartment and hitting the road again, but what can you do hey?

# 14

## Mongolia
## Just Turn Left at the Mountain!
### 3ʳᵈ October 2008

My brain is nothing more than a burnt-out piece of goat shit that is only capable of copying this handwritten diary I've been keeping for a few months. It's pretty crusty and tattered but at least I kept it dry.

12ᵗʰ July 2008: Another one that's hard to begin. We all ask the question "why?" at times in our lives. Maybe sometimes we pause for a few seconds and upon receiving no answers, we carry on about our day. Today though is different; "why?" is ever present. Sitting back and watching northern China go by out of the window aboard the K23 from Beijing to Ulaanbaatar, there is absolutely nothing else to do apart contemplate this. Why on earth am I going back to Mongolia exactly one year later? We all have choices and considering there are so many countries I haven't visited yet in the neighbourhood, it seems a kind of bizarre thing to be doing.

This time I'm not travelling alone. My mate Nathan from Canada is coming along. He actually left Canada for China when he was eighteen and is now twenty one. He speaks good Mandarin and is my inspiration to return to college and study Chinese properly in September. He is extremely tall and has holes in his huge shoes. Unnervingly he's sleeping with his eyes wide open on the top bunk of our compartment as he's been partying for two days non-stop. We are also sharing with a very nice Mongolian woman called Indra and all would be quiet except this giant happy Buddha of a man called Kishgee, who sleeps with a huge snore and a variety of interesting tones and whistles. He is obviously a very contented man.

As we coast through seemingly unpopulated Chinese towns, into green countryside and past old mud brick villages again the word "why?" comes floating back. I do know that I am super-exhausted after one year in Beijing with no break. I mean a full on explosion on all of your senses having taken some kind of continual mega-pounding. I do know that logically it works out as the best option after failing to get the visa renewed. More so though, I do know that I absolutely love Mongolia and that's all it takes really. Not a bad reason I guess! Aside from this, now the decision has been made, the objective is to return to Lake Khovsgol. There, we will be working with my now best mate Nagi on her family's ger camp known as Hirvesteg. It's tucked away along the shore of the lake near the mountains and the idea is to stay there until the Olympics finish, then we may stand at least some chance of getting a Chinese visa. Well, that's the plan anyway.

Back in Erlian again; the Chinese town just on the Mongolian border. Yes, this is without a doubt one of the longest and most tedious border crossings ever. The train stops and so does the air circulation. Passengers are kept in their compartments for at least an hour while passports are collected followed by departure cards. You choose to be either locked in your compartment while the wheels are being swapped over or get off and wait for two hours on the platform. Upon return to the train you then have to leave China and enter Mongolia, wait for the return of your passports, hand over your arrival cards and get your bags searched. The air gets heavy and you start to super heat. Toilets are off limits and Nathe paces up and down the aisle fiercely trying to control his bladder. All in all, the Erlian border crossing is always quite an experience.

Monday 14th: Great first day! So much is going on. It's really good to be back in Ulaanbaatar again and quite trippy, but most importantly is that feeling of freedom again, amaaaazing! Yes, yes! We have an apartment just out of town on the other side of the Peace Bridge compliments of our contact Batbayar who is presently sporting a big black eye. We really like it, though when jumping into our beds they both instantly collapsed. I also came back to find an enormous meat cleaver lying on mine. Hmmm… a bit strange that one! Got one month extensions on our visas sorted already, reeesult!

As per usual there are a lot of people here with absolutely nothing whatsoever to do. In the evening human forms lurk in the shadows. People lie unconscious on the pavement annihilated on vodka. We drew a large number of people in the supermarket as the cashier painfully slowly counted my change out in full public view. I could feel a lot of hungry eyes staring at that moment for sure. People don't change their clothes or wash. The bad cases don't even pull it out to piss. Followed back in the dark by three guys across the estate and one of them tried to come inside with us.

Mongolian guys are seriously hardcore, even the pissheads. Some are built like tanks. In China if you are barged into by someone (something that happens very often), people just keep on walking like nothing happened, avoiding a confrontation. In Mongolia I am more than happy to move out of the way of everybody and let them walk in a straight line. Guys are tough and the women really are some of the best-looking you will set eyes on, while Western backpackers flop around awkwardly in their lookalike sandals, t-shirts, shorts and designer hippy getup. Rich looking Mongolians blast around in their state-of-the-art 4x4s while a limbless guy squirms around on the floor covered in filth and blood. You can't ignore the weird state of poverty and wealth in this town for sure.

Wednesday 16th, 18hr bus journey to Moron: Knackered from yesterday's preparation, after packing and re-packing the gear, at 5.00pm we finally get on board the eleven seat tiny grey Russian minibus. This is typical of the out-of-town transport which resembles a 1970s Commer van. The packing is incredible. It's just the same as packing your rucksack; maxed-out and no space as they fit the possessions of seventeen people in. Gradually more and more people fill the tiny bus under an intense afternoon heat. A huge guy built like a brick shithouse who reckons he's a wrestler pushes his way in taking two spaces. He has the most enormous hands you will ever see and his wife sits opposite. It's really really hot in the bus, like a pressure cooker. There are six Mongolian women on board. Unlike China which is notorious as the land of the padded bra, Mongolian women are extremely well endowed and I can't quite believe my eyes. As we finally set off in this hot, sweating, packed to the max sardine can of a bus, every pot hole in the road puts a smile on my face so I guess it's just best to try look out of the window. This is travelling mate I can tell you!

Well, as per usual I spoke too soon. As we go up to someone's house to make the first of many stops I say to Nathe,
        "Hey! Look at the size of that guy out there. He's frigging massive!"
        The bus then suddenly slams to a halt, he pulls the door open, throws two big rectangular boxes in across everyone's lap so your chin rests on the top (it's a couple of bicycles in bits) and then literally jumps in on top of Nathan. We are all facing each other so that everyone's legs are interlocking. It's funny old life! There is absolutely zero space and you can feel peoples' bones pressing right into you and their muscles straining.

All night the smell wild rosemary fills the air and the large full moon illuminates our way. The driver stops at this all night diner so we can have tsee and buzz soup. The night is a blur; seventeen people in the back of the bus zoning in and out of consciousness, flopping around all over each other and an endless effort to find that unobtainable comfortable position. It feels like we have become one big sweating gelatinous mass and the experience seems to go on forever.

Everyone looks wasted in the morning. It's 6.00am when we hit another diner for breakfast and have goat buzz soup for the second time. Heading back to Moron via Rashant, a familiar sight and then it's out of the bus and a walk up and down Mount Tarjatdava as it's too steep and dangerous for the bus to go up fully loaded. At the top, we walk clockwise twice around an 'Ovo' or 'Duwo' (there seem to be a number of names for them); a pyramid of stones, wood, turquoise haddocks (the traditional blue silk prayer flag for a safe journey), animal skulls and vodka bottles. Shamanism is still practiced in Mongolia and people use Ovo's for good luck on the road.

After going through the small town of Tsonsengen, the bus finally pulls in at Moron. The bus station is buzzing, dusty and extremely hot. Why have I returned to a town called Moron? Hmmm, don't answer that question. Nagi's father Ulji Huttock meets us and invites us into his house, where he introduces his wife Tserenmadmid and Nagi's boy Tingis. Huttock is well known in town. Nagi previously said that before building Hirvesteg, he made a name for himself by setting up trade links with Russia in these parts.

"My Father had a really good trading business. He bought a lot of things like Kashmir sheep-skin, put them in five or six big trucks and used to take them to Russia across the ice of Lake Khovsgol in the winter. I remember he went away for one month or two months maximum and came back with Russian goods like clothes and sugar to sell in the small villages.

He was the first man to do that because the road through the mountain is the worst road in Mongolia. It's all mud and high tracks. No one had traded like that before. After that many people copied his idea. You could see these big Russian trucks in a line. It's dangerous and sometimes the trucks went through into the ice."

After negotiation after negotiation, Huttock helps us get a ride in a jeep up to Nagi's camp, some five hours further north.

Mongolian Time: We are unceremoniously dumped at someone's house in Khatgal, this small town idling on the southernmost part of Lake Khovsgol. We just assumed that the jeep was going all the way up, yeah right! Left at someone's house, waiting there well into the evening hours and filled with tiredness, we were tearing our hair out dying to push on. At the same time our kinda reluctant host just laid on his sofa watching Japanese sumo in Russian on his fuzzy black and white TV doing absolutely nothing apart from blag ciggies.

Mongolia time is completely from another dimension. You have to be ready for it. You have to absolutely not give a monkey's. If you arrange a time to meet someone they may well be very late, maybe two days late. If you make a deal it will then normally proceed to move in a completely different direction from how you anticipated. The people you made the arrangement with, may then just sit around and do absolutely nothing and it can be infuriating. If your plans succeed in Mongolia it's a major achievement. From Khatgal up the lake through the night in another Russian minibus, we finally make it to Hirvesteg. So mullered, but after a final bone-jarring journey we've arrived!

The first sight from the ger in the morning is a pool table, standing out in the open and exposed to the elements. This place could seriously be paradise. Hirvesteg is a really nice camp overlooking the lake. It has four log buildings. There is the main cabin which has a dining area for guests, a big kitchen around the back and a bedroom upstairs. There is the shower area (the water is heated by a large wood burner), a tool shed and a single empty hut standing apart, away by the shoreline. Aside from these few buildings, there are eighteen gers all ready to take on guests. There is only one more camp after this one and then there is nothing. The mountains are to the west of us. Mt Monkhasidag is visible to the far north of us; Russia!

We're having breakfast with Nagi. As she is telling us about the ger camp I ask
"So what kind of work do you want us to do then?"
"Oh, you will be managers of the camp!" is her simple reply.
At this moment a wave of shock goes through me from top to bottom, after all we are in a Mongolian camp. Holy shit! We are supposed to manage the whole camp; the workers, helping the guests and dealing with the money as well as teaching English to all the staff! Help! I was wondering how this trip was going to be different from last year. Here's your answer. In every way!

There is a canoe and a powerboat here, so it's easy to get out onto the water, including plenty of fishing tackle. There is horse riding, mountain biking and hiking. The most daunting thing for us is that we can't speak any Mongolian, how sad is that hey!

There are a few Western tourists that come this way but most are Mongolians, super hyper on a vacation they can hardly afford or rarely get. Feeling a bit intimidated by the whole experience today really. Oh for the comfort of noisy and unhard Chinese people. Once again,

Mongolians are tough. One family plays football outside our ger non-stop all day until darkness, phew! I watched one guy as he did some pull-ups on the frame work near our ger. He just didn't seem to get tired. Push-ups are easy and I can wrack off fifty no problem, but pull-ups, hmmm. I embarrassingly admit that I can do, shall we say, less than ten (if your laughing count how many you can do mate!). This guy easily did fifty pull-ups and was in no way tired.

Mad, mad fly-infested night in the ger, killing great black ones, loads of 'em. Oh, aside from that, you just can't imagine what it's like falling asleep in your own ger in Mongolia. It's a truly special feeling it really is, with the wood burner crackling and people singing traditional songs out in the distance.

Mad Bankers, Saturday 19th: Today was a chill-out day so I took myself for a long long walk along the shore. At this point, this has got to be one of the most tranquil and beautiful places on the map. The shore is white and the water a dazzling, dancing display of turquoise. Back at camp a group from the Chinggis Khaan Bank in UB are on day two of their holiday. There are twenty two of them and they are more than excited. Full of energy, they are generally 'all over the place' and quite a spectacle to behold. It's only the afternoon and they are already totally arseholed as a couple of them ride around the camp on the mountain bikes falling off every two minutes.

A big traditional meal has been arranged for them in the dining room and they insist that Nathe and I join them, oh dear! Jaja, the security officer, a giant of a man has steamed a whole goat in a milk churn under pressure, known as Khorhog. The president of the bank Mr Saintsogt Chamid insists that we sit at the head of the table with him, which to be honest is kinda nerve-wracking. The goat is taken out and ripped to pieces and everyone piles in with gusto, followed by the traditional vodka shots.

"This is the best meat" slurs Mr Chamid, handing me some dark grey greasy matter. "And this is the best vodka" he announces Standing up and raising his glass for the umpteenth time, everyone follows suit with drunken enthusiasm until the table is covered with animal carcass and empty vodka bottles.

Last year I managed to almost completely avoid vodka, but this year we have no choice. Utterly shitfaced, the first of many Mongolia fire parties starts up. The big blaze roars away like a beacon near the lake. The bankers stumble around, swinging burning branches and jumping over the fire, singing Mongolian songs and then turning up the sound system, dancing into the early hours. Holy shit! What a night!

329

Sunday: Quite sad to see the bankers go today. They all want to say goodbye and we have some new friends in Ulaanbaatar. The camp is quiet now. There is no reception for mobile phones here, no landline and no internet. There are some mythical hot spots where you just might be able get a signal. The best is out the back of the kitchen standing on the fence next to a tree, holding your phone up vertically at arm's length. The next is Tsegee's bedroom window ledge (Nagi's younger sister). I also discover a one bar reception in our ger that fades in and out like some vortex or portal to another reality.

Some of us went horse riding today. A great day though one of the horses did go absolutely nuts, ripped the fence to pieces and went running at top speed down the road with it. Some sight I can tell you!

Monday: Yes mate...and it's the first day as manager. Nathe and I are doing one day on and one day off and being the first one up in the morning, I sit up on the balcony above the dining hall and take in the scenery; the sun shines down on the lake and it's already hot and shimmering whilst the sound of birds and insects is the only audible thing. Monday morning! I mean you won't get a better way to start off the week really now will you? Moments of beauty and rareness, you can't miss them; a Mongolian woman in her purple padded dressing gown kneels outside her ger while mindfully combing her hair back.

The first chore of the day is getting Baska to throw away that rancid goat's head covered in maggots lying on the floor in the kitchen. Breakfast is rice pudding and dried beef. I get two English classes going in the afternoon. The first is an absolute beginner's class that most people attend including Jaja. He's got to be the hardest student I've ever had. I mean he's won six out of six of his wrestling tournaments, giving him the right to perform the eagle dance every time he competes from now on. The other class is more advanced with Nona, Nagi's other sister, Baska, a generally all round nice guy and Jaggi, Batbayar's cousin. Jaggi is in his second year training to be in the army and although quite young, is already seriously well 'ard!

In the evening we all play volleyball, badminton and an awesome game of football everyone gets stuck into. I must say it's kind of intimidating playing against the staff, especially when Amja the boat keeper (pronounced Amra), is running at you with the ball. In the end my only tactic, much to everyone's delight, is to grab hold of someone and let them drag me down the pitch in an effort to slow them down and stop them scoring. What a wicked, wicked day, with Nathe showing everyone how to play poker until the early hours.

330

Wednesday 23rd: Grey and overcast today. For the first time in so long I manage to think nothing. At about 1.00am Nagi and Amja return in a Russian mini-bus. They've been away from the camp for the past forty eight hours on a lightning trip to Moron to get supplies. I mean we've been living on next to nothing lately. Everyone has been waiting, coming out to greet them and to help unload. There are boxes and boxes of stuff from Moron market, including a blackboard for the classroom and three live goats....hmmm! To the kids, Christmas has come early and go nuts on a sugar overdose.

The next day Nathe wakes me up; the goats are already being slaughtered. Round the back of the kitchen suddenly, everyone is working at top speed. The legs are held and each goat is placed on its back, then a small incision is made in the stomach. You push your arm right in to find the artery just above the heart, pinch and it's all over.

The goat is then skinned and gutted very quickly. There is a separate operation going to clean all the guts and intestines. Bowels are cleaned out and it's all washed and wrapped up. The stomach is tied up on itself. Meat is held up on hooks round the back of the tool shed. Offal and blood are saved. It's a long process that lasts the morning and after, the guys roast the liver and toast with vodka. Amja promises me and Nathe the head roasted for dinner sometime. I really hope that this is not the case.

"Every part of the goat will be used" Nagi tells us. "Because people in the countryside have no money people keep everything, bones and skin. They may have a really small amount of money. If they do they will save it. If there is a sickness they won't have the money. They will say that will cost two cows or some goats and that will be enough.

Goats are expensive. These ones from Moron cost sixty dollars as they are nice fat ones. In Khatgal the grass is bad there and has no salt so the goats are too skinny. Because they are so expensive, often people will bring their own goat with them to kill while they are on holiday". Amazing hey? Phew, imagine taking your own pig down to Cornwall with you to keep outside your tent or caravan until breakfast time. Hmmm, I think not.

Well its 5:00pm and words can't possibly describe this present feeling. After returning from a lovely five mile stroll, dinner[1] still hasn't been served so I shove my head around the kitchen door to see what's been

---

[1] In England lunchtime is often referred to as 'dinner time'. The evening meal is commonly called 'tea time' though has nothing to do with drinking tea at all.

going on. Shockingly, Enkhee, one of the cooks, is stooped over the stove stirring two huge pots of bowels, intestines, tripe, giblets, you name it, it's all in there mate, stewing away in this grey, bubbling broth. At this point, deciding to take time out as this was very obviously what we were having, I go for a bit of a walk, trying to avoid a big anxiety attack and control my breathing. But hey, time waits for no one and within minutes there is a big hearty shout from the dining room,

"AAAAndy, Dinnnner!"

Inside, everyone is already there getting stuck in, sat around the first of two giant platters of brown and grey entrails. Serious! A serious situation indeed! Time stands still at this moment. I manage to get one photo off before having to turn away and lean against a post. Jaggi then heartily hands me a lump of meat, then a bowl of intestines stuffed with blood and in his heavy assertive voice simply says

"MEAT!"

Quickly following this, a rosy little innard soup comes my way.
"Hard work! Do it mate. Don't think. Look out of the window. Look at the sky. How nice it is today! Focus, focus, focus! Is that a horse over there? Look there's a bird on that tree." Yes, don't think about how completely strong the smell and flavour is and how it hits the back of your throat like a sledge hammer.
"Put it in your mouth. Don't chew so much, just bloody swallow it." I manage to do it though. I'm quite proud of myself, not retching even one time through the whole ordeal.

At this point, a second platter gets served up. It's really big and steaming away. No rice, noodles or potatoes to go with it, just a pure huge pile of entrails. There's so much of it (mercy), so I escape without anyone really noticing my disappearance too much. At this point the sheep's heads is being marinated in salty water. It looks hideous! The hair has been scorched off and it's floating around outside in a large margarine container. I mean what are you supposed to do? Eat an ear? Eat an eye? Hmmm decisions, decisions. I am assured by Nagi that it's delicious.
"It's good to cook nice head. Everybody likes eating the head." she insists. I tell you, I'm cooking chips in the ger tomorrow!

Half-moon reflected across the water. A clear sky of stars. Thunderclouds lighting up and moving slowly from the mountains across the lake up the north. That's what an evening is like while sitting next to the burner with the door open.

332

Another Mongolian Fire Party: Airag; the fermented mare's milk. This year it's later in season so it's a lot stronger. Huttock came yesterday with Tserenmadmid, bringing a    four litre orange juice container of it with him. Emerging from the ger in the morning, he whacks back at least half a litre and offers it to Nathe and I. It has a few tastes; kinda like being in a barn, sharp and zingy, like drinking liquid cheese and quite earthy. It definitely has a bite to it. If you get a good airag then you will definitely get really pissed, though it plays havoc with your guts, burbling precariously away for hours.

It's a quiet old Friday so Nathe and I build a big fire for something to do. As it gets dark everyone, including the neighbours, come down and the vodka comes out big time. We all form a big circle, joining hands and singing traditional songs. There is a party of nurses from UB and they have a seemingly unlimited supply of vodka, which goes round again and again and again. You just can't refuse. I used to try but it really upsets Mongolian people if you say no. Huttock and his wife are at the centre of everything and he makes speeches and toasts. Everyone gets super shitfaced and there is plenty of hugging going on. I'm just glad it's my day off tomorrow.

Saturday: Blaaaaaaagh! That frigging Mongolian vodka! It's seriously hardcore. It started arseing it down today so hiking up the mountain became fun and challenging; a perfect hangover remedy! Rain walking is amazing in this place, especially so high up. Damn! I missed the sheep's head! Upon returning, there's just the sad-looking skull on a plate, but lucky for me, they saved me a plate of windpipe and the roof of the mouth. Yum!

The pool table: This is truly a special table. Not only are you playing in the open air by the lake but you are playing surrounded by northern Mongolia. It is a special table in that when you pot a ball, they fall on the floor as there are no nets, hence are covered in dirt. There is one cue which is warped like a banana. There are two major ridges across the table causing the balls to jump in the air. The table is facing down a slope so often the balls will collect down one end. Often you will see the cue ball go up and then down the table several times. You can be playing with the sun in your eyes or against the wind, so in some ways I guess it's a bit like golf.

Be praised! Nagi knocks up a great lunch and we sing 'Wonderful World' by Ray Charles. There is a Khorhog on tonight. The milk churn under pressure hisses away and Jaja works hard to keep the stove hot enough. He takes it off and shakes the churn around and you can hear the stones clacking away inside. These are big rounded rocks which tenderise the goat, give it flavour and help to keep the temperature up.

The kitchen is an amazing place. The generator only gives us two hours of light every night as petrol or 'benzene' is more than valuable, so it's rationed out. After that everyone works using candle light. Vegetables and meat are never wasted. People eat when they can and it's hard work in there.

A wild stallion has his own pack of mares which he shepherds around proudly. He is brown with a big mane and is highly protective of them. Often they come though Hirvesteg and it's our job to get them off-site. Actually we do a lot of herding, especially the yaks from next door, who we have to shift twice daily. Anyway, a couple of horsemen came along today and took one of his mares. Shit did he freak! He attacked the horsemen non-stop until they were out of view. In the evening, a rival stallion came onto the scene and they fought all night, breaking up fences and making a right old din. The brown one was still there in the morning though (tough old boot).

Sleeping in this place is quite a trip. There are always tons of weird and bizarre noises going on through the night. A lone pisshead cried out in the woods. The other night in the early hours I went outside the ger to relieve myself with only my boots on. Across the field there was a snarling sound then a black shape, eyes illuminated by the star light came running out of the darkness at top speed. Diving back into the ger double-time, that sure was a narrow escape.

Mountain Trip to Renchinhumbe: We were never going to spend the whole time at the camp. This is the second stage of the trip. Now we have our shit together and know what we are doing (kind of), it's all about getting your head around moving on further. You just won't get a better chance to push your towny arse into something a bit more adventurous. After all, it's what it's all about hey? Renchinhumbe is a small village on the other side if the mountains further west. To get to it you have to push on up the lake towards Russia on horseback for a few days and then go left! Keep going left for a few days through the mountains until you get there. In order to get back you must go south and then take a right. Aaaaaah it's all just so straightforward!

Well before we do anything like building supplies up, we need a tent. Nagi lent us one but upon erecting it, we discovered that it was more like one of those one's you would put up in your garden next to a barby one summers evening for your kids to play in. It was also falling apart at the seams making us both feel quite depressed. Totally unable to get a tent from anywhere and fast running out of cash, we are forced to go back down to Khatgal to look for one, then go to the bank. It's a crap reality we have to deal with. I asked the locals here about buying a tent in Khatgal. They assure me that

"It may be possible!"

Trying to get a lift to Khatgal has been completely fruitless. 'Maybe!' is without a shadow of a doubt, maybe the most used word in Mongolia......maybe! In Mongolia 'maybe' actually means there is less than a five percent chance of it happening and is often used together with the word 'margash', which means 'tomorrow'. If you want something to happen and someone replies 'Margash! Maybe!' then face the reality that there is bugger all chance of anything happening whatsoever in the next century and find another solution as soon as possible.

We walked to another camp called Toilecht (which sounds just like the word toilet while clearing your throat), only to find that the lift that was offered never existed. The only alternative is to wait for a lift in the back of a lorry with Nona's mates, who are all presently on a serious mission of self-annihilation.

Another fire party, more vodka and more vodka; we're well into the vodka now. Over the track there is a small settlement consisting of two gers, a cabin and a shop. This is owned by a big woman called Nalmandach who has a toy boy called Batmyn, ten years younger than her. She is now completely used to our wailing pissed-up voices
"Naaalmaaaandaaach"
banging on her ger in the middle of the night to get her up for vodka, or our latest discovery of Russian AB beer in a three litre brown bottle. They also sell fish caught by Batmyn which they smoke by burning dung. Oh, and they have this great, always happy boy called Gansuch.

Sunday 3rd August: Waiting and waiting for this lift in the back of the lorry. Finally, at 8:00pm we set off. It's a small blue Russian flat bed. The back is divided into two areas by a three foot wide log and the end portion is filled with rocks. The open part nearest the driver's cabin is for the passengers. Thirteen of us fit into this space covered with a tarpaulin as shelter from a freezing cold evening. We are all squashed together and I'm really happy for the body heat as this open truck roars off into the darkness.

Jolted and battered, we come to this really steep hill that no one can get up. There are two big Russian lorries that are completely stuck. One has a trailer and is half-way up. Unable to get traction, the driver tries again and again, revving the engine hard and putting boulders behind the wheels to stop it rolling backwards. We all jump out and get to work throwing as many logs and wood into the trailer as possible and in the end everyone climbs on top in order to help give it some kind of purchase in the mud. Again and again he tries, but it's still getting nowhere. Finally he unhooks, tows the trailer up using a cable and we're off again. One way of killing a few hours I guess. Quite exiting really. Khatgal at 2am! Bloody cold, but found a nice ger! Knackered!

A bright, hot, sunny day mixed with a cool breeze. Waking up with a black tea, sitting outside the ger, we immediately go into Mongolian time. Stupidly we asked the owner, an old boy called Biar Magana, if he knows where we can buy a tent from. Of course, instead of just telling us where we can go, he's off into town looking for us. We wait for at least two painfully quiet hours while all we really want to do is get going. Now Biar Magana will do a great job asking everyone, but in his own time. Maybe he'll be having a smoke with his friends, a tea, lunch, or a great social. Who knows when he'll return!

Blowing out the whole Biar Magana thing, we quickly see that there is absolutely no way that a tent is going to materialise in Khatgal. It's just a bunch of shacks with a few shops in the middle of absolutely nowhere. Even worse is to come when I walk into the bank with my visa card. Yeh right! What a wanker! I do it every time. I'm always doing it and that is, for some strange reason, assuming you can use plastic in these tiny backwater towns. Next we pursue the absurd rumour of a supposed internet cafe in Khatgal. Well there is, but it's a run-down falling-apart shack and the town has no electricity.

Tuesday, 5pm(ish): Sitting in another Russian bus in Moron, it's another time of patience. The back wheel gave out and after being changed, we now appear to be going around picking more and more people up. In the end, the bus has twenty people in it. A child is sleeping on this guy Simon's lap and there is a box of thirty six eggs on mine. We have befriended Oggi, the owner of the guesthouse Garage 24 in Khatgal, who got us a cheap lift from Khatgal to Moron early this morning. The driver really put his foot down and seemed to control the bus amazingly well on these crap roads. In Moron, I was faced with the only ATM in town. It was old, out of date and unplugged, so we wiped off some of the dust and cranked it up and amazingly in a brief five minute window of opportunity, managed to get some cash out. Be praised! The internet worked in Moron, for ten minutes, just enough time to get an e-mail off to Mum!

Moron on a wet and raining grey day is a miserable old place. We found the oldest pool hall in the world with tables where the corner pockets come off in your hand and all the cushions had fallen apart. Some guys came in and shoved vodka in our faces while we were playing. You just can't escape it. There are no tents in Moron!

Wednesday: It's my birthday today and it's pissing it down! Looking to find a ride back up the lake to Hirvesteg, Nathe and I trudge to the centre of Khatgal, getting drenched with no chance of a lift, nice! Back at 24, Oggi really comes through though, lending us her tent for the next two weeks and unexpectedly we're off! Once again it's another Russian bus, snaking wildly at top speed through the mud and huge water filled pot holes. How these drivers keep these buses on the road, Lord only knows.

We get dropped off two thirds of the way up to Hirvesteg, so have to walk up the rest of the way in the rain. It's grey and lashing down with thick clouds across the mountains. Three women, Hishge, Olzi and their eighty five year old mother Shada, let us stay in their cabin for a while to dry off, giving us Tsee and biscuits. It's a real welcome stop-off and a really nice time that brightens us right up.

Finally, we arrive early evening back at Hirvesteg. They haven't had any customers at all while we've been away, so are playing cards in virtual darkness in order to save petrol for the generator. It's a really quiet season and things aren't going well. Nagi reckons they're gonna close the camp early and for that I feel really sorry. Eating is now minimal and we seem to have been eating a lot of bones and rice porridge on camp for a while now.

Over to Nalmandach's for a bottle of AB and I pour a birthday drink for everyone. Nagi then sends someone out to get a couple more bottles and then it just all goes downhill from then on. Five bottles of vodka later and all brain cells have been destroyed. Another bottle gets smashed and takes all the paint off the floor.

At some point Nagi tells us of her childhood, including the games she used to play. "When I was seven I went to a Russian school and the first thing I learnt was the word 'toilet' so I could go outside and play instead of staying in class. One of our games was to pretend to be a poor Russian family huddling around a candle to keep warm. We also played being dominated by your husband at gun point." I know, I know! Serious hey! All in all it was an awesomely great birthday I'll certainly never forget! Everyone sang happy birthday in Mongolian followed by toast after toast, hooray! Seriously mullered!

Planning and blagging: The trek into the mountains is just around the corner so that buzz is back. Haven't felt it for a while. There's nothing quite like building your kit up before going on a trip and the ger is filled with supplies which will be carried on the pack horse. Sewing extra bits on the tent, water proof as much as possible, big flower sacks one inside another to keep the doss rolls dry, meat, veg and what's in those cans? Hmmm, they look extremely suspect; we may well have bought dog food by accident.

Checked out the horses today; mine goes really fast and we galloped for the first time. We also met our guide Bimba; a short stocky guy who used to be in the army. Seems alright, though can't speak any English (could be a slight problem up there in the mountains). We've been told the weather is coming in and August is the rainy season. Why didn't anyone tell us that before? Korean fire party tonight, killed goat, had Khorhog, smashed again on vodka!

Mountain Trip to Renchinhumbe Day 1, 13/8/08: Thirteen is an unlucky number but Nona tells us that Wednesday is a lucky day in Mongolia, so that kinda balances things out then I guess. Amja, the boat man got seriously smashed last night and is still completely on one today. We're just on our way from Nalmandach's and about to set off, when there is a call from the nearby cabin. Inside are Amja and his mate Tomorr. They're blasting a bottle back at lunchtime, insisting Nathe and I have a big shot before we go, blaaaaagh! This is the second time that Amja has gone on one. Last time he was pissed for three days. He's also Nagi's bloke and I don't think he's quite top of the pops in her books at the moment. Apparently Mongolian guys can go on benders like this for weeks.

Last night I found Nagi alone outside smoking a ciggie. I could tell something had been bothering her all night and I asked her what was up.

"Amja has a real drinking problem. I didn't realise until we were together. Now I am embarrassed to be with him when he gets drunk. I trusted him and we agreed that he would not drink this summer on the camp but already he is drinking every day."

I must say that for anyone trying to find some sort of rehab, even miles away from nowhere in the mountains, Mongolia is the last place to try and dry-out. People show up with car loads of vodka, everyone has a few bottles stashed away at all times. Out here you have no chance!

Tomorr has a nice place though with beautiful wall hangings. His wife Paraham Docham just lies on the bed opposite and laughs as Nathe and I recoil from our over-sized lunchtime shots. As we leave on our horses, the sense of freedom is almost overwhelming. We are off at last! Our first camp tonight and it's a good one; good grub, good view, good everything. We're finally on our way. Nice!

Mountain Trip to Renchinhumbe Day 2: A pretty straight forward day pushing on up north. There aren't many people up here and we're definitely now entering a realm where people never enter into civilization. Stopping at a hut set slightly into the trees, three guys come out and the owner, a guy called Holt, is happy to invite us inside. Half of Holt's place is occupied by a 'charrack', a big old sledge, which is covered with furs and being used to sleep in. Bits of meat hang from the ceiling and they cook us a nice tsuivan. The lake freezes every year. Apparently the water is so clear you can look right through the ice, even if it's over four feet thick in places. It's easy to get across and flags are put up to guide trucks and cars across the ice safely. It must be totally amazing up here in the winter. Hmmm, now there's a thought!

In diminishing daylight and with the certainty of a storm approaching, Bimba gets off his horse, points to an old burnt-out fire pit and simply says, "Camp!" He then walks off to hang out at an overlooking hut with what must be some of his mates, leaving Nathe and I in a seriously bad mood. What a downer! We thought for sure we would be in the valley out of the wind by now, but oh no, we're on the edge of a bloody cliff and the water is mmmm, choppy to say the least.

There's sod all wood and the storm is rumbling and banging just a few miles away, very nice! The sky becomes as dark grey as it gets behind the mountains and as the wind suddenly drops there's an urgent feeling that some serious weather is imminently about to be dumped on our heads. After a brief reality check, we go at it as fast as possible. As the fire gets going, the storm hits, so we cook right thought it, shoving all the dry wood into the tent. You won't get a better meal as that, even if the meat turned out to be something similar to Chunky. Maybe it really was dog food after all.

Carrying water up and down the cliff is an experience. Washing the pots and pans in the lake also. The lake is rough, so you have to wash with every fourth wave, using handfuls of small pebbles as a scourer. Even so, it's easy to get caught out with the waves as Nathe found out. That water's frigging cold mate I can tell you. We're already completely filthy and sleep with the wood as the storm intensifies to unbearable proportions. The lake's completely heaving and bolt after bolt of lightning comes down around us.

Mountain Trip to Renchinhumbe Day 3: We've turned left now. The valley goes up and up into an endless bog, through an eerie forest with no sound. There was a forest fire here a few years back and it has a ghostly feel about it. No birds, nothing, just bog. I reckon horseback is really the only way to get through this pass and each footstep the horse makes is accompanied by a distinct sucking sound. It's a hard graft.

339

Camping in another thunderstorm, Bimba cooks for us tonight. Maybe he's already sick of the dog food as he blagged some bread and dried meat from a camp on the way up the valley. It rains hard as we eat, but I guess it means we have to slurp a bit more down. Simultaneous lightning and banging crashes around our ears the whole time. What a trip hey!

Mountain Trip to Renchinhumbe Day 4: Nice day! Sunny day! This is the best day yet. The valley opens right up until it's at least five miles wide with a big flat open plain down the middle. Way below us are more flat planes that seem to go on endlessly. It's a stunning, stunning place to go riding and take your horse as fast as you can go. I've never ridden like that before and one of those feelings you can't express as deeply as you would like. It's just seriously where it's at. We camp alongside people who are living in white makeshift tarpaulin tents. They come up into this area to cut grass for winter fodder as down below it is thin and short. Into the evening sunset, solitary figures swing their scythes from side to side in this quiet space between the hills. They leave the grass to dry in rows behind them then gather it in, taking it down in rough bales on horse drawn carts. This is life completely as we do not know it!

Mountain Trip to Renchinhumbe Day 5: Phew! What a day! Unbelievable really. Leaving the valley, the land changes into one big expanse, sloping gently downwards to the west. We are through the mountains and the sense of space feels fantastic. Slowly walking the horses; low, grey, swirling clouds and Bimba singing Mongolian songs along-side. I could ride all day like this. This is how life has always been; unchanged and timeless.

Finally in the distance the village of Renchinhumbe comes into view. This will be the furthest point we will reach in Mongolia this year and for sure it really is 'out there'.
So this guy on a motorcycle comes past with his radio on and Nathe's horse suddenly goes absolutely nuts, rears up and bolts. I mean they're off at the speed of light and all I can do is watch in total disbelief as Nathe tries desperately to stay on for dear life. In the end he comes off and his horse legs it, dragging the saddle along in the dirt. His pride is a bit dented, but Nathe is ok, just some road rash, phew!
This jolly guy called Batjargal stops on his Russian bike as he has seen everything, chilling out the whole situation. Bimba will have none of it though! After catching the runaway horse, he seems to blame Nathe for the whole incident, riding off in a strop. No support from our guide there then; nice one! We decide to walk into the village the rest of the way while Bimba is off in the distance with the pack horse. Just

as we get there though, Nathe says he wants to ride in. He strokes his horse, calming it, but as he mounts-up it goes apeshit and throws him off AGAIN, poor bastard. Bimba catches the horse a second time but now he's right pissed-off with Nathe. There's a big atmosphere and to make matters worse, the rain suddenly kicks in with a vengeance and Nathe has no waterproofs. He's definitely having a bad day. After going to the shop and buying some much needed supplies like cheapo Mongolian cakes, tea, noodles and oil, Bimba very reluctantly shakes Nathe's hand, though it seems like more of a sad and half-hearted gesture. We really do have to be friends out here after all.

Anyway, trudging behind Bimba in the rain, walking our horses behind us, we end up at his elder brother Batmuch's house who says we can stay there overnight, nice! It's a wicked place; the living room is beautifully decorated and the kitchen strangely has this giant laminated wall-sized photograph of fruit, wine and a huge burger and chips that makes us miss Western food big time. I mean we've been eating nothing but goat for weeks, so it's a kind of torture to see it. Batmuch makes byaslag, shed loads of it and has his own home industry going on.

His favourite pastime is sitting up on the roof of his shed where he can check out the area with half a pair of binoculars like a mini telescope. There's an amazing 360 degree view of the encompassing landscape. With a clear view of the mountains to the south, they disappear then re-emerge from cloudbanks blown by a strong wind. To the east are the green valleys and passes that await the return journey, while in the north and the west, the Steppe continues uninterrupted for mile after mile where the oncoming weather can be seen as far as the horizon. Sitting on Batmuch's shed roof, you will never feel so insignificant!

Batmuch also has a radio with short wave. After struggling away with the tuning for an hour or so, getting nothing but Russian, a Chinese English speaking station crackles into life delivering our first news in one month. Briefly we hear that a Cuban athlete threw his bronze medal down on the floor at the Olympics and got disqualified. No major disasters in Beijing though and we breathe a sigh of relief.

We also do a quick trip to someone's house to buy meat. They actually cut it all up in their living room. Phew, some butchers! Can you imagine what a whole cow looks like chopped up around the sofa and all over the coffee table? It's absolutely everywhere!

341

As the rain dies down Nathe and I go for a stroll around the village. I guess it's the rain but it really gives Renchinhumbe a strongly run-down and dilapidated feel about it. It's a small place that's engulfed by mountains and the surrounding space. Muddy tracks are littered with bones and many buildings are falling apart including the now boarded up local restaurant. The centre of the village seems to be a convergence spot for any pisshead in the area. One guy called Turtochtoch comes up and tries to give us his rolling tobacco, but then goes and drops it in this muddy puddle. It's such a bad feeling that we give him a packet of twenty and he's delighted, saying that he could never afford such a luxury. Three guys try and have a fight but they're just too arseholed. One guy falls over and crawls in the mud; quite a sad sight really. I mean it is still only the afternoon!

At this point Batjargal shows up on his bike with a big grin. He re-introduces himself all over again and is also shitfaced. It seems like absolutely everyone is ratted in this place. He's got such a good vibe though so it's no problem, seeing as we were having such a crap time earlier. All in all it's an amazing walk around. Later, back at Batmuch's house, Batjargal shows up yet again only this time even more off his pickle, having now decided to be our best mate. Still, it's a right old laugh and it swiftly turns into another one of those evenings. Batmuch's wife shows up, Niche Jerlach. She cooks us a nice noodle soup and then yes, you know it, the vodka comes out. I'm sure those shots are getting bigger. It's amazing how quick a bottle of vodka can be downed here and what's more amazing is how swiftly people can move onto the next one no matter what time of the day it is.

Mountain Trip to Renchinhumbe Day 6: Another Monday! As we ride slowly down a steep grassy plain into a river valley, the overcast sky clears from the mountains and they look like giant incisors pushing through the clouds. Mondays really don't get any better than this! The showers packed up long before we left Hirvesteg, so it seems to be forever since we got a shower in. I reckon we've definitely gone through the crust barrier by now. Maybe there's an Olympic crust medal waiting for us back in Beijing. Maybe it's been a month now, very nice! Camping on the river bank, some herdsmen bring in their yaks for the night, then come over in the dark and check us out. Food is getting better and better, though maybe we are just getting more and more hungry.

Mountain Trip to Renchinhumbe Day 7: Why, oh why, does my horse lead me into so many embarrassing situations? I mean, I've always been the unfortunate one who trips-over a step at the time when trying to be the coolest. In this respect my horse and I are utterly synchronised.

Today we were going through more bog and marsh. As she stepped down into a big pothole, a cloud of flies came out buzzing round her head and she was off like a rocket. When a horse bolts it's quite breathtaking and you'll never be more in-the-moment. Luckily, having thought this one through in advance, when she took off I just let her go for it, only gently pulling on the reigns. Eventually she calmed down and though we had legged it in a completely different direction, I was still on, yes yes!

Another time, while galloping past a load of herders, I waved and shouted "helloooo" only for my horse to pull-up and totally refuse to go through a small stream. I could hear them all laughing behind me. Oh the complete shame! Later on we approached a family riding towards us. At the last minute she veered-off under a tree and one of the branches was so low I got completely entangled in it, again, much to their delight. I was sure they were saying something like "Hey look at that Western guy. He has absolutely no idea how to ride a horse. How lame is that!"

I love being filthy dirty. I love my skin being the colour of the earth. I love striking camp and starting a fire. I love sleeping with the wood to keep it dry. I love washing the pots in the river. I love collecting wood. I love cooking the dinner. I love the taste of my tea in the morning (new improved smoked flavour). I love not caring one iota about my appearance and I love not having to spare a single thought about work, only where the next water hole is. Tonight's storm was so hectic that the only way to keep the fire going was to use ourselves to shield it from the rain. The meat got contaminated with maggots, so it was back to the dog food, nice!

Mountain Trip to Renchinhumbe Day 8: Laid out on the grass back at Hirvesteg it's hard to describe. It's sunny, cooler, and smaller? Colours seem more vivid, brighter. Although utterly filthy, I feel cleaner than ever, like some damaged chemicalled-out part of my brain has been repaired and the lights have been switched on again. At this moment I feel more alive than I ever have been. It's so completely quiet, like the laziest of lazy Sundays.

The first part of the four stage comedown is complete; from the wilderness to Hirvesteg. Next is Hirvesteg to Moron, then to UB, and from UB to Beijing (mercy!). Today was a hard graft. I never realised that bog and marsh could exist at forty five degrees up the side of a mountain, but it did and for hours. Eventually during mid-afternoon, the mountains opened up into one last spectacular valley giving itself up to Lake Khovsgol.

Bad night for Nagi! A group of tourists ordered Khorhog but the stones in the milk churn exploded turning the meat green, tasteless and inedible. So everyone's in Nagi's ger looking well pissed-off with this giant pile of green meat. It's been a crap season for her.

Not only that but the day after our return a Russian van shows up with eight people from the government sent to inspect the camp; a strange sight to see for sure as some of them are wearing suits, carrying briefcases or holding clipboards. After an hour of poking their noses into everything, Nathe and I watch from a distance as a heated argument ensues between Nagi and the most important looking people. Clearly things are not looking good for Hirvesteg.

After they leave and Nagi has had a chance to calm down via three cigarettes, we press her as to what had just gone down.

"They are the Health and Safety people. They come every year to check everything in all the camps. I am always fighting with them. I can't help it. I could be nicer but always everything we do is wrong. We are just doing what we can do. I say "We don't have a budget to make a nice camp as you are wishing, we are just doing what we can do". It's complicated to follow their rules and they are far from real life. I don't know how they make their standard.

They say all the tourist camps have to have white plates this diameter; everything has to be the same but we live in the mountains. What can we do? They say that workers cannot go into the kitchen. But you know how it is, workers need to come in and bring water and wood. A person that comes into the kitchen must wear special clothes and cover their boots. They say you have to have a professional chef and I say I have but I cook better than they do.

I then I have to pay a fine. I always have pay for something. Normally it's between 100-600 dollars. That's 100,000 tugrik for this fine and 600,000 tugrik for that fine. I say "Why are you giving me a shit time? They say it's their job to push you hard and they have to keep their standards."

Amazing! I mean it's hard enough scratching an existence together in Mongolia anyway without petty bureaucracy following you around. Even out here so far away from anything, it seems there's always someone who will squeeze every last penny out of you.

Herding the yak from the site in the evening, our neighbour the old shaman woman stares unnervingly at me from afar. A loan figure standing motionless almost silhouetted and lost amongst the changing colours of the landscape, she never alters her gaze, freaky! Purple clouds over the Russian mountains as the sun sets.

Vodka: As the staff leave, the camp gets quieter and quieter. It's cold and snow covers the mountains that we have just left. I bet this place is amazing in winter. Unfortunately, a couple of nights ago the vodka came out to see off Bimba, the shower attendant. Of course it continued the next day and then the next. Jaggi got kicked out of camp as he was continually arseholed and really had no idea what he was doing. At about 4pm, I noticed Amja surrounded by rubbish, passed out next to the outside loo (there's an overflowing skip nearby). Such a sad sight! Later from our ger, I see him picking slowly and forlornly along the shore line. He's been smashed for days and I wonder what must be going through his mind. He's in big trouble from the missus I can tell you. Later in the evening Amja came stumbling into the kitchen demanding his dinner and when he got it thrown in his face, he ate it from the floor, how sad is that? Bloody vodka!

"Mongolian people never used to drink vodka" Nagi tells us in an angered tone "It was brought in by the Russians. They can drink a lot but they keep working and keep managing. It's their special talent. Russian people can work and drink at the same time. Mongolians can't do this. They copied the Russians, but they didn't learn the technique. Russians don't drink like us, they drink and work.

Mongolians drink for one week and forget what they have to do. The big bad thing I see comes from nomadic culture because nomadic culture makes people very hospitable. Like if you visit someone's ger, even now, you can just walk in and they will give you tea or whatever they have. They will give you everything. If you stay overnight they will give you a place to sleep. Nomadic culture makes people very calm

Lots of young guys they don't have jobs, but if their body is healthy and their hands are working they should do something right? But they don't do anything. They will drink and make one trouble here with one family and then move to another. Also they get married and have kids, make a mess of someone's life and move away, they don't care. I see many guys like this. A lot of countries have drugs, but you don't see this happening in Mongolia. Here we have vodka instead."

Olympics: Huttock and a bunch of mates have come up from Moron. On a cold and raining afternoon the news that Mongolia has won two golds in the Olympics comes out and they are off, solidly all afternoon, standing in a big circle downing bottle after bottle. Unbelievable! It just never seems to end. Escaping after being given a couple of massive shots, I watch from the safety of above the dining hall, while they wrestle in the mud and another bottle comes out. They are elated. A serious mission lays ahead for these guys I reckon.

The Reindeer People: Huttock's mates have cleared off now and we are all starting to think about the journey home. It's so quiet and with every conceivable chore on camp done, I just don't know what to do with myself. Walking down the road, I'm not even able to choose which way to walk. I can't think! So I'm just standing there in a complete fit of indecision, when two people come loudly crashing across potholes on a Russian motorcycle. Up front is this enormously tall guy in a yellow traditional coat and on pillion, an old woman in pink with a headscarf on; quite a sight really. They suddenly pull up to a halt and the woman beckons for me to jump on the back.

It's amazing how your day can completely change at the click of your fingers. Before you know it we're off 'three's-up' down the road and there's me holding on to this old woman for dear life as we fly in and out of potholes and river beds at top speed. She laughs at the top of her voice and all I can do is continually shout

"OOOOOH SHIIIIIIT!"

Ending up at this enormous teepee, they invite me in. Talk about where it's at, I can tell you. They are probably the most well-known and talked about family around here; the Tsaatan People, herding reindeer and offering shamanic services. They are without a doubt the funniest bunch of people you will meet and its easy to feel an instant liking for them. The big guy is a wrestler called Ganzam Oomil. He is frigging massive, with cuts all over his face and teeth missing. The woman, Enchtoya, is his Mum and is a shaman. Later that evening inside the teepee, Nathe and I attended a ceremony with Enchtoya. People come from all over to attend, bringing offerings which must include a bottle of vodka. In a circle lit by candles she tells each one of us about our life's journey including our future.

I am in paradise but the comedown is severe. Reality is biting me on the arse today. It's not just the physical journey that lies ahead, but the work that needs to be done, like obtaining the correct documentation for a Chinese visa. Some task! What's the destination? A sofa in Beijing with a TV in front of it after having cooked a massive meal. It sure feels a long way away at the moment. To say it scares me is an understatement. In fact it makes me shake nervously when I think about it, especially when I hold out my hands at arm's length (though that might also have something to do with the accumulation of vodka).

Nathe and I got smashed last night and as I emerge out of the ger feeling utterly dreadful, an old Russian ship comes into view on the lake, moving directly towards us, full speed ahead. In this alcoholic oblivion, it's hard to take it all in. It's loaded with tourists and they are playing that old 70's pop song D.I.S.C.O at full volume. We watch in disbelief as it steams full ahead towards the camp before running aground. I mean you can hear the metal screeching and scraping across the bottom of the lake. A tug comes and strains to push the big ship free[2]. I mean it's really stuck! "Delectable....incredible....super sexy.....sweet as candy" is played on a loop at full whack the whole time. This is surely as surreal as it gets.

Some other Friday sometime: "Machine kaput!" is the only thing Huttock has to say this morning. We are going nowhere! Cabin fever has now set in big time. We watch our neighbours Munkhoo and his Father Batragcha shut up their cabin for the winter, leaving on foot. It maybe a long hike to Khatgal but I sure am envious of them as we shake hands goodbye. It's been quite a journey with Munkhoo and his family. A few days ago his Mother, Dawa Surum, broke her arm while picking berries in the mountains. Quite odd in that no one seemed to have a clue what to do and panicked. Inside their cabin, Dawa wailed in pain in the dark and cold. Some night that was, though luckily the virtually untouched medical pack really helped out, especially those Korean sleeping tablets. Anyway they finally got a machine to take her to Moron in the early hours and apparently she's fine now.

The only thing Nathe and I have to do is move rocks to complete the septic tank compliments of our favourite health and safety officers. There's no lift and no vehicles anywhere. Everyone has left. Time stands still. I walk all day in an effort to find a vehicle but there's no joy. Running into Bimba, our guide from the mountain trip, I remember he promised us a lift two days ago, but the jeep has seriously broken down. He then introduces me to a family nearby, though they only have space in their jeep for two and won't let me leave without giving me a double dose of vodka, aaaagh. Sits nicely on a single bowl of rice porridge! Really we want to leave with Huttock, Tserenmadmid and the kids, but that's seven people (and pigs can fly!) All day there are only two machines that pass by and even then the people couldn't help.

In the evening, we hear that the Reindeer Family have moved up the valley and their white jeep could be working. They do move around a lot and are soon to pack up, moving right across the mountains to where it will be slightly warmer during the winter. It's a way of life that goes way back and I feel deeply privileged to have even got to know them, let alone be on first name terms. As we head up the

---

[2] Being that Mongolia is a landlocked country and is over a thousand miles away from the sea it was surprising to hear about the Mongolian Navy (scary!). Mongolia actually has the worlds smallest navy consisting of one ship. Indeed the government published 'The Complete History of the Mongolian Navy' but it only took up one sheet of paper! The vessel that ran aground called the Sukhbaatar III was in fact that same ship. It was built especially to patrol the waters of Khovsgol in case of an invasion by Russia via Siberia but also takes tourists on pleasure cruises. To this day it has never seen any action!

valley, Nathe points out the reality that we are actually hiking into the mountains in Mongolia, in the dark, to find a shaman woman who can give us a lift in her jeep. Some thought hey! We find the camp and its truly brilliant seeing them again. The lift is on and I know they will keep their word. We are totally sorted, and feel like we really have made some new
friends.


Return trip: Hirvesteg to Khatgal, Khatgal to Moron, Moron to Ulaanbaatar, blaaaagh! So anyway, Ganzam shows up in his white jeep on a bright beautiful sunny Saturday morning bang on the dot at 9am. It's all smiles and Nathe and I say our goodbyes. We are finally off along with Huttock, Tserenmadmid and the kids. It's such a relief to be on the move. Ten minutes later though we stop. Mongolian drivers do seem to stop many times at the beginning of a journey and as a Westerner it can go beyond annoying. In fact it really is a sign of things to come. Little do we realise that this is just the start of the worst thirty hour little excursion into unpleasantness you will ever experience; just excruciating! You just don't get a normal journey in Mongolia, it's impossible!

Ganzam strips out the back seats and the occupants of the surrounding three gers all pile into the jeep with us. It's no problem this time though, as I get to sit up front for once with Tingis on my lap. Ganzam drives like a nutter and after a few hours as we drive through Khatgal to Garage 24, the front right wheel detaches itself and roles off ahead of us.

Hirvesteg to Khatgal complete! That was the tough one. We're out now and it's easy to get transport. Another Russian minibus takes us further for a few hours to Moron, which isn't a bad journey. How is it that Moron is really hot? Only four hours back up the road it was bloody freezing. We give our farewells to Huttock and the family. Sure hope we see everybody again. Been through a lot with them. It just proves that actions speak louder than words and language barriers can easily be broken if there's real feeling behind it.

Khatgal to Moron complete! Now is the big, big pain in the arse that we've been trying to forget will happen. I guess the plan is to go completely blank and mindless for the next twenty hours. As we are skint, I buy two bottles of water and two packs of Russian cakes for the journey and we make a tactical decision to sit on the back seats.

There is a train of thought that goes with this, though at this moment it is untried. Sitting on the back seats mean that:

1. You will have no one sitting on your lap all night.
2. You will have no large boxes or sacks on your lap either.
3. You will have no one talking and laughing loudly in Mongolian across you for hour after hour.
4. You won't have anyone snoring loudly either side of you.
5 You won't be squashed in with five or six people together on four seats.

However, it's a gamble sitting in the back, a real gamble. Although this is the seventh trip so far in one of these Russian minibuses, this position has not been fully tested out yet. We are already seven hours into the trip and the few hours from Khatgal has already revealed the following drawbacks:

1. It is beyond cramped in the back.
2 There are three seats and Nathe and I are also sharing with two others who are these nice Korean folk.
3. We are sitting over the wheel arch. Hmmmm, definitely not the best on these Mongolian roads.

At 4.00 pm we finally pull-out of this hot dust pit and we're off. The bus is nearly empty and we are full of hope that we are going to have a clean run to UB. After waiting for hours, there are no passengers and too many buses. It's just too late in the season and we're full of smiles. Yeah right! For the next three frigging hours (seriously), the bus driver then proceeds to prowl around Moron trying to pick-up as many passengers as possible and phoning people on his mobile phone. He even has a piece of paper with the names of would-be punters who he checks out. It's not just infuriating and totally annoying, more like utterly deflating.

During these three hours the driver very skillfully manages to pack the bus to capacity again. It's destroying! There is even a pregnant woman who is way down the line. Why on earth she's coming on this bone-shaking, body-jarring journey is beyond us, as is the driver's total refusal to let her sit up front in place of his friend. The nice bit of leg room that once existed vanished into the abyss, getting replaced by some boxes. We are all at last, placed into a discomfort that is to increase at a geometric rate within the hour. Yes, it was inevitable really; this submissive state of having no choice any more but to face the grim reality.

Alarmingly someone slammed my fingers in the door at the petrol station, the last of so many stops including two returns to the bus station and it was all downhill from then on.

The minibus at last leaves Moron at 7.30pm. Having so far been on the road for ten and a half hours, we are already mullered. By 8.30 my body is already in some serious pain; my calf muscles and knees are really throbbing and my back is contorted into some weird 3-D shape, fighting for every centimetre of space I can get with my Korean neighbour, a fight in the end no one could win. The pain goes on and on and on. There is no air. I am hallucinating by 12pm. Every bump we hit sends us flying and I am sure we are hitting giant green raised metal circles with great spikes shooting out at us. The batteries give out so we drive with no lights. I find some sweets on the floor all mushed up and the sugar rush is noticeable. At one stop we are standing outside and Nathe checks the time. Unbelievably it's just past twelve. Both of us are in shock. We are certain it should have been more like 5am. How did that happen? The last half an hour seemed like three or four hours and at that moment it feels like a crushing blow.

After a whole night, endlessly going on, in and out of pain barriers and weird states of consciousness, falling to pieces, we reach a familiar diner at 4am. To be honest it's a shithole and maddeningly the driver disappears for ages to pick people up and bring them to work, so we have to wait....again. It's unhandleable. It's not just fatigue, but my whole body is shaking with a sickness never experienced before. Nathe and I are beyond talking. I am just focused on shaking and pain. My feet don't belong in these shoes. They're crap imitation Merrells bought in Shenzhen and they really hurt. They superheat your feet and blister them up really badly, therefore they super-heat the rest of you. They make your feet smell so terrible that taking your boots off in the bus is not an option. I realise that I haven't changed my trousers in two months and have had two showers in six weeks.

And that crap f*ckin' diner! At 5am, seriously ill, coughing up and swallowing some rotten goat I ate. Swilling back water and unleashing in the worst outside-toilet-from-hell. Freezing cold on a warm sunny morning and shaking like a leaf. A foot-high mound of crap and toilet rolls, all piled up in one solidifying and gelatinous mass confronts me and there is the dread worry of just passing out in it. On and on; 6am, 6.15, 6.30, 7, 8, 8.30 and 9! I know I'm slim, but I'm really focused on how little we've been eating for the last few weeks. We were doing well on the mountain trip but since then there has been seriously nothing to eat, so now weakness is all-consuming. After making my belt smaller by well over an inch, at least my trousers are no longer in danger of falling down.

The last few hours of the journey are the worst. The driver stops again and again to talk to friends, fellow drivers, drop people off and unload and reload boxes and bags. At UB bus station, Nathe carried my big pack while I focused completely on staying upright until reaching the hotel.

Some Tuesday in Ulaanbaatar: What a trip! What day is it? What just happened? Laid up in bed with this sickness and exhaustion, trying to come to terms with the endless paperwork for a Chinese visa and sorting out transportation, it seems like a lot to deal with. We are in a hotel in the same area as last year opposite the train station. At night this place is terrifying; a guy jumped up and screamed in my face, this woman just pulled her kecks down and pissed behind this little bush next to the pavement. I can't believe the number of alcoholics here and how pissed-up people get. People can drink vodka all morning and pass out generally anywhere, such as on concrete, pavements, in shop doorways, supermarkets, childrens' playing grounds or just holes in the ground and amongst the detritus between the tenement blocks.

I came back to the hotel yesterday and asked Tzetsge, the waitress, if it was possible to order some food.
"No food!" was her blunt reply.
"Hmmm, why is there no food?" this is a restaurant after all, with a kitchen and menus knives and forks and things.
"The chef has gone!"
"Oh! When will she be back then?"
"Margash maybe! She has gone to the countryside!"

Getting back to China: This is it! This was the one that me and Nathe have been building up to. So many discussions about the 'what ifs' and 'maybes'; the anticipation of getting the job done and the effort of it all. Are we gonna make it? Rules and regulations are massive. In the hope that things have at least eased off, we go about the job with workmanlike conviction. It's amazing that no matter how mullered you get physically, you shove it to the back burner and do the job. I give myself a maximum of three hours a day until I feel like I'm gonna keel over. A shave and a shower just doesn't seem to cut any ice at the moment.

So, on Day One in UB we queue up at the Embassy to find that to get back to China you must have the following documents:

1. You need a copy of your hotel reservation in China, with the number of nights you will be staying.
2. You need copies of your entry and method of exit/your inward and outward journey.
3. You need a bank statement showing that you have 100 dollars for each day you will stay in China.
4. Passport, the right sized photos and a completely undamaged brand new 50 dollar bill. If it is damaged in any way, like a corner folded, you will be turned away.
5. Photocopies of everything.

The Embassy is open for three hours a day, three days a week from 9am to 12pm. If you are at the front of the queue and you've been there all morning, you will still be turned away at closing time so get there early. I also went to the train station ticket office for international departures. There is a train once a week, going on Friday, so we will have to be in UB for four nights in total. Oh well, we have a TV in our room with BBC World News and National Geographic, amazing! Talk about what the doctor ordered, I can tell you. Nathe and I have a fitful night; both of us have been going through our own personal journeys of hell trying to get our documentation together. Nathe is up all night trying to get things sorted. We end up with the most cobbled together load of cod shit you will ever see that we will nervously hand in to the Embassy tomorrow.

Back to the Embassy, we're outside standing in the queue at 8.30. By 10.30, at the front of the queue, this Aussie guy with a big smile, reckons there's absolutely no chance of us getting a visa using these documents. Nice! At 11am, having been completely rejected at the office, I run outside, catching a taxi to an internet cafe with a printer. At 11.50, returning with more documentation, the only way in is to bribe a guard with 5000 tugrik, enough for a bottle of vodka, and then queue-jump massively. This guy in front is freaking out because he reckons the staff behind the counter have lost his information and security remove him, just what you don't need hey? Amazingly, the guy behind the counter coolly and calmly looks at then accepts the documents and suddenly it feels like Liverpool has won the Champions League all over again.

Two-day trip back to Beijing: Of course! When the woman in the ticket office said the train to Beijing goes on Friday, it should have been obvious that she meant Saturday, you have to book a week in advance and it's already sold out. How foolish of me! Instead we find that the only remaining train is on Sunday and only goes to the border. It's an overnight sleeper train so from Erlian, we will then have to catch a Chinese sleeper bus for a second night to Beijing. Ah, those good old sleeper buses, the ones I vowed never take again, aaaaaaaagh! It goes on!

Can't remember much about the last few days in Ulaanbaatar. There was a beautiful little temple nearby, where the monks gave me a blessing for good health and an extra one for luck (they must have thought I needed it!) During a window of clarity, one afternoon I climbed the hills overlooking UB. It's truly beautiful up there and amazing to think you were looking at almost a third of the population of the whole country.

On the morning of departure, as we left the hotel, I decided to give the last bottle of vodka to the first person we came across, as by this time our livers really couldn't take it anymore. It was that and the fact that my guts were still saying no to most things. Opposite the front door were two likely looking guys sitting on a wall on the other side of the road. Never seen a bottle of anything being downed as quickly as that before! The first guy took around ten seconds to get the first half down his neck as did his friend with polishing the rest off, totalling about thirty seconds if you include the passing of the bottle. The last guy threw the empty bottle over his shoulder into the park with a huge grin on his face….and that was at eleven in the morning!

The trip back was, as it goes, a pleasant couple of nights. A sound couple from the UK, Chris and Martha shared a bottle of wine with us in the compartment. Nathe and I stood and looked out as we finally crossed the border back into China on Monday morning, both of us thinking that this was no ordinary start to the week. At 4.00am the following day we were back in Beijing, heading for the safety of the Red Lantern, through the rain and across the darkened empty streets. Now the real work begins; starting up all over again, (again!)

5795308R00201

Printed in Great Britain
by Amazon.co.uk, Ltd.,
Marston Gate.